BEYOND ALTERITY

EDITED BY
PAULA LÓPEZ CABALLERO AND
ARIADNA ACEVEDO-RODRIGO

AFTERWORD BY PAUL K. EISS

BEYOND ALTERITY

Destabilizing the Indigenous Other in Mexico

**THE UNIVERSITY OF
ARIZONA PRESS**

TUCSON

The University of Arizona Press
www.uapress.arizona.edu

© 2018 by The Arizona Board of Regents
All rights reserved. Published 2018

ISBN-13: 978-0-8165-3546-0 (cloth)

Cover design by Leigh McDonald
Cover art: Demián Flores, *La patria I*, Oil/canvas, 180 x 200 cm, 2010

Publication of this book is made possible in part by the proceeds of a permanent endowment created with the assistance of a Challenge Grant from the National Endowment for the Humanities, a federal agency.

Library of Congress Cataloging-in-Publication Data
Names: López Caballero, Paula, editor. | Acevedo Rodrigo, Ariadna, editor. | Eiss, Paul K., writer of afterword.
Title: Beyond alterity : destabilizing the indigenous other in Mexico / edited by Paula López Caballero and Ariadna Acevedo-Rodrigo ; afterword by Paul K. Eiss.
Description: Tucson : The University of Arizona Press, 2018. | Includes bibliographical references and index.
Identifiers: LCCN 2017042846 | ISBN 9780816535460 (cloth : alk. paper)
Subjects: LCSH: Indigenous peoples—Mexico—Ethnic identity. | Other (Philosophy)—Mexico.
Classification: LCC F1219.3.E79 B49 2018 | DDC 305.800972—dc23 LC record available at https://lccn.loc.gov/2017042846

Printed in the United States of America
♾ This paper meets the requirements of ANSI/NISO Z39.48-1992 (Permanence of Paper).

CONTENTS

ACKNOWLEDGMENTS

THE CONVERSATIONS and meetings that have made this book possible began to be formalized at the end of 2013 thanks to a Mellon–Latin American Studies Association (LASA) Seminars grant, which allowed us to fund three meetings in the course of 2014—the first at Departamento de Investigaciones Educativas at Centro de Investigación y de Estudios Avanzados (Cinvestav) in January, the second at a LASA panel and workshop (May), and the third at two round tables at the Reunión de Historiadores de México, Estados Unidos, y Canadá (September). Each of these was stimulating and useful, mainly because the collaborators on this book not only produced research of the highest caliber but also proved to be excellent interlocutors, always open, available, and patient. So our most sincere thanks to each of them.

We would also like to thank the anonymous reviewers who read two complete versions of the manuscript and undoubtedly made this into a better book. Thanks as well to the colleagues and friends who commented on the multiple drafts of this project: Andrew Cannesa, Alejandra Leal, Pablo Piccato, Francisco Quijano, Nitzán Shoshán, Mauricio Tenorio (who we must also thank for the marvelous title of the book), and David Wood, as well as those who took part in one or more of the meetings, even if they did not collaborate on the book: Jan Rus, Alejandro Araujo, Daniele Inda, Claudia Briones, and Peter Wade.

For both the planning of the meetings and the work of editorial coordination, we have fortunately been able to count on the support of our respective institutions: the Department of Educational Research at Cinvestav and the Center for Interdisciplinary Research in the Sciences and the Humanities at the National Autonomous University of Mexico. In addition, the project CONA-CYT 242433 "Thinking Alterity in Mexico," directed by Paula López Caballero, financed the translation of the introductory chapter. Our editor Kristen Buckles has been key to the whole process of preparing this book. We would like to thank her for her interest and confidence in us since we first presented the project in May 2014, as well as for her enormous skills on display throughout the whole editorial process.

Lastly, Ariadna thanks David Wood, who helped us at various junctures when we feared that too much was getting lost in translation. And Paula would like to thank Francisco Quijano for his critical readings at different stages and his generous day-to-day care of their baby, without which it would have been much more difficult to finish the project.

BEYOND ALTERITY

INTRODUCTION

Why Beyond Alterity?

PAULA LÓPEZ CABALLERO WITH
ARIADNA ACEVEDO-RODRIGO

THIS BOOK questions the way identification as indigenous has become tacitly, and almost automatically, associated with alterity. Coming from different disciplines with a range of methodologies and engaging with diverse topics, the contributors all share a common concern. Without denying the potential interest generated by studies that emphasize the difference and singularity of people (self-) identified as indigenous, we challenge the idea that those who identify or are identified as such are necessarily and constantly endorsing their alterity. Focusing on those practices, objects, and discourses where difference is more visible (that is, *cosmovisión*—language, customs, resistance, etc.) can be a restriction for the study of other social phenomena where that alterity is not obvious, but that are equally, or more, constitutive of social life. Rejecting the seductions of exoticism, this book does not conceive the alterity of indigenous persons as an explanation but as an object to be explained.

This epistemological problem finds an echo in past and present empirical evidence about groups that are identified as indigenous. For example, the results of the last national population census carried out in Mexico point out the question we are delineating (INEGI 2010), although we know that the abstraction involved in statistics means that they only yield indications and suggestions for grasping the chaos of the social. In this census the number of people identifying as indigenous was at its highest level since 1930, making Mexico the country with the largest indigenous population in the Americas. What is more, that total is higher than the combined indigenous populations from all the other countries that have material in their censuses about self-identification as indigenous.[1] In effect, this fraction has multiplied by a factor of 2.4 in comparison to the previous census, passing from 6.2 million people in 2000 to a little more than 15 million (equivalent to 14.9 percent of the national total) in 2010.

What is most interesting is that this sharp increase is due to the rise in the number of people who describe themselves as indigenous in response to a question in the census, despite their not speaking a native language (long the traditional criterion for inferring that someone is or is not indigenous). Between 2000 and 2010, this group went from 1.3 percent of the total national population to 8.9 percent. By contrast, the number of people who stated that they were speakers of a native language (SNL) went down, going from 7.1 percent to 6.7 percent of the population as a whole for the same period. But this is not the only novel finding. The sociodemographic characteristics of people who describe themselves as indigenous without being SNLs lead specialists to conclude that "they appear more like the national population as a whole in all the aspects analyzed: schooling, size of place of residence, relationship to the head of the household and migration" (Vázquez Sandrin and Quezada 2015, 197). It turns out that the number of people who feature in the census as indigenous in the twenty-first century in Mexico has increased, but that in both sociological and linguistic terms it is less and less possible to distinguish them from the majority population, whom we usually call mestizos. The explanations for this process have swung between a primordialist interpretation of identity (the changes would reflect a "loss" of [true] identity) to an instrumental one (people call themselves indigenous so as to get hold of resources). Our strategy is simply to wonder whether the problem is not our very definition of indigenous.

This problem, however, is not new. In a synthesis of the historiography on the urban Indians of New Spain, Castro Gutiérrez (2010) begins his study with an elementary question: "Who are [these urban Indians] and where do they come from?" What the sources allow us to establish is that "these natives . . . were barely distinguishable in their dress, trade and customs from the rest of the urban common people." Perhaps, suggests the author, this is where the difficulty of studying them lies, since they "represented *another way of being indigenous*, one that does not straightforwardly coincide with our preconceptions" (13, 14; italics added). The soothing haven of an alterity associated with groups that can be clearly differentiated, and are recognizable and stable for our contemporary eyes, seems to have been lost from the time of the early colonial city onward.

The forceful evidence offered by the chapters of this book makes clear that the problems that Castro Gutiérrez signals are not exclusive to his field of study or to "multicultural Mexico." In fact, we will see that the presupposition that tacitly associates identification as indigenous (or Indian) with alterity pervades the historiography and can come to dominate the empirical evidence, thus limiting the study of vast areas of social life. What do we do, then, with those practices where, as Castro Gutiérrez (2010) says provocatively, the actors studied "do not appear to be Indians"? (12). Do we give up looking at them because they are not "authentic," or because of the potential risk of reducing the effectiveness of political arguments from subaltern sectors? Do we include them in an analytic scheme that displaces that authenticity to the intimate and hidden terrain of everyday resistance, thus confirming that what is proper to being indigenous is finally to be, surreptitiously, "other"? Or do we simply accept that we have to modify our own notions of what it is to be indigenous?

Certainly, the social coordinates we use to navigate reality naturalize the association between *indigenous* and *alterity* as an incontrovertible fact: to be indigenous means to be other, to be *the* other. This alterity is reinforced at the national and international political levels, where commonly those movements identified as indigenous come to constitute, and constitute themselves through, alternative politics (ecological, communal, anticapitalist, etc.).[2] Equally, scientific literature has tended to replicate this common sense, if it has not been a major factor in its constitution, to such an extent that simply to imagine studying such societies without emphasizing their alterity sounds like nonsense, or worse, a denial of their reality. There might even be those who see an ethical problem here: the argument might question the validity of political claims made in the name of some indigenous collectivity, as if discussing the alterity attributed to such groups were equivalent to doubting their existence or their legitimacy.[3] So it is by no means redundant to make clear just how distant from our objectives is any idea of evaluating what is really indigenous or assessing the degree of authenticity of some group, person, practice, or discourse. Nor does this book claim to establish a more precise or definitive definition of what or who is indigenous. What are privileged here are not definitions but the social uses and contexts in which those identificatory categories take on meaning. One last thing we are not doing in this book is producing a linear narrative that would reconstruct either *the* history of the Indians from the conquest to the present or the values associated with indigenousness (race, language, ethnicity, etc.).[4] On the contrary, we avoid reducing this variability to a predefined trajectory, because the category *indigenous* is a permanent field of negotiation and dispute whose meanings are always volatile and elusive.

Aiming to question what today seems like a natural association between indigenous identification and alterity, the contributors to this book deploy different but complementary analytic moves. Section 1, "Land and Government," focuses on those social experiences that usually remain outside analysis because they do not coincide with the alterity that is in principle ascribed to groups called indigenous. The chapters in section 2, "Science," recover the historicity of the alterity associated with the category *indigenous*, showing its variability over time. As will be seen in the wealth of evidence collected in each essay, this separation between experience and category cannot be reduced to the opposition between practice and discourse. On the one hand, it turns out that historians often grasp the actors' experience through their discourses (in this book, Ducey, Acevedo-Rodrigo, Rockwell). On the other, the categories used by the sciences not only are performative of the reality they describe (López Caballero, Schwartz, Escalona) but are also grasped through the practices and objects that make that reality possible (Cházaro, García Deister).

This analytic distinction—experience, categories—comes close to the model put forward by Jenkins (1994; inspired by Barth 1969), which examines the functioning of forms of social identification and distinguishes between two registers: group and name.[5] The first refers to the social experiences that allow certain people to recognize themselves, or to be recognized, as part of a collectivity. The second refers to the categories that serve to indicate this belonging. The distinction is pertinent because "one [register] can change without the other doing so" (Jenkins 1994, 202). In our terms, this distinction allows us to see that a social marker of differentiation—for example, language or phenotype—can be operative even though social practices that are associated with it change. Or the other way around, the social marker of differentiation can cease to operate even though the social practices once associated with it continue to exist. In the following essays, each author gives a searching account of one facet of this problem as seen from their own field of knowledge. So in addition to the fine empirical detail of each text, the significant intervention that aims to go *Beyond Alterity* consists in laying out this lack of correspondence between experience and categories as part of the same phenomenon—that is, social and individual identification.

SOCIAL ACTORS BETWEEN EXPERIENCE AND CATEGORY

We will now go on to elaborate our debts to previous work, particularly on Mexico. If we look at the historical literature about the subjects that populated the Mexican rural world,[6] we find that the identification of actors has been an insufficiently addressed problem.[7] But one example that is crucially important for both its centrality and constant renewal is the historical work on campesinos and popular movements. Being interested in the actions of dominated groups, historians have reflected on how to characterize the actors in this history. Analytically, we can distinguish three main interpretative models, even if overlaps between them are common.[8] First, most classical accounts have tended to conceive the relationships of power between elites and dominated as essentially antagonistic and determined by economic factors. But in understanding the mobilizations as reactions to external pressures, the subjects appeared as rather passive and disconnected from the wider social context (Reina 1980).[9] A second model emphasizes that popular or subaltern mobilization is undertaken to negotiate domination (Joseph and Nugent 1994; Ruiz Medrano and Kellog 2010). Social actors appear, then, with their own motivations and strategies (more or less autonomous, depending on the author), playing a determinant role in how the hegemonic order became slowly imposed. Perhaps to counteract the "apotheosis of agency" (Van Young 1999, 243–44) that some of this historiography has tended to produce, a third model, which we might call culturalist, proposes to stress networks of collective meaning as a central explanatory factor of mobilization. Specifically, Van Young (2001) suggests that even if the actors are not merely reactive, as in the first model, their motivations and strategies are strongly determined by their culture, which is orientated exclusively to their local area and to the short term. By questioning the causes and effects of campesino mobilization, this literature makes it possible to delineate the social actors involved.

These problems are not exclusive to historians, who, one could claim, are methodologically determined by the limited testimony they manage to discern in the documents. We might think that the ethnographic method used in anthropology means that this discipline has the answers to the question of how people, specifically those (self-) identified as indigenous, identify socially. However, even within this discipline—and especially that part interested in indigenous groups in Mexico and Latin America—it also turns out to be difficult to abandon alterity as a point of departure. Anthropology was certainly defined for a long time by its object of study—the native or Indian. Today this definition is being left behind even if our fields of study are still dominated by the idea that anthropology is the science that studies difference (Pitarch 2008) or continuity (Lévi-Strauss 1962; Varela 2002).[10] There is a preliminary attempt at a better understanding of the alterity associated with the category *indigenous* in the study of indigeneity. In works on Latin America, the term *indigeneity* has a positive connotation and refers to the discourses and practices of subaltern groups that claim rights in the name of a singular inheritance that situates them as originary or native to their localities or territories. This inheritance, moreover, would express an alterity with regard to national identity (Graham and Penny 2014; Forte 2013). This focus stresses the contemporary and political dimensions of identification as indigenous and to that extent speaks to the contributions of this book. So a useful definition of indigeneity suggests that it be understood as "a relational field of governance, subjectivities, and knowledges that involves us all—indigenous and non-indigenous" and is to be found in the present and within "larger social fields of difference and sameness. [Indigeneity then] acquires its 'positive' meaning not from some essential properties of its own, but through its relation to what it is not" (De la Cadena and Starn 2007, 3, 4).

The texts in *Beyond Alterity* also conceive the singularity of indigenous groups as resulting from these articulations—government, subjects, knowledge(s)—and not as the conservation of fixed properties. Even so, this book distances itself from the indigeneity approach in two ways. Firstly, it shows that the indigenous/non-indigenous distinction does not always turn out to be so neat and tidy; indeed, it has not always been grounded on the same principles. For this reason, the book problematizes the not uncommon methodological habit of ascribing a "single will" to certain units of analysis (the people, the community, the ethnic group).[11] Secondly, as the anthropologist Canessa (2012; and more directly 2014) points out, indigeneity as a discursive field of struggle or resistance cannot continue to be understood independently of the wider political context, and in particular, of the position adopted by the nation-state. That is, indigeneity is not a question of two watertight and self-contained levels but of mutually constitutive ones.

This "racialized perception" (Washbrook 2012, 192) of the relationships between state and society, according to which local indigenous communities resist the domination of the necessarily non-indigenous state, has undergone criticism and analytic deconstruction for some time, albeit only to a small extent.

In this sense, we find important contributions in an array of literature that we group together under the term *political anthropology of identification*. The aim here is to question explicitly the ways in which people identify as indigenous, without assuming as an explanatory factor the very alterity that this category usually presupposes. We distinguish two main strategies for posing the problem in these works: on the one hand, plotting the historical variations of the forms of self-identification, and on the other, a recognition of the intersection and overlap between scales of analysis (community, state, nation, etc.) as a central element of explanation.

As for the first strategy, even as early as the 1970s, Friedlander (1975) was documenting the inherent tension within identification as indigenous in the everyday experience of the inhabitants of a village in Morelos. This form of identification functioned more as a mode of exclusion driven by the local agencies of the state than as an expression of a certain local belonging. In the same way, the indispensable work of Rus (1994) on what he accurately calls the "institutional revolutionary community" analyzes the mechanisms by which the presence of the state in the indigenous communities of Chiapas is achieved by consolidating—and not eliminating—local traditions, usages, and customs.[12] The historicity of the so-called indigenous identity is also explored in the early analysis of Frye (1996). In his research carried out in San Luis Potosí, the author develops what he calls a "history of indigenous identity" and describes how in this process, the postrevolutionary state and its rhetoric of belonging were central to the ways self-identification took place in the twentieth century. Historicizing the forms of identification, then, assumes that the markers of differentiation are not always the same and they do not always designate the same people. A similar argument is defended by Gabbert (2004), who offers a rich investigation on how identification as Mayan in Yucatán has varied in meanings and social positions from the sixteenth century to the present day.[13] In short, these authors offer solid arguments for engaging with the experience of those who are categorized as indigenous, shifting the analysis from identities to the study of the processes of identification. One important aspect of this literature is that identifications are inserted into wider classificatory systems. So it is fundamental to study those very taxonomies and the actors and spaces that permit their institutionalization.

Let us now turn to the second strategy—that is, to examine the intersection and overlap between scales of analysis. Nowadays it is a theoretical commonplace that the categories that form the analytic baggage of the social sciences are constructed and hence historical: national identity (Anderson 2006; Hobsbawm and Ranger 1983), class (Bourdieu 2013), gender (Beauvoir 1953; Butler 1993; Scott 1986), the people (Bhaba 1994; Eiss 2010) or popular culture (Williams 1982; Joseph and Nugent 1994), and race (Wade 2013; Martínez 2008, López Beltrán 2011). Perhaps one effect of this critical impulse has been the increasingly numerous studies that approach the state's institutional categories as political products and not as transparent reflections of reality (Loveman 2014; Angosto and Kradolfer 2012; Shor 2009; Lartigue and Quesnel 2003). In these works, attention is paid to the challenges, conflicts, and conditions faced by actors, generally within the state and administration, who defined the systems of classification. One conclusion is that in registering the population under certain categories (racial ones, for example, or linguistic ones in Mexico), certain social markers take on importance while others cease to be visible. This all contributes to a naturalization of divisions that are social and political. This analytic stance is consonant with a number of the chapters in the present book as it makes it possible to understand the alterity ascribed to the category *indigenous* as an "effect of the state" (Mitchell 1991, 95), or at least as the result of processes and conjunctures that refer more to the groups doing the classifying than to those being classified (see, for example, López Caballero and Escalona in the present volume).

To finish, let us mention the research that directly examines the categories of identification themselves. In the case of Mexico, it is the category *mestizo* that has undergone extensive critique, in particular because the term designates the national subject. Its historical character is generally accepted, allowing its genesis to be investigated (Bartra [1987] 2003; Basave 2002; Lomnitz 2001; Saada 2011; Tenorio Trillo 2009; Eiss 2016). In recent years, the identification of certain sectors of the population as descendants of Africans has been the object of analysis in Latin America; discussion has focused on mechanisms of visibility and the variation in the content of such identifications (Cunin and Hoffmann 2014; Wade 2013).

In short, this literature points out the importance of understanding social categories as political productions that impose "the legitimate definition of the divisions of the social world" (Bourdieu 1982, 112). In this sense, they have to be understood as languages of authority, as fields of struggle over the power to define, distinguish, and bring together. Further, the categories of identification have to be understood as a key aspect of the permanent process of legitimation of the nation-state, since through them there is an attempt to fix social subjectivities so that they become consonant with state and national belonging (Corrigan and Sayer 1985).

Now, like every category of identification (and perhaps more than most, given that it is seen as the transparent reflection of alterity), the word *indigenous* forms part of the cultural languages with which we navigate the world, and centrally, of the institutional and state languages that order the social world. Despite that, little work has been devoted to examining it while focusing on these characteristics.[14] But there is the useful reflection of Briones (2015), developed in her research into the Argentine Mapuche. From her point of view, "the emergence of particular styles of management of diversity [in each nation-state] cannot be understood as the automatic result of processes of intervention into realities that have been previously established and stabilized." On the contrary, Briones argues that these interventions have to be understood as "performativities of state action" that outline what is to be conceived of as "other," as "different"—a process she calls "national and regional formations of alterity" (59). Another important source for this perspective is the work of Segato (2007) on the politics of positive discrimination in Brazil, although here we do not fall back on the notion of race as she does. If "race is a sign," as this Argentine anthropologist says, this implies that "its meaning depends on . . . socially shared reading and a delimited historical and geographical context" (133). Hence using the category *indigenous* as a neutral term that refers in an absolute fashion to a clearly established social subject is highly problematic in analytical terms. It is not enough, then, to show that "Indians" are actors in social change, nor that "their" traditions or "their" culture have changed over time. The limit of these approaches is not that they are false but that they leave the category *indigenous* intact, whether using it as a term that refers to something stable and clearly identifiable in the world or even invoking it as an explanation of the phenomenon under investigation.

In conclusion, the essays collected here are not limited to refining the details of a picture that is already well-known—the history, culture and traditions of "indigenous groups." Rather, in dialogue with the perspectives we have just outlined, the contributors to the present volume offer their chisels, sharpened by their deep knowledge of their fields of knowledge, to sculpt the multiple faces of the object of study that here slowly takes on form: identification as indigenous *beyond alterity*. In the following two sections, we will detail the contents of each chapter and summarize their contributions to rethinking the problem of alterity.

WHEN EXPERIENCE EXCEEDS ALTERITY

Probably from the sixteenth century onward, but certainly in the eighteenth century, governors and campesinos of what were called the *pueblos de indios* sold, bought, rented, and inherited parcels of land within the territorial limits of each village, mostly, but not exclusively, to and from their neighbors. Spaniards, mestizos, and *mulatos* often crop up in these transactions. From the late colonial period and during the nineteenth century, the population of rural Oaxaca and Guerrero paid taxes and worked temporarily or permanently in other regions. They used the colonial and national courts to denounce the authorities for corruption and to settle intergenerational conflicts or those between indigenous nobles and the campesinos. In Veracruz, they took up arms, negotiated with the generals during the independence struggles, and at times managed to impose their own priorities. A century later, speakers of Zapotec, Chinantec, Nahuatl, and Totonac in Oaxaca and Puebla sustained village schools, whether by taxes or by other means, with Spanish as the language of instruction; they also regularly demanded that the state authorities send trained teachers and supplies. It was almost always the inhabitants of the municipalities who paid the teachers' salaries. In postrevolutionary Tlaxcala, command of Spanish, where Nahuatl was spoken, was a resource that was constantly made use of by the inhabitants of the municipalities, even if this proficiency was perfected not in school but in the socialization given by engagement in the political and agrarian affairs of the town. And in some Mayan ejidos in contemporary Yucatán, parcels of the ejido legally defined as land in common use are exploited as individual property. Or, the other way round, land legally apportioned as individual parcels maintains an important degree of collective organization for production.

These are some of the situations carefully recorded by the contributors to the section "Land and Government." As the forceful empirical material in these chapters shows, these are central practices in the social life of those pueblos identified as indigenous, even though they seem at odds with common conceptions and the historiography has classified them as irrelevant exceptions or dismissed them outright as nonexistent. Giving an account of the variety of these practices, actors, spheres, and institutions is then a prime achievement of the works gathered together here.

But the valuable contributions of these works can also be put into dialogue with a double problematic. The authors of this volume grant a central explanatory weight in their arguments, on the one hand, to the internal diversity of the collective entities they study (pueblo, community) and, on the other, to their deep imbrication with other analytic levels (region, state, federation). The combination allows them, and us, to document, with great refinement, the challenges posed by the units of analysis we work with and that are often freighted with a widely endorsed but tacit definition of who is Indian, the premises of which must be examined.

In relationship to the first problematic, both Kourí and Torres-Mazuera give an account of the multiplicity of the forms of land ownership. Drawing on empirical evidence that is separated by three or four hundred years, they show this multiplicity in both the colonial *pueblos de indios* and in Mayan ejidos in the south of Yucatán in the present day. In chapter 1, Kourí indicates that common sense from colonial legislators to twenty-first-century historians (and even contemporary anthropologists, as the chapter by Torres-Mazuera confirms) sees corporate landholding in the *repúblicas de indios* as a function of the "communalism, cohesion, and a spirit of egalitarian solidarity" that are supposed to be inherent to indigenous culture (31). By contrast, Kourí shows that land distribution and use by the *repúblicas de indios* in New Spain were hierarchical and unequal, and that "de facto—and in some places de jure—private property in at least portions of the *tierras de repartimiento*" was a "prevalent condition in late colonial pueblos" (48). Kourí considers it an error to conclude, from the evidence of the political autonomy of the *pueblos de indios*, and of their solidarity in the face of external threats to communal property, that they were necessarily egalitarian and cohesive. If private property was much more extensive than we have been wont to believe, then the nineteenth century disentailment of land need not have been such a radical rupture as is painted by the story of imposed privatizations and dispossession that are then the causes of the 1910 revolution. Hence, the whole of the agrarian history of Mexico needs to be rethought.

Similarly, in chapter 6, Torres-Mazuera finds that in their discussion of the ejidos of the contemporary Yucatán, legal and agrarian anthropologists assume a continuity of communal landholding and a link with what is indigenous ("usages and customs" associated with "indigenous . . . *cosmovisiónes*"; 152) that cannot be maintained in the light of historical and ethnographical evidence of major breaks in the history—for example, those caused by the introduction of the ejidos after the revolution, or by the multiple changes in agricultural production since the 1970s, or by the programs of liberalization of ejido lands since the 1990s that have allowed them to be bought and sold. Openly disputing the more normative interpretations of law in general, and agrarian law in particular, this chapter focuses its analysis not so much on property regimes but on the social relationships of property where the distinction between private and communal is not the most important one in operation. The result is that, at least within the agrarian sphere, neither the *pueblo de indios* nor the *ejido* look like even approximately homogeneous entities. This questions the relevance of speaking about the *pueblo de indios* or the *ejido* as though they were subjects with univocal agency or certain fixed properties.

The second aspect of this problematic has to do, as we said, with the imbrication between analytic levels. In spite of the sophistication of the available interpretative models, one constant that traverses them is the characterization of the subaltern actors as singular or distinct. It is as though the effort of historiography to restore them as agents of history inevitably granted their intentions, strategies, and methods a high degree of autonomy.[15] The chapters in this book share the same analytic gesture that tries to go beyond this "effect of othering," showing the constant interaction between social actors that come from very diverse spheres and physical spaces (López Caballero 2009).

In chapter 2, Guardino's historiographical reexamination of the period 1750–1850 takes issue with Van Young's thesis that the parochialism, traditionalism, and isolation of the rural world gave rise to an ethos of disconnection from national projects. To do this, he proposes to "reconcile" the evidence that the inhabitants of the towns "were inward-looking and oriented toward tradition" with evidence of "their engagement with forces beyond their villages" in the economic, political, legal, and even religious spheres (64). These demonstrations challenge the emphasis given in the literature to the separation between geographical and analytical levels, since in order to sort out even the most local issues, the inhabitants of the rural world had to get involved in regional and national politics.

Along these lines, in chapter 3, Ducey documents the decisive role played by the inhabitants of the former *pueblos de indios* in the war of independence, thereby contesting a historiography that has seen them as irrelevant or indifferent to this process. Focusing on the Gulf Coast between 1811 and 1821, he argues that the long war had an even stronger impact than blueprints for change in bringing together a coalition of socially and ethnically diverse actors and in expanding their political horizons. As former Indians, now citizens, became legally equal to Spaniards and, crucially at a time of conflict, could bear arms, they managed to obtain recognition for the colonial, corporate forms of local government (cabildos) in exchange for their support for insurgents. However, it would be wrong to overemphasize the historical continuity of the colonial cabildos, given their service to the insurgency and the new circumstances in which they operated, including migration, indictments against "unpatriotic Spaniards," and the adoption of a novel language of rights. Additionally, Ducey concludes that "the practice of the war produced a devolution of power to the village [cabildo] while at the same time ensuring that rural politics were more connected to the outside world" (101).

In chapter 4, Acevedo-Rodrigo outlines the continuing efforts to support public elementary schools (with teaching in Spanish, the official national language) in towns and villages with a majority of indigenous language speakers in the Puebla and Oaxaca Sierras. These schools were both the cause and effect of the pueblo's internal inequalities—for example, in teaching literacy to a minority while at the same time contesting inequalities vis-à-vis other pueblos by providing the local government with enough literate officials to defend collective interests. These regions' liberalism, even if dubbed "popular" in the literature, was not very different from that of the elite insofar as education was concerned; equality was tenaciously claimed and some small advances took place even in the midst of persistent hierarchies.[16]

For their part, the Nahuatl speakers of the Malintzi region (Tlaxcala) interviewed by Rockwell in chapter 5 rarely attended school but nevertheless valued this experience as the basis that allowed them finally to master, in a self-taught fashion, written Spanish, which they deployed in government, in the Church, or at work. Rockwell endorses the already established criticism of the literacy thesis that posits a "great divide" distinguishing "oral" from "literate" (130) culture and places the Indians on the side of orality, whether to run down their backwardness or to celebrate their cultural resistance. Through historical documentation and ethnographic work she shows the profound interpenetration of the oral and written spheres, such that the lettered men of Malintzi contrast knowledge(s) fixed in memory and those recorded on paper to test the veracity of both. Rockwell concludes that writing was not an external phenomenon; rather, there was "an internal process of the appropriation of writing" and, even more, "literacy was transformed in the process" (142).

In short, private landholding, participation in national politics, and writing in Spanish are not exceptions or anomalies but constitutive features of social experience in rural localities, even if they exceed the attributes usually associated with the category of indigenous; they undo its frontiers and perhaps add new contents to it. Nevertheless, in the present day it becomes practically impossible to question two related ideas: first, that there is a central division in Mexican society that distinguishes Indians from non-Indians, and second, that the root of this divide is precisely the former's quality as others, their alterity. It remains to be understood, then, how this idea has gradually become fixed, even becoming a cliché or something commonplace that seems to require no explanation. Let's look at the responses offered by section 2, "Science," in this respect.

FIXING DIFFERENCE THROUGH SCIENTIFIC PRACTICES

If the nineteenth century began with the abolition of the legal category of the Indian, it is well-known that it ended with the construction of a new category erected on the social remnants of the old one; this would no longer be legal but medical, archaeological, and anthropological. Chapters in section 2 elaborate on the origins and new uses of some of the attributes that commonly appear as "proper" or "essential" to indigenous groups and that seem to make it possible for Indians to be clearly distinguished from those who are not. These chapters examine precise historical moments where the category *indigenous* and the alterity supposedly intrinsic to it are stabilized.

Despite their different methodological horizons and themes, the chapters of this section share at least two assumptions that traverse the analyses.[17] They do not assume the existence of a set of fixed properties that recognize and define the Indian so that subsequently this figure can be analyzed, represented, or interpreted by scientists and intellectuals.[18] On the contrary, the five chapters of this section consider that these discourses contributed centrally to the definition of the very social and conceptual order they were studying.[19] In chapter 8, López Caballero examines an intense controversy in the main academic journals of the 1940s in which it appears that knowing who was indigenous and how such a subject ought to be defined was an ongoing task. The chapter takes a sociohistorical approach to the categories of identification and shows that the period 1940–1948 was a key time for both the institutionalization and professionalization of Mexican anthropology, with a slow consolidation of an official *indigenista* politics, and a key period for the strengthening of a concept of the Indian that would endure down to our own day. Similarly, the case studied by Schwartz in chapter 9 illustrates the "cognitive dissonance" (226) between academic definitions of the Indian and the social and economic evidence available about such groups. The historian reconstructs the first experiment in integrated regional development carried out by the Instituto Nacional Indigenista (INI) in response to the massive population displacement that took place with the building of the Miguel Alemán dam in the 1940s, and in which anthropologists and *indigenistas* were heavily involved. She demonstrates that the anthropologists who took charge of this project thought it was self-evident that the inhabitants were indigenous and therefore concluded that these groups were "historically rooted in the land" (227). In fact, many of the inhabitants came from other regions and many others were constantly migrating to and from different parts of the country. Thus, within the framework of the rise of the INI and its attempts to justify its existence, the difficulties faced by the anthropologists came not only from lack of finance, infrastructure, or political will, but also from an othering of the subjects they were dealing with.

These chapters concur on a second point: that the study of science cannot be carried out only—and not even principally—through an examination of canonical texts, treatises, theories, and schools, but instead should be carried out through a discussion of the very practices and objects of research. This allows it to escape from a more classical history of ideas, devoted in large part to the political sphere.[20] Cházaro's chapter 7 takes as its point of departure the instruments with which doctors measured the pelvises of Mexican women in the middle of the nineteenth century. She analyzes two medical projects from the second half of the that century: the measurement of what were then called "jammed pelvises" and the measurement of skulls and bones with a view to explaining human variation. Cházaro's argument shows that these studies and the instruments and objects used gave material form to an idea of a "Mexican race" that was different from the Indians. In this process of definition, the indigenous element was seen not just as "degenerative" but also as adaptive in evolutionary terms, permitting individuals to adjust to their environment. This chapter finishes in the 1920s, so making clear the continuities between pre- and postrevolutionary scientific projects.

Escalona's analytic horizon in chapter 10 is also about the role scientists have played in ordering the world through their research practices—in this case, the work undertaken by the Harvard Chiapas Project in the 1950s. Making use of the project's internal documentation, field notebooks, and correspondence, the author examines in detail how Evon Vogt's scientific project in Chiapas was central to the elaboration and stabilization of the idea of Mayan civilization. He explains how in ethnographic practice itself, an idea of Mayan culture was taking shape that would take in all the rural societies of Chiapas, Yucatán, and Campeche, from the archaeologists' classic period down to the present day.

Finally, in chapter 11, García Deister explains how in practice it becomes impossible for contemporary genomics to establish an "indigenous type" that would serve as a means to distinguish it from the rest of the population, usually identified as mestizo (273). She brings out the contested dimension of the category of the Indian and its meanings in contemporary Mexico, showing that the lack of precision in the category is not a consequence of insufficient scientific advance that will eventually be overcome with time but rather is constitutive of the category as such. These specialists attribute a double role to the Amerindian component of the mestizo genome: it makes the latter genetically unique but also makes the population that carries it susceptible to diabetes and obesity. Cutting-edge research in genomics thus continues to reproduce an idea of the indigenous that stresses at one and the same time a valuable aspect and a pathological one.

Additionally, these chapters nourish race studies. This is one of the few fields where there is a productive intersection between science studies—interested mainly in the so-called natural sciences (Latour 1988; Latour and Woolgar 1986)—and indigenous studies. Certainly, for Latin America the history of the idea of race and racialization is a relatively recent optic of analysis.[21] The authors in this section concur in understanding race as a subset of a wider ensemble of categories that have to do with the social management of alterity. This latter can be fixed through a multiplicity of social and cultural markers that might or might not refer to the idea of race. Hence, there is a dialogue here with those studies that have been interested in the history of race and racialization in Latin America, but the chapters do not limit themselves to the discussion of this concept.

Cházaro's chapter explores how, in the measuring of pelvises, skulls, and bones, an idea of the Mexican race, which was singular and different from the European race in particular, took on materiality and would eventually migrate from obstetrics to anthropology, from Mexican women to the indigenous subject. For her part, López Caballero shows that, on the one hand, the term *race* will be used throughout the 1940s, even as its definition will move farther away from the idea of inheritance. But on the other hand, far from simply replacing the idea of race, culture will incorporate many of the values previously mobilized by the former term, particularly the idea of innate features (even if they are now cultural rather than physical). Escalona's chapter, by contrast, does not explicitly discuss the idea of race, but rather that of Mayan civilization, understood as a system of principles that organize the social and ritual life of those identified as Mayan. In making these organizing principles a chronological and geographical constant, the alterity of these groups was reinforced, even if the difference was no longer thought of in biological or hereditary terms. Lastly, the essay by García Deister does not refer to the term *race* at all, as it is not used by the scientists in the field she is studying.[22] Instead, these scientists make use of the notion of ancestry to try to distance themselves from a linear association between biology and identity, even if in their language and practice it is impossible to cast off the social categories of differentiation (specifically, indigenous and mestizo in the case of Mexico).

In conclusion, as a whole, the perspectives we have detailed here, like pieces of a puzzle, contribute to destabilizing the identification as indigenous and begin to separate it from the alterity with which it would seem to be consubstantial. In more abstract terms, the contribution of this book is that it analytically separates experience from category. When we consider the people who we usually group together or who group themselves together under the category *indigenous*, we need to ask, What are they doing beyond the identification that the category induces? Also, what is the historicity of the category itself, beyond the people who are so designated? Through these two analytic strategies, all of the works gathered together here add to our concern to approach those groups designated as indigenous *beyond alterity* and to show that being other is only one of many possibilities—socially determined—for the people identified as indigenous. But in addition, as Eiss pinpoints in the epilogue, destabilizing that alterity necessarily presupposes going "beyond Occidentalism." In fact, the implicit—and more existential—doubt that underlies this project concerns the Western "self" that "is implicitly constructed, stabilized, or confirmed in such processes of indigenization" (291). This effort to redefine the categories that we navigate with is, we hope, one more contribution to the dismantling of what Bauman (1989, 61) has called the intrinsic logic of racism: "Man is before he acts: nothing that he does can change what he is."

NOTES

This introduction was translated by Philip Derbyshire.

1.   For an analysis of these results, see Vázquez Sandrin and Quezada (2015). According to these authors, the twelve countries that have up-to-date information in this regard and included a question about "self-description" are Argentina, Bolivia,

Brazil, Chile, Colombia, Costa Rica, Ecuador, Guatemala, Honduras, Panama, Paraguay, and Venezuela.

2. Consider, for example, the current challenge by the Congreso Nacional Indígena (indigenous National Council) in Mexico to have an independent indigenous candidate in the next presidential elections in 2018.

3. Even though in this book there is no work examining social movements who base their demands on indigenous belonging, the politicization of indigenous identity as the basis of rights (which often goes under the name of "strategic essentialism") has to be understood as one more use of the category that takes place in precise historical contexts of enunciation. Along these lines, the politicization of indigenous identity should be considered as an object of study that needs to be explained, not as a factor explaining social movements.

4. Instances of this sort of chronological account can be found in, for example, Gotkowitz (2011, 11–38) and Loveman (2014) for Latin America; and for Mexico, Bonfil (1972), Knight (1990), López (2010, 2–12), Sanz (2011), and more recently in Martínez Casas et al. (2014), even if this last text tends to align its narrative with a political program that critiques the ideology of *mestizaje* as a mechanism of oppression.

5. A more elaborate commentary on this literature and on the analysis of the category *indigenous* can be found in López Caballero (forthcoming).

6. We have already seen that Castro Gutiérrez (2010) points out how difficult it was in the history of Mexico to perceive and recognize people identified as indigenous outside of the rural context.

7. Important exceptions are Washbrook (2012) and Viqueira (2002), both on the region of Los Altos de Chiapas, and on Michoacán, Boyer (2003), and the book edited by Roth-Seneff (2015), especially the chapter by Castro Gutiérrez.

8. For a more detailed discussion of this historiography, see Rugeley (2002), Reina (2011), and Guardino in this book.

9. In the historiography of the Mexican Revolution, this perspective breaks down into two modalities: the populist, in which the masses and the leaders form a unity against the elites, and the revisionist, which rejects the popular character of the movement, conceiving it as a manipulation of the masses by the leaders (see Boyer 2003).

10. Without pretending to be exhaustive, some demonstrations of how cultural continuity and alterity continue to pursue anthropologists concerned with the indigenous populations of the continent can be found in the idea of the "hard nucleus" (*núcleo duro*) of culture (López Austin 1996), very close to that of "cultural logic" (Dehouve 1993; Good 2004). Both ideas have a structuralist background that presupposes a cultural frame that survives through time and defines the singularity of the group under study (for an excellent critique of this postulate, see Bazin 2009). The notion of "ontologies" badly conceals its structuralist inheritance and once more refers back to a postulate of alterity (no longer of mental structures but of forms of conceiving oneself and the nature/culture distinction supposedly structuring Western thought). See Descola (2013), Viveiros de Castro (2014), and De la Cadena (2010). And lastly, the term "epistemologies of the south" (De Sousa Santos

2009) and its derivatives in, for example, "Mayan epistemology" also presuppose a persistence not so much of culture but of resistance. This model is close to that of "change for continuity" (Hernández 2001; Recondo 2007), according to which continuity would be the aim of the social practices of the actors under investigation.

11. For example, in the chapters by Kourí and Torres-Mazuera. In addition, see Purnell (1999), Marino (2016), Baitenmann (2011), and Eiss (2010).

12. See also Hernández (2001), who explores the articulations between applied anthropology, indigenous politics, and indigenous identity in Chiapas during the twentieth century, or Vázquez León (2010), who interrogates "Purépecha identities" under the sign of contemporary multicultural norms. In our book, see chapter 8 by López Caballero, chapter 9 by Schwartz, and chapter 10 by Escalona.

13. Also see Schlossberg (2015), who deals with the production of indigenous authenticity among Michoacán artisans, and Muehlmann (2013), who analyzes the historical and political construction of indigenous identity in the Colorado River Delta. López Caballero (2017), for her part, shows how the inhabitants of Milpa Alta in Mexico City continue to identify as "autochthonous" without calling themselves indigenous. In the present volume, see chapter 5 by Rockwell and chapter 9 by Schwartz.

14. For a historical perspective, see the valuable work of Martínez (2008) on the notions of race and lineage in colonial America and the research of Giudicelli (2010), where he analyzes how the incipient ethnology of the nineteenth century reactivated the colonial administrative categories from the north of Mexico, converting them into ethnonyms of what, since then, have been called "ethnic groups."

15. One example of this presupposition is the work of Van Young (2001, 402, 483), for whom the subaltern actors are characterized by their "localocentrism" and rooted in particular world views. A second example is Mallon (1995, 97), who, by contrast with Van Young, argues that campesinos played an important role in national projects and at the same time considers that these actors produced a "communitarian liberalism" fundamentally different from that of the elite, thus implying that they had a strong degree of autonomy.

16. The blurring of boundaries between people and the elite, between indigenous and non-indigenous that is outlined in the chapters by Guardino, Ducey, and Acevedo-Rodrigo, suggests how useful it would be to initiate a dialogue between this history of popular participation and conceptual history. Although the latter has centered on the elites, and the former on subordinate groups, both share a questioning of the existence of a fixed or "authentic" definition of liberalism that allows the latter to be divided into fundamentally elite or popular versions (Palti 2006; Ávila 2007).

17. A third similarity that has been widely maintained in other works is that the national sphere cannot be the privileged level of analysis, given the systematic interactions and exchanges with actors situated beyond the borders of the state (Tenorio Trillo 1999; Said 1978).

18. We can see this perspective, for example, in Earle's work (2007, 3). She explains that the objective of her book is "to tell a coherent story about the place of 'the Indian' within Spanish American elite nationalism," as though this has been

an objective reality even if its representation has varied over time. See also Rozat (2001, 12), who additionally opposes the "representations of the Indian" to the "real Indians of the country," which leads to the extreme position of assuming that it is representation that is inaccessible or variable and not "the real Indians." For other examples of the representation of the Indian in literature, see Taylor (2009) and Lund (2012); in cinema, Arroyo (2011) and Lienhart (2004); in international festivals, Tenorio Trillo (1996); and in popular culture, Pérez Montfort (1994). In contrast, see Achim (2017) for the early history of the National Museum and the change of status of its exhibit *From Idols to Antiquities*. For the history of anthropology in Mexico, the fundamental contribution by Lomnitz (2001) shows how Mexican anthropology and nationalism were slowly knitted together out of the same yarn, thus contributing to the definition of the indigenous other.

19. A similar thesis is explored for the period dominated by the figure of Lázaro Cardenas, who at the same time he was driving forward the policies of the Departamento de Asuntos Indígenas (Department of Indian Affairs) was fixing a stable representation of the indigenous subject founded on "a glorious past, [and] in a communitarian present, that is at the same time poverty stricken and homogeneous" (López Hernández 2013, 70). Also see Giraudo (2016), Plá (2011), and López Caballero (2015).

20. See, for example, the fundamental article by Brading (1988); although he gives a close examination of the work of Gamio, this author focuses mainly on the political impact his figure had. Also in the inspiring work of Palacios (1998, 2008), the theoretical or programmatic discussions are not accompanied by an analysis of the concrete exercise of the production of knowledge. See also the detailed investigation by Urías Horcasitas (2007), who reconstructs the history of racialist and racist thought in the sphere of scientific and political ideas in Mexico from the nineteenth century to the 1950s.

21. See among others, Appelbaum, Macpherson, and Rosemblatt (2003), Gotkowitz (2011), Knight (1990), Stepan (1991), Urías Horcasitas (2007), and Wade (2015).

22. For a discussion of the use of race in genomics studies and its problematic relationship with identity, see Abel and Sandoval-Velasco (2016) and Nelson (2016).

REFERENCES

Abel, Sarah, and Marcela Sandoval-Velasco. 2016. "Crossing Disciplinary Lines: Reconciling Social and Genomic Perspectives on the Histories and Legacies of the Transatlantic Trade in Enslaved Africans." *New Genetics and Society* 35 (2): 149–85.

Achim, Miruna. 2017. *From Idols to Antiquity: Forging the National Museum of Mexico*. Lincoln: University of Nebraska Press.

Anderson, Benedict. 2006. *Imagined Communities: Reflections on the Origin and Spread of Nationalism*. Rev. ed. London: Verso Books. First published 1983.

Angosto, Luis Fernando, and Sabine Kradolfer, eds. 2012. *Everlasting Countdowns: Race, Ethnicity and National Censuses in Latin American States*. Newcastle: Cambridge Scholars Publishing.

Appelbaum, Nancy P., Anne S. Macpherson, and Karin Alejandra Rosemblatt, eds. 2003. *Race and Nation in Modern Latin America*. Chapel Hill: University of North Carolina Press.

Arroyo, Claudia. 2011. "Fantasías sobre la identidad indígena en el cine mexicano del periodo postrevolucionario." In *Identidades. Explorando la diversidad*, edited by Laura Carballido, 149–70. Mexico: Universidad Autónoma Metropolitana (UAM)–Anthropos.

Ávila, Alfredo. 2007. "Liberalismos decimonónicos: de la historia de las ideas a la historia cultural e intelectual." In *Ensayos sobre la nueva historia política de América Latina, siglo XIX*, edited by Guillermo Palacios, 111–45. Mexico: Colegio de México.

Baitenmann, Helga. 2011. "Popular Participation in State Formation: Land Reform in Revolutionary Mexico." *Journal of Latin American Studies* 43 (1): 1–31.

Barth, Fredrik. 1969. *Ethnic Groups and Boundaries: The Social Organization of Culture Difference*. Oslo: Universitetsforlaget.

Bartra, Roger. (1987) 2003. *La jaula de la melancolía. Identidad y metamorfosis del mexicano*. Mexico: Grijalbo.

Basave Benítez, Agustín. 2002. *México mestizo. Análisis del nacionalismo mexicano en torno a la mestizofilia de Andrés Molina Enríquez*. Mexico: Fondo de Cultura Económica.

Bauman, Zygmunt. 1989. *Modernity and the Holocaust*. Cambridge: Polity.

Bazin, Jean. 2009. *Des clous dans la Joconde. L'anthropologie autrement*. Toulouse: Anacharsis.

Beauvoir, Simone de. 1953. *The Second Sex*. New York: Knopf.

Bhaba, Homi K. 1994. *The Location of Culture*. London: Routledge.

Bonfil Batalla, Guillermo. 1972. "El concepto del indio en América: categoría de situación colonial." *Anales de Antropología* 9: 105–24.

Bourdieu, Pierre. 1982. "La force des representations." In *Ce que parler veut dire*. Paris: Seuil.

———. 2013. *Distinction: A Social Critique of the Judgement of Taste*. New York: Routledge.

Boyer, Christopher. 2003. *Becoming Campesinos: Politics, Identity and Agrarian Struggle in Postrevolutionary Michoacán, 1920–1935*. Stanford, CA: Stanford University Press.

Brading, David. 1988. "Manuel Gamio and Official *Indigenismo* in Mexico." *Bulletin of Latin American Research* 7 (1): 75–89.

Briones, Claudia. 2015. "Madejas de alteridad, entramados de estados-nación: diseños y telares de ayer y hoy en América latina." In *Nación y alteridad. Mestizos, indígenas y extranjeros en el proceso de formación nacional*, edited by Daniela Gleizer and Paula López Caballero, 17–61. Mexico: UAM and Ediciones Educación y Cultura.

Butler, Judith. 1993. *Bodies That Matter: On the Discursive Limits of Sex*. New York: Routledge.

Canessa, Andrew. 2012. *Intimate Indigeneities: Race, Sex, and History in the Small Spaces of Andean Life*. Durham, NC: Duke University Press.

———. 2014. "Conflict, Claim and Contradiction in the New 'Indigenous' State of Bolivia." *Critique of Anthropology* 34 (2): 153–73.

Castro Gutiérrez, Felipe. 2010. "Los indios y la ciudad. Panorama y perspectivas de investigación." In *Los indios y las ciudades de la Nueva España*, edited by Felipe Castro Gutiérrez, 9–33. Mexico: Universidad Nacional Autónoma de México (UNAM).

Corrigan, Philip Richard, and Derek Sayer. 1985. *The Great Arch: English State Formation as Cultural Revolution*. Oxford: Blackwell.

Cunin, Elisabeth, and Odile Hoffmann, eds. 2014. *Blackness and* Mestizaje *in Mexico and Central America*. Trenton, NJ: Africa World Press.

Dehouve, Danielle. 1993. "À la recherche du sens perdu. La lutte contre l'oubli chez des Nahuas du Mexique." In *Mémoire de la tradition*, edited by A. Becquelin, M. Antoinette, and D. Dehouve, 51–70. Nanterre: Société d'ethnologie.

De la Cadena, Marisol. 2010. "Indigenous Cosmopolitics in the Andes: Conceptual Reflections Beyond 'Politics.'" *Cultural Anthropology* 25 (2): 334–70.

De la Cadena, Marisol, and Orin Starn, eds. 2007. *Indigenous Experience Today*. New York: Berg.

Descola, Philip. 2013. *Beyond Nature and Culture*. Chicago: University of Chicago Press.

De Sousa Santos, Boaventura. 2009. *Una epistemología del Sur. La reinvención del conocimiento y la emancipación social*. Buenos Aires: Siglo XXI Editores, Consejo Latinoamericano de Ciencias Sociales.

Earle, Rebecca. 2007. *The Return of the Native: Indians and Myth-Making in Spanish America, 1810–1930*. Durham, NC: Duke University Press.

Eiss, Paul. 2010. *In the Name of* el Pueblo*: Place, Community, and the Politics of History in Yucatán*. Durham, NC: Duke University Press.

———. 2016. "Mestizo Acts." *Latin American and Caribbean Ethnic Studies* 11 (3): 1–9.

Forte, Maximilian. 2013. *Who Is an Indian? Race, Place, and the Politics of Indigeneity in the Americas*. Toronto: University of Toronto Press.

Friedlander, Judith. 1975. *Being Indian in Hueyapan: A Study of Forced Identity in Contemporary Mexico*. New York: Saint Martin's.

Frye, David. 1996. *Indians into Mexicans: History and Identity in a Mexican Town*. Austin: University of Texas Press.

Gabbert, Wolfgang. 2004. *Becoming Maya: Ethnicity and Social Inequality in Yucatán Since 1500*. Tucson: University of Arizona Press.

Giraudo, Laura. 2016. "Piégés dans la 'race indienne': maîtres d'école, inspecteurs et communautés rurales dans le Mexique post-révolutionnaire." In *Régimes nationaux d'altérité. États-nations et altérités autochtones en Amérique latine, 1810–1950*, edited by Paula López Caballero and Christophe Giudicelli, 179–206. Rennes: Presses Universitaires de Rennes (Coll. Les Amériques).

Giudicelli, Christophe. 2010. "Historia de un equívoco. La traducción etnográfica de las clasificaciones coloniales. El caso neovizcaíno." In *Fronteras movedizas. Clasificaciones coloniales y dinámicas socioculturales en las fronteras americanas*, edited by Christophe Giudicelli, 139–71. Zamora, Mexico: Colegio de Michoacán, Centro de Estudios Mexicanos y Centroamericanos.

Good, Catherine. 2004. "Ofrendar, alimentar y nutrir: los usos de la comida en la vida ritual nahua." In *Historia y vida ceremonial en las comunidades mesoamericanas: los ritos agrícolas*, edited by Johanna Broda and Catherine Good, 307–20. Mexico: Instituto Nacional de Antropología e Historia, Consejo Nacional para la Cultura y las Artes, Instituto de Investigaciones Históricas-UNAM.

Gotkowitz, Laura. 2011. "Introduction: Racisms of the Present and the Past in Latin America." In *Histories of Race and Racism: The Andes and Mesoamerica from Colonial Times to the Present*, edited by Laura Gotkowitz, 1–53. Durham, NC: Duke University Press.

Graham, Laura R., and H. Glenn Penny, eds. 2014. "Performing Indigeneity: Emergent Identity, Self-Determination, and Sovereignty." In *Performing Indigeneity: Global Histories and Contemporary Experiences*, edited by Laura R. Graham and H. Glenn Penny. Lincoln: University of Nebraska Press, 1–53.

Hernández, Rosalva Aída. 2001. *La otra frontera: identidades múltiples en el Chiapas poscolonial*. Mexico: Centro de Investigaciones y Estudios Superiores en Antropología Social (CIESAS) and Miguel Ángel Porrúa.

Hobsbawm, Eric, and Terence Ranger. 1983. *The Invention of Tradition*. Cambridge: Cambridge University Press.

INEGI. 2010. *Censo de Población y Vivienda*. Mexico: Instituto Nacional de Estadística y Geografía.

Jenkins, Richard. 1994. "Rethinking Ethnicity: Identity, Categorization and Power." *Ethnic and Racial Studies* 17 (2): 197–23.

Joseph, Gilbert M., and Daniel Nugent, eds. 1994. *Everyday Forms of State Formation: Revolution and the Negotiation of Rule in Modern Mexico*. Durham, NC: Duke University Press.

Knight, Alan. 1990. "Racism, Revolution and *Indigenismo*: Mexico, 1910–1940." In *The Idea of Race in Latin America*, edited by Richard Graham, 71–113. Austin: University of Texas Press.

Lartigue, François, and André Quesnel, eds. 2003. *Las dinámicas de la población indígena: cuestiones y debates actuales en México*. Mexico: CIESAS.

Latour, Bruno. 1988. *The Pasteurization of France*. Cambridge, MA: Harvard University Press.

Latour, Bruno, and Steve Woolgar. 1986. *Laboratory Life: The Construction of Scientific Facts*. Princeton, NJ: Princeton University Press.

Lévi-Strauss, Claude. 1962. *La pensé sauvage*. Paris: Plon.

Lienhart, Martin. 2004. "*La noche de los mayas*: Indigenous Mesoamericans in Cinema and Literature, 1917–1943." *Journal of Latin American Cultural Studies* 13 (1): 35–62.

Lomnitz, Claudio. 2001. *Deep Mexico, Silent Mexico: An Anthropology of Nationalism*. Minneapolis, MN: University of Minneapolis Press.

López, Rick. 2010. *Crafting Mexico: Intellectuals, Artisans, and the State After the Revolution*. Durham, NC: Duke University Press.

López Austín, Alfredo. 1996. *Los mitos del Tlacuache*. Mexico: Instituto de Investigaciones Antropológicas–UNAM.

López Beltrán, Carlos, ed. 2011. *Genes (&) mestizos: Genómica y raza en la biomedicina mexicana*. Mexico: Instituto de Investigaciones Filosóficas-UNAM and Ficticia Editorial.

López Caballero, Paula. 2009. "The Effect of Othering: The Historical Dialect of Local and National Identity Among the *Originarios*, 1950–2000." *Anthropological Theory* 9 (2): 171–87.

———. 2015. "Las políticas indigenistas y la 'fábrica' de su sujeto de intervención en la creación del primer Centro Coordinador del Instituto Nacional Indigenista (1948–

1952)." In *Nación y alteridad. Mestizos, indígenas y extranjeros en el proceso de formación nacional*, edited by Daniela Gleizer and Paula López Caballero, 69–108. Mexico: UAM and Ediciones Educación y Cultura.

———. 2017. *Indígenas de la nación. Etnografía histórica de la alteridad en Mexico (Milpa Alta siglos XVII–XXI)*. Mexico: Fondo de Cultura Económica.

———. Forthcoming. "La inevitable volatilidad del 'ser' indígena en México. Por una praxeología de las identificaciones a partir de la identificación como 'indígena.'" Unpublished manuscript, last modified September 10, 2017. Microsoft Word file.

López Hernández, Haydée. 2013. "De la gloria prehispánica al socialismo. Las políticas indigenistas del cardenismo." *Cuicuilco* 20 (57): 47–74.

Loveman, Mara. 2014. *National Colors: Racial Classification and the State in Latin America*. Oxford: Oxford University Press.

Lund, Joshua. 2012. *The Mestizo State: Reading Race in Modern Mexico*. Minneapolis, MN: University of Minnesota Press.

Mallon, Florencia. 1995. *Peasant and Nation: The Making of Postcolonial Mexico and Peru*. Berkeley: University of California Press.

Marino, Daniela. 2016. *Huixquilucan. Ley y justicia en la modernización del espacio rural mexiquense, 1856–1910*. Madrid: Consejo Superior de Investigaciones Científicas.

Martínez, María Elena. 2008. *Genealogical Fictions: Limpieza de Sangre, Religion, and Gender in Colonial Mexico*. Stanford, CA: Stanford University Press.

Martínez Casas, Regina, Emiko Saldívar, René D. Flores, and Christina A. Sue. 2014. "The Different Faces of *Mestizaje*: Ethnicity and Race in Mexico." In *Pigmentocracies: Ethnicity, Race, and Color in Latin America*, by Edward Telles and the Project on Ethnicity and Race in Latin America, 36–80. Chapel Hill: University of North Carolina Press.

Mitchell, Timothy. 1991. "The Limits of the State: Beyond Statist Approaches and Their Critics." *The American Political Science Review* 85 (1): 77–96.

Muehlmann, Shaylih. 2013. *Where the River Ends: Contested Indigeneity in the Mexican Colorado Delta*. Durham, NC: Duke University Press.

Nelson, Alondra. 2016. *The Social Life of DNA: Race, Reparations, and Reconciliation After the Genome*. Boston: Beacon.

Palacios, Guillermo. 1998. "Postrevolutionary Intellectuals, Rural Readings and the Shaping of the 'Peasant Problem' in Mexico: El Maestro Rural, 1932–1934." *Journal of Latin American Studies* 30 (2): 309–39.

———. 2008. "Intelectuales, poder revolucionario y ciencias sociales en Mexico (1920–1940)." In *Historia de los intelectuales en América Latina. De la conquista al modernismo I*, edited by Carlos Altamirano and Jorge Myers, 583–605. Buenos Aires: Katz.

Palti, Elías José. 2006. "The Problem of 'Misplaced Ideas' Revisited: Beyond the 'History of Ideas' in Latin America." *Journal of the History of Ideas* 67 (1): 149–79.

Pérez Montfort, Ricardo. 1994. *Estampas de nacionalismo popular mexicano: ensayos sobre cultura popular y nacionalismo*. Mexico: CIESAS.

Pitarch, Pedro. 2008. "El imaginario prehispánico." *Nexos* 372 (29): 49–54.

Plá, Dolores. 2011. "Más desindianización que mestizaje. Una relectura de los censos generales de población." *Dimensión Antropológica* 18 (53): 69–91.

Purnell, Jennie. 1999. *Popular Movements and State Formation in Revolutionary Mexico: The Agraristas and Cristeros of Michoacán*. Durham, NC: Duke University Press.

Recondo, David. 2007. *La política del gatopardo: multiculturalismo y democracia en Oaxaca*. Mexico: CIESAS.

Reina, Leticia. 1980. *Las rebeliones de campesinos en Mexico (1819–1906)*. Mexico: Siglo XXI Editores.

———. 2011. *Indio, campesino y nación en el siglo XX mexicano. Historia e historiografía de los movimientos rurales*. Mexico: Siglo XXI Editores.

Roth-Seneff, Andrew, Robert V. Kemper, and Julie Adkins, eds. 2015. *From Tribute to Communal Sovereignty: The Tarascand and Caxcan Territories in Transition*. Tucson: University of Arizona Press.

Rozat Dupeyron, Guy. 2001. *Los orígenes de la nación: pasado indígena e historia nacional*. Mexico: Universidad Iberoamericana, Departamento de Historia.

Rugeley, Terry. 2002. "Indians Meet the State, Regions Meet the Center: Nineteenth-Century Mexico Revisited." *Latin American Research Review* 37 (1): 245–58.

Ruiz Medrano, Ethelia, and Susan Kellog, eds. 2010. *Negotiation Within Domination: New Spain's Indian Pueblos Confront the Spanish State*. Boulder: University Press of Colorado.

Rus, Jan. 1994. "The '*Comunidad Revolucionaria Institucional*': The Subversion of Native Government in Highland Chiapas, 1936–1968." In Joseph and Nugent 1994, 265–300.

Saada Granados, Marta. 2011. "Mexico mestizo: de la incomodidad a la certidumbre. Ciencia y política pública posrevolucionarias." In López Beltrán 2011, 29–64.

Said, Edward W. 1978. *Orientalism*. New York: Vintage Books Editions.

Sanz, Eva. 2011. *Los indios de la nación. Los indígenas en los escritos de intelectuales y políticos del Mexico independiente*. Madrid: Frankfurt am Main; Mexico: Iberoamericana, Vervuert, Bonilla Artigas, and Universidad de Alcalá.

Schlossberg, Pavel. 2015. *Crafting Identity: Transnational Indian Arts and the Politics of Race in Central Mexico*. Tucson: University of Arizona Press.

Scott, Joan W. 1986. "Gender: A Useful Category of Historical Analysis." *The American Historical Review* 91 (5): 1053–75.

Segato, Laura Rita. 2007. *La nación y sus otros*. Buenos Aires: Prometeo.

Shor, Paul. 2009. *Compter et classer: Histoire des recensements américains*. Paris: École des Hautes Études en Sciences Sociales.

Stepan, Nancy. 1991. *The Hour of Eugenics: Race, Gender, and Nation in Latin America*. Ithaca, NY: Cornell University Press.

Taylor, Analisa. 2009. *Indigeneity in the Mexican Cultural Imagination: Thresholds of Belonging*. Tucson: University of Arizona Press.

Tenorio Trillo, Mauricio. 1996. *Mexico at World's Fairs: Crafting a Modern Nation*. Berkeley: University of California Press.

———. 1999. "Stereophonic Scientific Modernisms: Social Science Between Mexico and the United States, 1880–1930." *The Journal of American History* 86 (3): 1156–87.

———. 2009. "Del mestizaje a un siglo de Andrés Molina Enríquez." In *En busca de Molina Enríquez. Cien años de "Los grandes problemas nacionales,"* edited by Emilio Kourí, 33–64. Mexico: Colegio de México.

Urías Horcasitas, Beatriz. 2007. *Historias secretas del racismo en Mexico (1920–1950)*. Mexico: Tusquets Editories.

Van Young, Eric. 1999. "The New Cultural History Comes to Old Mexico." *Hispanic American Historical Review* 79 (2): 211–47.

———. 2001. *The Other Rebellion: Popular Violence, Ideology, and the Mexican Struggle for Independence, 1810–1821*. Stanford, CA: Stanford University Press.

Varela, Roberto. 2002. "Naturaleza/cultura, poder/política, autoridad/legalidad/legitimidad." In *Antropología jurídica. Perspectivas socioculturales en el estudio del derecho*, edited by Esteban Krotz, 69–109. Barcelona: Anthropos, UAM.

Vázquez León, Luis. 2010. *Multitud y distopía. Ensayos sobre la nueva condición étnica en Michoacán*. Mexico: UNAM, Programa Universitario Mexico Nación Multicultural.

Vázquez Sandrin, Germán, and María Felix Quezada. 2015. "Los indígenas autoadscritos de México en el censo 2010: ¿revitalización étnica o sobreestimación censal?" *Papeles de Población* 21 (86): 171–218.

Viqueira, Juan Pedro. 2002. "La comunidad indígena en Mexico en los estudios antropológicos e históricos." In *Encrucijadas chiapanecas. Economía, religión e identidades*, edited by Viqueira Juan Pedro, 47–74. Mexico: Tusquets and Colegio de México.

Viveiros de Castro, Edoardo. 2014. *Cannibal Metaphysics*. Minneapolis, MN: Univocal.

Wade, Peter. 2013. "Blackness, Indigeneity, Multiculturalism and Genomics in Brazil, Colombia and Mexico." *Journal of Latin American Studies* 45 (2): 205–33.

———. 2015. *Race: An Introduction*. New York: Cambridge University Press.

Washbrook, Sarah. 2012. *Producing Modernity in Mexico: Labour, Race, and the State in Chiapas, 1876–1914*. Oxford: Oxford University Press.

Williams, Raymond. 1982. *The Sociology of Culture*. New York: Schocken.

PART I

LAND AND GOVERNMENT

CHAPTER 1

THE PRACTICES OF COMMUNAL LANDHOLDING

Indian Pueblo Property Relations in Colonial Mexico

EMILIO KOURÍ

ORPORATE LANDHOLDING in colonial Mexican villages (*repúblicas de indios*) has long been defined ex ante as possessing a series of characteristics presumably inherent to indigenous culture: communalism, cohesion, and a spirit of egalitarian solidarity. Communal property holding thus understood has commonly been regarded as the supreme institutional expression of indigenous cultural identity and practice, and hence as a defining aspect of indigeneity. Against this view, this essay offers a broad reinterpretation of the long history of land tenure in the pueblos, going back to the sixteenth century. Through a critical analysis of a wide array of sources, it argues that the structure of land use in villages was from the start hierarchical and profoundly inequitable, and also that de facto private property rights over (communal) lands had been a feature of pueblo society long before the disentailment law of 1856 and subsequent decrees provided a legal path to privatization. Judging from this evidence, it seems clear that equitable and inclusive access to communal land by the members of village corporations was never a salient feature of indigenous social organization.

THE *REPÚBLICA DE INDIOS*

Modeled juridically to resemble Spanish towns, Mexican colonial villages were at first largely an extension, under changing political circumstances, of pre-existing indigenous institutions. Tenochtitlán had been vanquished, but the

Spaniards were few and the territory vast, so out in the countryside, the lords who ruled would continue to do so. Local forms of social organization decisively shaped the initial constitution of the pueblos, even as these began to conform to the municipal norms laid out by Spanish legislation in the wake of the conquest. Certain parallelisms in form—as well as prior experience with imperial demands—made the transition relatively uncomplicated, but there is no doubt that in the first instance, the pueblos essentially reprised many well-established practices of pre-Hispanic stock. It is important to identify the most salient of these, but not without first recalling—and endorsing—the wise caveat of Alonso de Zurita, a sixteenth-century Spanish royal judge who compiled extensive descriptions of native ways and means: "I must say at the outset, however, that it is impossible to state a general rule as concerns any part of Indian government and customs, for there are great differences in almost every province . . . Consequently, if what I say here appears to contradict some other information, the cause must be the diversity that exists in all things in every province" (Zurita 1963, 86).

Considered in abstraction, there are two aspects of local indigenous social organization worth highlighting, at least for the most densely populated areas of New Spain, where the majority of colonial pueblos were to be established. Although their specific manifestations would change considerably over time, their imprint was to be lasting. The first was the expressly hierarchical character of the local social order, in terms both of rulership and of the categorization of place and space. Rural society was aristocratic in nature, with lords and nobles exercising their dominion over commoners, serfs, and slaves. In the Nahua-speaking central valleys, the *altepetl*—akin, in some ways, to a county—was the main human association, a lordship headed by a *tlatoani* in association with a hereditary class of nobles (*pipiltin*) ruling over various groups of commoners and dependents with diverse sets of tribute and labor obligations. High administrative, religious, and judicial functions were the preserve of the nobles. The *altepetl* had also a territorial component, within which the local nobility exercised a broad jurisdiction. This territory, as will be seen, was also hierarchically subdivided. Oaxaca's Mixtecs and Zapotecs were organized in similar fashion, with hereditary kings of divine origin and a supporting nobility commanding a people and a territory stratified socially and spatially. Likewise, Yucatec Maya society at the time of the conquest was composed of discrete, multilayered polities with a territorial domain governed by hereditary lords (the *batabs*).

These hierarchical conceptions ordered the space under the lords' jurisdiction in a number of ways. There were head settlements—usually where the lord resided—and subject settlements, with lines of authority drawn accordingly. In the *altepetl*, the outlying hamlets were called *calpullis*, or "little villages"—often dispersed, nonnucleated settlements—with their own subordinate officials. The head town would sometimes contain several barrios, each also a *calpulli*. Social obligations (tribute, labor services, etc.) were structured following that axis of power, from the hinterlands toward the center as well as from the bottom up. Across the entire territory of the lordship, land was also categorized in this manner, with an elaborate set of differential rights and uses reflecting the society's pyramidal orientation. Despite profound changes over the following centuries, the character of village social relations would long be conditioned by this foundational stratification.

A second generalizable aspect of pre-Hispanic rural organization concerns internal political autonomy. Although imperial rule was or had been a fact of life in many parts of the region, the lordships had a remarkable degree of autonomy in the internal conduct of their own affairs—political, religious, judicial, or economic. Where the Aztecs held sway, the payment of tribute was the principal requirement, and most local polities were otherwise largely unaffected. This indirect form of rule meant that within the lords' jurisdictions self-government—albeit of a hierarchical sort—prevailed. This established tradition of relative local self-rule the Spanish Crown found at first very amenable. It served to counter the aristocratic pretensions of ambitious conquistadors and *encomenderos*, plus it meshed well with peninsular views regarding both the prerogatives of town governments and the residual rights of conquered nobilities. Efforts would later be made to curtail the power of the native nobility and restrict the range and scope of the Indian towns' jurisdiction, but the principle of limited self-government embodied in the old indigenous polities survived the transition to Spanish rule and became a defining feature of the new colonial pueblos. The pre-Hispanic lordships had designated assets to provide for their collective obligations, internal and external, and the pueblos would, as well. The defense of this political space of municipal autonomy would be a recurrent theme in the history of the pueblos.

Around the middle of the sixteenth century, the *repúblicas de indios* began to take shape as a structure of local government for the indigenous pueblos. The old hierarchies of place were by and large maintained, with head and subject towns together making up a pueblo, though some formerly dependent villages managed to attain the legal status of pueblo and obtain *repúblicas* of their own. Secession was a constant, if often latent, ambition among subject villages, which surged out into the open—with frequent success—in the second half of the eighteenth century. The *repúblicas* got a governor and a town council (one or more mayors and a number of councilmen), all seated in the head town, and the subject towns got a local councilman. They also established a community treasury (*caja de comunidad*), out of which they would pay for their various civil obligations. In general terms, the lords took up the governorships and the nobles (labeled as *principales*) the various council positions, all of which underscored a sense of continuity. In addition, sundry other minor officials were maintained, in accordance with local custom. Spanish law required the *repúblicas* to be elected, but the lords and *principales* managed at first to retain control of the government by limiting high office holding to those of their rank. In some places (e.g., central Mexico) the nobility lost power and importance during the second half of the sixteenth century, and the commoners (*macehuales*) took over the republics. Here, other hierarchies would henceforth prevail, with wealth, not status, as the main basis of rank. In other places (e.g., parts of Oaxaca and Yucatán) the nobility held on to the town governments until at least the close of the seventeenth century, and in some Yucatecan cases, possibly for another hundred years or more.[1] In other respects, the form of Indian town government remained unchanged—except for minor modifications—until the collapse of the Spanish Empire.

In regard to the socioeconomic and institutional history of pueblos, however, these formal continuities hide far more than they reveal. The pueblos' story would be one of change and adaptation, often radical and generally improvised. In the words of a historian who has pondered this issue, "Eighteenth century pueblos barely preserved the essential features of their predecessors . . . ; despite the nearly static image provided by persistent formal structures and a conservative legal framework, [the *pueblos de indios*] were constantly undergoing deep changes in every conceivable field, political, social, economic, spatial or otherwise" (García Martínez 1990, 105). The root causes were demographic (a precipitous collapse, followed by spatial reorganizations, then a gradual population recovery) and economic (the development of Spanish towns, markets, and enterprises, including haciendas). As populations shifted and the business of colonialism sprouted, pueblos disappeared, merged, moved, reconfigured themselves, or were born anew, yielding in due course a social and institutional landscape that may have resembled the old one superficially but was in fact profoundly different.

The Spanish invasions brought war, chaos, hunger, and enslavement to many quarters of native society, and these had a tangible demographic impact, but it was the European diseases—smallpox, measles, typhus, influenza, and malaria—that wreaked the deadliest havoc among the indigenous population. The epidemics struck in successive waves, silent tsunamis wiping out millions of Indians along the way. Two particularly devastating ones hit New Spain in the sixteenth century, one in the mid-1540s, another in the late 1570s. Historians have long debated the approximate magnitude of this demographic collapse, but by all accounts it was colossal, in some ways impossible to comprehend fully. A high estimate for the core area of indigenous settlement in New Spain—from the isthmus of Tehuantepec to the northern edge of Mesoamerica—places the decline's proportion at 33:1 (25 million to 750,000, 1519–1630), and a lower one at 15:1 (11 million to 750,000).[2] Needless to say, the fabric of village social relations was in many places torn irreparably; and as it was rewoven, the warp and weft would no longer make the same pattern.

In the face of steep population declines, and in the hope of tightening control over Indian subjects, Spanish authorities began a program of forced resettlement, first between 1550 and 1564, and again from the mid-1590s to around 1606. As whole villages disappeared and many a hamlet became abandoned, these *congregaciones* sought to consolidate surviving populations, moving pueblos to more suitable locations, placing *sujeto* dwellers into *cabeceras*, merging previously distinct communities into newly configured ones. Nucleated residential patterns, long a Spanish desideratum, took hold in many villages as a result of this process. Resettlement was sometimes resisted and not always successful; on the whole, however, the *congregaciones*—and native reactions to them—rearranged the social and political geography in core regions of Indian New Spain (Cline 1949; Gerhard 1972, 1975, 1977; Gibson 1985; and Simpson 1934). In the process, lands previously under the jurisdiction of the old lordships/pueblos became easily available for Spanish colonization, providing fertile ground for the growth of the hacienda.

Significant as they were, these prescribed transformations failed to produce the kind of municipal and residential stability that Spanish officials had ostensibly sought to establish for Indians. Other, more powerful forces would conspire against that, keeping colonial pueblos in a slow but continuous flux. The main impetus was the evolution of economic and demographic conditions after 1650, and especially during the eighteenth century. The notable growth of urban centers and of Spanish-controlled enterprises—mines, haciendas, cattle ranches—in the course of that period boosted the expansion of regional market economies, and hence also the competition over productive resources. Inside the pueblos, the sustained recovery of Indian populations—already palpable by the late 1600s—produced a similar effect. The most salient political consequence of these twin developments was perhaps the erection of numerous new municipal *cabeceras—pueblos de indios* in their own right, the bulk of them after 1750. This process unfolded in two distinct ways, each reflecting important aspects of the changing constitution of late colonial Mexican villages.

The most common route to pueblo status involved a kind of municipal fission, the secession of *sujeto* villages. Hundreds of new self-governing pueblos were created in this way. As noted, the autonomist impulse was far from new, but it acquired unprecedented vigor at this time, and Spanish authorities ultimately yielded to it, mainly for fiscal reasons. Beyond the old desire for self-rule, a confluence of several factors pushed many *sujetos* in this direction. Pervasive inequity between the *cabecera* and its *sujetos* in the allocation of tribute and labor obligations had long rankled dependent villages, as had the discretionary powers enjoyed by *cabildos* in the management of communal assets, which sometimes involved acts of malfeasance. Land, in particular, was often a bone of contention, especially where pueblos faced hacienda encroachment (a subject examined in the following section). The rise of village populations exacerbated these tensions and simultaneously offered a potential escape, since the larger *sujetos* could now show that they had enough qualified inhabitants to request their own *cabildos*.

The "progressive promotion of *sujetos* to *cabecera* status" was seldom achieved without some discord, and conflicts over boundaries and the proper division of communal assets formerly under the jurisdiction of the *cabecera* could become bitter and protracted (Gibson 1985, 190).[3] Still, late colonial Spanish officials by and large acquiesced, hoping for better fiscal accountability, and mindful of the villages' newly pressing demographic realities. Meanwhile, the rising economic elites in the newly emancipated pueblos savored the prospect of running their own town governments. Secession prospered in regions with different economic geographies: in Oaxaca's Mixteca, where the hacienda was not a threat, and in what is now Morelos, where sugar estates were growing in size and importance. Between 1646 and 1800, the number of *cabeceras* in Morelos rose from thirty-three to ninety-four, a rate of increase that mirrored that of New Spain as a whole. Elsewhere, a well-studied case is that of Tlapa, an old agricultural headtown in Guerrero that had seventy subject villages in 1767. Three decades later, "This vast jurisdiction had totally disintegrated and most of the subject villages had attained the rank of *pueblo cabecera*" (Dehouve 1984, 381; see also Gerhard 1975, 575; Pastor 1987, 175–78; Sánchez Santiró 2001).[4]

Another set of new pueblos arose not from the independence of established *sujetos* but from new settlements populated by migrants. Indian mobility—seasonal and permanent—was an old and widespread phenomenon, with roots going back well beyond the conquest.[5] Under Spanish rule, flight from oppressive communal obligations or disadvantageous village conditions was always a possibility, the corporatist prescriptions of colonial law notwithstanding. Along with the expansion of commercial and business activity, population growth after the early seventeenth century intensified these internal demographic movements, redrawing once again the human and institutional geography of the countryside. Despite the "closed" and "localocentric" character sometimes ascribed to colonial village corporations, their boundaries—in terms of social relations—were in fact rather porous (Wolf 1957).[6] Over time, people came and went, settling down and then moving on, and even full-fledged membership in a pueblo did not always imply permanent residency. Indians moved to cities, worked in mines and textile factories, and labored as hired hands in cattle ranches and agricultural haciendas. They also rented farm-fields from Spanish estates and colonized idle lands of uncertain ownership that appeared to be unoccupied and accessible. There they established permanent settlements—hamlets, ranchos, or *rancherías*—devoted at least in part to family agriculture. And it wasn't just Indian migrants who formed these new dwelling sites but also mestizos and *mulatos* moving along the widening interstices of an increasingly complex colonial economy. The emergence of many such places of diverse origin and legal standing in the course of the eighteenth century attests to the central importance of mobility and migration in shaping the evolution of institutional life in rural Mexico. Some of these informal settlements would grow in size, become organized, and in time attain the status of a *pueblo de indios*.

Tenampulco, in the Sierra de Puebla, is a good case in point. An eighteenth-century hamlet populated by arriving Indians and *mulatos rancheros*, it rose on the abandoned site of an old *altepetl* and pueblo that had completely collapsed at the close of the sixteenth century. According to the region's historian, the old Tenampulco "absolutely ceased to exist as a pueblo or as an organized settlement of any type during the seventeenth century" (García Martínez 1990, 109). Toponymic continuity aside, there was nothing in common between the two Tenampulcos, separated as they were by a gap of one hundred years. By the 1730s, the new migrant settlement had been recognized as a subject of Xonotla. A 1736 epidemic nearly wiped out the inhabitants of the hamlet, which was then practically abandoned for over two decades. In the late 1750s the survivors returned, and a third Tenampulco sprouted vigorously, seceding from Xonotla in 1777 to become its own *pueblo de indios*, even though a majority of its members were in all likelihood *mulatos* or *pardos*. Other eighteenth-century pueblos were constituted in similar fashion.[7]

In 1800, self-governing villages of recent creation far outnumbered those originating in the sixteenth century. By one count, "Approximately two thirds of the more than a thousand pueblos existing in the second half of the eighteenth century had been established only a few decades earlier as separate and individual corporations" (García Martínez 1990, 107). In addition, this dynamic process of "place making and place breaking" produced numerous other new settlements, which—unlike Tenampulco—did not achieve a political standing that would grant them self-rule (Amith 2005, chap. 6). By the close of the eighteenth century, these unincorporated ranchos and *rancherías* populated by Indians and *castas* of various sorts were nevertheless a very significant feature of rural society.[8] One of them, the *ranchería* of Mapastlán, had been formed by migrant *mulatos* and mestizos who worked on a hacienda of the same name and rented lands from a nearby pueblo, Anenecuilco. They were also muleteers, occasional mine workers, and ranch hands. In 1834, Mapastlán (later renamed Ayala) became a pueblo, and—in one of many historical ironies—old Anenecuilco was made its *sujeto* (Sotelo 1943, 212; and Hernández 1991, 46–47).[9] It was there, in 1911, that Emiliano Zapata would issue his famous Plan de Ayala, the clarion call for what soon turned into a struggle to reclaim the ancestral land and self-rule rights of the pueblos—rights that, as it turns out, Mapastlán/Ayala had never itself possessed.

The ironies of Ayala point to the tortuous, uneven, and often discontinuous history of colonial pueblo corporations, which stands in contrast to its own representation: a complicated web of discrete historical developments smoothed out into a hazy narrative emphasizing institutional stasis, unbroken rootedness, enduring identities, and fundamental solidarity. Most eighteenth-century pueblos were not old, and those that were—formal resemblances notwithstanding—no longer functioned much as they once had. In regard to the institutional trajectory of the pueblos, flexibility is a better characterization than resilience: they bent and twisted in the face of continuous challenges but were unable then to spring back into their previous shape. To be sure, there were significant signs of continuity with the past, some deceptive and others not. But the breaks were just as clear and important, if not more so. The principle of limited local self-government remained essential and became, like the *repúblicas*, more widespread, although its basis had changed substantially. In most pueblos, the aristocratic rule of their origins had become a thing of the past, replaced by a rising economic elite largely of commoner roots. Social hierarchies thus maintained a defining importance. The formal structures of governance no longer denoted these distinctions, but they were nevertheless very real, and not hard to find. Village land tenure and use arrangements placed them in sharp relief.

THE LANDS OF THE COLONIAL PUEBLOS

The organization of land tenure in pre-Hispanic lordships was extraordinarily diverse, locally as well as regionally, but it is possible to identify certain common categories: the lands devoted to the temples, the patrimonial lands of lords and nobles, the lands assigned to office holders, and the lands given to the commoners. Of these, only the last two would be of lasting importance in the constitution of colonial pueblos. Temple lands were diverted to other uses and owners with the imposition of Christianity, and lands devoted to the cult of the saints in colonial villages had in general a very different origin (the *cofradías*, or Indian confraternities). The lands belonging to the nobility were for the most part recognized by the Spaniards as private property, with title to them issued in the form of royal grants (*mercedes*). Their right of entailment, however, was a different matter; except in a few places (e.g., Oaxaca), it was completely eliminated, and over time the territories of the old lords were by and large alienated. In parts of Oaxaca where the lords (caciques) had their privileges validated, many of the entailed estates of their *cacicazgos* were maintained until the end of colonial rule, worked by tenant farmers (*mayeques* or *terrazgueros*) or rented to ranchers and villages. But elsewhere, on the whole, the old noble lands became indistinguishable from other kinds of private property, fee simple holdings that could be freely disposed of. The two remaining general categories—official and commoner lands—would form the core of the village corporations.[10]

In the course of the sixteenth century, colonial authorities sought to shape pueblo land tenure in the mold of Spanish towns, importing their categorization of public or communal lands: *propios y arbitrios* (town council lands, to fund governance and taxes), *ejidos y dehesas* (woodlands and pastures on the edge of town, for collective use), and *terrenos comunales* (farming lots for the use of town members). The transition was not especially complicated in legal terms, because these distinctions roughly replicated some already in existence locally. Official lands would become *propios* (tribute was organized in a different manner), and commoner lands would be divided into ejidos and *tierras del común* (later called *tierras de común repartimiento*), in accordance with their use. In practice the shift was far from seamless, because local land tenure arrangements were remarkably diverse (and because some pueblos retained much more land than others), and so many indigenous corporations never fully conformed to the norm. Not every town, for instance, would have its own ejido. Still, that would be the new model for colonial pueblos, and to some extent the *congregaciones* of the sixteenth century enabled its implementation.

A larger, more significant, and less well understood transition involved the gradual delimitation of the old jurisdictional domain of the lordships, the reduction of the new pueblos' sphere of administrative control to the boundaries of their recognized communal lands. Before, lordships appear to have exercised a broad set of jurisdictional powers over both a people and a territory, and the latter extended well beyond the confines of communal property—including lordly and religious lands, as well as other areas not currently under any specific category of use. Communal lands (as described above) formed a part of the lordship but were by no means the extent of it. Spanish colonial practice would sharply redefine these terms. Unoccupied lands—whatever the reason—were often regarded as *baldías* (idle) or *realengas* (belonging to the Crown) and were thus granted to—or purchased by—Spaniards and well-positioned Indians, freeing them from any administrative oversight by Indian *repúblicas*. Likewise, Spaniards residing within the territory of an Indian pueblo were exempted from the authority of its cabildo. Jurisdiction and territoriality thus shrank as they coalesced. As Spanish authorities validated the pueblos' property rights to their primordial possessions, the constitution of the *repúblicas* made their domain coterminous with it. In this way, and unlike the lordships that had preceded them, colonial Indian pueblos would be comprised only of communal territory, and the reach of Indian municipal government would go no further than that.[11]

The precise demarcations of a pueblo's communal lands were often a work in progress. The upheavals of the sixteenth century—sharp demographic declines, the spread of Spanish and Indian private estates, the *congregaciones*—kept many a pueblo's territorial boundaries in a state of flux. Numerous decrees regulating the size, composition, and utilization of Indian communal lands, while often protective in their intent, added to the confusion on the ground, establishing mandates that could not or would not be met (and providing a basis for protracted litigation).[12] During the decades of fast population loss, many pueblos sold vacant lands, particularly in areas where commercial agriculture and ranch-ing faced good prospects. Tax debts were often cited as part of the reason. Rentals were also common, and in some cases these, too, would lead to the per-manent alienation of communal property. Where Spanish economic enterprises were fast on the rise (e.g., parts of central Mexico), pueblo holdings tended to shrink in size, sometimes considerably. In other places, though, Indian *repúblicas* acquired additional land, by purchase or royal grant, thereby enhancing their patrimony (Gibson 1985, 268–83; Taylor 1972, chap. 3; García Martínez 1987; Simpson 1952; Chevalier 2006; and Nickel 1988, 48–59).[13]

From the late 1500s through the early 1700s (and later in certain regions), the Crown ordered a series of *composiciones de tierras*, compulsory title regularization programs designed to raise much needed revenues to cover the rising expense of imperial conflicts in Europe and the Americas. Private landowners were the initial target, but pueblos were eventually included. Costly as they were, these transactions allowed numerous haciendas and ranches—and many pueblos, as well—to obtain clean title to their lands, effectively legalizing previous de facto or irregular holdings. At the same time, efforts were made to establish and enforce a core land area to which every pueblo was entitled (the townsite, or *fundo legal*, as it would later be called). First in 1567, and once again in 1687 and 1695, royal decrees codified the minimum extension of *tierras por razón de pueblo* (lands held by virtue of being a pueblo), finally set at six hundred varas in each cardinal direction, measured from the town church. Variously interpreted and consistently contested by adjoining proprietors, this mandate enabled eighteenth-century pueblos with core settlement areas smaller than the norm to demand larger allotments, and many did so successfully.[14] The ruling applied only to *cabeceras*; in addition to their *fundo legal*, most pueblos had other, noncontiguous lands, including those of the *sujetos*. As subject towns seceded and became pueblos in their own right, they could request their own six hundred varas square, setting off endless litigation with established neighbors, including other pueblos.

In these ways, colonial villages gradually defined their territorial proper-ties. Conflicting claims and unresolved disputes became—and would long remain—an endemic feature of the lay of the land. On the whole, it is impos-sible to generalize about the evolution of pueblo landholdings following their constitution as colonial corporations. By the eighteenth century, some pueb-los had large territories, other very small ones; there was great variance not only across regions but within them. And what this all meant in local terms depended fundamentally on the quality of the lands held, on the land-person ratio, and on the manner of its allocation. Each pueblo had its own land story to tell. In terms of the social organization of communal land use, however, certain striking commonalities do emerge.

The first involves the disposition and control of the *tierras de común repartimiento*, farmlands held by village members to provide for themselves and their families. The bulk of a village's arable lands were usually occupied in this way, divided into lots (one, or more often, a scattered series of them) assigned—in theory—to each head of household. According to Spanish law, these lands were communal, meaning that they belonged to the collective, with individual members having only the right to work them. Town governments, the *repúblicas*, were entrusted with their fair administration and would—again, in principle—allocate and reallocate them to ensure that everyone's basic needs were attended to. There would be little or no individual private property within the village jurisdiction. Underlying this design was a strong colonial paternalism, but also a sense that it closely corresponded with essential cultural norms rooted in native societies. This was how indigenous people had long organized much of their basic agricultural production (in the *calpullis*), or so it was supposed, and pueblo landholding structures were intended to preserve and take advantage of that. True, there were also native forms of estate serfdom (the *mayeques*), but these Spanish royal authorities would initially seek to curtail, fearing the development of an American feudalism of the sort desired by the conquistadors. Village agriculture was thus imagined—and codified—as embodying an ethos of collectivist egalitarianism in the use of land, notwithstanding the rank distinctions that pueblo corporation would inherit from the lordships (which the Spaniards would, to a degree, seek to suppress). A 1532 letter from the audiencia of Mexico to the king captures this well: "In most communities few [citizens] have private lands except the native lords or their descendants. Very few commoners or tributaries own land. Most land is communally owned and worked. Communal lands serve to maintain the native nobility, to support their churches and celebrations, and now to pay tribute to Your Majesty" (Taylor 1972, 73).

This image of communal landholding norms was from the start by and large a fantasy, which outside observers and interpreters of pueblo life would long adhere to and village leaders were wise to perpetuate. The hierarchical character of pueblo government would often translate into an inequitable apportioning of communal farmlands, not just in terms of size but, crucially, also in terms of quality. Rank and office had their prerogatives, which were quite often self-reinforcing. This may not have mattered as much as long as the population was declining, but it would have serious consequences later on. As the native nobility lost political influence (where it did), local power passed into the hands of a class of relatively well-to-do commoners, whose ascendancy was also marked by privileged and disproportionate access to the landed resources of the community. By the second half of the eighteenth century, most, if not all, villages were almost certainly stratified in this fashion, with regional variations deriving mostly from local economic circumstances and culture-specific land management practices. This has long been recognized, to one or another degree, by most historians of colonial rural society, although the notion of a vague egalitarian village ethos somehow manages to persist.

What is less recognized—even though the evidence is no less compelling—and probably more significant is the widespread development of essentially private property relations within communal lands *de común repartimiento*. These were exclusive and extensive personal rights over portions of a village's territory, exercised not only by nobles or *principales* but also by many a *macehual*. It is not known for certain whether this represented an evolution of landholding trends already incipient among pre-Hispanic commoners or was instead the result of a gradual extension—in a colonial context—of accepted nobility property rights to other segments of village society.[15] In this regard, as in so many others, regional differences are bound to be notable. What is more certain, in any case, is that de facto private property in nominally communal lands was a common fact of life in many eighteenth-century Mexican pueblos, a practice that contradicts prevailing general characterizations, then and now, of the nature of village social relations in the colonial period.

Pueblo legal norms ratified the old rights of usufruct and inheritance that were an established part of commoner agriculture in pre-Hispanic *calpullis*, and there they drew the line. Villagers could make use of communal farmlands and pass them on to their heirs; claims to specific plots within the communal zone were thus acknowledged to have a certain consuetudinary validity, which both cabildos and Spanish officials were generally careful not to question. Beyond possession, though, commoners were not supposed to have any other personal rights over village lands, which belonged de jure to the pueblo as a whole; they could not sell, buy, or mortgage what was not in the end their own. However, a study based on Nahuatl language wills from late sixteenth-century Culhuacan, a village in the outskirts of Mexico City, found a very active land market involving commoners and nobles alike in the purchase and sale of pueblo lands. While these terse early testaments raise many more questions than they can answer, they do suggest that these people "viewed their land as their personal property," regardless of its communal status (Cline 1986, 149).[16] Likewise, in notarial records from the 1590s, commoners from Cholula requested permission to sell *calpullali* (communal lands) to Spaniards, "often employing the argument that such lands were of poor quality, that the land(s) in question had not been worked for many years, that they were ancient family possessions, and that they needed the cash to help with the planting of other lands they were working." The sale was approved, "recognizing the prior right of the individual to dispose of property acquired by inheritance" over the right of the village to its formally inalienable communal lands (Harvey 1984, 90).[17] Town governments were entitled to take back farm lots that were unused, abandoned, or for which there were no heirs, and there is evidence that sometimes they did, but it is also apparent that their effective domain over these *tierras de repartimiento* was limited.

It may well be that these early cases (which were surely not unique) reflect a moment of relative land abundance, during which the sale of small parcels, whatever their legal standing, was of no great concern. There were enormous land tenure changes in central Mexico during these decades (and well into the seventeenth century), with nobles appropriating and selling old *altepetl* lands along with some patrimonial holdings of their own, and Spaniards buying—or grabbing—anything and everything they thought they could use. At the same time, as will be seen, many town governments were renting or selling their *propios*, and in the context of that great flurry of new activity, the petty land transactions of the *macehuales* would have been both understandable and relatively insignificant. All the same, these transactions are an important early indication of a radical gap between legal norms and social practices in the organization of communal village landholding. Perhaps in other parts of New Spain—where social and economic conditions were markedly different—this process did not get underway until later, but by the second half of the eighteenth century, a nearly full range of de facto personal rights (to rent, mortgage, and sell) over lots of communal property existed there, as well. Several case studies illustrate this well.

In the region of Guadalajara, "Private ownership of land within Indian society was widespread by the eighteenth century" (Van Young 1984, 23). In socioeconomic terms, these pueblos were highly stratified corporations, with a wealthy elite, a middling sector of communal farmers, and often a group of poor residents who had difficulty gaining access to land. The population was growing, the economy was expanding, and the lure of business opportunities placed great pressure on the allocation of communal resources. In this context, "Many village Indians who achieved relative wealth, be they commoners or caciques, did so primarily on the basis of acquiring land, mostly by purchase." An illustrative example is that of Francisco Miguel, an Indian commoner from the pueblo of Santa Cruz (Tlajomulco). At his death in 1743, his will listed "eighteen separate parcels of arable land"; eleven he had purchased from other Indians, and three he had inherited. Some of the rest perhaps he had received "through his right as a vecino of the pueblo" (287). He owned two houses, farming implements, and a number of other assets. In addition, various fellow villagers owed him money and other services. Other such wills painted a similar picture. Sales among Indian villagers were most common, but transactions involving outsiders were not unheard of. All in all, pueblo lands changed hands frequently, but for various reasons most of these transfers were not publicly recorded, and so "the sales of land by Indians and other village dwellers which appear in local notarial registers are only the tip of the iceberg" (289). North of Guadalajara, in parts of Zacatecas (e.g., Tlaltenango), there were pueblos where villagers habitually rented out their communal *repartimiento* farmlands to other parties instead of cultivating them as they were supposed to. There, too, village members were understood to have extensive property rights over their parcels. Periodic royal efforts and frequent official exhortations to regulate the sale of village lands and to correct their inequitable internal allocation, all largely ineffectual, are an additional indication that these social practices were both widespread and entrenched (Menegus Bornemann 1999, 97–101).[18]

In the Valley of Mexico the pattern was more or less the same: private rights and a skewed distribution of village land. Within many late eighteenth-century pueblos, "A sizable minority held nothing more than their house lots; half the community members or a little more had additional agricultural plots, but insufficient to produce subsistence for the average family; another minority enjoyed generally adequate subsistence holdings; and a tiny elite had extensive lands" (Tutino 1984, 187). At Acolman, for instance, "The Indian elite . . . treated their holdings as private property, as Indians had been doing throughout central Mexico from the sixteenth century" (183). And it wasn't just the village elites who could exercise some of these rights, though they clearly were in a much stronger position to do so. A telling example comes from Yautepec, in the lowlands of north-central Morelos:

In 1798 an Indian named María Luisa Suasa ceded her solar [communal lot] to a
mulatto, Juan Tilapa, who paid her a sum of forty or fifty pesos. The two parties
evidently viewed their transaction as a sale, rather than a lease. Nevertheless,
Tilapa, and later his widow, Rita Valero, paid the town's Indian gobernador four
pesos per year as interest on a censo perpetuo imposed on the solar. Tilapa and
Valero did not use the land themselves; instead they rented it to a succession of
modest mestizo and mulatto sugarcane cultivators, each of whom paid fifteen
pesos per year in rent. In 1808, the newly elected gobernador of Yautepec . . . seized
the solar and declared it communal property, but in fact appropriated it for his
own use. (Martin 1985, 165–67)

By the late eighteenth century, many Indian towns in the sugarcane zone
of Morelos—in particular, the *cabeceras*—had a very high percentage of non-
Indian residents, some of whom had become community members (e.g., "Indians" by virtue of marriage), many who had not. All the same, a good number of
these *vecinos* had parcels of communal land. In Cuautla, for instance, "Several
claimed outright ownership of their plots, while others rented from individual
Indians rather than from the community" (Martin 1985, 165).[19]

Out in Oaxaca, where villages were far more cohesive in ethnic terms, and
where the hacienda was for the most part an unimportant institution, private
rights over communal lands were nevertheless also strong. A study of the Mixteca region found "a general privatization of communal lands taking place since
the seventeenth century, when commoners became able to buy and sell *repartimiento* parcels as if these were fee simple properties" (Pastor 1987, 127). In
the eighteenth century, "Parcels change hands with relative ease and increasing
frequency, as do town lots, which were also productive possessions" (147). By
the close of the colonial period, farmlands had quoted prices: "a market in
lands was germinating" (263). In some pueblos, there were rich *macehuales* who
owned large numbers of parcels, more than a few town lots, and several teams
of oxen. This was, however, only a "relative privatization" (148), because its scope
was generally restricted to those within the pueblos. Real estate transactions
faced no difficulty or opposition as long as they did not involve outsiders, and
in many cases town governments actively mediated the process. There is ample
documentation showing that the *repúblicas* "bore witness to and legalized illegal sale contracts between commoners, on the argument that since the seventeenth century it had become customary to allow 'relatives' to sell inherited
parcels to each other" (179). In this way, village officials exercised their statutory

jurisdiction over communal territories while simultaneously recognizing the bounded—yet very real—private property rights of individual members of the pueblo. Overall, the trend toward privatization meant that "the *república* has increasingly fewer effective rights over *repartimiento* lands, and therefore also less of an opportunity to redistribute them, because Indians without heirs tend to sell their parcels before they die, and are increasingly determined to defend their possessions in Spanish courts if the town government threatens to reclaim them" (127–28, 147–48, 178–81, 262–64, 326, and 339–44).[20]

Another study, this one focusing on the Valley of Oaxaca, reached very similar conclusions. It found that "eighteenth century records of land purchases and sales by macehuales are numerous," and also that "natives frequently rented land out or let it out on shares, which provided a partial solution to local imbalances in property ownership without forcing landless townsmen to abandon their homes" (Taylor 1979, 74-5). References to village lands mortgaged by individual Indians also appeared in the archival records. This was clearly not the historical practice of communal landholding that the revolution's lawmakers had in mind during the 1910s and 1920s, when they set up the modern ejido, declaring it to be modeled after the traditional forms of land tenure organization in the old Mexican pueblos. As the author of this study keenly observes, "An individual Indian in colonial Oaxaca had much more freedom in disposing of his lands than the modern ejido tenure allows" (75).

Even in distant Yucatán, in so many ways quite different from the other Mexican regions examined here, private property gained a strong foothold in colonial villages. The image of Mayan land communalism is an old and enduring one, buttressed by the notion that the kind of farming practiced there—family-based slash-and-burn field-rotation agriculture—was naturally well suited for collective landholding. Diego de Landa's ([1566] 1994) description in his influential *Relación de las cosas de Yucatán* comes to mind: "The lands, for now, are communal, and thus the first to occupy them possesses them" (40). In fact, the organization of lowland Mayan landholding was then fairly complex and—as a number of recent analyses have documented—by the eighteenth century it had come to include a remarkably open market in private parcels within village territories.[21] There, as elsewhere, lands of patrimonial origin—belonging to groups of relatives of putative noble ancestry—were considered private property, and were freely bought and sold with the express approval of local cabildos and the sanction of the Indian court, where many such transactions were recorded. Unlike in Oaxaca, there was in general no restriction regarding the legal or residential status of buyers, and although *repúblicas* were usually given the right of first refusal, numerous Spaniards acquired land in this way.

Over time, commoners joined this market, trading not only in private holdings otherwise acquired but also in parcels nominally belonging to the *común repartimiento*. According to one study focusing on the hinterlands of Merida, "The evidence indicates that indigenous proprietorship grew through the eighteenth century by means of a simple mechanism involving the issuing of 'papers,' which caciques and their cabildos handed out to the Indians in their pueblos as protection for the crops they each had within communal areas" (Güémez Pineda 2004, 755). With the imprimatur of the cabildos, these documents were soon turned into land titles, allowing holders to claim those parcels as private property, to will them as such, or to sell them. In 1805, a Spanish court officer argued that such titles ought to be considered illegal and invalid, because the lands in question were juridically communal. Caciques and other individual Indians, the officer explained, had appropriated them "by means of spurious papers written in their languages by their scribes, violating royal regulations and stripping pueblos of these assets, forcing inhabitants to pay rent to those who bought portions not only of their communal farmland, but also of their ejidos" (AGN, Tierras 1359, file 5, 16v–18v; quoted in Bracamonte y Sosa and Solís Robleda 1996, 163). In the final years of colonial rule, the Indian court in Yucatán tightened its requirements for the approval of Indian land sales, mostly to no avail. Cabildos continued to approve transactions on their own, as they had at times done all along, and notarial records show that village land sales were also conducted by means of "good faith" contracts between individuals, without any mediation—or obstruction—from town authorities. Not surprisingly, there were also well-established rental arrangements involving various types of village land, including *de repartimiento*, for both milpa (maize, beans, etc.) and commercial crops. All in all, the communal pueblos of northwestern Yucatán appear to have had one of the most developed and least restrictive systems of Indian village land ownership and transfer anywhere in colonial Mexico.

De facto—and in some places also de jure—private property in at least portions of the *tierras de repartimiento* was thus a prevalent condition in late colonial pueblos, if not earlier. Although this is what recent research consistently confirms, general accounts of the period, if they mention private rights at all, treat them as an inconvenient fact—a practice that was somehow incongruous, perhaps a kind of deviation, and in the last analysis therefore a marginal development.[22] As such, this remains mostly a buried aspect of village social relations under Spanish rule, notwithstanding its far-reaching analytic importance. Juxtaposed with standard histories of village land tenure and politics in the nineteenth century, which emphasize state-mandated and market-driven privatizations imposed on mostly unwilling communal pueblos as the trigger of the revolution, these colonial antecedents acquire a deep significance. The baseline from which the supposedly radical land tenure transformations of the nineteenth century are measured and interpreted is an idea of how communal landholding functioned back in the colonial period (and for some, also before the conquest). In this manner, a contrast is established between the more or less stable social norms regarding collective land rights in the past and their disruption, with disastrous consequences, in the century following independence. But if—as it turns out—private property rights of various sorts were already a normal fact of life in many eighteenth-century communal villages, the old argument no longer holds together, and thus the history of how the evolution of communal forms of land tenure shaped village society and politics in the nineteenth century needs to be told in a different way. More detailed research is needed on property relations inside colonial pueblos, but what there is already points clearly in a revisionist direction.

Besides the *tierras de común repartimiento*, colonial villages were structured to hold two other broad categories of land. One was the ejido, collective woodlands and pastures offering members a variety of much-needed resources (e.g., timber, firewood, grasses, etc.). Very little is known concretely about ejido use, or about the existence of ejidos in all or most pueblos. It is simply assumed that such lands existed (the law said they had to) and were always enjoyed communally— that is to say, without differential access rights to their most valuable resources, which is unlikely. A far more important category, in institutional terms, was that of the *propios*, lands set aside to support village governance and the fulfillment of a diverse set of collective obligations, internal and external. These would have included tribute, internal administration, church-related costs, and village feasts, the last two of which became, in many places, partly the province of the *cofradías*. In addition to land, some *repúblicas* also owned mills, herds, or other such assets, but council lands were always the main source of revenue for village treasuries.[23] A typical strategy, adapted from Spanish towns, would consist of renting the *propios*—often to outsiders—to generate income; long-term leases (*censos perpetuos*) to haciendas or ranchos produced a stable inflow of money, but they effectively withdrew those territories from the communal land base. When they could, the *repúblicas* also bought more land, adding to their rental stock. Marketing crops grown collectively on council lands was another common municipal enterprise. In some regions, the sale of *propios* was not uncommon prior to the eighteenth century, when populations were still low and the *repúblicas* were hard-pressed to meet their colonial obligations, though sales involving motives far less noble were also not unheard of.[24]

As with *repartimiento* lands, there are certain commonalities worth highlighting in the management of council lands. These reflect in part some of the same distinctive aspects of social organization that shaped communal farmland use—above all, hierarchical rule. Poor accountability, the discretional use of official resources, the uneven distribution of municipal burdens and benefits, self-dealing (in the rental of *propios* or in the sale of municipal crops, for instance), favoritism, and outright theft—these were in many cases the effects of sustained elite control over the assets belonging to the *repúblicas*. In the words of one student of colonial pueblos, "The Indian communities of colonial Mexico were sharply differentiated between the few who controlled the allocation of resources and the majority dependent on their decisions" (Tutino 1984, 182). Another found ample evidence—in the hinterlands of Guadalajara—of "the private utilization of communal funds by caciques, principales, and alcaldes, including the income from the rental of communal lands which such men were in a position to make," and also "enough instances of outright expropriation of common lands, particularly by caciques, to make it clear that this was not an unusual practice" (Van Young 1981, 290–92). And yet another concluded that "without question the Indian leaders of late colonial Morelos abused their power and appropriated community resources for themselves, their close associates, or favored gente de razón" (Martin 1985, 173).[25] In these regions and others, personal wealth (relative to the vast majority of village members) and high office holding (or close links to it) were more often than not closely correlated.

Still, the management of municipal assets was much more than simply an extension—onto a different set of communal resources—of the naturalized inequity that often governed the allocation and appropriation of *repartimiento* lands, because it had also a significant political dimension. In addition to affording opportunities for personal enrichment, council lands generated many of the fiscal resources that made possible the survival of village governments. At stake in the administration of those assets was the effective preservation of self-rule, and this, as noted, had long been a defining aspiration of the pueblos, old and new. This meant that elites would fiercely defend their pueblos' assets and jurisdiction even as they took private advantage of them. These were the spaces upon which their domination was founded, and maintaining them was therefore a vital endeavor. Without pueblos there would be no formal—and little practical—Indian privilege, relatively modest as that often was. Of course, the value of autonomy encompassed far more than self-interest, but that was not a minor part of it. The preservation of local identities, traditions, and cults was also deeply meaningful (and a primary source of legitimacy), and that, too, depended on retaining a sphere of institutional autonomy, which council properties were intended to underwrite. On this, systematic official improbity notwithstanding, elites and commoners could come together, making "the collective enterprise of survival" an endlessly renewable source of fundamental village cohesion (Farriss 1984).

The protection of communal property—and through it, of self-government—by village officials was often an exercise in creativity, determination, and persistence in the face of increasingly powerful external forces. A good example comes from the late eighteenth century, when Bourbon officials sought to impose strict fiscal regulations on the *cajas de comunidad* of the *repúblicas*, limiting religious expenses, instituting detailed accounting reviews, and effectively expropriating any surpluses. Instead of surrendering their control over council properties, many pueblos placed communal assets in the hands of their *cofradías*, thus avoiding—at least in part—the loss of local autonomy that the new Spanish legislation entailed.[26] Communal defense had also an important territorial dimension, and pueblos fought—in and out of court—to preserve, regain, or even extend their rightful boundaries, clashing with private landholders as well as with neighboring pueblos. Such actions involved asserting corporate jurisdiction and property rights against external claims not only over council property but also over *repartimiento* and ejido lands.

This is precisely the type of scenario that well-worn phrases like "the defense of community" or "the defense of communal lands" usually denote, and there is no question that this kind of struggle has a large and storied place in the history of village landholding, during the colonial period and beyond. But it should be clear by now that communal defense—understood in this way—conveys nothing regarding the internal distribution of communal property and is thus not incompatible with the prevalence of entrenched systems of differential and even private rights over pieces of that property. The pueblos were at once political bodies and landholding spaces, and although one could not exist without the other, each had an internal logic of its own, which could, and did, differ considerably. This distinction—which the previous pages have sought to elucidate—is crucial to understanding the complex history of pueblo institutions. It helps to explain why, for instance, pueblos in which a large number of members lacked enough lands for basic subsistence rented some of their best lands to outsiders (or to well-placed insiders), or why gross disparities in the allocation of village land rights did not preclude the formation of united fronts against outside threats to the territorial or jurisdictional integrity of the collectivity.

The pride of self-government, the pull of a rooted group identity, the ritual performance of social cohesion, the ability to stage collective action—none of these manifestations of life in political community reflected or required a particular distribution of village farmland rights. Nor did they have to, even if the term *community* would suggest otherwise. Despite their conflation in the law and in formal descriptions (belonging to a pueblo means equitable access to its communal farmland), village political membership and village land tenure rights in the zones of *común repartimiento* developed in separate and very different directions. One would become formally—and in some ways also substantially—inclusive, while the other one would not.

By the late eighteenth century, Indian village land tenure patterns had long been highly stratified, and population growth made the inequities a rising source of tension. Some pueblos became rife with internal conflicts, many without clear resolution. People could and did leave, from the top and bottom of the social scale, moving to haciendas and ranchos or to the cities. And yet the pueblos lived on, battling to keep those social spaces—hierarchical and partly privatized but also cohesive and familiar—that constituted them. Modern historians have puzzled over the mixture of conflict and solidarity found in landholding pueblos, suggesting—among various arguments—that the externalization of internal social conflicts served an integrative function and maintained more than a semblance of cohesion (Van Young 1984; also Taylor 1979, 152–70; and Mallon 1995, 64–65). This may well be, but the paradox in question is best grasped as the expression of two overlapping yet ultimately distinct spheres of social organization within the village communities—one concerning land allocation, the other, self-government. And in regard to landed property rights, it seems clear that indigenous culture had little to do with an imagined communalist ethos.

NOTES

1.   The preceding analysis draws on a vast literature exploring these issues. On preconquest and sixteenth-century indigenous social hierarchies, see, e.g., Carrasco and Broda (1982), Carrasco (1996), and Soustelle (1955). On central Mexico, see, e.g., Gibson (1967, 1985), Lockhart (1992), García Martínez (1987), Harvey and Prem (1984), Zavala and Miranda ([1954] 1981), Altman and Lockhart (1984), Zavala ([1935] 1988),

Taylor (1979), Cline (1986), Haskett (1991), Horn (1997), and Ouweneel and Miller (1990). On Oaxaca, see, e.g. Spores (1967, 1984), Whitecotton (1977), Terraciano (2001), Taylor (1972), Pastor (1987), Romero Frizzi (1990, 1996), Chance (2001), and Carmagnani (1992). On lowland Yucatan, see, e.g., Farriss (1984), Roys (1943), Bracamonte y Sosa and Solís Robleda (1996), Chamberlain (1948), Quezada (1993), Patch (1993), Fernández Tejedo (1990), Restall (1997), and Thompson (1999). On Chiapas, see, e.g., Wasserstrom (1983), McLeod and Wasserstrom (1983), de Vos (1994), García de León (1993), Gosner (1984), and Ruz (1985). For a general overview, see Adams and McLeod (2000); older, but still useful, is Wauchope (1964–76, esp. vols. 6–8). An old classic, now in many places outdated but still important, is Chevalier (2006).

2. On the demographic collapse, see Sánchez Albornoz (1984, 4–14); for the higher estimate, see Borah and Cook (1963); for the lower estimate, Sanders (1992); also Rosenblat (1967). On epidemics, see Crosby (1972).

3. The phrase is Gibson's.

4. Also, for a general picture, see Gerhard (1972).

5. For a discussion of indigenous mobility in central Mexico, before and after the conquest, see Lockhart (1976, 102–3, 119–21). For a broader examination of the relationship between colonial migration and indigenous community, see Farriss (1978); also the essays in Robinson (1981, 1990). An important case study of migration and community formation is Amith (2005).

6. See also Wolf (1986). For a critique of the idea of the closed community, see also Peter Guardino's essay in this volume.

7. On Tenampulco, see García Martínez (1990, 1987). On migrants and pueblos, see also Mentz (1988).

8. Amith (2005) explores the historical development of Palula (Guerrero), a community formed by migrant tenant farmers in the eighteenth century on the site of an extinguished sixteenth-century *sujeto* bearing the same name.

9. On the migration of non-Indians into Morelos and their involvement with the pueblos, see Martin (1984). In one final irony, in the 1930s Ayala would claim for its ejido part of the lands that Anenecuilcans had long considered part of their historical domain.

10. On preconquest and early sixteenth-century land tenure organization, see, e.g., Gibson (1985, 257–70), Harvey (1984, 84–85), Cline (1986, chap. 8), Dyckerhoff (1990), and López Sarrelangue (1966). On Oaxaca's *cacicazgos*, see Taylor (1972, chap. 2) and Pastor (1987).

11. This argument is in large measure derived from García Martínez's (1992) insightful essay. See also Hoestra (1990).

12. The extensive colonial legislation on colonial pueblos can be consulted in *Recopilación de las leyes de los reynos de las Indias*; and Ventura Beleña ([1787] 1991) and Solano (1984). Also see López Sarrelangue (1966, 9–13). On ejidos, see Martínez Báez (1931).

13. On the particular case of Yucatán, see Bracamonte y Sosa (2003, chaps. 3–4).

14. On *composiciones de tierras*, see, e.g., Torales Pacheco (1990) and Osborn (1973). On the *fundo legal* legislation and its effects, see Wood (1990), Sánchez Santiró (2001,

151–64), Borah (1983, 136–38), and Miranda (1966, 168–81). On both subjects, see also Gibson (1985, 285–99) and Taylor (1972, chap. 3).

15.   For a discussion of *calpulli* norms regarding *macehual* landholding in preconquest central Mexico, including other sources, see Harvey (1984, 86). For a broader outlook, including the sixteenth century, see Cline (2000, 205–9); also the essays in Carrasco and Broda (1982).

16.   See Cline (1986, chap. 8): "In the colonial period," she concludes, "people bequeathed their land to heirs and ordered it to be sold completely without reference to the *calpulli*" (149). In another text, Cline (2000, 206) observes that "however much the prehispanic system of land tenure emphasized corporate, inalienable landholdings, by the late sixteenth century individual men and women treated land as their private property to do with it as they wished."

17.   Referring to transaction records collected in Reyes García (1973).

18.   On Spanish laws intending to regulate the sale of pueblo lands, see, e.g., Van Young (1984, 68).

19.   Also the essays in Mentz (2009).

20.   For a different, more traditional view of pueblo landholding practices, see Carmagnani (1992).

21.   This discussion is based primarily on Güémez Pineda (2004); Bracamonte y Sosa and Solís Robleda (1996, 135–80), and Patch (1993, chap. 4). On the workings of the Indian court, see Borah (1983).

22.   For recent examples, see Knight (2002, 116–23, 222) and Velázquez (2010).

23.   On communal cattle herds, see, e.g., Mendoza García (2002).

24.   See, e.g., Haskett (1990, 135–37) and Taylor (1972, 70–74).

25.   On the wealth of late eighteenth-century *principales* and rich *macehuales* in the Mixteca Alta, see Pastor (1987, 323–35 and 339–44).

26.   Later, in 1804, the assets of the *cofradías* were expropriated by royal decree in order to finance the wars in Europe, but Indian confraternities were by and large spared. On *cofradía* types, functions, property, and administration, see Mendoza García (2002; 2005, chap. 3), Pastor (1987, 246–59), Bechtloff (1996), Chance and Taylor (1985, 1–26), Korsbaek (1996), Lavrin (1990), and Tanck de Estrada (1999).

REFERENCES

Adams, Richard E. W., and Murdo McLeod, eds. 2000. *Mesoamerica*. The Cambridge History of the Native Peoples of the Americas, vol. 2, part 2. Cambridge: Cambridge University Press.

Altman, Ida, and James Lockhart, eds. 1984. *Provinces of Early Mexico: Variants of Spanish American Regional Evolution*. Los Angeles: University of California, Los Angeles, Latin American Center Publications.

Amith, Jonathan D. 2005. *The Möbius Strip: A Spatial History of Colonial Society in Guerrero, Mexico*. Stanford, CA: Stanford University Press.

Bechtloff, Dagmar. 1996. *Las cofradías en Michoacán durante la época colonial*. Zinacantepec: Colegio Mexiquense.

Borah, Woodrow. 1983. *Justice by Insurance: The General Indian Court of Colonial Mexico and the Legal Aides of the Half-Real.* Berkeley: University of California Press.

Borah, Woodrow, and Sherburne F. Cook. 1963. *The Aboriginal Population of Central Mexico on the Eve of the Spanish Conquest.* Berkeley: University of California Press.

Bracamonte y Sosa, Pedro. 2003. *Los Mayas y la tierra: propiedad indígena en el Yucatán colonial.* Mexico: Miguel Ángel Porrúa, Centro de Investigaciones y Estudios Superiores en Antropología Social (CIESAS) e Instituto de Cultura de Yucatán.

Bracamonte y Sosa, Pedro, and Gabriela Solís Robleda. 1996. *Espacios mayas de autonomía: El pacto colonial en Yucatán.* Mérida, Mexico: Universidad Autónoma de Yucatán.

Carmagnani, Marcello. 1992. *El regreso de los dioses: El proceso de reconstitución de la identidad étnica en Oaxaca, siglos XVII y XVIII.* Mexico: Colegio de México.

Carrasco, Pedro. 1996. *Estructura político-territorial del imperio tenochca. La Triple Alianza de Tenochtitlan, Tetzonco y Tlacopan.* Mexico: Colegio de México and Fondo de Cultura Económica (FCE).

Carrasco, Pedro, and Johanna Broda. 1982. *Estratificación social en la Mesoamérica prehispánica.* Mexico: Instituto Nacional de Antropología e Historia (INAH).

Chamberlain, Robert Stoner. 1948. *The Conquest and Colonization of Yucatan, 1517–1550.* Washington, DC: Carnegie Institution of Washington Publication.

Chance, John K. 2001. *Conquest of the Sierra: Spaniards and Indians in Colonial Oaxaca.* Norman: University of Oklahoma Press.

Chance, John K., and William B. Taylor. 1985. "Cofradías and Cargos: An Historical Perspective on the Mesoamerican Civil-Religious Hierarchy." *American Ethnologist* 12 (1): 1–26.

Chevalier, François. 2006. *La formation des grands domaines au Mexique: Terre et société aux XVIe-XVIIe-XVIIIe siècles.* Paris: Khartala.

Cline, Howard F. 1949. "Civil Congregations of the Indians in New Spain, 1598–1606." *Hispanic American Historical Review* 29 (3): 349–69.

Cline, Sarah L. 1986. *Colonial Culhuacan, 1580–1600: A Social History of an Aztec Town.* Albuquerque: University of New Mexico Press.

———. 2000. "Colonial Central Mexico." In Adams and McLeod 2000, 187–222.

Crosby, Alfred W., Jr. 1972. *The Columbian Exchange: Biological and Cultural Consequences of 1492.* Westport, CT: Greenwood.

Dehouve, Danièle. 1984. "Las separaciones de pueblos en la región de Tlapa (siglo XVIII)." *Historia Mexicana* 33 (4): 379–404.

de Landa, Diego. (1566) 1994. *Relación de las cosas de Yucatán.* México: Consejo Nacional para la Cultura y las Artes (CONACULTA).

de Vos, Jan. 1994. *Vivir en frontera: La experiencia de los indios de Chiapas.* Mexico: CIESAS.

Dyckerhoff, Ursula. 1990. "Colonial Indian Corporate Landholding: A Glimpse from the Valley of Puebla." In Ouweneel and Miller 1990, 40–55.

Farriss, Nancy M. 1978. "Nucleation Versus Dispersal: The Dynamics of Population Movement in Colonial Yucatan." *Hispanic American Historical Review* 58 (2): 187–216.

———. 1984. *Maya Society Under Colonial Rule: The Collective Enterprise of Survival.* Princeton, NJ: Princeton University Press.

Fernández Tejedo, Isabel. 1990. *La comunidad indígena maya de Yucatán, siglos XVI y XVII.* Mexico: INAH.

García de León, Antonio. 1993. *Resistencia y utopía: memorial de agravios y crónica de revueltas y profecías acaecidas en la Provincia de Chiapas durante los últimos quinientos años de su historia, tomo 1.* Mexico: Ediciones Era.

García Martínez, Bernardo. 1987. *Los pueblos de la sierra: el poder y el espacio entre los indios del norte de Puebla hasta 1700.* Mexico: Colegio de México.

———. 1990. *"Pueblos de Indios, Pueblos de Castas:* New Settlements and Traditional Corporate Organization in Eighteenth Century New Spain." In Ouweneel and Miller 1990, 103–16.

———. 1992. "Jurisdicción y propiedad: Una distinción fundamental en la historia de los pueblos indios del México colonial." *Revista Europea de Estudios latinoamericanos y del Caribe* (53): 47–60.

Gerhard, Peter. 1972. *A Guide to the Historical Geography of New Spain.* Cambridge: Cambridge University Press.

———. 1975. "La evolución del pueblo rural mexicano: 1519–1975." *Historia Mexicana* 24 (4): 566–78.

———. 1977. "Congregaciones de indios en la Nueva España antes de 1570." *Historia Mexicana* 26 (3): 347–95.

———. 1993. *The Southeast Frontier of New Spain.* Norman: University of Oklahoma Press.

Gibson, Charles. 1967. *Tlaxcala in the Sixteenth Century.* New Haven, CT: Yale University Press.

———. 1985. *The Aztecs Under Spanish Rule: A History of the Indians of the Valley of Mexico, 1519–1850.* Stanford, CA: Stanford University Press.

Gosner, Kevin. 1984. "Las élites indígenas en los Altos de Chiapas, 1524–1714." *Historia Mexicana* 33 (4): 405–23.

Güémez Pineda, Arturo. 2004. "El poder de los cabildos mayas y la venta de propiedades privadas a través del Tribunal de Indios: Yucatan (1750–1821)." *Historia Mexicana* 54 (3): 697–760.

Harvey, Herbert R. 1984. "Aspects of Land Tenure in Ancient Mexico." In Harvey and Prem 1984, 83–102.

Harvey, Herbert R., and Hanns J. Prem, eds. 1984. *Explorations in Ethnohistory: Indians of Central Mexico in the Sixteenth Century.* Albuquerque: University of New Mexico Press.

Haskett, Robert. 1990. "Indian Community Land and Municipal Income in Colonial Cuernavaca." In Ouweneel and Miller 1990, 130–41.

———. 1991. *Indigenous Rulers: An Ethnohistory of Town Government in Colonial Cuernavaca.* Albuquerque: University of New Mexico Press.

Hernández, Alicia. 1991. *Anenecuilco. Memoria y vida de un pueblo.* Mexico: Centro de Estudios Históricos, Colegio de México.

Hoestra, Rik. 1990. "A Different Way of Thinking: Contrasting Spanish and Indian Social and Economic Views in Central Mexico (1550–1600)." In Ouweneel and Miller 1990, 60–86.

Horn, Rebecca. 1997. *Postconquest Coyoacan: Nahua-Spanish Relations in Central Mexico, 1519–1650.* Stanford, CA: Stanford University Press.

Knight, Alan. 2002. *Mexico: The Colonial Era.* New York: Cambridge University Press.

Korsbaek, Leif. 1996. *Introducción al sistema de cargos.* Toluca: Universidad Autónoma del Estado de México.

Lavrin, Asunción. 1990. "Rural Confraternities in the Local Economies of New Spain." In Ouweneel and Miller 1990, 224–49.

Lockhart, James. 1976. "Capital and Province, Spaniard and Indian: The Example of Late Sixteenth Century Toluca." In *Provinces of Early Mexico: Variants of Spanish American Regional Evolution,* edited by Ida Altman and James Lockhart, 99–123. Los Angeles: UCLA Latin American Center Publications.

———. 1992. *The Nahuas After the Conquest: A Social and Cultural History of the Indians of Central Mexico, Sixteenth Through Eighteenth Centuries.* Stanford, CA: Stanford University Press.

López Sarrelangue, Delfina E. 1966. "Las tierras comunales indígenas de la Nueva España en el siglo XVI." *Estudios de Historia Novohispana* 1 (1): 131–48.

Mallon, Florencia. 1995. *Peasant and Nation: The Making of Postcolonial Mexico and Peru.* Berkeley: University of California Press.

Martin, Cheryl E. 1982. "Haciendas and Villages in Colonial Morelos." *Hispanic American Historical Review* 62 (3): 407–27.

———. 1984. "Historia social del Morelos colonial." In *Morelos: Cinco siglos de historia regional,* edited by Horacio Crespo, 81–93. Mexico: Centro de Estudios Históricos del Agrarismo en México, Universidad Autónoma del Estado de Morelos.

———. 1985. *Rural Society in Colonial Morelos.* Albuquerque: University of New Mexico.

Martínez Báez, Antonio. 1931. "El ejido en la legislación de la época colonial." *Universidad de México* 2 (8): 112–17.

McLeod, Murdo, and Robert Wasserstrom, eds. 1983. *Spaniards and Indians in Southeastern Mesoamerica: Essays on the History of Ethnic Relations.* Lincoln: University of Nebraska Press.

Mendoza García, Jesús E. 2002. "El ganado comunal en la Mixteca Alta: de la época colonial al siglo XX. El caso de Tepelmeme." *Historia Mexicana* 51 (4): 749–85.

———. 2005. "Poder político y económico de los pueblos chocholtecos de Oaxaca: municipios, cofradías y tierras comunales." PhD diss., Mexico: Centro de Estudios Históricos, Colegio de México.

Menegus Bornemann, Margarita. 1999. "Los bienes de comunidad de los pueblos de indios a fines del periodo colonial." In *Agricultura mexicana: crecimiento e innovaciones,* edited by Margarita Menegus Bornemann and Alejandro Tortolero, 89–126. Mexico: Instituto Mora and Colegio de México.

Mentz, Brígida Von. 1988. *Pueblos de indios, mulatos y mestizos, 1770–1870: los campesinos y las transformaciones protoindustriales en el poniente de Morelos*. Mexico: CIESAS.

————, ed. 2009. *Historia de Morelos: tierra, gente, tiempos del Sur. La sociedad colonial, 1610–1780*. Vol. 4. Morelos: H. Congreso del Estado de Morelos.

Miranda, José. 1966. "La propiedad comunal de la tierra y la cohesión social de los pueblos indígenas mexicanos." *Cuadernos Americanos* 25 (149): 168–81.

Nickel, Herbert J. 1988. *Morfología social de la hacienda mexicana*. Mexico: FCE.

Osborn, Wayne S. 1973. "Indian Land Retention in Colonial Mextitlán." *Hispanic American Historical Review* 53 (2): 217–38.

Ouweneel, Arij, and Simon Miller, eds. 1990. *The Indian Community of Colonial Mexico: Fifteen Essays on Land Tenure, Corporate Organizations, Ideology, and Village Politics*. Amsterdam: Centrum voor Studie en Documentatie van Latijns Amerika.

Pastor, Rodolfo. 1987. *Campesinos y reformas: La Mixteca, 1700–1856*. Mexico: Colegio de México.

Patch, Robert W. 1993. *Maya and Spaniard in Yucatan, 1648–1812*. Stanford, CA: Stanford University Press.

Quezada, Sergio. 1993. *Pueblos y caciques yucatecos, 1550–1580*. Mexico: Centro de Estudios Históricos, Colegio de México.

Restall, Matthew. 1997. *The Maya World: Yucatec Culture and Society, 1550–1850*. Stanford, CA: Stanford University Press.

Reyes García, Cayetano. 1973. *Indice y extractos de los protocolos de la notaría de Cholula (1590–1600)*. Mexico: INAH.

Robinson, David J., ed. 1981. *Studies in Spanish American Population History*. Boulder, CO: Westview.

————, ed. 1990. *Migration in Colonial Spanish America*. Cambridge: Cambridge University Press.

Romero Frizzi, María de los Ángeles. 1990. *Economía y vida de los españoles en la Mixteca Alta, 1519–1720*. Mexico: INAH and Gobierno de Oaxaca.

————. 1996. *El sol y la cruz: los pueblos indios de Oaxaca colonial*. Mexico: CIESAS.

Rosenblat, Ángel. 1967. *La población de América en 1492: viejos y nuevos cálculos*. Mexico: Colegio de México.

Roys, Ralph L. 1943. *The Indian Background of Colonial Yucatan*. Washington, DC: Carnegie Institution of Washington.

Ruz, Mario Humberto. 1985. *Copanaguastla en un espejo: Un pueblo tzeltal en el Virreinato*. San Cristóbal de las Casas: Centro de Estudios Indígenas, Universidad Autónoma de Chiapas.

Sánchez Albornoz, Nicolás. 1984. "The Population of Colonial Spanish America." In *Colonial Latin America*, edited by Leslie Bethell, 4–14. The Cambridge History of Latin America, vol. 2. Cambridge: Cambridge University Press.

Sánchez Santiró, Ernest. 2001. *Azúcar y poder: estructura socioeconómica de las alcaldías mayores de Cuernavaca y Cuautla de Amilpas, 1730–1821*. Mexico: Universidad Autónoma del Estado de Mórelos.

Sanders, William T. 1992. "The Population of the Central Mexican Symbiotic Region, the Basin of Mexico, and the Teotihuacan Valley in the Sixteenth Century." In *The Native Population of the Americas in 1492*, edited by William Denevan, 85–150. Madison: University of Wisconsin Press.

Simpson, Lesley B. 1934. *Studies in the Administration of the Indians in New Spain*. Berkeley: University of California Press.

———. 1952. *Exploitation of Land in Central Mexico in the Sixteenth Century*. Berkeley: University of California Press.

Solano, Francisco de, ed. 1984. *Cedulario de tierras: Compilación de legislación agraria colonial (1497–1820)*. Mexico: Instituto de Investigaciones Jurídicas, Universidad Nacional Autónoma de México (UNAM).

Sotelo Inclán, Jesús. 1943. *Raíz y razón de Zapata, Anenecuilco*. Mexico: Etnos.

Soustelle, Jacques. 1955. *La vie quotidienne des Aztèques à la veille de la conquête espagnole*. Paris: Hachette.

Spores, Ronald. 1967. *The Mixtec Kings and Their People*. Norman: University of Oklahoma Press.

———. 1984. *The Mixtecs in Ancient and Colonial Times*. Norman: University of Oklahoma Press.

Tanck de Estrada, Dorothy. 1999. *Pueblos de indios y educación en el México colonial, 1750–1821*. Mexico: Colegio de México.

Taylor, William B. 1972. *Landlord and Peasant in Colonial Oaxaca*. Stanford, CA: Stanford University Press.

———. 1979. *Drinking, Homicide, and Rebellion in Colonial Mexican Villages*. Stanford, CA: Stanford University Press.

Terraciano, Kevin. 2001. *The Mixtecs of Colonial Oaxaca: Ñudzahui History, Sixteenth Through Eighteenth Centuries*. Stanford, CA: Stanford University Press.

Thompson, Philip C. 1999. *Tekanto: A Maya Town in Colonial Yucatan*. New Orleans, LA: Tulane University, Middle American Research Institute.

Torales Pacheco, María Cristina. 1990. "A Note on the *Composiciones de Tierra* in the Jurisdiction of Cholula, Puebla (1591–1757)." In Ouweneel and Miller 1990, 87–102.

Tutino, John. 1984. "Provincial Spaniards, Indian Towns, and Haciendas: Interrelated Sectors of Agrarian Society in the Valleys of Mexico and Toluca, 1750–1810." In Altman and Lockhart 1984, 177–94.

Van Young, Eric. 1981. *Hacienda and Market in Eighteenth-Century Mexico: The Rural Economy of the Guadalajara Region*. Berkeley: University California Press.

———. 1984. "Conflict and Solidarity in Indian Village Life: The Guadalajara Region in the Late Colonial Period." *Hispanic American Historical Review* 64 (1): 67–79.

Velázquez, G. E. 2010. *Nueva historia general de México*. Mexico: Colegio de México.

Ventura Beleña, Eusebio. (1787) 1991. *Recopilación sumaria de todos los autos acordados de la real audiencia y sala del crimen de esta Nueva España*. Mexico: Instituto de Investigaciones Jurídicas, UNAM.

Wasserstrom, Robert. 1983. *Class and Society in Central Chiapas*. Berkeley: University of California Press.

Wauchope, Robert, ed. 1964–76. *Handbook of Middle American Indians*. Austin: University Texas Press.

Whitecotton, Joseph. 1977. *The Zapotecs: Princes, Priests, and Peasants*. Norman: University of Oklahoma Press.

Wolf, Eric. 1957. "Closed Corporate Peasant Communities in Mesoamerica and Central Java." *Southwest Journal of Anthropology* 13 (1): 1–18.

———. 1986. "The Vicissitudes of the Closed Corporate Peasant Community." *American Ethnologist* 13 (2): 325–29.

Wood, Stephanie. 1990. "The Fundo Legal or Lands *Por Razón de Pueblo*: New Evidence from Central New Spain." In Ouweneel and Miller 1990, 117–29.

Zavala, Silvio. (1935) 1988. *Las instituciones jurídicas en la conquista de América*. Mexico: Porrúa.

Zavala, Silvio, and José Miranda. (1954) 1981. "Instituciones indígenas en la Colonia." In *La política indigenista en México: métodos y resultados*, vol. 1, edited by Antonio Caso, Gonzalo Aguirre Beltrán, and Ricardo Pozas Arciniega, 207–313. Mexico: CONA-CULTA and Instituto Nacional Indigenista.

Zurita, Alonso de. 1963. *Life and Labor in Ancient Mexico: The Brief and Summary Relation of the Lords of New Spain [Breve y sumaria relación de los señores de la Nueva España]*. Translated and with an introduction by Benjamin Keen. New Brunswick, NJ: Rutgers University Press.

CHAPTER 2

CONNECTED COMMUNITIES

Villagers and Wider Social Systems in the Late Colonial
and Early National Periods

PETER GUARDINO

A FEW YEARS ago I came across a book in our university library called *The Forgotten Village*. The book combines over one hundred photographs of life in a Mexican village around 1940 with a story by John Steinbeck (1941). As exciting as this discovery was, I was even more pleased when I realized that the photographs were actually movie stills, and after a little sleuthing I was able to find the film itself. The movie is a bit of an odd bird. Steinbeck wrote a fictional screenplay, and then the filmmakers convinced many indigenous peasants in a Mexican village to play people like themselves. The Mexican government cooperated, and the resulting film vividly illustrates the attitudes of Mexico's early twentieth-century *indigenista* social reformers toward the country's indigenous inhabitants.

In the movie, an epidemic is killing the village's children. The government schoolteacher and his young protégé, Diego, try to convince the villagers to summon modern medical aid, but the villagers are suspicious of outsiders and prefer to trust their traditional healer. Diego defies his parents and leaves to seek help. Diego's journey takes him past various signs of modernity until he reaches an urban hospital and convinces a doctor to take a medical team to the village. The team quickly discovers bacteria in the village well, and they disinfect it. The villagers, however, refuse to allow the outsiders to treat their children with modern techniques and instead riot, forcing the medics out. Diego again defies his parents, kidnapping his very ill sister to allow the doctor to save her life. His parents exile him, but the authorities promise to educate him so that he can help other peasants, presumably by bringing them modernity (Millichap 1983, 50–56; Simmonds 1996, 57–58). Here I obviously cannot do justice to this movie, which often sparks heated discussion in my classes. For now, just note how it paints a strong dichotomy between traditional, insular villagers and a more dynamic outside world.

The idea that the lives of indigenous peasants were centered on their villages is also expressed very strongly in *The Other Rebellion*, Eric Van Young's (2001) book on popular violence during Mexico's independence war. In this influential tour de force, Van Young combines extensive research with deep knowledge of contemporary social theory. One of the book's key arguments is that the political horizons of Mexico's indigenous peasants were extremely restricted. Van Young even coins a new term for this. The word, *campanillismo*, derived from the Italian word for bell towers, signals the "tendency to see the social and political horizon as extending metaphorically only as far as the view from their church bell tower" (383). This is a terrifically memorable image.

Steinbeck and Van Young both stress the cultural gap between a largely urban, "national" society and a rural, traditional peasantry, seconding a kind of cultural common sense that is widely accepted even beyond the ivory tower. Rural people all over the world are commonly seen as traditional and parochial. In Mexico, indigenous peasants often have portrayed themselves in exactly the same way, stressing their connections to the past and customs established since time immemorial. Indigenous peasants have also emphasized the distinction between villagers and the outside world, and they sometimes exaggerate their lack of sophistication.

As Paula López Caballero points out in her chapter in this volume, the work of early twentieth-century anthropologists was shaped by similar ideas, and these anthropologists thus believed that indigenous peasants could best be understood through studies focusing on their communities. The strongest current in the anthropological study of peasants was led by Robert Redfield, and his peers and students made community studies the dominant mode of inquiry. Although Redfield (1956, 68–72) himself pointed out that there were often significant links between the "great tradition" associated with nations and urban life and the "little tradition" lived in communities, he and those who emulated him did not make those connections central to their work. The resulting community studies often reinforced the more general cultural prejudice that rural people were insular.[1]

The inward orientation of indigenous peasant villagers is also a strong motif in the thousands of documents that government officials, village priests, and travelers have written about peasants. For centuries peasants have been repeatedly portrayed as parochial, backward, and simply uninterested in the great events of the world. For government officials this has been a constant source of frustration, and that frustration has made the experience of dealing with peasants an often bitter one.

The concept that before the revolution indigenous peasants viewed their lives through the lens of tradition and centered their lives on their villages fits a great deal of evidence. Indigenous peasants themselves, government officials, and many early twentieth-century ethnographers saw things this way. There is nothing surprising about this image, and it fits with our own cultural beliefs about rural people. Nevertheless, there are reasons we should be less than content with this picture. Even sixty years ago some anthropologists pointed out an interpretive problem with this image. Moreover, much recent scholarship about peasant politics in the nineteenth century paints a very different portrait of peasant behavior.

One of the first anthropologists to forcefully reject the idea that Mexican peasants were inwardly oriented and largely divorced from the concerns of urban society was Eric Wolf. Although Wolf (1957, 1–18) actually coined the phrase "closed corporate community," he argued that peasants were very much part of a wider world that extracted value from them.[2] Wolf seems to have believed that the community studies that were the staple of his discipline drastically underestimated how much communities belonged to a larger web of social, political, and economic relationships, and he stressed those relationships in his multiple writings on the peasantry. In 1956 Wolf boldly argued that communities form part of a complex society and could "thus be viewed no longer as self-contained and integrated systems in their own right" (1975, 51).[3]

Evidence that communities were vitally connected to the social fabric of wider society later arrived from another quarter. In the 1970s and 1980s, historians like Jean Meyer (1973) and Leticia Reina (1980) discovered that there had been an astounding number and variety of peasant rebellions in the nineteenth century. Dozens of those movements involved peasants from many villages and peasants allied with people who were not peasants. Neither fact fit easily with earlier images of indigenous peasant communities. Early efforts to understand these rebellions tended to follow the lead of contemporary theory about rural movements (Tutino 1986; Katz 1988, 521–61; Coatsworth 1988, 21–62).

Researchers sought structural reasons why peasants from many villages might simultaneously take action, and to a lesser extent they looked for temporary congruences between the interests of these peasants and those of the other actors involved in the revolts.

Soon, though, historians researching these rebellions began to write about how peasant political culture was related to wider political cultures. They found that the words of at least some indigenous peasants were recorded, and that in those documents peasants expressed their concerns using vocabularies that connected them to wider political discourses. This was not surprising when peasants' allies were conservatives, as church-state conflict and the liberals' campaign against communal property made those alliances quite logical. However, some peasants also associated with the liberals, up to then considered almost the natural enemies of peasants. They spoke of citizenship, popular sovereignty, and municipal autonomy.[4] When historians investigated more routine forms of peasant politics, such as lobbying, judicial activity, and village elections, they also found that indigenous peasants had multiple political engagements with institutions, groups, and discourses beyond the boundaries of their villages. These engagements were unequal, as peasants occupied the bottom rung of just about any hierarchy imaginable to people in nineteenth-century Mexico. Yet peasant political activity was often creative and effective, and, more importantly, individual peasants and communities often showed a keen awareness of the wider political environment that shaped their lives.[5]

Thus we have two general interpretations, one that argues that indigenous peasants were basically insular and traditional, and another that indicates that indigenous peasants often worked politically with their peers in other villages and also with institutions and actors beyond the peasantry. In this essay I will try to show how evidence that peasants were inward-looking and oriented toward tradition can be reconciled with the evidence of their engagement with forces beyond their villages. I will mostly use material from my earlier work on late eighteenth- and early nineteenth-century Guerrero and Oaxaca. I will also draw on work by various historians about different regions stretching up into the beginning of the twentieth century. Rather than discussing geographic specificity, I will sketch the circumstances and factors that gave rise to different kinds of political behavior.

Peasants often had to consider the world beyond their villages, parrying threats and using resources from that wider world. More importantly, the distinction between what is internal and external to villages pales next to the multiple ways in which these things are interwoven. Peter Wade (2007, 51) notes that many contemporary anthropologists resist the idea of a clear division between neat, bounded localities and external, global forces. We need to resist this idea even when investigating the past, because the very political institutions and cultural practices that people often have seen as local and traditional have been actually continuously produced and modified by people living their lives in local spaces in conjunction with wider forces and initiatives.

Community politics were central to indigenous peasants, as communities protected peasant rights and peasants owed numerous obligations to their communities. These communities were patriarchies, and generally during the colonial period, a small set of respected elders annually chose village officials. Men became elders by working their way up through a series of posts called the cargo system, and families also owed the community labor for public works and to support religious life. Communities collected the colonial tribute, and after independence they often collected a similar personal tax. Most obviously, communities were the guardians of peasant agrarian resources, including fields, pasture, woods, and water.

Villages were very much political entities, and the strength of their connection to the wider political world can be seen in the most potent symbols of peasant political culture. Documents were important talismans that represented the authority of higher level officials. Even for illiterate peasants, legal documents took on, in the words of Romero Frizzi (1996, 176), a "sacred and political role."[6] Reading in Mexican archives, I am struck by how often indigenous peasants caught up in passionate disputes brandished these pieces of paper, which were carried by messengers on long journeys through difficult terrain, buried away from the prying eyes of outsiders, or eagerly sought in government archives. Moreover, staffs of office, the most important symbols of the legitimacy of village officials, were also explicitly seen as originating in higher authority. Again and again peasants stated that the staffs they carried had been given them by the king.[7] Authorities often bestowed these staffs on elected village officials in ceremonies that emphasized this connection.

The connection between village officials and higher authority was more than symbolic. District administrators sometimes intervened in the selection of village officers, often arousing bitter opposition. Moreover, the internal processes through which communities chose officials were not always consensual or harmonious. Before independence in some Oaxacan villages, there were sharp conflicts between noble villagers and commoner villagers. Sometimes the young also clashed with the old, particularly over the distribution of village burdens. Disputes also broke out between head towns and subject communities. Some inhabitants defied the authority of village officials, and others accused them of corruption or dereliction of duty. In all of these clashes, one side or another appealed to higher authority. The archives are full of thousands of such cases, suggesting that many, many indigenous peasants were aware that they might convince authorities to see their side of a dispute.

Postindependence governments intervened in community political life in new ways. Most states no longer recognized colonial indigenous governments, and indigenous peasants had to compete in municipal politics, bringing them into close contact with peasants from other communities and mestizos or whites from market towns.[8] Village governments often continued to exist without official sanction. Indigenous peasants still needed to administer village lands and organize religious devotions. Municipal governments and district administrators, far from working to make real the nominal extinction of village governments, often collaborated in maintaining them or deliberately turned a blind eye to their survival because village governments were the best means of keeping order and collecting taxes. The officials of outlying settlements nominally represented a municipal town council dominated by non-Indians, but sometimes they were clearly seen as representatives of an ethnic polity. Under centralism, district administrators supposedly appointed justices of the peace to keep order in villages, but for indigenous villagers those justices occupied the top rung of the cargo system.[9]

Both before and after independence, there were congruences between political culture inside and outside villages. The cargo system was very closely related to the Hispanic municipal tradition of *cargas consejiles*, unpaid posts that rotated among all men, and for this reason Spanish, creole, and mestizo judges never raised their eyebrows about it. Although nobility inside indigenous peasant communities had a somewhat different ideological base than nobility in Spanish culture, there were significant similarities, and again Spanish judges had little difficulty with the concept. After independence there were new congruences. Steve Stern (1995, 194–97) has pointed out that politics in colonial peasant communities had long included strong tendencies toward both hierarchy and egalitarianism. The new republican political ideologies espoused by the state after independence fit well with the latter, particularly on the issue of hereditary privileges. Moreover, alternation in office, which had long been important in indigenous communities, also fit well with the new values espoused by the state.[10] All of these congruences are not coincidence. They are a product of the ways in which, during the long colonial period, Spanish and indigenous actors *together* created the institutions that we know as indigenous villages, and that creation continued to happen after independence.

Taxes weighed heavily on indigenous families. The heaviest taxes were levied within communities, usually in the form of labor rather than cash. The cargo system took vast quantities of time away from the economic activities of peasants. Villagers also owed communities labor for agricultural plots whose produce was used for community expenses. Village authorities demanded yet more labor for public works. Young families sometimes worked in rotation to provide parish priests with household help. Communities also collected taxes for higher levels of government. All of these taxes, both internal and external, sometimes generated disputes and resistance, and usually when that happened, someone appealed to higher authority.

Indigenous peasants had a set of cultural and religious beliefs that connected them to both their ancestors and their descendants, holding out the promise of an eternal life that would include both. Indigenous villagers displayed great reverence for the patron saints of their villages. Patron saints were the most important symbols of village identity and sometimes were considered to be the actual owners of village lands (Van Young 2001, 483).[11] Villagers feted the saints in costly annual celebrations and also carefully guarded, lovingly cleaned, and richly clothed their images. Indigenous peasants lavishly adorned their churches.

Religious practices and beliefs varied, yet all villagers were explicitly Catholic, members of a Church that stretched over much of the globe. Each village belonged to a parish staffed by a priest, and such priests were rarely Indians. These priests oversaw religious practices and education, and only they could administer sacraments. Sometimes villagers paid priests cash for specific services. Other villages supported priests through customary relationships that mostly compensated the priest with goods and labor. Villages sometimes withheld payment to protest poor treatment or sought to negotiate lower payments. More often, though, villagers clashed with each other over the form of payment. Younger villagers actually supplied most labor owed to priests under customary arrangements, and they sometimes sought relief by asking for a strict fee schedule instead. In contrast, older villagers favored customary arrangements because they shifted the burden onto the young.

Priests and the masses they said were central to key collective rituals, especially patron saint feasts, so peasants needed their cooperation on such occasions.

Yet these collective rituals sometimes included pre-Hispanic elements and always represented an ostentatious baroque Catholicism, which did not sit well with many late eighteenth- and early nineteenth-century priests (Van Young 2001, 482; Gruzinski 1985, 175–201; Taylor 1996, 250–58). Often priests criticized as "barbaric" activities that would not have been out of place in seventeenth-century Europe, practices that previous pastors had encouraged or even established. What priests saw as evidence of local idiosyncrasy and adherence to tradition had once been both new and aligned with European forms of Catholicism. Some priests tried mightily to introduce more contemporary forms of Catholicism. Yet it is important to understand that more contemporary forms of Catholicism also appealed to at least some peasants. Often it was indigenous peasants who denounced the continuance of earlier customs that were no longer favored by authorities.[12] Indigenous peasants and priests frequently found it desirable to take their disagreements about religion and how it should be supported outside the village, to either diocesan authorities or government courts.[13]

Many villages were far from harmonious, and tensions often broke out into the open. Men and women struggled over what they owed to each other and to each other's parents. Families clashed over agrarian resources and status in village politics. Indigenous peasants quarreled about how the many burdens of communal life should be distributed. Moreover, villagers argued about religious beliefs or the importance of rival religious patrons. In all of these kinds of conflicts, only one of the contending parties was supporting the status quo, and that means that many peasants were interested in change. Moreover, in all these conflicts, indigenous peasants turned to authorities and resources outside their villages for help. Probably the average peasant family simply wanted to live decent lives, but for many families this desire brought them into a wider political arena. Peasants, their families, and their villages were suspended in a dense web of connections to the outside world. Therefore, political, economic, and religious changes outside villages presented different groups within villages with both threats and opportunities (Stern 1987, 13–14).

Up until now I have been trying to explain why life inside peasant communities actually generated political behavior oriented toward the world outside communities. For the rest of this piece, I will survey the forms this political behavior took and show how the discourses and ideologies of this outwardly oriented behavior were intimately connected to aspects of peasant culture we would normally assume to be traditional bulwarks of autonomy. Peasant political culture was constantly changing, and it was contested within villages (Falcón

2002, 88). Villages had their own internal political histories, and they were also subject to varying influences from the outside. Thus in a given village, people could interpret the same events in very dissimilar ways, and they could justify different kinds of responses.

Although indigenous peasant culture varied regionally and even from village to village, there are general statements we can make with some confidence. Peasants seem to have valued village unanimity greatly, considering political meetings that did not involve the whole village to be illegitimate by nature.[14] Age was enormously important in village politics. Peasants also had a strong respect for tradition and custom. Of course, all of these core values were subject to interpretation. More than one group might claim to represent the village's voice, age was only worthy of respect if the elders acted as responsible patriarchs, and it could be difficult to distinguish legitimate custom from the corruption of recent innovation.

Some key features of indigenous peasant culture were directly related to the wider political culture it was part of. When peasants pursued their interests through the courts, they needed to engage the wider political culture. As Enrique Florescano (1997, 289) points out, the judicial system was a kind of school where Indians "learned to manage the laws, the procedures, and the legal memory of the conqueror." Colonial law helped transform native society in profound ways, as Susan Kellogg (1995) has pointed out.

Catholicism was very important to peasants, and the notion that the Church was under attack could be profoundly unsettling. In colonial Mexico, loyalty to the king seems to have also been quite fundamental to peasants, although it was not a personal loyalty to whatever blue blood then occupied the throne. Indian peasants saw the king as a rather abstract, if benevolent and fatherly, figure who guaranteed their access to land and was the ultimate source of justice. This idea was reinforced in the constant judicial activity in which peasants approached the king as humble petitioners, and it was even reiterated during village riots through variations on the famous phrase "Long live the king and death to bad government!" The authorities promoted this ideal through the pomp and circumstance of the courts and the elaborate ceremonies that marked the royal succession (Minguez 1995, 17).

Both Catholicism and the king were essential to the participation of indigenous peasants in the suddenly violent politics of 1810–1821. John Tutino (1986, 41–98) and Brian Hamnett (1986, 26–34) have shown how population pressure, rising prices, and increased commercialization reduced living standards and security for many peasants before 1810. As shopkeepers or hacienda administrators, European Spaniards were often the point men of these structural changes, giving a human face to the pressures and transactions that eroded living standards. Yet, as Van Young (2001) points out, these structural pressures do not by themselves explain the actions of peasants, which were also motivated by how political events in Spain and Mexico City looked through the prism of peasant political culture. Napoleon Bonaparte's attempt to usurp the Spanish throne and the European Spaniards' coup in Mexico City together let loose a veritable flood of propaganda, rumors, and conspiracy theories. France was already seen as a source of heresy, and many people found the idea that the unpopular European Spaniards were conspiring with the French to attack the Church and turn New Spain over to Napoleon quite plausible. Under these circumstances, the imprisoned Fernando VII became a kind of millenarian figure identified with the restoration of justice.

Up to this point I have mostly followed Van Young's interpretation, which I believe captures how many indigenous peasants came to understand the situation. However, Van Young (2001) does not recognize how much many people who were not indigenous peasants also shared these beliefs. Instead he argues that their monarchism and that of the peasants "touched different emotional chords and expressed different social aspirations" (493). Certainly people who were not peasants had different social aspirations, but the emotional chords struck by the monarchy were quite similar. Monarchy and religion were intertwined, and sermons linked New Spain's religious destiny with the king's fate (Casaus y Torres 1808). The sense of crisis deeply affected people from many walks of life, and both the king and Catholicism held similar places in their vision of political, religious, and social order. For instance, in May 1810 Bishop Antonio Bergoza y Jordán ordered Oaxaca's parish priests to be alert to Joseph Bonaparte's "seductive emissaries that try to pervert loyal Americans with tricks" and make them accomplices of "their enormous crimes, of the usurpation of the Crown of our legitimate Sovereign, of their own apostasy of the Catholic religion, of the violation, profanation, and robbery of churches, of the looting of cities and villages, of the burning of houses, the death of our brothers, and of all the crimes imaginable."[15]

The fate of the king is here linked very closely to threats that must have resonated very much with peasant community life. What we see here is not the basically bloodless, rationalist, Western thinking that Van Young (2001, 459–60) attributes to creoles. In fact, the line between official propaganda warning that Napoleon might recruit traitors and the millenarian rumors circulating in the peasantry was very thin indeed. Together they prepared the ground for the calls to arms issued by Hidalgo and Morelos. These leaders at first did not advocate a total break with Spain and the construction of a republican state. Instead they offered to defend the king's rights and the Catholic faith, and sometimes they even encouraged the millenarian image that the king was traveling incognito with their armies (Lemoine 1965, 169). The division between indigenous peasant millenarianism and creole elite nationalism did not begin to materialize until later (Landavazo 2001, 135–79).

The rural insurgency temporarily brought together disaffected people and groups, including many indigenous peasants. Certainly there was confusion and conflict within the fragile insurgent alliance, and indigenous peasants and other members of the rural poor did not always confine their violence to the European Spaniards. Moreover, as Michael Ducey shows extremely well in his chapter in this book, the war developed a momentum of its own that carried many people to new political terrain altogether.[16] The war finally ended more from exhaustion than through victory for anyone.

After independence most Mexican politicians were uncomfortable with the fact that many Mexicans farmed communal lands and often did not even speak Spanish. Some politicians believed that breaking up indigenous communal landholding or placing natives and native lands under the control of local elites would hasten the construction of a unified national state. Others believed that indigenous peasants could gradually become Mexicanized if they were simply given a chance to participate in state making through local governments. A third set of lawmakers saw melding Hispanic and indigenous forms of government as the only practical way to keep order and collect taxes in the countryside (Caplan 2003, 272–74).

Much change occurred even where this third view drove policy. In Oaxaca, lawmakers in the 1820s allowed every village, no matter how small, to retain its local government. They even legitimized the cargo system. However, they assigned new duties to village governments, and they arranged for authorities to be elected through universal male suffrage. In some villages universal male suffrage led to fierce generational conflict. Some younger men insisted on strict adherence to state electoral law, and sometimes they won office as a result. However, the elders still had great prestige, and within a few years, a compromise was reached under which elections followed state law but village elders had great influence over the electorate. Here republican law was melded with traditional forms of authority (Guardino 2000; 2005, 234–38).

The brief insurgency of the young was ended, but a second, more profound change occurred. In most villages noble peasants had enjoyed special privileges in the cargo system. These controversial privileges had sparked many eighteenth-century lawsuits. After independence, both the privileges and the conflicts ended. The state constitution abolished all hereditary privileges, and the nobles' privileges, already unpopular, now were indefensible (Guardino 2000; 2005, 231–33). The cargo system became more egalitarian, since now privileges could only be earned by years of service. The development shows how the very different motives of Hispanic politicians and indigenous peasants could converge. For politicians, inherited privileges were not compatible with Enlightenment ideals. For peasant commoners, they were incompatible with the ideal of a harmonious and predictable accumulation of power through community service. Indigenous peasant commoners probably did not read the French philosophes, but they certainly benefited from the philosophes' popularity.

In some states, peasant local government became linked to the early nineteenth-century debate between federalism and centralism. Generally federalists favored larger numbers of municipalities and centralists favored appointed government in the countryside. In some regions federalist regimes approved so many municipalities that indigenous peasants could control or exercise significant influence in some. When the centralists came to power in the mid-1830s, they replaced municipalities with appointed justices of the peace, sometimes exposing peasant lands to rapacious local elites (Guardino 1996, 150–54). In many other districts, administrators found it expedient to appoint indigenous peasants as justices of the peace, as it was useful to have someone local in charge of collecting the head tax. Yet there was often a sharp disjuncture between the indigenous peasants that officials thought would make good justices of the peace and the peasants that indigenous political culture judged fit for leadership. Villages wanted the post to be filled by men chosen by the elders, or at the very least men who had climbed the cargo ladder. District administrators preferred bilingual men who were typically younger. In the end, villages won out because justices of the peace could not govern effectively without the support of the elders and those serving in lower cargos. Many district administrators began confirming justices that had already been chosen by the village elders (Guardino 2005, 238–41; 2000; and 1996, 103).[17]

Benito Juárez became governor of Oaxaca after federalism was restored in the late 1840s. Juárez, born a Zapotec Indian peasant, had by then more or less fully assimilated into the provincial political elite, and as governor he was not particularly favorable to Indian peasants. Moreover, he later became Mexico's most famous liberal leader when the liberals were strenuously attacking communal land tenure. Yet Juárez clearly understood how useful it was to allow indigenous peasants some political autonomy. In 1848 Juárez wrote that

> the villages of the state have had the democratic custom of electing on their own the functionaries who with the names of alcaldes and regidores kept the villages clean, kept order, and administered the communal funds. This beneficial custom was strengthened by the federalist system, giving the villages the power to elect the members of their ayuntamientos and repúblicas, and codifying the duties and rights of those bodies. For this reason the republican representative federal system was well-received in the villages of the State, and the centralist system that abolished those bodies caused universal disgust, contributing to the fall of that system that damaged us so much. With the reestablishment of federalism the villages have recovered not only their ayuntamientos and repúblicas, but also the right to elect them following their past customs, leaving local government organized in a way that, far from obstructing, instead expedites the march of the general administration of the State. (*Esposición que en cumplimiento del Artículo 83* 1848, 12)

Although Juárez exaggerates how much indigenous peasants in Oaxaca accepted the introduction of liberal, republican, local government, his words do in many ways correspond to the evidence about the experience of indigenous peasants with centralism. Once again we see how peasant communities that seem at first glance to be bulwarks of local autonomy and tradition were actually being constantly recreated in interaction with larger political trends and institutions.

Juárez argued that peasant discontent with centralism contributed to its downfall, but there is little evidence of severe peasant resistance to centralism in Oaxaca. It seems that Juárez was referring to something else. The neighboring region that later became Guerrero experienced massive peasant rebellions in the 1840s, and those rebellions helped overthrow centralism. This region, which belonged at the time to Mexico, Puebla, and Michoacán, had a different experience with postindependence government. Those state governments never officially sanctioned municipal government in every village. Still, many indigenous villages had their governments recognized in the 1820s but lost that recognition when the centralists took power in the 1830s. In the district of Chilapa, where a creole and mestizo local elite competed for land with peasant villages, the local elite consolidated its political control and began settling longstanding land disputes in its own favor. By 1842 the area was in flames, and a few months later the rebellion spread to many other districts after the centralist government demanded a vastly increased head tax from the peasants.

These indigenous peasants allied themselves with a strong federalist movement. Peasants, or at least the village leaders who drafted letters and proclamations, came to associate federalism with increased local autonomy and low taxes, and these indigenous peasants participated in the 1846 movement that restored the federalist constitution (Guardino 1996, esp. 147–77). The 1840s rebellions affected neighboring regions of Oaxaca, and this is undoubtedly what Juárez was referring to when he said that peasant discontent with centralism contributed to its downfall (Reina 1980, 235–37; Smith 2012, 137–41).

I have argued that social structures made it more or less inevitable that some peasants would look outside their villages for solutions to their problems. Moreover, the ways in which peasants understood their lives made the idea that they might find allies in government or among other social groups plausible. Now I will offer a few further points about the interpretative and theoretical issues involved in understanding peasant politics.

The first issue is quite a big one. Who, exactly, are we talking about here? Do the statements that political movements issued necessarily represent the voices of common peasants? After all, I have already argued that peasant communities were hardly harmonious and consensual places.[18] Even in the case of peasant legal petitions, we often see the action of what William Taylor (1996, 382–84) calls "legal entrepreneurs," the often bilingual and literate peasants who wrote petitions and organized judicial actions (Yannakakis 2003). For instance, in my research on the 1840s rebellions in Guerrero, all of the dozens of letters and proclamations I turned up were actually written in Spanish, not one of the area's indigenous languages. Is it possible that peasant leaders were saying one thing to the state, nonpeasant allies, and even their counterparts in far-flung villages while they were making entirely different arguments to the commoners of their own villages? This seems unlikely. The concepts in the political documents are clearly related to those found in peasant petitions and testimonies captured during more routine political processes. Yet the most convincing clue that the letters and proclamations are closely related to broader peasant political sensibilities comes from an unexpected quarter.

When peasants took problems to court, they had to present written petitions that were usually produced by village scribes or lay lawyers, called *tinterillos* (literally, inkpot men). After the initial petition, individual peasants were often called to testify in person. Their testimony almost never contradicts the legal petitions composed on their behalf, and when they do not match perfectly, the difference is usually one of tangential details. This leads me to imagine the process of producing legal petitions, and probably the letters and proclamations composed during rebellions as well, as one in which individual peasants and peasant leaders spoke while the scribes recording the argument translated them not just from an indigenous language into Spanish but also into the legal and political idiom that would make the arguments comprehensible to their intended audiences.

Imagining this process leads directly to the issue of hegemony. Social scientists researching different eras and regions have examined how the state and elites shape political and social conflict by establishing a common discursive framework. Social scientists have often argued that hegemony does not prevent conflict so much as it sets the boundaries of debate. William Roseberry (1994, 360–61) suggested that

> we use the concept *not* to understand consent but to understand struggle, the ways in which the words, images, symbols, forms, organizations, institutions, and movements used by subordinate populations to talk about, understand, confront, accommodate themselves to, or resist their domination are shaped by the process of domination itself. What hegemony constructs, then, is not a shared ideology but a common material and meaningful framework for living through, talking about, and acting upon social orders characterized by domination.

Similar visions of hegemony have become quite common in historical works on Mexico.[19]

As we write about the efforts of elites to form and impose hegemonic projects, on the one hand, and the ways in which crafty subalterns reinterpret and resist those projects, on the other, we enter a linguistic terrain that privileges a conscious instrumentality. This instrumentality is perhaps most visible in the image of political repertoires (Tilly 1984). Thinking about political repertoires forces us to consider innovation, improvisation, and learning. However, it also assumes that there is a musician choosing the tunes played. Although certainly both elites and subalterns often thought about how to convey their messages and achieve their aims, we should also keep in mind that words and actions have cultural meanings and fill emotional needs (Van Young 1993, 4, 17). Still, as Romana Falcón (2002, 80–81) points out, there is little doubt that subaltern actors were quite capable of making conscious choices about what they would say to move others to listen to them.[20]

Eric Van Young (2001) points out another possibility to be taken into account. Sometimes even when peasants and their allies worked together or even used the same words they did not in fact truly understand each other. They were engaged, in Van Young's words, in "dialogues of the deaf" (493, 500). After all, if the most important ideas and symbols that peasant political culture shared with the political culture of other groups could be interpreted flexibly, different groups could have quite divergent interpretations of the same nominal positions. This phenomenon is very close to the idea of "double mistaken identity" that James Lockhart (1992) introduced in his work on the early encounter between Nahuas and Spanish colonialism. Lockhart points out that sometimes "each side takes it that a given form or concept is essentially one already known to it, operating in much the same manner as in its own tradition, and hardly takes cognizance of the other side's interpretation." Yet Lockhart goes on to say that the initial misunderstanding eventually led to a genuine rapprochement, "leading to forms that cannot be securely attributed to either parent culture" (445–46).

Indigenous peasant villages were a prominent feature in the social and cultural landscape of Mexico's nineteenth-century countryside. In these villages peasants worked, raised families, and worshiped. Many probably aspired only to live these lives without too much sound and fury. However, peasants often had to interact with economic forces and political actors outside their villages. They needed to seek sources of income and they needed to appeal to powerful outsiders, both to adjudicate disputes within the village and to moderate the demands placed on them by the state and powerful outsiders. Furthermore, indigenous peasant political culture was quite cognizant of the need to interact with the wider polity. Indigenous peasants went to court often, and sometimes they rebelled. Both during the colonial period and afterward, peasants phrased their concerns in ways that made sense to judges and political elites. After independence they even constructed alliances with peasants from other communities. Although their social aspirations were often centered on their home villages, by necessity, their political horizons stretched much farther than they could see from the village bell tower.

ACKNOWLEDGMENTS

This chapter began life several years ago as a talk given in different versions at Harvard University; the University of California, San Diego; and Northwestern University. I am grateful to the various colleagues who commented on those versions. More recently it has benefited from the comments of the members of project "Rethinking Change, History and Indigenity," especially Ariadna Acevedo-Rodrigo, Paula López Caballero, Gabriela Torres-Mazuera, and José Luis Escalona Victoria.

NOTES

1. On Redfield, see Taylor (1999, 82) and Roseberry (1995, 156–57). See also Silverman (1979) and Viqueira (2002, 47–74). Redfield's most important work was *The Folk Culture of the Yucatan* (1941).

2. See the analysis of Redfield and Wolf in Michael Kearney (1996).

3. This was first published in Wolf (1956).

4. See Mallon (1995), Thomson (1999), Guardino (1995, 185–213; 1996), Ducey (1999a; 2001, 525–50; 2004), Falcón (2002), and Rugeley (1996).

5. See Guarisco (2003; 2008, 167–220), Güémez Pineda (2007, 89–129), Tecuanhuey Sandoval (2007, 337–68); Salinas Sandoval (2007, 369–410), Serrano Ortega (2007, 411–40), Escobar Ohmstede (1996, 1–15; 1997; 1998a; 1998b), Caplan (2003, 255–93; 2010), Purnell (2002, 213–37), Guardino (2005; 2000, 119–30), and Birrichaga (2008, 221–57).

6. See also Taylor (1996, 433) and Yannakakis (2008, 54–56). In her contribution to this book, Elsie Rockwell emphasizes the crucial importance of such documents in village life in twentieth century Tlaxcala, as well as current consciousness of a long history of producing and preserving such documents.

7. See, for example, AGN, Criminal, vol. 306, fols. 144–45v; and AVA, Penal, file 407, 1789.

8. See Caplan (2003), Escobar Ohmstede (1997; 1998a: 151–52), and Ducey (2001).

9. See Ducey (2001, 531–33; 1997, 72–73), Guarisco (2003, 268), Escobar Ohmstede (1997, 309), and Guardino (2005, 238–41).

10. Biblioteca Nacional, Fondo Álvarez, fol. 1, doc. 18.

11. Thus, for instance, sometimes when villages rented land to outsiders, they specified that the rent should be paid in goods like wax for the candles of the village's patron saint, or in some cases cash that was likewise spent to support the religious rituals honoring the saint. AGEO, Colonial, vol. 2; AGEO, Real Intendencia I, vol. 6, file 2; Romero Frizzi (1996, 222); Van Young (2001, 489).

12. See, for instance, AVA, Penal, file 334, 1791 (1789); AGN, Clero Regular y Secular, vol. 188, file 12, fols. 203v–4; AVA, Penal, file 414, 1798; AVA, Civil, file 576, 1798.

13. Daniela Traffano (2001) has done wonderful work in the diocesan archive in Oaxaca.

14. See, for example, AVA, Penal, file 678, 1838; AVA, Penal, file 887, 1848; AVA, Penal, file 894, 1848; AVA, Penal, file 1070, 1853; AVA, Penal, file 1079, 1853.

15. Biblioteca Nacional, Fondo Manuel Martínez Gracida, vol. 68.

16. Another good discussion of the evolution of peasant insurgent ideas during the war is found in Ducey (1999b).

17. Thus we see the paradox of Miguel Francisco, justice of the peace of Jocutla, Guerrero. Francisco, like all justices of the peace, was supposedly named to his post by the district administrator. Yet when he was imprisoned in a land dispute, he wrote to the state government demanding that he be released and allowed to take up his post again, because, in his words, "The village saw fit to appoint me." Archivo de la Cámara de Diputados del Estado de México, file 1840, book 104, file 272.

18. See, for instance, Emilio Kourí's contribution to this volume.

19. See for instance, many of the essays in Joseph and Nugent (1994), as well as Connaughton, Illades, and Pérez Toledo (1999, 14, 28). Notably similar concepts are important to some works that do not explicitly refer to the theoretical term. Thus in describing the social order of New Spain, Felipe Castro Gutiérrez (1996, 21) speaks of "una especie de guión," upon which characters improvised their everyday performances.

20. The issue of subaltern deceit is explored quite creatively from a different angle in James Scott (1985).

REFERENCES

ARCHIVES

Archivo de la Cámara de Diputados del Estado de México
Archivo de Villa Alta (AVA), Oaxaca
    Fondo Civil
    Fondo Penal
Archivo General del Estado de Oaxaca (AGEO)
    Fondo Colonial
    Fondo Real Intendencia
Archivo General de la Nación (AGN)
    Fondo Clero Regular y Secular
    Fondo Criminal
Biblioteca Nacional
    Fondo Álvarez
    Fondo Manuel Martínez Gracida

PRINTED PRIMARY SOURCES

Casaus y Torres, Ramón Francisco. 1808. *Sermon en accion de gracias a Dios nuestro senor por las gloriosas hazanas de la invicta nacion espanola para la restauracion de la monarquia, y restitucion de nuestro amado soberano el Sr. D. Fernando VII. a su trono . . . Predicado el dia 10 de septiembre de 1808 en la iglesia de San Agustin de Antequera de Oaxaca.* Mexico: D. M. de Zuñiga y Ontiveros.

Esposición que en cumplimiento del Artículo 83 de la Constitución del Estado hace el Gobernador del mismo al soberano Congreso al abrir sus sesiones el 2 de julio del año de 1848. 1848. Oaxaca: Impreso por Ignacio Rincón.

SECONDARY SOURCES

Birrichaga, Diana. 2008. "Los espacios del poder local. (Re)Configuración de los grupos políticos en los pueblos texcocanos, 1820–1850." In *Prácticas populares, cultura política y poder en México, siglo XIX,* edited by Brian Connaughton, 221–57. Mexico: Universidad Autónoma Metropolitana and Casa Juan Pablos.

Caplan, Karen. 2003. "The Legal Revolution in Town Politics: Oaxaca and Yucatán, 1812–1825." *Hispanic American Historical Review* 83 (2): 255–93.

———. 2010. *Indigenous Citizens: Local Liberalism in Early National Oaxaca and Yucatán.* Stanford, CA: Stanford University Press.

Castro Gutiérrez, Felipe. 1996. *Nueva ley y nuevo rey: Reformas borbónicas y rebelión popular en Nueva España.* Zamora: Colegio de Michoacán and Universidad Nacional Autónoma de México.

Coatsworth, John. 1988. "Patterns of Rural Rebellion in Latin America: Mexico in Comparative Perspective." In *Riot, Rebellion and Revolt: Rural Social Conflict in Mexico,* edited by Friedrich Katz, 21–62. Princeton, NJ: Princeton University Press.

Connaughton, Brian, Carlos Illades, and Sonia Pérez Toledo, eds. 1999. *Construcción de la legitimidad política en México: sujetos, discurso y conducta política en el siglo XIX.* Mexico: Universidad Autónoma Metropolitana, Colegio de México, Universidad Nacional Autónoma de México, and Colegio de Michoacán.

Ducey, Michael. 1997. "Liberal Theory and Peasant Practice: Land and Power in Northern Veracruz, 1826–1900." In *Liberals, the Church, and Indian Peasants: Corporate Lands and the Challenge of Reform in Nineteenth-Century Spanish America,* edited by Robert H. Jackson, 65–94. Albuquerque: University of New Mexico Press.

———. 1999a. "Hijos de pueblo y ciudadanos: Identidades políticas entre los rebeldes indios del siglo XIX." In Connaughton, Illades, and Pérez Toledo 1999, 127–51.

———. 1999b. "Village, Nation, and Constitution: Insurgent Politics in Papantla, Veracruz, 1810–1821." *Hispanic American Historical Review* 79 (3): 463–93.

———. 2001. "Indian Communities and Ayuntamientos in the Mexican Huasteca: Sujeto Revolts, Pronunciamientos, and Caste War." *Americas* 57 (4): 525–50.

————. 2004. *A Nation of Villages: Riot and Rebellion in the Mexican Huasteca, 1750–1850*. Tucson: University of Arizona Press.

Escobar Ohmstede, Antonio. 1996. "Del gobierno indígena al ayuntamiento constitucional en las huastecas hidalguense y veracruzana, 1780–1853." *Mexican Studies/Estudios Mexicanos* 12 (1): 1–15.

————. 1997. "Los ayuntamientos y los pueblos de indios en la Sierra Huasteca: Conflictos entre nuevos y viejos actores, 1812–1840." In *La reindianización de América, siglo XIX*, edited by Leticia Reina, 294–316. Mexico: Siglo XXI and Centro de Investigaciones y Estudios Superiores en Antropología Social (CIESAS).

————. 1998a. *De la costa de la sierra: Las huastecas, 1750–1900*. Mexico: CIESAS.

————. 1998b. "El federalismo en las Huastecas durante la primera mitad del siglo XIX." In *Política y diplomacia en el siglo XIX mexicano*, edited by Luis Jáuregui and José A. Serrano Ortega, 65–83. Historia y nación: Actas del Congreso en homenaje a Josefina Zoraida Vázquez, vol 2. Mexico: Colegio de México.

Falcón, Romana. 2002. *México descalzo: Estrategias de sobrevivencia frente a la modernidad liberal*. Mexico: Plaza y Janés.

Florescano, Enrique. 1997. *Etnia, estado y nación: Ensayo sobre las identidades colectivas en México*. Mexico: Aguilar.

Gruzinski, Serge. 1985. "La 'segunda aculturación': el estado ilustrado y la religiosidad indígena de la Nueva España (1775–1800)." *Estudios de Historia Novohispana* (8): 175–201.

Guardino, Peter. 1995. "Barbarism or Republican Law: Guerrero's Peasants and National Politics, 1820–1846." *Hispanic American Historical Review* 75 (2): 185–213.

————. 1996. *Peasants, Politics and the Formation of Mexico's National State: Guerrero, 1800–1857*. Stanford, CA: Stanford University Press.

————. 2000. "Me ha cabido en la fatalidad: Gobierno indígena y gobierno republicano en los pueblos indígenas: Oaxaca, 1750–1850." *Desacatos* (5): 119–30.

————. 2005. *The Time of Liberty: Popular Political Culture in Oaxaca, 1750–1850*. Durham, NC: Duke University Press.

Guarisco, Claudia. 2003. *Los indios del valle de México y la construcción de una nueva sociabilidad política, 1770–1835*. Toluca: Colegio Mexiquense.

————. 2008. "Indios, cultura y representación política durante el primer federalismo. El caso del valle de México." In *Prácticas populares, cultura política y poder en México, siglo XIX*, edited by Brian Connaughton, 167–220. Mexico: Universidad Autónoma Metropolitana and Casa Juan Pablos.

Güémez Pineda, Arturo. 2007. "La emergencia de los ayuntamientos constitucionales gaditanos y la sobrevivencia de los cabildos mayas yucatecos (1812–1824)." In *Ayuntamientos y liberalismo gaditano en México*, edited by Juan Ortiz Escamilla and José A. Serrano Ortega, 89–129. Zamora: Colegio de Michoacán and Universidad Veracruzana.

Hamnett, Brian. 1986. *Roots of Insurgency: Mexican Regions, 1750–1824*. Cambridge: Cambridge University Press.

Joseph, Gilbert, and Daniel Nugent, eds. 1994. *Everyday Forms of State Formation: Revolution and the Negotiation of Rule in Modern Mexico*. Durham, NC: Duke University Press.

Katz, Friedrich. 1988. "Rural Rebellions After 1910." In *Riot, Rebellion and Revolt: Rural Social Conflict in Mexico*, edited by Friedrich Katz, 521–61. Princeton, NJ: Princeton University Press.

Kearney, Michael. 1996. *Reconceptualizing the Peasantry: Anthropology in Global Perspective*. Boulder, CO: Westview.

Kellogg, Susan. 1995. *Law and the Transformation of Aztec Culture*. Norman: University of Oklahoma Press.

Landavazo, Marco Antonio. 2001. *La máscara de Fernando VII: Discurso e imaginario monárquicos en una época de crisis, Nueva España, 1808–1822*. Mexico: Colegio de México, Universidad Michoacana de San Nicolás de Hidalgo, and Colegio de Michoacán.

Lemoine, Ernesto. 1965. *Morelos: Su vida revolucionaria a través de sus escritos y otros testimonios de la época*. Mexico: Universidad Nacional Autónoma de México.

Lockhart, James. 1992. *The Nahuas After the Conquest: A Social and Cultural History of the Indians of Central Mexico, Sixteenth Through Eighteenth Centuries*. Stanford, CA: Stanford University Press.

Mallon, Florencia. 1995. *Peasant and Nation: The Making of Postcolonial Mexico and Peru*. Berkeley: University of California Press.

Meyer, Jean. 1973. *Problemas campesinos y revueltas agrarias (1821–1910)*. Mexico: Secretaría de Educación Pública.

Millichap, Joseph R. 1983. *Steinbeck and Film*. New York: Frederick Ungar.

Minguez, Victor. 1995. *Los reyes distantes: Imágenes del poder en el México virreinal*. Castello: Universitat Jaume I., Servei de Publicaciones, and Diputació de Castelló.

Purnell, Jennie. 2002. "Citizens and Sons of the Pueblo: National and Local Identities in the Making of the Mexican Nation." *Ethnic and Racial Studies* 25 (2): 213–37.

Redfield, Robert. 1941. *The Folk Culture of the Yucatan*. Chicago: University of Chicago Press.

———. 1956. *Peasant Society and Culture: An Anthropological Approach to Civilization*. Chicago: University of Chicago Press.

Reina, Leticia. 1980. *Las rebeliones de campesinos en México (1819–1906)*. Mexico: Siglo XXI.

Romero Frizzi, María de los Ángeles. 1996. *El sol y la cruz: Los pueblos indios de Oaxaca colonial*. Mexico: CIESAS and Instituto Nacional Indigenista.

Roseberry, William. 1994. "Hegemony and the Language of Contention." In Joseph and Nugent 1994, 355–66.

———. 1995. "Latin American Peasant Studies in a 'Postcolonial' Era." *Journal of Latin American Anthropology* 1 (1): 150–77.

Rugeley, Terry. 1996. *Yucatán's Maya Peasantry and the Origins of the Caste War*. Austin: University of Texas Press.

Salinas Sandoval, María del Carmen. 2007. "Ayuntamientos en el Estado de México, 1812–1827: Proceso de adaptación entre el liberalismo y el Antiguo Régimen." In *Ayuntamientos y liberalismo gaditano en México*, edited by Juan Ortiz Escamilla and José A. Serrano Ortega, 369–410. Zamora: Colegio de Michoacán and Universidad Veracruzana.

Scott, James. 1985. *Weapons of the Weak: Everyday Forms of Peasant Resistance*. New Haven, CT: Yale University Press.

Serrano Ortega, José Antonio. 2007. "Ciudadanos naturales. Pueblos de indios y ayuntamientos en Guanajuato, 1820–1827." In *Ayuntamientos y liberalismo gaditano en México*, edited by Juan Ortiz Escamilla and José Antonio Serrano Ortega, 411–40. Zamora: Colegio de Michoacán and Universidad Veracruzana.

Silverman, Sydel. 1979. "The Peasant Concept in Anthropology." *Journal of Peasant Studies* 7 (1): 49–69.

Simmonds, Roy. 1996. *John Steinbeck: The War Years, 1939–1945*. Lewisburg, PA: Bucknell University Press.

Smith, Benjamin T. 2012. *The Roots of Conservatism in Mexico: Catholicism, Society and Politics in the Mixteca Baja, 1750–1962*. Albuquerque: University of New Mexico Press.

Steinbeck, John. 1941. *The Forgotten Village*. New York: Viking.

Stern, Steve J. 1987. "New Approaches to the Study of Peasant Rebellion and Consciousness: Implications of the Andean Experience." In *Resistance, Rebellion, and Consciousness in the Andean Peasant World, 18th to 20th Centuries*, edited by Steve J. Stern, 3–25. Madison: University of Wisconsin Press.

———. 1995. *The Secret History of Gender: Women, Men, and Power in Late Colonial Mexico*. Chapel Hill: University of North Carolina Press.

Taylor, William. 1996. *Magistrates of the Sacred: Priests and Parishioners in Eighteenth-Century Mexico*. Stanford, CA: Stanford University Press.

———. 1999. "¿Eran campesinos los indios? El viaje de un norteamericano por la historia colonial mesoamericana." *Relaciones* 20 (78): 79–110.

Tecuanhuey Sandoval, Alicia. 2007. "Puebla 1812–1825: Organización y contención de ayuntamientos constitucionales." In *Ayuntamientos y liberalismo gaditano en México*, edited by Juan Ortiz Escamilla and José A. Serrano Ortega, 337–68. Zamora: Colegio de Michoacán and Universidad Veracruzana.

Thomson, Guy. 1999. *Patriotism, Politics, and Popular Liberalism in Nineteenth-Century Mexico: Juan Francisco Lucas and the Puebla Sierra*. With David LaFrance. Wilmington, DE: Scholarly Resources.

Tilly, Charles. 1984. "Social Movements and National Politics." In *Statemaking and Social Movements: Essays in History and Theory*, edited by Charles Bright and Susan Harding, 297–317. Ann Arbor: University of Michigan Press.

Traffano, Daniela. 2001. *Indios, curas y nación. La sociedad indígena frente a un proceso de secularización: Oaxaca, siglo XIX*. Turin: Otto Editore.

Tutino, John. 1986. *From Insurrection to Revolution in Mexico: Social Bases of Agrarian Violence, 1750–1940*. Princeton, NJ: Princeton University Press.

Van Young, Eric. 1993. "The Cuautla Lazarus: Double Subjectives in Reading Texts on Popular Collective Action." *Colonial Latin American Review* 2 (1–2): 3–26.

———. 2001. *The Other Rebellion: Popular Violence, Ideology, and the Mexican Struggle for Independence, 1810–1821*. Stanford, CA: Stanford University Press.

Viqueira, Juan Pedro. 2002. "La comunidad indígena en México en los estudios antro-pológicos e históricos." In *Encrucijadas Chiapanecas*, edited by Juan Pedro Viqueira, 47–74. Mexico: Colegio de Mexico and Tusquets Editores.

Wade, Peter. 2007. "Modernity and Tradition: Shifting Boundaries, Shifting Contexts." In *When Was Latin America Modern?*, edited by Nicola Miller and Stephen Hart, 49–68. New York: Palgrave MacMillan.

Wolf, Eric. 1956. "Aspects of Group Relations in a Complex Society: Mexico." *American Anthropologist* 58 (6): 1065–78.

———. 1957. "Closed Corporate Communities in Mesoamerica and Central Java." *Southwestern Journal of Anthropology* 13 (1): 1–18.

———. 1975. "Aspects of Group Relations in a Complex Society: Mexico." In *Peasants and Peasant Societies: Selected Readings*, edited by Teodor Shanin, 50–68. Baltimore: Penguin.

Yannakakis, Yanna. 2003. "*Indios ladinos*': Indigenous Intermediaries and the Negotiation of Local Rule in Colonial Oaxaca, 1600–1769." PhD diss., Philadelphia: University of Pennsylvania.

———. 2008. *The Art of Being In-Between: Native Intermediaries, Indian Identity, and Local Rule in Colonial Oaxaca*. Durham, NC: Duke University Press.

CHAPTER 3

INDIGENOUS COMMUNITIES, POLITICAL TRANSFORMATIONS, AND MEXICO'S WAR OF INDEPENDENCE IN THE GULF COAST REGION

MICHAEL T. DUCEY

O
NE OF the challenges in understanding the role of indigenous actors in Mexican history is the tendency to characterize them as being stubbornly attached to tradition while at the same time serving as a fount of revolutionary potential. Historians of Mexico's nineteenth century have frequently commented on this dualistic nature of indigenous political action, coining phrases to describe this Janus-faced behavior: "liberal syncretism," "political bilingualism," or "popular liberalism."[1] This interplay of tradition and innovation is a useful paradigm for approaching the recent studies of the nation's independence. Historians have either aimed to create a "new political history," as in the works of François-Xavier Guerra (1992) and Jaime Rodríguez O. (1996), that generally leaves village actors on the margins, or they have stressed the violent social upheaval of the lower classes. Eric Van Young's (2001) work represents the finest example of this second tradition, placing the lower classes at the center of his analysis but in isolation from the transformative political events of the times. Thus, in the leading currents in the historiography, indigenous actors are either irrelevant—as one commentator puts it, "Independence without Insurgents" (Granados 2010)—or indifferent to the grand political projects of 1810–1821.

By the turn of the nineteenth century, indigenous pueblos had already experienced profound changes under the pressures of the previous century's economic and demographic trends as well as the political innovations of Enlightenment reformers who aimed to transform pueblos into tax-paying participants in a productive economic order. As seen in Kourí and Guardino's discussions of land tenure and village government in this volume, the practices often identified as traditional were themselves products of constant innovation and adaptation to the demands of the viceregal government and economy. The inhabitants of the *repúblicas de indios* had experienced frequent political assaults on their political autonomy as the Crown tightened tax collection and the supervision of day-to-day affairs in rural New Spain (Van Young 1988, 199–204; Ducey 2004, 30–46; Tanck de Estrada 1999, 17–74, 581–82). In this chapter I stress the inventiveness of local actors confronted by the dissolution of political systems constructed around their colonial subordination. The insurgency disrupted hierarchies of power, class, and caste, permitting the emergence of new political agents from within the indigenous villages and marginal Afro-mestizo rancheros to challenge the colonial order during the long years of the insurgency. In an effort to bring *indios* back into the new political history of Mexican independence, I illustrate how the leadership of local insurgencies tailored their actions to accommodate the interests of indigenous communities.

One of the problems we face in understanding the idea of the indigenous is that it is largely a one-way discussion; we know what political operatives proposed to indigenous villagers and how they mobilized them, but rarely do we get the other side of the dialogue. The following pages describe how insurgents and counterinsurgent loyalists strove to win over residents of indigenous villages. It is not a simple monologue, however. First, a close reading of the documents can reveal the perceptions of political actors of what the inhabitants of the *pueblos de indios* wanted. And second, we can observe what actually appealed to villagers and finally what kept them fighting even after the "national" leadership of the insurgency had been defeated.

The surviving documents from the Gulf Coast region reveal the interplay between local traditions and new initiatives that produced a series of negotiations and unspoken consensus concerning how indigenous people would manage the state and their communities. I review three critical processes that both illustrate the impact of indigenous actors on independence and also problematize the identity of *indios* as it was transformed in the violent upheaval of the period. These phenomena are the outbreak of the insurrection in the pueblos during 1811 and 1812, the insurgent efforts to create a new government that could claim legitimacy and demand loyalty from the pueblos between 1812 and 1815, and finally the long guerrilla war that lingered until 1821. These three moments can serve as a means of observing the actions of regional leaders and their followers as they seized opportunities to both challenge subordination and transform the projects that emanated from the Spanish government and the centers of insurgent leadership. Inherently tied to these processes was the question of what the political identity of *Indian* meant: the relation between subject and king became a problem fiercely debated, not just with words but also with muskets. Both sides of the military divide redefined the meaning of *Indian* during the war, forcing a breakdown of the traditional rules of ethnic subordination that maintained the term as a signifier of a conquered tribute payer excluded from honorable militia service and always subordinate to Spaniards.

SPEAKING FOR THE KING AND THE PUEBLO

An unexpected result of the constitutional crisis of the Spanish monarchy, and, more broadly, the events that resulted from the French Revolution and the Napoleonic Wars, was the opening of political avenues for traditional institutions to adopt new forms of political language centered on a vague concept of the nation. Since the 1790s the royal government had exhorted loyal subjects to guard against internal subversion and foreign invaders, demanding sacrifices to maintain the Spanish war effort, first against the French, then the English, and, after 1808, Napoleon and his heretical hordes.

Royal officials and the clerical establishment propagated a new rhetoric of national emergency emphasizing broad threats to an ambiguously defined nation and the Catholic religion. The long years of war in Europe promoted constant mobilizations to defend the monarchy, reaching a crescendo in 1808 when Napoleon forced Fernando VII to abdicate the crown in favor of his brother. Marco Landavazo (2001, 37) has carefully described the popular fervor in defense of Fernando VII, documenting the outpouring of donations for the cause. Furthermore, he notes how the support for the captive king motivated "social sectors that were traditionally subordinated, marginal or politically passive in this movement of universal enthusiasm" (83). The crisis unfolded in an environment where impossible things could and did happen: the king had disappeared and a foreign invasion was imminent.

The debates surrounding the rights of the kingdom and the dilemma of the missing monarch for the legitimacy of the viceregal government were not limited to creole elites. While much of the literature concentrates on the role of the Spanish town councils in the cities, and especially that of the city of Mexico, constitutional debates spread from the center to the outlying *ayuntamientos* and even Indian cabildos. The Spanish juntas rewrought the language of the monarchy as they organized against the French. The frequently used argument that appeared in European circles describing an end to three hundred years of tyranny, for example, referring to the loss of ancient privileges under the Habsburgs and the Bourbons, took on new meanings on this side of the Atlantic: the language of resistance to the French transformed into challenges to the legitimacy of Spanish domination.[2] As Peter Guardino notes in the previous chapter, the monarchy provided a symbolic connection between the actions of indigenous villagers and the wider colonial order. While the colonial village may seem tightly circumscribed to local affairs, conflicts with Spanish officials, neighboring landlords, or even other towns drove villagers to seek out patrons, or at least sympathetic listeners, in the viceregal capital. On a concrete level of practical administrative politics, villagers were attuned to events beyond the town borders that might affect their interests.

In Misantla and Papantla, the increasing emergencies degraded the already rather porous boundaries between *indio* and other *casta* groups. One of the critical distinctions that the Bourbon reformers maintained was that service under arms in the colonial militias should exclude people classified as Indian, and increasingly they excluded free colored men (known as *pardos* or *morenos* at that time) from serving as officers (Vinson 2001, 41). In Papantla, in the aftermath of a particularly violent uprising in 1787, Crown commanders lamented the close ties between Indian villagers and *pardo* militiamen and ordered a rigorous reformation of the local militia companies (Ducey 2014b, 32–35; 2004, 45).[3] During the last decades of imperial rule, the Bourbons had attempted to better regulate and control the privileges of coastal militia, tighten military discipline, and reenforce the traditional racial boundaries by limiting the opportunities for advancement into the officer ranks open to *casta* rank-and-file soldiers. The invasion threats and the outbreak of the insurrection in the interior brought rapid changes that undermined the reformers' vision of a disciplined and racially segregated militia. Facing the emergency, the government formed new militia companies with the innovation of including indigenous villagers. While at first the Viceroy Venegas called only for the enrollment of the "propertied classes," in June of 1811 the government adopted a new policy of enlisting men of all racial categories into new village militia companies (Ortiz Escamilla 2008b, 178–79). Local officials were often skeptical of the wisdom of mustering the indigenous population for armed service; for example, the subdelegate of Huejutla wrote that indigenous villagers were not accustomed to the demands of military life and that it would "bring them to the precipice of committing the crime of infidelity."[4] But beyond the extraordinary rigors of militia service, it also served as an invitation for villagers to reconsider their subordinate status of Indian as colonial subjects.

The fervent professions of allegiance to the absent king had a very heterodox content depending on who and when they were made. The insurgency began with frequent declarations of loyalty to Fernando VII, prompting some historians to interpret the phenomenon as a mask held up by the leadership to persuade the unwashed masses to follow them. Or it is seen as an expression of "naive monarchism" often associated with "primitive rebels" to use Hobsbawm's term (1969, 26–27).[5] The apparently irrational attachment to the person of the king rested on the vision of the monarchy as the fount of justice and the head of the body politic; as Landavazo (2001) points out, the removal of the king transformed the nation into a headless creature, doomed to fail. Furthermore, villagers saw the king's justice as a check on the arbitrary power of low-level royal officials, and its absence exposed his Indian subjects to the abuses of local usurpers.

When the insurrection broke out, the rebels did not repudiate the customary tropes of legitimacy but rather appropriated them for their own. This position may seem unsustainable to modern observers, but the events since the king's imprisonment and abdication left plenty of room for doubts. Fernando came to the throne after the disastrous rule of his father, Carlos IV, and inspired hope that the young monarch would finally bring relief to the long-suffering subjects of the far-flung Spanish Empire. To have him snatched away and replaced by a French pretender provoked dismay and led many to believe that traitorous Spanish allies of Napoleon ensconced in the government were the root of the crisis. In New Spain, the situation was made even more ambiguous when a coalition of Spanish merchants and conservative judges of the Audiencia militarily overthrew the unpopular viceroy José de Iturrigaray because he seemed to be on the verge of supporting the call to establish a self-governing junta with the town councils for the viceroyalty. The unprecedented deposition of the viceroy lacked any legal basis; the participants merely declared that they acted in the name of the people (Rodríguez O. 2009, 1:141, 144–45; Warren 1996, 29). While the Spanish uprising against the French was greeted with universal approval in Mexico, the steady advance of Napoleon's army seemed to indicate that Spanish resistance had failed and that the kingdom would soon fall to the usurper. While the debates over the nature of sovereignty and the rights of town councils to represent the people may have struck rural villagers as obscure, we should not be surprised that the language of the crisis filtered into the indigenous villages. The belief that the Spanish were on the verge of surrendering the kingdom to Napoleon who would, in turn, abolish the Catholic faith was widespread, and the clergy, seeking to inspire patriotic efforts from parishioners promoted an atmosphere of impending danger for the faith.

Once the insurrection broke out in Mexico, years of crisis had firmly embedded the hysterical language of the *patria* in danger throughout the land. The government demanded acts of loyalty from the *repúblicas de indios* as a new round of emergency mobilizations began.[6] Rumors of treasonous motives quickly spread, sowing doubts about the intentions of local administrators. Eric Van Young (2001, 148, 339, 352–53) and others (Ducey 2014a, 432, 445–46) have documented the widespread belief that Spaniards planned to murder innocent villagers at any moment.

The methods by which the insurrection spread revealed how the popular actors embraced insubordination as a form of loyalty to Church and king. Rebel officers and representatives, bearing commissions from the leadership of the movement and claiming to act in defense of the king's rights, presented themselves in the *pueblos de indios* bearing invitations to rally the population "for the King, religion, but against the *gachupines*."[7] While government loyalists were often mystified by the rapid and apparently universal spread of rebellion, relying on the usual tropes of "infectious contagion," the insurgency expanded as local factions responded to the call of an uprising that presented itself as the legitimate government of the kingdom.[8] The means of subversion were not mysterious; the movement seduced the indigenous governments and the new militias via correspondence that called on them to defend the king and arrest Spanish officials. Insurgent operatives actively recruited Indian governors, making concrete offers of increased autonomy and economic benefits.[9] The arrival of subversive emissaries suddenly transformed the leaders of the indigenous town councils into central actors in politics beyond their communities as both sides aspired to win them over.

The insurrection expanded the political horizons and opportunities of the pueblos. Although village dissidents previously had searched for allies in the viceregal government to challenge their local enemies, during 1810 and 1811 they were suddenly confronted with a situation where two groups claimed to be representatives of the *gobierno superior*. Both forcefully clamored for their adhesion to the *causa justa*, using similar language promising to defend the king and the true religion against their enemies. For the insurgents, the enemies were the *peninsulares* and the Crown officials that the pro-French Manuel Godoy had appointed. The slogan "Long live the king and death to bad government" obviously raises questions about naïve monarchism and the subversive intent of popular slogans, but there was no doubt about its revolutionary consequences as the insurgents came to power in the towns of the Gulf Coast.[10]

Within indigenous communities, the new politics of choice created dilemmas and opportunities. On the one hand, there was the chance to settle scores with the Crown officials who had done little to endear themselves in the villages.[11] The invitations confirmed what many rural residents had long suspected: Spanish officials were illegitimate scoundrels. The atmosphere of fear that had enveloped the political landscape added urgency to the demand for action. In the absence of the monarch, the Spaniards could not be trusted, and there would be no restraints to Spanish abuses once the recourse of the figure of the king´s justice disappeared. But the invitation to join the insurrection was also fraught with danger; it was a declaration of war, after all. Plenty of evidence exists indicating that when forced to choose, many actors opted for neutrality or a lukewarm adherence to whoever held the upper hand in the locality. Indigenous villagers could be extremely cagey when presented with the choice of insurgency or loyalism, often seeking the path that would maintain their community autonomy (Ortiz Escamilla 1997, 94, 99). At the same time, the existence of options also heightened the tensions within communities; economic inequality and internal factionalism with roots in the last decades of the colonial period were exacerbated by the outbreak of war in the countryside. The political fallout of choosing insurgency fractured indigenous pueblos, as historical local divisions became identified with the overarching projects of rebellion or loyalty.

INDIGENOUS ACTORS AND THE NEW POLITICAL ORDER

Both insurgents and counterinsurgents confronted the necessity to create new forms of government in an effort to consolidate their legitimacy; in the case of the royalist, this took the form of the Cortes de Cádiz (the Spanish parliament called to confront the war with France) and the constitution that it produced in 1812. Cádiz has captured the imagination of historians in recent years; Jaime

Rodríguez O. (2009; 1996) has been prominent among those who called our attention to the centrality of the transatlantic constitutional process that it represented.[12] Central to the concern of this study is the effort by the lawmakers in the constitutional assembly to transform the relation between subject and monarch. This is especially notable in the case of the indigenous population of the Americas, who were granted full citizenship rights. The Spanish American delegates who attended the assembly in Cádiz strenuously argued in favor of the broadest possible extension of rights in order to increase the number of delegates from the American territories of the Spanish Empire. Marixa Lasso (2006, 343–46), for example, has demonstrated how creole delegates became staunch advocates for the inclusion not only of the indigenous population but also of the descendants of Africans in the Americas. While the push to include the African population as full citizens failed in the face of opposition from the delegates of the Spanish peninsula, in the case of the indigenous population, the constitution declared them citizens. In language that no doubt must have struck many as remarkable, article 5 of the constitution declared, "That all free men born and residing in the dominions of Spain and their descendants are Spaniards" (Spain, Cortes generales y extraordinarias [1812] 1961, 293). By constitutional fiat the term *Spaniard* now signified membership in a political nation and not ethnic origin. The eighteenth article of the constitution extended citizenship rights to those who traced their bloodlines to either Spain or the Americas; that is, it included the indigenous population but excluded the descendants of Africans. The articles struck down a central tenet of a society based on hierarchy and subordination of the *indio*.

Another key innovation of the Spanish Charter was the abolition of colonial indigenous governments (*repúblicas de indios*) and the creation of *ayuntamientos* in all localities that had at least one thousand inhabitants. Rather than create town councils following historical precedents, the constitutional system proposed a modern system of representation based on the new organs of government serving as the expression of the interests of all of the citizens in a given territory. These institutions displaced the indigenous institutions organized on the principle of corporate representation and historical tradition. On the one hand, the new arrangement offered small towns an autonomous governing body based on popular suffrage, independent of the traditional centers of power that the *repúblicas* represented; on the other, they were no longer ethnically exclusive. The *repúblicas* excluded the participation of non-indigenous residents from voting or holding office, but the new *ayuntamientos* prescribed that all male citizens could vote and take office, permitting the possibility that local creole or mestizo elites could claim control of village affairs. In the towns where the viceregal government held sway, new town councils came into existence, and the new citizens voted in surprisingly high percentages. In the case of Mexico City, the new institutions proved to be a thorn in the side of the viceregal government, becoming centers of opposition to the actions of the counterinsurgency administration of Félix María Calleja (Warren 1996, 34–36; Guedea 1996, 181–83). In parts of northern Veracruz, however, loyalist officials oversaw the establishment of new town councils and viewed them in a more favorable light. Local administrators had considerable leeway in deciding which towns met the criteria for creating new councils and considered them as potentially useful in mobilizing resources for the government (Ducey 2007, 184). The initiatives that promised autonomy to the new *ayuntamientos* were often offset by the rising costs placed upon indigenous communities to supply money and goods to maintain the war effort. The counterinsurgency effort enabled the local elites to gain new powers as commanders of militia companies that became central to Calleja's counterinsurgency program (Ortiz Escamilla 1997, 80–81, 111; Archer 1992, 290, 295). The new militia companies founded in response to the insurrection assumed the power to create their own "provisional taxes" in each community, permitting them to gain fiscal independence and also shifting the costs of the war to local communities (Ortiz Escamilla 2008a, 197). Thus the elevation of indigenous villagers to the status of Spanish citizens came at the same time that political authority gravitated to noncivilian spheres. The constitutional experiment came to an abrupt end in 1814 as a result of Fernando VII's repudiation of the charter shortly after returning from his imprisonment in France, meaning that the military transformation had a more profound impact than the introduction of constitutional *ayuntamientos*.

At the same time, the constitutional reforms were not implemented in the wide swath of rebel-controlled territory along the coast of Veracruz, essentially from the point north of the port of Veracruz to the territory south and west of the port of Tuxpan. During this period, insurgents also struggled to create an administration that could sustain the war, strengthen its claims to legitimacy, establish relations with the outside world, and eventually move to an open demand for independence. As the insurgent leaders occupied more territory, and in the face of an increasingly concerted counterinsurgency effort, it became imperative to regularize and coordinate the disparate groups contained within the movement. Organizing a regional government proved problematic for the insurgents; the leadership had few mechanisms to impose its will on the villages, forcing them to negotiate with their followers to accomplish their ends. As a result, the insurgent leadership tended to be fairly accommodating in their relations with indigenous communities.

The rebels offered a deal to the local communities: in exchange for recognizing their legitimacy and authority as *repúblicas de indios*, they expected loyalty and military support against the counterinsurgent government. Unlike the Constitution of Cádiz, the insurgents did not create new town councils; rather they left the historic cabildos intact and recreated an order that maintained traditions of autonomy. There was an unstated consensus that the *república* should remain unchanged, reflecting the power that the custom of village independence exercised in the political world view of the rebels. Confirming Emilio Kourí's observations made in chapter 1, the practices of local autonomy proved to be a remarkably powerful model for rural insurgents, demonstrating an ability to bend under the intense pressures of a counterinsurgency war. As the Mexico City government reclaimed many of the principal towns of the Gulf region, the rebels who refused to put down their arms formed rebel *repúblicas de indios* in the remote areas of the forest. Sovereignty here devolved upon the *cabildo indígena*, and local insurgent commanders were willing to recognize it.

On a national level, rebel leadership of José María Morelos aspired to establish a more coherent project by calling for a constitutional congress. The centrality of the pueblo institutions may be seen in the way in which the insurgents organized elections to choose deputies for the Congress of Chilpancingo in 1813. The electoral records specify that the votes were cast by corporate entities, not by individuals; the governors, the *república*, and sometimes the *escribano de república* attended the *juntas electorales*, and the town scribe or governor signed as the representative of the commons. In the case of Papantla, the military commander received Morelos's call for the elections and proceeded to organize them by summoning the town councils of the indigenous communities to meet and hold elections.[13] The towns in turn sent delegates to Papantla to select a representative for the entire district.[14] The corporatist elections sought to maintain a compact with the rebellion's indigenous allies, promising them a continuity of autonomy in exchange for their loyalty. In the better-known and -documented elections in Michoacán and Guerrero, the *repúblicas* voted as corporations as well. The Michoacán records demonstrate how the participants perceived the electors as more than just the occupants of a political post; for example, the representative chosen in the election that took place in San José Taximaróa (in Michoacán) is described in the following terms: "To whom the pueblo gives and confers all its power, full, complete and sufficient, according to what is required and needed, and they declare the illustrious Don Antonio Manzo de Cevallos, as Elector, in whose voice, once united with the Congress, and in the presence of its sovereignty, will be able to represent these inhabitants in all affairs concerning their happiness" (Hernández y Dávalos [1877] 1985, 154).

The language of sovereignty is fused with the idea of acting as a holder of a power of attorney for the town; a role that was very common in the world of lawsuits and community legal defense was now ritualistically projected into the arena of political representation and national sovereignty. The creation of the insurgent congress confirmed historic political practices of the indigenous communities even as it diverted them to the innovative purpose of legitimizing a national armed political movement.

At least symbolically, elections were a method of reestablishing a hierarchy between the pueblos in rebellion. They were ritualized events performed with the participation of a representative of the local insurgent authorities; in the case of Papantla, it was the insurgent subdelegate who invited the population to vote after a public reading of General Morelos's formal instructions. In addition to the missive from General Morelos, the representatives of the insurgency took the opportunity to exhort the assembled communities to explain the call to form the congress and inspire the patriotic sentiments of the voters.[15] The communities proceeded to elect a representative who in turn participated in an electoral council in the district seat to choose a representative who would later attend a provincial conclave and name a representative to the new national congress. This elaborate tiered system emphasized the political ties between region, province, and nation in which representatives from the pueblos participated in a kind of pilgrimage to the new national congress. It incorporated pueblos adopting traditional aspects of indigenous governance and fusing them to a new project national in scope.

Ultimately, the reluctance to meddle in the system of local government reflects the dependence of the insurgents on the pueblos for survival. The project was conservative: the colonial cabildo organized the elections, and the constitution of Apatzingán that resulted from them maintained the structures of local town rule unmolested. While the constitution contains extensive sections dedicated to the congress, executive, and judicial branches of the new government, it makes no modification in town administration. In contrast, the Cádiz document spelled out the characteristics and functions of municipal government, creating a uniform model of rule.[16]

Elections were merely symptomatic of the insurgent attitudes toward the pueblos in almost every sphere of governance. During the years specified above, the insurgent leadership under Ignacio Rayón sent an envoy, a priest holding the military rank of colonel, Antonio Lozano, to Papantla to organize a civil administration and to instill a modicum of military discipline in the disparate militias that had adhered to the "American" cause. As with any administration, one of the central challenges was to establish a coherent administration over the fiscal resources that were available to the insurgents. This proved to be a profound weakness of the rebel administration; they never were able to establish a tax base in the communities they controlled in spite of the elaborate ceremonies of elections undertaken in 1813. At the same time, the traditional taxes that had sustained royal government evaporated as a result of the insurrection itself. The end of tribute payments was the first act undertaken in rebel-controlled zones, and the collection of revenue that the Crown had traditionally extracted from the towns, the tobacco monopoly, and *alcabalas* (an excise tax on commerce), came to a grinding halt. The lack of a revenue base had repercussions in the colonel's efforts to establish military discipline, local insurgent commanders found their own ways of extracting cash to sustain their companies independent of the regional commanders. The exceptions to this general trend confirm the rule: Nicolás Bravo and Guadalupe Victoria were able to dominate local commanders by virtue of their control over the "taxes" extracted from merchants who wanted to move goods down the Mexico-Veracruz road, which they controlled (Ortiz Escamilla 2008a, 135, 152–56). These resources enabled them to favor loyal commanders with munitions and money. But the region under Lozano's command did not have an easily blackmailed commercial class, forcing him to appeal to the indigenous communities for voluntary donations in lieu of regular sources of tribute.

Colonel Lozano's pleas to the indigenous towns are revealing; they were sent to the *hijo gobernador* and his *república* of each town. The language is clearly traditionalist, rooted in the gendered relationship between the corporate leader and the *gobierno superior*. Typical of these letters between Lozano and the indigenous pueblos, one may encounter the following terms: "My sons Governors and judges of the towns: . . . Your beloved fatherland exhorts and requests that you lend us your aid and the duty that you, as true and recognized sons of the fatherland, have demands it now that, more than ever, you need its protection."[17] The paternalist discourse offering protection in exchange for fiscal support in the name of the nation in danger recalls the frequent calls for "donations" used by the Spanish monarchy since 1790; here the incipient insurgent state adopted it yet again. The context, however, was distinct. Lozano emphasized the role of the insurgent forces in protecting the Indian republics from government reprisals. The language of ever-present danger and imminent ruin still had traction in the rebel discourse in 1813, and not without foundation, since government forces often carried out reprisals when they reoccupied rebel towns. What is evident here is that local rebel commanders had limited powers to extract money from the towns. His exhortations emphasized the "voluntary" nature of his requests.[18]

Tensions between the towns and armed bands of insurgents were constant, and regional leaders had a difficult time reigning in abusive rebel chiefs. Just as pueblos asserted their autonomy from superior echelons of government, the bands of armed men essentially chose the officers who led them. In many cases, the pueblos named the local commander and expected him to protect the town at all costs. The insurgent leadership often granted them formal rank in the "American" army as an inducement to adhere to the cause, but unlike a professional force, rank did not indicate subordination to higher-ups. Their authority rested on the loyalty of their men.[19]

The insurgent civil administrations proved to be extremely limited in terms of the actual power they exercised fiscally and politically, reflecting their relative weakness vis-à-vis the pueblos they hoped to lead into a new era. Even as the insurgents embarked on the radical move toward republicanism, abandoning the dream of Fernando VII's return, they did not seek to redefine the role of the indigenous pueblo and the centrality of the indigenous in determining one's political identity. It was a revolution that, perhaps more out of necessity than conviction, cobbled together a coalition of pueblos and new political actors— including indigenous villagers, rancheros, and *pardo* militiamen—into a project of nation.

WAR IN AN INDIGENOUS SOCIETY

The insurgency took another turn after 1815. The government's counterinsurgency campaign had reversed the initial success of the rebels in the cities of the Bajío and began a slow march to restoring government supremacy over the viceroyalty. Counterinsurgency leaders dedicated themselves to eliminating centers of insurgent administration. On the Gulf Coast, the Mexico City government committed resources to forcing Nicolás Bravo to abandon Coscomatepec and

Lozano to flee Papantla, but pacifying the countryside beyond the towns was a much tougher nut to crack. Félix María Calleja's dogged campaigns succeeded in dispersing the well-organized armies under Morelos and ultimately put the insurgent congress to flight. The long, drawn-out guerrilla war that followed was fundamentally a war organized by the pueblos and came to obey the logic of local allegiances and enmities (Guardino 1996, 64–68). The cantankerous independence that the pueblos demonstrated toward rebel efforts to establish military and civil control may have hampered the ability of the insurgent leadership to marshal resources against the government, but as a result, when rebel administrative centers fell, the local villages maintained their will to fight. The autonomy within the insurgent camp guaranteed that pacification would take more than defeating rebel armies on the field of battle.[20]

The guerrilla war that followed made a virtue of the necessity that had kept local commands autonomous; small pockets of rebels held out, but when pressured they abandoned the principal towns and took refuge in the lush forests of the Gulf Coast. Due to their independence, the defeat of one rebel band did not affect the ability of others to continue; and while they could, and did, come together for offensive operations, these were ad hoc actions coordinated between equals. Government pacification campaigns were slow and costly. As the soldiers loyal to Mexico City reoccupied the traditional administrative towns, the population of the towns divided over whether to accept amnesties and stay in the government-controlled towns or flee to the hills. Many of the rebel combatants took to the forests with their families, becoming the nuclei of new communities formed in opposition to the loyalist administrative centers. As towns divided as a result of the conflict, the tensions within villages, between factions and political and economic hierarchies, became patently evident. The pattern became so common that each progovernment town seemed to be shadowed by a corresponding insurgent camp.

The insurgents were more than armed bands of men; entire families removed themselves from the government-controlled territories to continue the struggle. It was as much a migration as a military movement. The slash-and-burn agriculture practiced in the underpopulated coastal lands was adaptable to mobility; indigenous dissidents established their milpas farther into the forest, seeking to hide them from government patrols. Insurgent peasants rebuilt their modest huts, raised large community structures, and, in Palo Blanco, even built their own church. Insurgents near Coahuitlán, in the Sierra de Papantla region, built "on the crest of a hill a great house with the trappings of a church, although it had no image, it was well protected against animals with a fence, and the façade was decorated with flowers and a star and there were many graves."[21] In addition to erecting the physical infrastructure of pueblos, they recreated the model of the autonomous *república de indios*: electing a town council from among their members. When the military forced the surrender of the community in Palo Blanco, they presented a list of amnestied rebels specifying certain individuals as *gobernador*, *alcaldes*, and *escribanos*.[22] Indigenous renegades of the period insisted on maintaining pueblo structures intact even as war converted them into refugees in their own territory. In previous chapters we have seen how new pueblos emerged as a result of migration, demographic expansion, and internal divisions between *cabeceras* and *sujeto* villages; rebels built on these processes to create new communities to continue their challenge to the colonial order. The historic model of the pueblo creation provided a powerful organizing tool demonstrating how age-old traditions were bent to new purposes.

The refusal of these small-town insurgents to lay down their arms in spite of the privations and difficulties they faced once the resurgent royalist government had decapitated the national movement raises the question of what kept them fighting. There are several possible answers: they feared reprisals from royalist commanders, many of whom (as landowners and merchants) had been on the receiving end of rebel depredations, or perhaps local leaders were able to maintain a cohesion among their own followers through a combination of threats, communal and family loyalty, and personal charisma. The insurgency had also sparked local feuds within the region that would not necessarily end even with a royal pardon. But more than fear of reprisals, it seems that the experience of the war and the new language of rights had transformed the way indigenous people conceived of their relation to the state. In this period of intense violence, the history of indigenous autonomy and communal organization became even more central to local identities and individual survival. The leadership of the rural insurgency had internalized the language of national emergency and uncompromising violence, and, as the defense of the cause became intertwined with defense of the pueblo, the political landscape saw the emergence of new meanings of *pueblo* and its relation to the body politic.

Even as it seemed to be in remission throughout the viceroyalty, the insurgency saw the consolidation of two groups of political actors that were to play central roles in the years following independence. On the one hand, loyalist officers cemented their new roles as key political actors. Colonel Carlos María Llorente, for example, used his position to seize lands and settle loyal militiamen who had served him during the long war on the property as tenants. It was the beginning of a political dynasty that held sway in the region of Tantoyuca for much for the nineteenth century (Gómez Cruz 2009, 73–75). The commander of Huejutla, Colonel Álvarez de Güitian, also demonstrated the independence of local commanders by defying direct orders from viceroys while accumulating a fortune.[23] Brian Hamnett (1986, 178, 184) has noted that, on a grander scale, Generals Joaquín de Arredondo and José de la Cruz established their own feudal domains in their respective provinces.

The insurgent side of the equation saw the emergence of new popular actors within the indigenous community that now were versed in political practices that went beyond the boundaries of the colonial *pueblo de indios*. Throughout the war, rural Mexico was the stage for a political debate unlike any in its history; government pamphlets and newspapers circulated in the pueblos, and insurgents wrote responses and held public meetings to reply to them. Colonel José Joaquín de Aguilar, the leading insurgent commander after the exit of Antonio Lozano, engaged in a give-and-take with local loyalist commanders writing circulars to refute royalist propaganda.[24] Another frequent practice was the public rejection of government amnesty offers, in which rebel commanders would muster out the troops and read them the offer, prompting the soldiers to formally refuse it with a "solemn oath in favor of liberty and independence."[25] Aguilar even replied to government amnesties with offers of his own pardon to "the Americans under arms supporting the tyrant in the town of Chicontepec."[26] During his long years as the leading insurgent in the province, Guadalupe Victoria kept the cause alive by promoting a radical language of equality and republicanism.

The political activities of the community level commanders are not easy to trace, yet they are the ones who kept the insurgency going long after the national leadership had perished or surrendered. One revealing case may be found in the papers associated with an indigenous insurgent by the name of Mariano Olarte, who came to be the principal commander of the rump of the rebellion surviving in the camps of the Papantla region. Olarte, along with many members of his family, had followed his father, Serafín Olarte, into the insurrection when he rose up in May of 1812. Mariano became the leader of the local insurgency when his father died in an ambush in 1819. During the next two years, Olarte struggled to keep the movement going in the face of frequent government offensives, yet at the same time he took the time to pen several proclamations to denounce his enemies and exalt the objectives of the cause. Following the traditions laid down by Aguilar, Olarte organized public denunciations of the government and published "Amnesties" mocking the royalist commanders who pursued him through the forests of his home region (Ducey 2004, 82–88).

The sources that exist concerning how insurgents strived to motivate their small town followers are sparse, but what we can observe is that an oral culture of exhortation existed and animated the insurgents to keep fighting and also spreading the insurgent gospel to the ranks. These incidents demonstrate that political activities during the war breached the divide between literate and oral culture discussed by Elsie Rockwell in chapter 5. Aguilar carried out an oral performance and then committed it to text, while we can imagine that Olarte's scornful writings reflected the ridicule royalist leaders were subjected to around insurgent campfires. Both instances reveal how public readings of political tracts had become part of the political landscape. When Colonel Aguilar held his public repudiations of government amnesties, they served as spaces to promote the cause and also to reenforce group solidarity within the beleaguered forces of the rebellion. The central element to point to here is that the political actors in rural Mexico had learned to publicly promote alternative projects, appropriating the style and language of royalist propaganda and turning against the Crown. The insurgency demonstrates how porous the divide between village and city was. The initial expansion of the movement came as villages consciously chose alliances with outsiders based on their evaluation of who had the right to rule. The war itself flooded the communities with competing political plans and ultimately spawned a new generation of local middlemen who could speak the new lingo and couch it in terms that connected to their local followers. The actors described in the previous chapter cut their teeth on the violent and rapidly changing reality of the collapsing colonial order.

CONCLUSIONS

During the colonial era, indigenous towns engaged in an active political life in which factions competed for the control of local offices and sought out the support of important administrators both in the region and in the viceregal capital. The Crown and its local representatives frowned upon political factionalism, seeing it as a symptom of disorder in the body politic, and so dissidents phrased their denunciations of government abuses in terms of the individual excesses of the local administrators rather than making systemic critiques. The war permitted discontented indigenous villagers to adopt the language of *patria* and religion to their own small-town realities. The insurgents presented themselves as the true government, a friend at court, where villagers could find support for their political aspirations. Suddenly demands were no longer made in terms of this or that abusive subdelegate, priest, or tax collector but as indictments of the irreligious and unpatriotic Spaniards. Factionalism within the pueblos was also catapulted into new political arenas where "national" actors actively promoted the political participation of their followers, providing a new and explosive context to small-town feuds.

The participation of indigenous people in the insurgency defies easy categorization. Clearly the actors were immersed in a political culture rooted in the old regime of New Spain, but the profound impact of the long war cannot be denied. The crisis produced a situation where both rebels and government agents bombarded indigenous actors with news, pleas for political loyalty, military mobilization, and financial support. The ideology of the insurgent actors borrowed from both the traditions of the colonial era and the new discourses that emerged after 1808. The crisis-inspired rhetoric defined the nation in terms of xenophobia, but the line of inclusion versus exclusion left the indigenous population within the nation. The need to curry favor with the pueblos led the insurgents to maintain intact corporate identities, and the practice of the war produced a devolution of power to the village while at the same time ensuring that rural politics were more connected to the outside world. One observes that, intertwined with the new constitutional precepts guiding state formation and practices of citizenship, there was a certain bedrock of consensus to accommodate the pueblos. This consensus was not so much ideological as it was a common approach to governance, reflecting a shared political culture exposed to the stress of revolution. In coming to a consensus, the villagers constructed a project rooted in local practices even as they framed them in the new language of national identity and political rights, setting the stage for Indians to claim membership in the nation while interpreting the rules for their participation to incorporate existing traditions into the new forms of citizenship.

NOTES

1.   Annino (1995, 74) characterizes indigenous reactions to political change in the period as "*sincretismos liberales*"; Thomson (1997, 12) uses "political bilingualism" to describe the attitudes of Nahuas in the Sierra de Puebla toward liberalism in the mid-nineteenth century, while Mallon (1994, 74) adopts the phrase "popular liberalism."

2.   Ávila, Ortiz Escamilla, and Serrano (2010, 101, 103–5) provide a useful summary of the political rhetoric of the moment and beliefs that the kingdom was about to be delivered to Napoleon's hands.

3.   The records describing the reorganization of the companies by Colonel Ildefonso Arias de Saavedra are to be found in AGN-IG, 414A, file 8; and for information about ties between *pardo* militiamen and Indian villagers during the riot, see AGN Criminal, vol. 315, file 2.

4.   De la Vega, Huejutla, January 7, 1812, AGN-OG, vol. 21, file 19, fol. 184. The subdelegate was engaged in a conflict with the local militia commander, Agustín Villegas, who was pushing for more Indian militiamen. It should also be noted that the prohibition on militia service was sometimes violated. Indians can be found in the ranks of the colonial militia.

5.   Hobsbawm (1969, 26–27) further argued that the social program of premodern rebels centered on the restoration of the "good old order" that often included the benevolent (but distant) king; Van Young (2001, 463–66) describes the attitude of the insurgents as being one of "naive monarchism." On this topic, Scott (1990, 96–103) provides a valuable challenge to the traditional understanding of the term.

6.   *Informe de juramento de "los sujetos principales Españoles de este pueblo, con el Gobernador y República de Indios,"* Juan Baptista Bausa, Juan Tomás Rodolfo, Juan Vidal de Villamil, and Joseph Rodríguez to Virrey Venegas, Papantla, January 29, 1811, AGN-OG, vol. 829, fols. 94–95; Ortiz Escamilla 2010, 27.

7.   Juan Antonio Sánchez to Captain Antonio Cortés, January 11, 1811. AGN-IG, vol. 149, fol. s.n.

8.   For example, one Spanish merchant referred to "the contagious venom of the insurrection." Testimony of Diego Santander, May 13, 1811, AGN-Criminal, vol. 250, file 8, fols. 356 and 368.

9.   Besides the obvious attraction of arresting despised subdelegates and tax collectors, the rebels offered favorable resolutions of land conflicts, the end of tribute, and generally increased autonomy (Ducey 2014a, 439, 444).

10. Silva Prada (2003, 33–34, 42–43) has an interesting discussion of the limits of loyalty in popular declarations of "*viva el rey*," indicating the subversive nature of the slogan had a long tradition in New Spain.

11. A deep historical tradition has carefully mapped out the tensions that the late colonial period had produced in the indigenous villages—increasing fiscal burdens, demographic pressures, appropriations of pueblo resources preserved in the *cajas de comunidades* and *cofradías*, declining political autonomy, and ecological pressures (Tanck de Estrada 1999; Arrioja Díaz Viruell 2011; Ouweneel 1996; Van Young 1988; Guardino 1996; Marichal 1999).

12. Escobar (2011, 151–82) has published an excellent review of the impact of Cádiz on local communities in the region studied here.

13. The circular ordering the election in the Gulf Coast region may be found in "Copia de la orden circular del Exmo. Sr. D. José María Morelos que ha remitido el Sr. Brigadier D. Nicolás Bravo el 28 de julio desde Coscomatepec y se ha recibido en

esta comandancia hoy el día de la fha. 15 de agosto de 1813," Papantla, AGN-INF, vol. 84, file 2, fols. 20–21.

14. Lozano to Peredo, August 16, 1813, AGN-IVir, vol. 84, file 2, fol. 21r.

15. Hernández y Dávalos ([1877] 1985, 135–60) provides numerous examples. In Huetamo, for example, the subdelegate "harangued" the assembly, explaining that the circular calling for elections "demonstrates the love, duty and efficacy with which his Excellency [Morelos] pursues our homeland's good and happiness, establishing a wise and just congress, that will not only sustain our rights but also create laws that will govern us" (144).

16. See articles 309 to 323 of the "Constitución política de la monarquía española" (Spain, Cortes generales y extraordinarias. [1812] 1961).

17. August 2, 1813. AGN-INF, vol. 84, file 2, fol. 9.

18. In a request that "the Indians of the pueblos" contribute five *reales* each to purchase powder, he stressed *"es con toda su voluntad."* Lozano to Peredo, August 14, 1813, AGN-INF, vol. 84, file 2, fol. 19v.

19. Testimony of Ignacio José Uribe, Ixhuatlán, January 17, 1815, AGN-INF, vol. 34, file 5, fol. 161r, for example, declared that he received the title of captain at the request of the Indians of his town and that Osorno confirmed him in the post.

20. See Serrano Ortega (2001, 83, 85), or to use a phrase of Van Young (2001, 140), Mexico experienced a "feudalization" of its political order. Archer (1992, 293) points out that the lull in the fighting after 1815 did not necessarily signify pacification and came at a great cost for local society.

21. Captain Ignacio de Zúñiga to de la Concha, Coyunta, January 20, 1819, AGN-OG, vol. 124, fol. 75. On the Huasteca rebel settlements, see *Gaceta del Gobierno de México* (1813, 166–67); and AGN-OG, vol. 4, fols. 27–28.

22. See Lt. Col. José María Lubían, "Lista que manifiesta los individuos de la comprensión de Palo Blanco y Sombrerete que han impetrado la real gracia de Indulto desde 10 de diciembre de 1817," February 27, 1818, AGN-OG, vol. 122, fols. 6–8. All family members, not just male adults, appear in the lists of rebels granted amnesty; see "Lista de indultados," AGN-OG, vol. 725, fols. 340-46.

23. Álvarez sometimes pretended not to have received communications from the viceroy and in other cases insisted that he did not have the resources needed to carry out the orders he did receive. AGN-OG, vol. 65, fols. 145, 146–47, 232–36, 245–46. On November 15, 1815, for example, then viceroy Calleja accused Álvarez of sending false reports and exaggerating the precarious situation of his command. AGN-OG, vol. 67, fol. 357; vol. 67, fol. 359.

24. Letter of José Joaquín Aguilar, "Cuartel general por la nación de la sierra y costa de Barlovento," December 2, 1816, AGN-OG, vol. 65, fols. 57–60.

25. Aguilar to *"los Americanos que sostienen las armas del tirano en el pueblo de Chicontepec,"* August 14, 1815, AGN-OG, vol. 65, fol. 266.

26. Ibid. He also sent the same invitation to the government troops stationed in la Mesa de Coroneles, July 14, 1815, Tlaxcalantongo, AGN-OG, vol. 67, fols. 277–78.

REFERENCES

ARCHIVES

Archivo General de la Nación (AGN)
Criminal
Indiferente de Guerra (IG)
Indiferente Vireinal (IVir)
Infidencias (INF)
Operaciones de Guerra (OG)

PRINTED PRIMARY SOURCES

Gaceta del Gobierno de México. 1813. 4 (259): 166–72.

Spain, Cortes generales y extraordinarias. (1812) 1961. "Constitución política de la monarquía Española" (1812). In *El pensamiento constitucional hispanoamericano hasta 1830*, edited by the Academia Nacional de Historia, 5:291-395. Caracas: Ediciones Guadarrama.

SECONDARY SOURCES

Annino, Antonio. 1995. "Nuevas perspectivas para una vieja pregunta." In *El primer liberalismo mexicano: 1808–1855*, edited by Maricela Fonseca, 45–91. Mexico: Instituto Nacional de Antropología e Historia.

Archer, Christon I. 1992. "The Militarization of Mexican Politics: The Role of the Army, 1815–1821." In *Five Centuries of Mexican History: Papers of the VIII Conference of Mexican and North American Historians, San Diego, California, October 18–20, 1990*, edited by Virginia Guedea and Jaime E. Rodríguez O., 285–302. Mexico: Instituto de Investigaciones Dr. José María Luis Mora.

Arrioja Díaz Viruell, Luis Alberto. 2011. *Pueblos de Indios y tierras comunales. Villa Alta, Oaxaca: 1742–1856.* Zamora: Colegio de Michoacán.

Ávila, Alfredo, Juan Ortiz Escamilla, and José Antonio Serrano. 2010. *Actores e escenarios de la Independencia. Guerra, pensamiento e instituciones, 1808–1825.* Mexico: Fondo de Cultura Económica.

Ducey, Michael T. 2004. *A Nation of Villages: Riot and Rebellion in the Mexican Huasteca, 1750–1850.* Tucson: University of Arizona Press.

———. 2007. "Elecciones, constituciones y ayuntamientos. Participación popular en las elecciones de la tierra caliente veracruzana, 1813–1835." In *Ayuntamientos y liberalismo gaditano en México*, edited by Juan Ortiz Escamilla and José Antonio Serrano Ortega, 173–211. Zamora: Colegio de Michoacán and Universidad Veracruzana.

———. 2014a. "Indios, insurgentes y súbditos: autoridad e insurrección en los pueblos indígenas de la costa del barlovento veracruzana y la sierra Huasteca, 1810–1812." In *México a la luz de sus revoluciones*, edited by Laura Rojas and Susan Deeds, 427–54. Mexico: Colegio de México.

————. 2014b. "La territorialidad indígena y las reformas borbónicas en la tierra caliente mexicana: los tumultos totonacos de Papantla de 1764–1787." *Historia Social* (78): 17–43.

Escobar, Antonio. 2011. "'Ha variado el sistema gubernativo de los pueblos.' La ciudadanía gaditana y republicana fue ¿imaginaria? para los indígenas. Una visión desde las Huastecas." In *Poder y gobierno local en México 1808–1857*, edited by María del Carmen Salinas Sandoval, Diana Birrichaga, and Antonio Escobar, 153–91. Zinacantepec: Colegio Mexiquense, Colegio de Michoacán, and Universidad Autónoma del Estado de México.

Gómez Cruz, Filiberta. 2009. "De arrendatarios a condueños: La lucha indígena contra los Llorente en la Huasteca Veracruzana durante el Segundo Imperio." *Ulúa, Revista de Historia, Sociedad y Cultura* (13): 71–87.

Granados, Luis Fernando. 2010. "Independencia sin insurgentes. El bicentenario y la historiografía de nuestros días." *Desacatos* (34): 11–26.

Guardino, Peter. 1996. *Peasants, Politics, and the Formation of Mexico's National State, Guerrero, 1800–1857*. Stanford, CA: Stanford University Press.

Guedea, Virginia. 1996. *La insurgencia en el departamento del norte. Los llanos de Apan y la sierra de Puebla, 1810–1816*. Mexico: Universidad Nacional Autónoma de México and Instituto de Investigaciones Doctor José María Luis Mora.

Guerra, François-Xavier. 1992. *Modernidad e independencias: Ensayos sobre las revoluciones hispánicas*. Mexico: Editorial MAPFRE and Fondo de Cultura Económica.

Hamnett, Brian. 1986. *Roots of Insurgency: Mexican Regions, 1750–1824*. Cambridge: Cambridge University Press.

Hernández y Dávalos, Juan E. (1877) 1985. *Historia de la guerra de independencia de México*. Vol. 5. Mexico: Instituto Nacional de Estudios Históricos de la Revolución Mexicana.

Hobsbawm, Eric J. 1969. *Bandits*. New York: Pantheon Books.

Landavazo, Marco Antonio. 2001. *La máscara de Fernando VII. Discurso e imaginario monárquicos en una época de crisis. Nueva España, 1808–1822*. Mexico: Colegio de México, Universidad Michoacana de San Nicolás de Hidalgo, and Colegio de Michoacán.

Lasso, Marixa. 2006. "Race War and Nation in Caribbean Gran Colombia, Cartagena: 1810–1832." *American Historical Review* 111 (2): 336–61.

Mallon, Florencia. 1994. *Peasant and Nation: The Making of Postcolonial Mexico and Peru*. Berkeley: University of California Press.

Marichal, Carlos. 1999. *La bancarrota del virreinato. Nueva España y las finanzas del Imperio español, 1780–1810*. Mexico: Fondo de Cultura Económica.

Ortiz Escamilla, Juan. 1997. *Guerra y gobierno: Los pueblos y la independencia de México*, Colección Nueva América. Mexico: Instituto Mora, Colegio de México, Universidad Internacional de Andalucía, and Universidad de Sevilla.

————. 2008a. *El teatro de la guerra. Veracruz, 1750–1825*. Castelló de la Plana: Publicaciones de Universitat Jaume I.

————. 2008b. "Los gobiernos realistas de Veracruz." In *Revisión histórica de la guerra de independencia en Veracruz*, edited by Juan Ortiz Escamilla, 177–96. Xalapa: Universidad Veracruzana and Gobierno del Estado de Veracruz.

————. 2010. *Veracruz en armas. La guerra civil, 1810–1821. Antología de documentos*. Veracruz 1810–1825. Antología de documentos, vol. 1. Xalapa: Universidad Veracruzana and Editorial del Gobierno del Estado de Veracruz.

Ouweneel, Arij. 1996. *Shadows over Anáhuac: An Ecological Interpretation of Crisis and Development in Central Mexico, 1730–1800*. Albuquerque: University of New Mexico Press.

Rodríguez O., Jaime E. 1996. *La independencia de América Española*. Mexico: Fondo de Cultura Económica.

————. 2009. *Nosotros somos ahora los verdaderos españoles. La transición de la Nueva España de un reino de la monarquía española a la República Federal mexicana, 1808–1824*. 2 vols. Zamora, Michoacán: Colegio de Michoacán.

Scott, James C. 1990. *Domination and the Arts of Resistance: Hidden Transcripts*. New Haven: Yale University Press.

Serrano Ortega, José Antonio. 2001. *Jerarquía territorial y transición política*. Zamora, Michoacán: Colegio de Michoacán and Instituto Mora.

Silva Prada, Natalia. 2003. "Estrategias culturales en el tumulto de 1692 en la Ciudad de México: Aportes para la reconstrucción de la historia de la cultura política Antigua." *Historia mexicana* 53 (3): 18–63.

Tanck de Estrada, Dorothy. 1999. *Pueblos de indios y educación en el México colonial, 1750–1821*. Mexico: Colegio de México.

Thomson, Guy P. C. 1997. "*Pueblos de Indios* and *Pueblos de Ciudadanos*: Constitutional Bilingualism in 19th Century Mexico." Paper presented at the Workshop on Political Culture and Ideology in Nineteenth- and Twentieth-Century Mexico. Oxford, St. Anthony's College, May 2.

Van Young, Eric. 1988. "Moving Toward Revolt: Agrarian Origins of the Hidalgo Rebellion in the Guadalajara Region." In *Riot, Rebellion and Revolution: Rural Social Conflict in Mexico*, edited by Friedrich Katz, 176–204. Princeton, NJ: Princeton University Press.

————. 2001. *The Other Rebellion: Popular Violence, Ideology, and the Mexican Struggle for Independence, 1810–1821*. Stanford, CA: Stanford University Press.

Vinson, Ben, III. 2001. *Bearing Arms for His Majesty: The Free-Colored Militia in Colonial Mexico*. Stanford, CA: Stanford University Press.

Warren, Richard. 1996. *Vagrants and Citizens: Politics and the Masses in Mexico City from Colony to Republic*. Wilmington, DE: Scholarly Resources.

CHAPTER 4

HAPPY TOGETHER?

"Indians," Liberalism, and Schools in the Oaxaca and Puebla
Sierras, 1876–1911

ARIADNA ACEVEDO-RODRIGO

THIS CHAPTER is about public elementary schools from 1876 to 1911 in two regions that have been considered rural and indigenous: the northern sierras of Oaxaca and Puebla. It is often implied that these schools must have been practically nonexistent or very ineffective given that the 1910 national literacy rate barely reached 20 percent, and it was often lower in rural areas with a significant number of speakers of indigenous languages. Yet it is clear that the number of schools in what today would be considered the countryside was not negligible, and the historical sources to study them are abundant (Loyo 1999, 3, 9). It is less clear how significant they were.

I contend that the Spanish-speaking schools of late nineteenth-century liberalism mattered because, at least in certain towns and villages, they proved meaningful to speakers of indigenous languages who made considerable efforts to keep and improve them. I further argue that we will not understand their role so long as the historiography remains trapped in normative and anachronistic criteria that measure certain results (e.g., literacy rates but not qualitative changes that are significant in the rural context) against the yardstick of the hopes of nineteenth-century elites, or against current expectations of what elementary education is for.[1] In the first section of this chapter, I show that these schools have not received enough attention, although some historiographical trends should make future studies of them more likely, and I unpack the assumptions underlying historians' claims that they were nonexistent, ineffective, or inappropriate. Having questioned such premises, the second and third sections look afresh at the documentary evidence of the locally and nationally relevant roles these schools did play, and ask what the promise of equality and progress embodied by liberal education looked like in the rural world. A closing section suggests that "Indians" and liberal republican schools could be happy together, even if they lived an inherent tension: aspirations of equality resulted in the production of hierarchies within and between the localities studied, together with the promise of social mobility for a few, and in a form of subordinate inclusion of the rural municipalities in the Mexican state.

MAKING SCHOOLS VISIBLE IN "INDIAN" MEXICO

A strong historiographical trend has questioned the idea that national projects, including nineteenth-century liberalism, necessarily excluded or marginalized indigenous peasants, as we can see in the chapters by Guardino and Ducey in this volume. This literature has also provided us with a better grasp of local government so that we now have a better standpoint from which to examine the relationship between liberal schools and speakers of indigenous languages. Yet this historiography has considered schools only briefly, even when the importance of education for the liberal project is emphasized.[2]

In the last three decades, historians researching the 1876–1911 period known as the Porfiriato have sought to free it from the condescension of its revolutionary successors. Yet schools in the countryside, where the vast majority of those considered indigenous were believed to live, have only partially benefited from the new interpretations. Studies on postrevolutionary rural education argued that the experience of prerevolutionary schooling had been a crucial factor in local responses to postrevolutionary education (Vaughan 1997, 78–85; Rockwell 2007; Giraudo 2014, 173, 175). Some of the recent history of education during the Porfiriato has likewise recognized the importance of elementary schooling in the countryside, but only Mexico State has two book-length studies on the topic.[3] In any case, this research has not produced a challenge to the generalized view, outside the historiography of education, that rural elementary schooling during the Porfiriato was insignificant, even if this view rests more on the notion that this was an elitist regime, or on its contrast with postrevolutionary education, than on an analysis of the empirical evidence.[4]

In sum, historiographical trends on liberalism and the reassessment of the Porfiriato and education would suggest that we need a debate on prerevolutionary schools in the countryside, and yet the topic of liberal education in "Indian" Mexico remains elusive. Perhaps in order to be able to comprehend nineteenth-century schools, and to place them squarely in a broader narrative of the social and political history of Mexico, we need to question the pervasive idea that they were insufficient, ineffective, or inadequate.

When analysts consider that rural or "indigenous" education was neglected before the 1910 revolution, they are right if they mean that the federal government did not invest in it. However, municipal and state governments did; in 1875, 65 percent of Mexico's 8,103 private and public schools were sustained by municipalities (Díaz Covarrubias [1875] 2000). In the following decades, some (perhaps a majority) of these schools passed on to state-level administration, and only after 1921 did some schools become federal. In other words, the absence of federal schooling before the revolution does not mean that there was little public education, as has often been implied. It is accurate to state that schools before the revolution were not normally labeled as schools for Indians or peasants, nor did they belong to a proto-*indigenista* or rural policy.[5] Generally, there was no such labeling, because a republican government was supposed to provide the same instruction for all, irrespective of race or condition. However, it is wrong to conclude that nobody invested in education in the countryside, or for Indians, or that such investment was insignificant. This view either reproduces the centralist perspective of postrevolutionary officials, who ignored or underestimated municipal and state education, or anachronistically imposes *indigenista* and ruralist criteria onto pre-1910 schools.[6]

Assumptions historians make about the incompatibility between liberal schooling and Mexican rural life seem to have a sound logical basis. Why would peasant speakers of indigenous languages be interested in schools with Spanish as the only language of instruction, and focused on conventional subjects of little use in the rural world such as the three Rs, history, geography, and civics? The assumption here is that liberal schools were out of place in the Mexican countryside. The problem with seeing these schools as mere postcolonial or urban impositions is the sheer amount of time, money, and effort put into them by the inhabitants of the Oaxaca and Puebla Sierras, as attested by documentation preserved in municipal and state archives. If schools were really so inappropriate for these milieus, how do we account for all the energy invested in them? Who defines what is appropriate? We need to ask anew what schools did and what interest those described as peasant and indigenous had in them.

STUBBORN HIERARCHIES IN THE LIBERAL REPUBLICAN SCHOOLS OF OAXACA AND PUEBLA

By the early 1890s, instruction provided by municipal and state governments was in principle free, compulsory, and nonreligious (Meneses 1998, 167–543, 652–68). It also had to be equal for all, irrespective of class, race, and language; in this sense the liberal schools of the Porfiriato were republican.[7] Arguments pointing to indigenous difference or specificity were generally rejected for being discriminatory.[8] Thus the issue of whether schoolchildren were indigenous or not was not a major concern either of the educational congresses or of the laws and regulations passed. In fact, in Puebla it was absent from the legislation and school regulations, and only rarely did it become a matter of debate. In Oaxaca, exhortations to civilize Indians via public instruction, together with complaints about the difficulties of doing so, appeared much more frequently than in Puebla (Ruiz and Traffano 2006), but educational legislation only made a brief reference to the "indigenous race" while still classifying schools according to local conditions as I discuss below. Were there observable consequences of the measures taken in Oaxaca to make instruction more appropriate for their region? Did the Puebla Sierra benefit from the absence of policies designed especially for the indigenous population?

It is common to think of the sierras as "isolated" and "backward," but the northern sierra of Puebla and the Ixtlán Sierra of Oaxaca were in fact renowned for their effective support for liberal and patriotic struggles from the 1855 Revolution of Ayutla, through the 1860s European intervention, to the Revolution of Tuxtepec that took Porfirio Díaz to the country's presidency in 1876 (Thomson 1999, 197; McNamara 2007). Being strongholds of liberalism, these two regions provided schooling that might have been as good as it got in the nineteenth-century Mexican countryside.[9] Below we will see what was and what was not achieved.

In Oaxaca, the way educational legislation sought to adapt to its environment probably reinforced existing hierarchies, even if they were often contested. Trying to adjust to scarce resources, the 1889 law created a ladder of three different classes of schools, which roughly corresponded to political-administrative

TABLE 4.1. Terminology for political-administrative levels and authorities in Oaxaca and Puebla during the Porfiriato

OAXACA STATE GOVERNMENT	PUEBLA STATE GOVERNMENT
The district capital (*cabecera de distrito*) was the seat of the *jefatura política* / *jefe político*	
Municipal head town (*cabecera municipal*) or *Ayuntamiento* / Municipal president (*presidente municipal*) [These were all pueblos]	Municipal head town (*cabecera municipal*) / Municipal president (*presidente municipal*) [These could be pueblos or higher-status *villas*]
Agencia municipal / *Agente municipal* [These were all pueblos]	*Junta auxiliar* / *Presidente auxiliar* [These were all pueblos]

hierarchies (see table 4.1), and mentioned the "indigenous race" only for third-class schools. In this manner, school quality, political-administrative status, and race hierarchies were conflated. How were these hierarchies defined? How did they affect actual practice?

Both in the 1889 and 1893 legislation, first-class schools were to teach five grades and open in the state capital and some district capitals. The other district capitals would have second-class schools with four grades, while all other localities (*ayuntamientos* and the lower-rank *agencias municipales*) would have third-class schools with only three grades. Additionally, the 1893 Oaxaca legislation made an explicit reference to pupils "of the indigenous race" in section III of article 11, which described third-class schools as those with a single teacher and fewer subjects than second- and first-class schools, in order to give greater attention to the "study of the national language in those schools in which the majority of pupils belong to the indigenous race" and "to compensate" for the shorter time children spent in school (Ruiz 2001, 111). Although there was no explicit definition of the "indigenous race," the assumption was that members of this race were those who spoke languages of pre-Hispanic origin. An additional assumption, included in the 1891 report that informed the 1893 legislation, was that it was to the "indigenous class" that school attendance was most onerous because they needed their children's help in the fields.[10]

By referring to the "indigenous race" only with regard to third-class schools, the legislation assumed that it was *ayuntamientos* and *agencias municipales*, and not the more important district capitals (which were entitled to have second- and first-class schools), that would cater to speakers of indigenous languages, thereby contributing to the projection of a language-based, indigenous versus non-indigenous distinction onto the existing political-administrative hierarchy.[11] However, practice sometimes contradicted such projections. For instance, in the district capital of Ixtlán, and others in the northern sierra, there were plenty of speakers of indigenous languages; throughout the district of Ixtlán, teachers reported a majority of Zapotec speakers.[12] Moreover, as we will see in the next section, Zapotec- and Chinantec-speaking pueblos, whether they had *ayuntamientos* or *agencias municipales*, often sought to upgrade their schools and sometimes managed to obtain second-class schools or more qualified teachers.

What was the situation of schools in the district of Ixtlán? During the Porfiriato, the total number of boys' schools in the district varied between sixteen and thirty, and there were only three girls' schools; the total population varied between 26,000 and 32,000. They did not fare badly compared to Oaxaca City and Oaxaca State. In 1889 Ixtlán had roughly one school for every 1,320 inhabitants: a very similar ratio to that of the whole state in 1895, one school per 1,305 people. In fact, in 1905 Ixtlán did better than Oaxaca State: its ratio increased to roughly one school per one thousand inhabitants, whereas the whole state had gone down to 1:1,940.[13]

If we look at schools' internal organization, Ixtlán still held its own. The 1893 law added a distinction between schools with "perfect" and "economical organization."[14] In the first there was one teacher per grade, as prescribed by the ideal of the graded school, which began to be introduced in Mexico in the 1890s. The latter category had half or fewer of the teachers needed due to lack of funds. None of the schools in the district of Ixtlán had a "perfect organization." The best the district capital schools managed during the Porfiriato was one teacher, who doubled as head teacher (*director*), and one assistant (*ayudante*). However, Ixtlán was not doing worse than the city of Oaxaca, where it appears that only the model school attached to the teacher training college had one teacher per grade. Indeed, most schools in the country had a single teacher and only one classroom (López López 2015).

Within Ixtlán district, political-administrative status was a rough predictor of the type of schools a locality would have, and hierarchies could occasionally be altered. In the cases of Ixtlán and Ixtepeji, classification of schools corresponded to their administrative status. Each locality had one boys' school (staffed by male teachers) and one girls' school (staffed by female teachers) throughout the Porfiriato. By 1892 the boys' and girls' schools at the district capital of Ixtlán had been upgraded to first-class (including a college-trained schoolmaster for the boys), whereas those of the *ayuntamiento* of Ixtepeji were second-class; still, this was the best an *ayuntamiento* that was not a district capital could aspire to.[15] Most remaining *ayuntamientos* and all *agencias municipales* except Guelatao had third-class schools.[16]

There were many ways in which some hierarchies prevailed. Teachers in third-class schools were not paid as well and had less training than teachers in second- and first-class schools; their programs could be limited to the three Rs, but some taught geography, history, and civics as well. In 1903 educational authorities in Oaxaca City still considered that it was not worth sending Enrique Rebsamen's new writing-reading method to schools with no formally trained teachers, thereby reinforcing the lower status of third-class schools and decreasing their students' chances of learning to read and write at the same time, as prescribed by the new method.[17] In the next section, we will see how such discrimination was contested. But let us first look at the situation in Puebla.

Puebla's legislation did not classify schools as in Oaxaca and remained silent on the matter of the "indigenous race," but its schools nonetheless responded substantially to the hierarchies of political-administrative division. In Zacatlán, Tetela, and Zacapoaxtla (all districts of the Puebla Sierra), district capitals excelled and municipal head towns followed suit; they all had one boys' and one girls' school throughout the period. Pueblos governed by *juntas auxiliares* made an effort, and some did quite well. As in Ixtlán, the hierarchy was defined by teachers' salaries, experience and training, the number of subjects taught, the number and condition of books and materials, and whether or not the school had an assistant as well as a headmaster. Civic festivals organized by patriotic boards (*juntas patrióticas*) and teachers were more elaborate at the district capital than in municipal head towns; pueblos generally did not even aspire to have their own festival but would attend the head town's.[18]

The only exception to the higher status of district capitals was Xochiapulco, a series of Nahuatl-speaking squatter barrios that had acquired municipal status after their support for the Revolution of Ayutla, and together with the district capital of Tetela had been at the vanguard of Puebla's patriotic liberalism. The municipal school in Xochiapulco was renowned not only for having a (Methodist) college-trained teacher, a library, a school museum, and a basic meteorological station used for science lessons, but also for its patriotic festivals involving weeks of preparation and public readings before the actual events (Thomson 1998).

Elsewhere, the usual political hierarchies stood. Differences between municipal head towns existed according to their unequal economic and social status, but perhaps the greatest differences within localities of the same administrative status were those between pueblos. In the municipality of Cuetzalan, for instance, Nahuatl-speaking San Miguel Tzinacapan stood out as the pueblo with the best relation with the head town, and no major internal or external land disputes. They had not sent soldiers to the national guard but contributed to liberal efforts with taxes and food, and had by far the best attended and most stable school of the municipality's four pueblos, including Spanish-speaking Xocoyolo.

Puebla's figures speak for themselves. In 1875, when Mexico had a school (private or public) for every 1,110 inhabitants, the state of Puebla boasted one school per 809 inhabitants, much better than Oaxaca's ratio of 1:1,717.[19] I have no figures for the whole of the state of Puebla at the end of the Porfiriato, but in the districts of Zacatlán, Zacapoaxtla, and Tetela, it is clear that the number of schools had increased modestly and mainly in favor of the pueblos governed by *juntas auxiliares*, and sometimes in favor of the smaller localities (barrios).

Both in Puebla and in Oaxaca, a majority of school-age children were not enrolled. For the Puebla Sierra, I calculated that between 14 and 20 percent of school-age children were registered during the Porfiriato, and almost all of them attended school regularly. In the state of Oaxaca in 1900, according to official figures, 27 percent of school-age children were enrolled and 21 percent actually attended a school. For the district of Ixtlán, figures were lower: 19 and 16.5 percent enrolled in 1895 and 1900, respectively, and 13 percent attended both in 1895 and in 1900 (López López 2015, 93–96). It is clear that only a minority received education, yet as I argue in the next section, this was not an insignificant minority.

In sum, if we look at the aggregate of individual children's figures, Puebla's silence on anything indigenous and its refusal to divide schools into three classes from best to worst as in Oaxaca does not seem to have brought much greater opportunities; social hierarchies persisted stubbornly, with small percentages of children attending schools in both regions. However, some subtle differences are worth noting. Literacy figures suggest that the simultaneous introduction of reading and writing was faster in Puebla than in Oaxaca. Further research should ask to what extent this had to do with practices such as not sending the most advanced literacy methods to Oaxaca's third-class schools, as mentioned above.[20]

Finally, Oaxaca, the land of Benito Juárez and Porfirio Díaz, did worse in school numbers and no better in attendance figures than the Puebla Sierra. Governor Mucio Martínez of Puebla (1892–1911), a ruthless repressor of opposition voices, probably did not have any more positive a view of the rural population than Emilio Pimentel, the governor of Oaxaca (1903–1911), who had shown little faith in the intellectual capacities of the masses during the 1880s debates on compulsory education and substantially reduced school budgets during his administration (Chassen-López 2004, 414–18; Martínez Vásquez 2012, 79–83). The difference lay in who controlled the budget. Whereas Puebla municipal head towns and pueblos had kept control of school funding and spent what they raised, those of Oaxaca could only plead with the state government for their share of the educational budget. All in all, the study of these two regions suggests that for localities with sufficient resources and much interest in schools, municipal control was best.[21]

FIGHTING IGNORANCE AND HIERARCHIES

Before 1889, municipal and district authorities in Oaxaca were fully in charge of schools, except for budget decisions made by the state government. After 1889, the state government increasingly centralized educational administration (Traffano 2007), but local authorities, including *principales* (elders who sometimes held the highest authority) and parents, continued to participate in some school matters and to contest state government decisions.[22] While the Oaxaca administration was clear about the school hierarchy, *ayuntamientos* and *agencias municipales* fought against it by demanding funds for their schools, and often by supplementing the meager ten monthly pesos allocated by the state budget for the teachers' salary with another five raised locally through donations, in order to get better teachers.[23] More frequently, judging by the greater number of cases documented in the state archive, the local government paid half and the state government the other half.[24] The latter generally sent books but no utensils such as blackboards, ink, or paper. The cost of buildings and their maintenance, as well as the provision of furniture, was the responsibility of the municipalities and *agencias*. The state budget was not always reliable: a school that received funding one year may not receive any the following year, or it might receive it a few months late.[25] This led to pueblos paying teachers' salaries themselves or closing schools, in contrast to the more stable trajectories of municipal schools in the Puebla Sierra.

School provision, then, could be irregular, but pueblos had a memory of their past education, which they invoked when they sought to reopen a school. In fact, many files labeled in the state archive as "openings" of schools were reopenings, suggesting that officials overlooked previous histories of schooling, just as post-revolutionary educational policy would often do from the 1920s onward. In 1885, for instance, the *agente del común* and eight *principales* of San Miguel Aloapam requested permission to open a school, explaining that they had not had one since 1874.[26] When requesting an allocation in the state's educational budget, the most frequent arguments were the need to be enlightened, not to remain "ignorant" or "backward," and the fact that they paid their taxes punctually.[27] The examples of Guelatao, San Miguel Amatlán, Zogochi, San Miguel del Río, and others below further show pueblo and head-town involvement in school administration.

The case of Guelatao deserves attention because it was an *agencia municipal* (of around four hundred inhabitants in 1889) and therefore lower in the hierarchy than Ixtlán or Ixtepeji, and would have normally had only one third-class boys' school. However, Guelatao had a second-class boys' school and a girls' school. The state government at some point allowed it a share of the budget similar to that of the *ayuntamientos*. Perhaps it helped that Guelatao was (former president) Benito Juárez's birthplace, but there is evidence to qualify suspicions that they received special treatment as a generous concession. Firstly, when plans were made for a better school to be opened as part of the celebrations marking the centenary of Juárez's birth in 1906, they were thwarted by the revival of a land conflict with Ixtlán, and Governor Pimentel's disinterest in education (McNamara 2007, 157–68). Secondly, the inhabitants of Guelatao had a history of participation in their schools. For instance, in 1886 a meeting was convened at which local authorities, parents, and "other residents" held a vote to appoint a teacher for the girls' school, choosing from four candidates. The procedure was referred to as a "popular vote" and there was "unanimous" support for Señorita Dominga Ramos. Perhaps attesting to the higher status of Guelatao in relation to other *agencias municipales*, all of the local authorities and a few other men, who may have been *principales* or ordinary citizens, could sign their names and did so in the meeting's minutes.[28] It is hard to establish whether or not these practices ended as the state government centralized school administration from 1889 onward (regulations are silent on the matter), but perhaps they only stopped being registered and still took place. In any case, throughout the Porfiriato, local authorities generally wrote to the state government to propose as teacher a person they knew, to ask for renewals of the appointments of those who did a good job, and sometimes to argue in favor of replacing a bad teacher.[29]

A not-uncommon case was that of San Miguel Amatlán, where, after a meeting of the *ayuntamiento* in 1885, *vecinos*, *principales*, and the secretary (signing in the name of the illiterate municipal president) wrote to the state government to request the teacher be replaced because of his frequent absenteeism, which meant children "were playing" rather than "making progress" and therefore "wasted their time."[30] Their choice of words was no mere mimicking of official parlance; the introduction of the graded school from the 1890s onward gave a very concrete form to abstract ideas of progress. Children were now supposed to be grouped in grades—that is, homogenous groups with a specific age and ability—and to pass yearly exams to gain entry to the next level. As education became more rigidly divided into stages, it was clearer whether individual pupils were getting behind or making adequate progress, and teachers and parents began to discuss schooling in these terms.[31]

Such involvement in schools raises the question of what the uses of schools and literacy were for the authorities and for the wider population. As in the case of Tlaxcala villages, explored by Rockwell's chapter in this book, in Oaxaca and Puebla, the government of even the smallest village needed at least one of its members to be literate; administration, litigation, and conflict management required a considerable amount of records and correspondence to be kept. Leaving these duties to outsiders who might not defend pueblo interests and could abuse their power was always a risk. Having a school was also a marker of status for a pueblo, both setting it above other localities and distinguishing it in the eyes of municipal, state, and national authorities. The fact that school status depended on the political-administrative level, even if not rigidly so, made good schools desirable; they could help villages gain a measure of autonomy from a head town or even obtain an administrative upgrade.[32] Finally, the promise of individual social mobility, if not the most obvious use of an education at the time, was already present in these sierras.

Zogochi and San Miguel del Río were aware of the advantages of schools. In 1896 Zogochi argued that, being located at the geographical center of the "*pueblos del rincón*"—and being the most densely populated among them, as well as the most "ignorant," with only two literate people—they should have a school.[33] In 1887 José Demetrio Sánchez, who was the municipal president of San Miguel del Río, and a secretary representing the illiterate alderman José Hernández signed a letter apparently written by a scribe well versed in republican rhetoric but also cognizant of what mattered to these pueblos. After extolling the virtues of enlightenment and progress, including the role of instruction in bolstering morality and hard work, their request to open a school stated that it was thanks to the one they used to have that many in the town knew how to read and write and were therefore able to "know" their "patriotic legislation" and their "rights and duties." They also pondered the bad prospects of a town without a school: "[it] will play a sad role in comparison with other towns. Its illiterate citizens will be useless even for taking the simplest of official posts and will always be at the mercy of [better educated] strangers."[34] After providing a map of an adequate schoolroom, an inventory of furniture, and a promise to pay half of the teacher's monthly salary of thirteen pesos, San Miguel del Río reopened its school the same year.

Villages in Puebla were acquainted with the issues spelled out in San Miguel del Río's letter. In fact, in the Puebla Sierra, in sometimes all-illiterate pueblo governments known as *juntas auxiliares* (see table 4.1), it was common for male, first-language Spanish speakers from the municipal head town to become village secretaries and double as teachers. Their mere presence could undermine the power of the school to become a tool of greater pueblo autonomy vis-à-vis the head town. Additionally, although these teachers-secretaries were supervised by local authorities, some were much criticized, labeled as caciques, and sometimes ousted under charges of embezzlement, illegitimate increase of taxes, or labor exploitation. Often such conflicts took the form of a pueblo faction opposing not only the teacher-secretary turned cacique but also the pueblo council that had collaborated with him or allowed him to abuse his power, thereby showing that, much as political differences could cause opposition to local governments and consequent changes in who was in charge and even in how authorities were selected, the distinction between literate and illiterate was another relevant division.[35]

In Ixtlán, teachers did not seem to double as secretaries. However, it was common for them to stand for local office in the village where they taught, or in another in the same district, and they left the school when they were voted in. Many went back to teaching after doing paid work elsewhere or after unpaid municipal service.[36] This practice might have derived from the fact that in the late colonial period, and perhaps later, the post of teacher was considered part of the services to local government that adult men were obliged to provide, further pointing to the deep imbrication between schools and pueblo or head-town government.[37] Additionally, in contrast to teachers in the Puebla Sierra, those in Ixtlán might more often have been men who had Spanish as their second language (Guardino 2005, 51–52, 107–11).

Local governments had to look after their interests and keep the population's support, but they were always additionally concerned with developing a good relationship with the higher authorities, and one of the means to do so was through the school. This could be the case even when the pueblo authorities were illiterate. According to an 1885 account of Chinantec-speaking Santiago Comaltepec, the municipal president had had the initiative to build a schoolhouse and the community provided the labor. The inauguration of the building was attended by the *jefe político* (the district administrator), district judges, and local authorities. As recorded by Secretary Pedro Palancares in the inauguration's minutes, the illiterate municipal president of Comaltepec, José Domingo López, gave a speech in Spanish using the same type of rhetoric as in the numerous petitions for schools in the rest of the district. For López the "instruction of the popular masses is the beginning of all civilization and of intellectual, material and moral progress."[38] If Palancares's description of the event was at all accurate, there is no reason to believe that illiterate authorities did not advocate, or at least help produce, the rhetoric registered in the minutes they signed.[39] In any case, whatever these villagers had in their hearts and minds, the illiterate men whose names were recorded in pueblo minutes and petitions, and who provided funds and labor for the upkeep of school buildings and furniture, showed significant support for education. Comaltepec's event closed with bell ringing, fireworks, and hoorays that showed "the pueblo's enthusiasm." Celebrations like this had a political use vis-à-vis the higher authorities, by demonstrating a pueblo's capacity for civilization and endorsement of educational policies. It was a statement that advocated joining a broader community beyond the pueblo's confines.

As seen above, only a minority of children attended schools in these rural areas, as was the case in Tlaxcala, according to Rockwell's chapter in this book. Were schools merely serving a self-reproducing local elite? It is difficult to tell until we have much more research at the village or town level.[40] However, schools' promises of individual advancement of one's children, even of those not belonging to the local elite, should not be ruled out as a further motivation to sustain schools. Whereas in the early nineteenth century the Guelatao-born and Zapotec-speaking Juárez (by his own account) had only learned to read and write properly in the city of Oaxaca, the boys and girls of Guelatao during the Porfiriato could learn the basics in their own pueblo (Juárez 2010, 33–35). Reaching higher education in Oaxaca or Mexico City was not easy, but neither was it impossible for young men. Juárez and Ignacio Manuel Altamirano (a Nahuatl-speaking scholarship boy who studied in Toluca under Ignacio Ramírez and became a prominent radical liberal) were in fact favorite contemporary examples of the benefits of educating Indians; they were also symbols of the promise of equality embodied by public instruction.

Of course most people, including women, not only lacked the fame and fortune of Juárez or Altamirano but also never occupied a post requiring literacy. Yet some might have benefited from a little schooling; their gains might have been modest, but they were probably meaningful. Young women had very little chance of attending school in this period, even if they seemed to have fared slightly better in the Puebla Sierra than in Ixtlán.[41] However, in 1891 Adelaida Perzabal, a domestic worker from the district capital of Ixtlán, signed with a trembling hand a letter directed to the state governor, requesting that her thirteen-year-old son be accepted at the correctional school in Oaxaca City. We do not know whether Perzabal went to school in her hometown or was taught elsewhere to sign her name, nor whether she could read. However, historians of reading and writing have often assumed that those who were able to sign could read because reading was taught for two or three years before writing was introduced, which was the case in Mexico before the 1890s (Acevedo-Rodrigo 2008). We know Perzabal did not write the letter, as the handwriting of the body of the document shows a sure hand, as opposed to the woman's shaky signature. But whether she was able to read the letter herself or had it read by a scribe, she was able to present a document arguing the reasons to request a place for her son in Oaxaca and to write her name.[42] Exceptional or not, these were important experiences hidden behind the low school enrolment and literacy rates of the time.

Finally, these schools reproduced economic, social, and political hierarchies, but they were also capable of partially contesting some of these same hierarchies. They fulfilled needs that benefited all, insofar as government administration was carried out, and more directly benefited a small group of individuals, whether it was the lucky few who made it to the bright lights of the cities, all those who had civil posts requiring literacy, the many men who signed petitions, or the humble woman who occasionally signed a letter. Where the Oaxaca State government saw very low attendance (for example, 10 or 15 percent of school-age children) and therefore a reason to close the school and invest the money elsewhere, local governments and many literate and illiterate parents saw the need for a school and pleaded with the government to reopen theirs so that children would not end up being "pitifully behind."[43] Education was one issue in which the most self-serving interests might have dovetailed with the national interest.

THE PUEBLO'S PROGRESS: SCHOOLS AS A FORM OF SUBORDINATE INCLUSION

Schools were too much part of the good government of a respectable pueblo to be the miserable institutions of critics' complaints.[44] District and municipal head towns had to live up to the expectations that their higher status conferred, whereas *agencias municipales* or *juntas auxiliares* needed to parade their progressive credentials and keep or improve their status. When authorities and parents argued in favor of a school, they were showing their support for education and thereby for the country's general progress. Indeed, sustaining schools was a form of endorsing inclusion of the pueblo or head town in the greater national community, and further confirms Guardino's argument in this book that the rural "Indian" pueblos of the nineteenth century were, of necessity, connected communities rather than the isolated villages of some accounts.

Members of the pueblos and head towns seem to have done better at fighting hierarchies without than within. Inclusion was far from egalitarian, and promises of equality did not manage to blur deep-seated hierarchies. Seen from the point of view of individuals, these schools obviously excluded many, and many probably excluded themselves or their children for sound reasons that educational policy did not manage to address. However, if we look at the village or town level, these schools were not about "exclusion" or "marginalization," terms that are very common in Mexican discussions of indigenous populations.[45] What I have recounted in this chapter for the Ixtlán and Puebla Sierras is best described as their "subordinate inclusion" in the Mexican state.[46] This should modify the view that prerevolutionary schools were irrelevant or insignificant in the history of citizenship in Mexico.

Evidence for the municipalities here discussed attests to an understandable but very underestimated interest in schooling among those known as Indians. I hope to have shown by now that, with all their vices and virtues, "Indians" and schools were happy together. Schools were no beacons of equality, but as Kourí demonstrates in his chapter in this book, neither were indigenous pueblos. Perhaps the powerful and often unexamined normative language we have attached to "Indians" and schools has blinded us to their actual social history. It is a long history, and we would do well to start writing it.

ACKNOWLEDGMENTS

I thank Paula López Caballero, Leticia Reina, Elsie Rockwell, Carlos Escalante, Aleida García, David Wood, and the anonymous reviewers for their careful reading and invaluable comments on previous versions of this chapter.

NOTES

1. The imposition of normative criteria is not only a historians' problem but it is also pervasive in educational theory; see Hunter (1994, 1–31).

2. Reina's (2004) book is representative of much of the recent history for this period—a comprehensive study of nineteenth-century Oaxaca that recognizes the importance of Spanish literacy for local administration but does not reflect on the existence and impact of schools (242–43, 246–47). Partial exceptions to this rule come from studies on popular liberalism and popular political culture; Thomson (1998; 1999) saw schools as crucial tools for the penetration of liberalism in the Puebla Sierra but still did not examine them in depth, and Guardino (2005, 109–12, 163–64) has warned against facile assumptions of Indian resistance to instruction in Villa Alta, Oaxaca.

3. For a discussion of the literature on prerevolutionary schools in the countryside, see Acevedo-Rodrigo (2011a). In their assessment of indigenous issues in the history of education, Sigüenza and Fabián (2013) regret the scarcity of research on the Porfiriato. The two books for Mexico State are those by Bazant (2002), which examines municipal and state schools (most of which were rural), and Escalante (2014), which is focused on a rural municipality of Mazahua speakers.

4. On unexamined assumptions about the Porfiriato, including the elite-popular and urban-rural divides, see Tenorio (2006, 18–19, 48, 53), who, nonetheless, fails to account for elementary schooling in the countryside except to mention the absence of studies explaining why it was mostly municipal (31–32, 111). Lomnitz (1999, 286) consulted relevant history of education (i.e., Vaughan 1997) and still dismissed the role of prerevolutionary schooling in the history of citizenship.

5. Partial exceptions are Yucatán and the failed 1910 educational project of the Sociedad Indianista; see Eiss (2004) and Urías (2001).

6. Even as acute an observer as Knight (1990, 79–83) seemed to imply that there was little schooling for "Indians." In his defense, it must be noted that his chapter was written in 1992, just before the relevant historiography of education took off. Nonetheless, this view was common at the time, and it is what many historians and anthropologists who are not specialized in education, and educationalists

unaware of recent historiography, think about Porfirian schooling even today. See also Bertely (1998, 74, 93–94) and Eiss (2004, 122).

7. This school policy further confirms Brading's (1988) claim that Mexican liberal patriotism was a form of classical republicanism.

8. In an 1883 debate, the future minister of public instruction, Justo Sierra, argued in favor of a school that gave equal treatment for all, including Indians, against the positivist argument of Francisco Cosmes, who believed schools were inappropriate for indigenous populations (for linguistic reasons and because of parents' need for children to work, among other factors) and therefore a waste of time. Sierra's view was enshrined in the national educational congress of 1889, which issued recommendations for all public schools (Acevedo-Rodrigo 2011b; Stabb 1959, 414–16).

9. Note, for instance, that the situation in Chiapas was much bleaker, with a very unequal distribution of resources putting speakers of indigenous languages at a disadvantage (Washbrook 2012, 158, 166–68).

10. Mention of the "indigenous race," as well as the classification of schools, had been proposed by educationalist Enrique Rebsamen in his visit to Oaxaca and in his subsequent 1891 report, whose suggestions were followed in the 1893 law (Rebsamen 1891, 24–27).

11. The legislation did not include any reference to the use of indigenous languages. See Acevedo-Rodrigo (2011b) and Heath (1972) for language issues at the time.

12. AGPEO-IP-Ixtlán, box 2 bis, file 24, "Exp. 580," 1904. See also the references to the 1892 and 1894 Memorias in footnote 16.

13. The Ixtlán figures are my own calculations from the following sources: BB-UABJO-DIP, Junta de Vigilancia, Actas de visita, box 1, 1886–1891, file 5, "Exp. Villa Juárez," April 1889; Pimentel (1907); Chassen-López (2004, 241); Oaxaca State figures come from López López (2015, 124).

14. "Ley reglamentaria de instrucción pública," April 1893 in Ruiz (2001, 111). For full transcriptions of Oaxaca's nineteenth-century educational legislation, see Ruiz (2001).

15. Historically, Ixtepeji had had greater religious, political, and economic status than Ixtlán. Indeed, the fact that Ixtlán and not Ixtepeji had been made capital of the district in 1857, together with land disputes, fed a deep rivalry between the two municipalities. Additionally, Ixtepeji men were soldiers in the liberal struggles of 1855–1876 (McNamara 2007, 40). On Ixtlán-Ixtepeji rivalries, see Chassen-López (2004, 441) and Pérez García ([1956] 1996, 134–46). For details of Ixtepeji's high status: BB-UABJO-DIP, Junta de Vigilancia, Actas de visita, box 1, 1886–1891, file 5, "Exp. Villa Juárez," April 1889.

16. Unless otherwise stated, the information in this and the following paragraphs comes from "Memoria del ramo de instrucción pública del distrito de Ixtlán de Juárez. 1892," a full transcript of which can be found in Traffano (2016), and AGPEO-IP-Ixtlán, box 1, file 28, "Exp. 17. Memoria relativa al ramo de instrucción primaria en el distrito de Ixtlán. Año de 1894"; and file 35, "Memoria sobre el ramo de instrucción, correspondiente al distrito de Ixtlán. 1897–1898." For additional

information on Ixtlán capital, see AGPEO-IP-Ixtlán, box 6, file 5, "Exp. 119," 1897, and file 24, "Exp. 49," 1898.

17. AGPEO-IP-Ixtlán, box 1, file 34, "Ixtlán. 1898," January 18, 1898; and box 2 bis, file 18, "Exp. 506. Ixtlán. 1903." On the introduction of the simultaneous teaching of reading and writing in this period, see Acevedo-Rodrigo (2008).

18. The evidence for the Puebla Sierra in this and subsequent paragraphs, unless otherwise stated, comes from Acevedo-Rodrigo (2017), which is primarily based on municipal archives.

19. Puebla's was also a favorable ratio compared with the 1:2,056 ratio in Portugal, and similar to Belgium's 1:893, although it was far from the impressive 1:277 in the United States (Díaz Covarrubias [1875] 2000, 109–17; Chassen-López 2004, 241).

20. In 1900 in the district of Ixtlán, 7 percent of the population could read and write and a further 1 percent could only read; in the state of Oaxaca, 8 percent could read and write and 3 percent could only read. Literacy figures for the Puebla Sierra in 1900 have been calculated at an average of 20 percent, excluding those who could only read (although some municipalities had a rate as low as 7 percent); the state of Puebla had 15 percent who could read and write and 1 percent who could only read. In 1921 Puebla State had 27 percent literacy, while Oaxaca had 18 percent (*Censo General de la República Mexicana* 1902; *Censo General de Habitantes* 1921; Acevedo-Rodrigo 2017).

21. This hypothesis is reinforced if we compare the cases of Oaxaca and Puebla with those of Mexico State, Tlaxcala, and Chiapas; see Acevedo-Rodrigo (2011a).

22. *Principales* were at the top of a form of local government that integrated older custom with newer, legally recognized forms of organization. In my research on the late nineteenth century, I have not found enough documentary evidence to judge the extent of *principales'* power in this period, but see Guardino (2005, 47–56) for a description of it in late colonial Villa Alta (a neighboring district to the east of Ixtlán) and Reina (2015) for the coexistence of customary forms of selecting authorities and elections prescribed by liberal legislation in Oaxaca during the Porfiriato.

23. AGPEO-IP-Ixtlán, box 1, file 9, "Santiago Xiacú," January 14, 1891; and file 11, "Trinidad," January 29, 1891; box 2 bis, "Cinco Señores."

24. See, for instance, AGPEO-IP-Ixtlán, box 4, file 8, Yahuiche, 1892–1893.

25. AGPEO-IP-Ixtlán, box 2 bis, file 10, "Exp. 631," 1901.

26. AGPEO-IP-Ixtlán, box 2, February 26, 1885.

27. See, for instance, AGPEO-IP-Ixtlán, box 2 bis, file 8, "Exp. 624. San Juan Chicomezúchil," September 1901.

28. Local selection of teachers may have derived from earlier conflicts in which higher authorities had difficulties finding suitable people and left the task to the pueblos (Guardino 2005, 108). For the Guelatao 1886 meeting, see AGPEO-IP-Ixtlán, box 2, file 19, "Exp. 19. Guelatao de Juárez. February 4, 1886."

29. AGPEO-IP-Ixtlán, box 4, file 27, Atepec, February 14, 1883; box 2, file 8, "Cinco Señores, March 10, 1886"; and box 6, file 11, "Exp. 598. Trinidad Ixtlán. 1896," Nexicho, July 10, 1896.

30. AGPEO-IP-Ixtlán, box 2, file 17, "Exp. 17. San Miguel Amatlán, July 26, 1885"; see also file 28, "Exp. 28. Tepanzacualco."

31. See also the Ixtlán schoolmaster's concerns in "Memoria del ramo de instrucción pública del distrito de Ixtlán de Juárez. 1892," in Traffano (2016).

32. See Rockwell (1994, 188) for the use of schools to upgrade villages' status in Tlaxcala.

33. AGPEO, box 5, file 12, "Exp. 600. Zogochi," February 6, 1896.

34. AGPEO-IP-Ixtlán, box 2, file 47, "Exp. 19," September 29, 1887.

35. On village factionalism during the period 1750–1850 in Villa Alta, see Guardino (2005, 47–56, 231–45). On the importance of the literate/illiterate divide (and bilingualism/monolinguism) in local government and its relation with higher levels of government in Chiapas, see Washbrook (2012, 173–76) and Rus (1994).

36. See, for instance, AGPEO-IP-Ixtlán, box 4, file 30, May 4, 1894; box 6, file 15, "Exp. 57. 1898"; and box 6, file 2, "Exp. 105. Abejones."

37. Such imbrication of civil government in public instruction is unsurprising, since as early as the mid-eighteenth century, schools passed from mainly religious hands to increasing control of civil governments (Tanck de Estrada, 1999), prefiguring the liberal state instruction of the second half of the nineteenth century.

38. AGPEO-IP-Ixtlán, box 2, "Exp. 7. Comaltepec. 1885."

39. I have no direct evidence of illiterate authorities of Ixtlán discussing letters' contents with scribes or secretaries, but in the light of Rockwell's evidence in this book, there is no reason to believe their contribution was negligible.

40. For the Puebla Sierra, it is not possible to work out whether the Nahuatl and Totonac-speaking pupils were the children of the most prominent men in the locality because of their lack of inheritable surnames, or because of the use in whole municipalities of just a handful of surnames that were shared by families of low and high socioeconomic levels. For the Ixtlán district there might be enough use of inheritable surnames to trace this matter, but we do not yet have studies of specific villages that allow us to do so.

41. For state figures and opinions of girls' schooling in 1875, see Díaz Covarrubias ([1875] 2000, 109–23); for Ixtlán, Pimentel (1907); and for Puebla, Acevedo-Rodrigo (2017). For petitions to open girls' schools in Ixtlán, see AGPEO-IP-Ixtlán, box 2, file 49, "Exp. 17. Pueblos y haciendas de Xiacui, Capulalpan, Natividad, San Pedro Nolasco y Castresana"; and box 6, file 6, "Exp. 116. Jaltianguis, 1897."

42. AGPEO-IP-Ixtlán, box 1, file 9, "Adelaida Perzabal to State Governor, Oaxaca de Juárez," August 28, 1891.

43. AGPEO-IP-Ixtlán, box 2 bis, file 10, "Exp. 631," Jaltianguis, January 31, 1901.

44. School inspectors presented a bleak picture of instruction throughout the nineteenth century, but as historians we would do well to take them with a pinch of salt. See, for instance, Staples (1999, 56) and BB-UABJO-DIP, Junta de Vigilancia, Actas de visita, 13 files covering 1886–1891.

45. For such discussions among anthropologists in the 1940s, see López Caballero's chapter in this volume. For historians' recent use of these terms, see, for instance, Falcón (2002, 15–16, 36–37) and Alvarado and Ríos (2011).

46.   I borrow the term "subordinate inclusion" from Taylor and Wilson (2004, 160–61), who coined it to discuss citizenship in Latin America.

REFERENCES

ARCHIVES

Archivo General del Poder Ejecutivo de Oaxaca, Instrucción Pública en los Distritos, Distrito de Ixtlán (AGPEO-IP-Ixtlán)

Biblioteca Burgoa, Archivo Histórico de la Universidad Autónoma Benito Juárez de Oaxaca, Dirección de Instrucción Pública (BB-UABJO-DIP)

PRINTED PRIMARY SOURCES

Censo General de Habitantes, efectuado el dia 30 de noviembre de 1921. 1921. Secretaría de la Economía Nacional. Mexico: Dirección General de Estadística.

Censo General de la República Mexicana verificado el 28 de octubre de 1900 conforme a las instrucciones de la Dirección General de Estadística. 1902. Mexico: Secretaría de Fomento.

Díaz Covarrubias, José. (1875) 2000. *La Instrucción Pública en México.* Facsimile edition of the original published in Mexico in 1875 by the Government Press. Mexico: Miguel Ángel Porrúa.

Juárez, Benito. 2010. *Apuntes para mis hijos.* Edition prepared by Héctor Cuauhtémoc Hernández Silva. Mexico: Fondo de Cultura Económica (FCE).

Pimentel, Emilio. 1907. *Compilación de decretos y cuadros estadísticos de la Sección de Instrucción Pública del Estado.* Oaxaca: Gobierno del Estado.

Rebsamen, Enrique. 1891. *Informe sobre la reorganización de la escuela práctica anexa a la normal de Profesores del estado de Oaxaca.* Oaxaca: Imprenta del Estado.

Ruiz, Francisco José. 2001. *La educación oaxaqueña en sus leyes.* Oaxaca: Instituto Estatal de Educación Pública de Oaxaca (IEEPO).

Traffano, Daniela. 2016. *"Por la muy merecida importancia que la enseñanza ha obtenido . . ." Documentos sobre instrucción pública en Oaxaca a finales del siglo XIX.* Oaxaca: Carteles Editores.

SECONDARY SOURCES

Acevedo-Rodrigo, Ariadna. 2008. "Ritual Literacy: The Simulation of Reading in Rural Indian Mexico." *Paedagogica Historica* 44 (1–2): 49–65.

———. 2011a. "Muchas escuelas y poco alfabeto: La educación rural en el Porfiriato, México, 1876–1910." In *Campesinos y escolares. La construcción de la escuela en el campo latinoamericano, siglos XIX y XX,* edited by Alicia Civera, Juan Alfonseca, and Carlos Escalante, 73–105. Mexico: Colegio Mexiquense and Miguel Ángel Porrúa.

———. 2011b. "La ignorada cuestión del idioma: La educación en los pueblos indígenas de Puebla, México, 1876–1930." In Alvarado and Ríos 2011, 431–68.

———. 2017. "Lingering Liberalism. Indians, Education, and Government in Puebla, Mexico, 1875–1940." Unpublished manuscript, last modified May 1, 2017. Microsoft Word file.

Alvarado, Lourdes, and Rosalina Ríos, eds. 2011. *Grupos marginados de la educación, siglos XIX y XX*. Mexico: Instituto de Investigaciones sobre la Universidad and la Educación de la Universidad Nacional Autónoma de México (UNAM).

Bazant, Mílada. 2002. *En busca de la modernidad: Procesos educativos en el Estado de México, 1873–1912*. Zinacantepec: Colegio Mexiquense.

Bertely, María. 1998. "Educación indígena del siglo XX en México." In *Un siglo de educación en México*, vol 2, edited by Pablo Latapí, 74–110. Mexico: FCE.

Brading, David. 1988. "Liberal Patriotism and the Mexican Reforma." *Journal of Latin American Studies* 20 (1): 27–48.

Chassen-López, Francie. 2004. *From Liberal to Revolutionary Oaxaca: The View from the South, Mexico 1867–1911*. University Park: Pennsylvania State University Press.

Eiss, Paul. 2004. "Deconstructing Indians, Reconstructing *Patria*: Indigenous Education in Yucatan from the *Porfiriato* to the Mexican Revolution." *Journal of Latin American Anthropology* 9 (1): 119–50.

Escalante, Carlos. 2014. *Mazahuas, campesinos y maestros. Prácticas de escritura, tierras y escuelas en la historia de Jocotitlán, Estado de México (1879–1940)*. Zinacantepec: Colegio Mexiquense.

Falcón, Romana. 2002. *México descalzo. Estrategias de sobrevivencia frente a la modernidad liberal*. Mexico: Plaza Janés.

Giraudo, Laura. 2014. "No era un desierto. La Secretaría de Educación Pública y la educación rural en el estado de Veracruz, periodo posrevolucionario." In *Historia de la educación en Veracruz. Construcción de una cultura escolar*, edited by Luz Elena Galván Lafarga and Gerardo Antonio Galindo Peláez, 171–96. Mexico: Universidad Veracruzana and Secretaría de Educación del Estado de Veracruz.

Guardino, Peter. 2005. *The Time of Liberty: Popular Political Culture in Oaxaca, 1750–1850*. Durham, NC: Duke University Press.

Heath, Shirley Brice. 1972. *Telling Tongues: Language Policy in Mexico, Colony to Nation*. New York: Teachers College Press.

Hunter, Ian. 1994. *Rethinking the School: Subjectivity, Bureaucracy, Criticism*. St Leonard's, NSW, Australia: Allen and Unwin.

Knight, Alan. 1990. "Racism, Revolution, and *Indigenismo*: Mexico, 1910–1940." In *The Idea of Race in Latin America, 1870–1940*, edited by Richard Graham, 71–114. Austin: University of Texas Press.

Lomnitz, Claudio. 1999. "Modes of Citizenship in Mexico." *Public Culture* 11 (1): 269–63.

López López, Edmundo. 2015. "La introducción de la escuela graduada en la educación elemental de la ciudad de Oaxaca, 1889–1905." Master's thesis, Departamento de Investigaciones Educativas, Centro de Investigación y de Estudios Avanzados (Cinvestav).

Loyo, Engracia. 1999. *Gobiernos revolucionarios y educación popular en México, 1911–1928.* Mexico: Colegio de México.

Martínez Vásquez, Víctor Raúl. 2012. *La educación en Oaxaca: 1825–2010.* Oaxaca: IEEPO.

McNamara, Patrick. 2007. *Sons of the Sierra: Juárez, Díaz, and the People of Ixtlán Oaxaca, 1855–1920.* Chapel Hill: University of North Carolina Press.

Meneses, Ernesto. 1998. *Tendencias educativas oficiales en México.* Vol. I, *1821–1911.* Mexico: Centro de Estudios Educativos and Universidad Iberoamericana.

Pérez García, Rosendo. (1956) 1996. *La sierra Juárez,* vol. 1. Oaxaca: Instituto Oaxaqueño de las Culturas.

Reina, Leticia. 2004. *Caminos de luz y sombra. Historia indígena de Oaxaca en el siglo XIX.* Mexico: Centro de Investigaciones y Estudios Superiores en Antropología Social (CIESAS) and Comisión Nacional para el Desarrollo de los Pueblos Indígenas.

————. 2015. *Cultura política y formas de representación indígena en México, siglo XIX.* Mexico: Instituto Nacional de Antropología e Historia.

Rockwell, Elsie. 1994. "Schools of the Revolution: Enacting and Contesting State Forms in Tlaxcala, 1910–1930." In *Everyday Forms of State Formation: Revolution and the Negotiation of Rule in Modern Mexico,* edited by Gilbert M. Joseph and Daniel Nugent, 170–208. Durham, NC: Duke University Press.

————. 2007. *Hacer escuela, hacer estado. La educación pos-revolucionaria vista desde Tlaxcala.* Mexico: Colegio de Michoacán, CIESAS, and Cinvestav.

Ruiz, Francisco José, and Daniela Traffano. 2006. "'Porque sólo la ilustración puede desterrar de esos pueblos los vicios y la inmoralidad que los dominan': Indígenas y educación en Oaxaca." *Revista de História* 1 (154): 191–220.

Rus, Jan. 1994. "The '*Comunidad Revolucionaria Institucional*': The Subversion of Native Government in Highland Chiapas, 1936–1968." In *Everyday Forms of State Formation: Revolution and the Negotiation of Rule in Modern Mexico,* edited by Gilbert M. Joseph and Daniel Nugent, 265–300. Durham, NC: Duke University Press.

Sigüenza, Salvador, and Graciela Fabián. 2013. "Historia de la educación indígena en la configuración del Estado nacional y la ciudadanía en México." In *Multiculturalismo y educación, 2002–2011,* edited by María Bertely, Gunther Dietz, and María Guadalupe Díaz, 81–115. Colección Estados del conocimiento. Mexico: Consejo Mexicano de Investigación Educativa.

Stabb, Martin S. 1959. "Indigenism and Racism in Mexican Thought, 1857–1911." *Journal of Inter-American Studies* 1 (4): 405–23.

Staples, Anne. 1999. "Una falsa promesa: la educación indígena después de la Independencia." In *Educación rural e indígena en Iberoamérica,* edited by Pilar Gonzalbo, with Gabriela Ossenbach, 53–64. Mexico: Colegio de México.

Tanck de Estrada, Dorothy. 1999. *Pueblos de indios y educación en el México colonial, 1750–1821.* Mexico: Colegio de México.

Taylor, Lucy, and Fiona Wilson. 2004. "The Messiness of Everyday Life: Exploring Key Themes in Latin American Citizenship Studies." *Bulletin of Latin American Research* 23 (2): 154–64.

Tenorio, Mauricio. 2006. *El Porfiriato*. Mexico: FCE, Centro de Investigación y Docencia Económicas.

Thomson, Guy. 1998. "'*La republique au village*' in Spain and Mexico." In *Nation Building in Nineteenth-Century Latin America: Dilemmas and Conflicts*, edited by Hans-Joachim König and Marianne Wiesebron, 137–62. Leiden: Research School CNWS.

————. 1999. *Patriotism, Politics and Popular Liberalism in Nineteenth-Century Mexico: Juan Francisco Lucas and the Puebla Sierra*. With David LaFrance. Wilmington, DE: Scholarly Resources.

Traffano, Daniela. 2007. "'La creación y vigilancia de las escuelas municipales continuará a cargo de las autoridades [. . .] Ciudadanía, escuela y ayuntamientos.'" In *Los pueblos indios en los tiempos de Benito Juárez*, edited by Antonio Escobar, 69–90. Mexico: UABJO and Universidad Autónoma Metropolitana.

Urías, Beatriz. 2001. "Etnología y filantropía. Las propuestas de 'regeneración' para indios de la Sociedad Indianista Mexicana, 1910–1914." In *Modernidad, tradición y alteridad. La ciudad de México en el cambio de siglo (XIX-XX)*, edited by Claudia Agostoni and Elisa Speckmann, 223–40. Mexico: Instituto de Investigaciones Históricas, UNAM.

Vaughan, Mary K. 1997. *Cultural Politics in Revolution: Teachers, Peasants, and Schools in Mexico, 1930–1940*. Tucson: University of Arizona Press.

Washbrook, Sarah. 2012. *Producing Modernity in Mexico: Labour, Race and the State in Chiapas, 1876–1914*. Oxford: Oxford University Press.

CHAPTER 5

TODOS TENEMOS LA CRISMA DE DIOS

Engaging Spanish Literacy in a Tlaxcalan Pueblo

ELSIE ROCKWELL

BEYOND THE ORAL/LITERATE DIVIDE

OFFICIAL DISCOURSE, as much as academic discourse, still tends to define populations considered indigenous in any nation as primarily rural, agrarian, isolated, and traditional. In this context, the dichotomy between purportedly "oral" and "literate" cultures continues to be reproduced with contrary signs: at times the oral is seen as a dearth, the lack of written culture, and at times it is seen as a valuable depository of "indigenous world views." This "great divide" literacy thesis has been deeply questioned by the work of many scholars; studies of the uses of writing in many places not only trace links between language, literacy, and power, but also reveal ways in which communities resisted authority by strategic use of written documentation.[1] In my ongoing research, I contribute to this field a perspective based on my historical and ethnographic research on local appropriations of Spanish literacy by speakers of Nahuatl in the Malintzi region of Tlaxcala, Mexico. In relation to the theme of this volume, it is noteworthy that older inhabitants of this region refer to themselves as *mexicanos*, in the sense of speakers of the Mexicano language, as Nahuatl was known historically, and not as *indigenas*, which they regard as pejorative.

In this chapter, I propose to examine the challenges of engaging the dominant Spanish language as described by elders of the Malintzi region of Tlaxcala. My conversations with several *vecinos* of Cuauhtenco, who spoke only the local language as children in the 1930s and came to master Spanish as adults, has modified my understanding of the complexities involved in dealing with a diglossic environment in which Spanish is the high status language used in all written communication and public spaces and Mexicano is low status, currently used in private local settings.[2]

Multiple studies have shown that colonized peoples of Spanish America were immersed in worlds of writing.[3] In central Mexico, they had vigorous long-term written cultures, which were largely destroyed through the Spanish conquest. In colonial times, scribes reproduced enduring elements of pre-Hispanic writing (especially symbolic, territorial, and genealogical representations) and interwove them with the alphabetic inscription of native languages and of Spanish. Within relationships marked by colonial power, communities had to deal with an extremely varied and dense network of official documentation imposed by the Spanish ecclesiastical and governmental apparatus; however, they also generated their own literacies.

The Malintzi region of Tlaxcala, located between the Gulf of Mexico and the nation's capital, is a territory that had been traversed and transformed by the Teo-Chichimec, Spanish, and French invasions, railroads and modern textile mills, the nineteenth-century civil wars, and the 1910 revolution. Although enjoying a relatively privileged status as a *república de indios* during colonial times, Tlaxcala was in no way an isolated region. In fact, it was not considered indigenous at all by the state during most of the twentieth century; for example, it was not an object of *indigenista* policies. Nevertheless, through five centuries of intense demographic and economic restructuring, the speakers of the Mexicano language living on the slopes of the Malintzi volcano have reproduced and reinvented communal ways of dealing with the dominant social order, including the world of Spanish literacy.[4]

Several conceptual tools brought to bear on this study help both to make sense of the particularities of this case and to notice the commonalities with other contexts. My theoretical perspective has drawn on French historians of written culture and recent work in anthropological linguistics. The concept of cultural appropriation, as developed by Roger Chartier (1995), points to the multiple transformations in the manners of reading and understanding texts that occur as different collectivities take up and make their own the textual forms and literacy practices of those in power. Michel de Certeau's (1984) term *scriptural economy* reveals heterogeneous literacy configurations produced in contexts marked by unequal power relations, and uncovers ways in which terrains are controlled through strategies from above and navigated through tactics from below. "Orality insinuates itself, like one of the threads of which it is composed, into the network—and endless tapestry—of a scriptural economy" (de Certeau 1984, 132, cited by Collins and Blot 2003, 30). Various authors have made ample use of de Certeau's work in discussing an alternative view to the "literacy thesis," stressing the plurality of literacies and their relation to colonial and national governance (Collins and Blot 2003). The very separation of the oral and the literate, as of indigenous and non-indigenous, is thus seen as part of the "regimes of language" (Kroskrity 2000) of modern states.

In anthropological linguistics, a new understanding of multiple spatialities and temporalities in asymmetric multilingual contexts has uncovered the shifting values and activities that diverse writings entail, in contexts of intense oral interaction and social mobility (Blommaert, Collins, and Slembrouck 2005; Kell 2011). This research has broken up closed conceptual boundaries once thought to be firmly in place. No longer can local cultures or literacies be isolated out of broader contexts and past histories as objects of inquiry; they need to be examined through lenses that capture both distal and proximal flows that account for present meanings and practices, including those transactions and interpretations enveloping the appropriation of writing.

My conversations with village elders in Cuauhtenco opened a window onto the complexities of gaining access to written Spanish through minimum schooling and diverse paths in accommodating to the scriptural economy of a particular location and timeframe.[5] Cuauhtenco is one of the villages on the slopes of the Malintzi volcano, a village subject to the municipal *cabecera* of Contla.[6] For centuries it has struggled to keep land that it claimed as communal, and thus has maintained a fairly strong community organization; as in many localities, external interests also intervened in these affairs, often operating through local caciques. While never harmonious, collective action nevertheless led several successful struggles for land and water rights of the region's rural peoples (Rockwell 2014). Cuauhtenco's history may be unlike that of other communities, yet it also speaks to deeper processes that have occurred in all regions of the world.

A COLLECTIVE MEMORY OF LITERATE ANCESTORS

The elders we interviewed in Cuauhtenco knew that local knowledge of writing did not begin after the revolution of 1910. Century-long struggles for land rights had involved many *vecinos* as intermediaries with authorities. A recurrent theme in their accounts was the regard for literate ancestors, particularly those who had succeeded in carrying through the successive trials and administrative affairs in the late nineteenth and early twentieth centuries, and who had reached a level of legal expertise deemed unattainable in present times. Stories converged around Juan de la Rosa Cuamatzi, who won a trial (*amparo*) in 1892 in the Supreme Court against the state governor, Próspero Cahuantzi, who was accused of having invaded communal lands (some had copies of the document to verify this fact). Juan Felix Maldonado spoke of his wife's grandfather, Agustín Reyes, who had worked with Juan de la Rosa Cuamatzi during the "first trial" and continued to lead the struggle while de la Rosa was sent to jail. Juan's version refers to the large number of books and documents that Agustín possessed, including copies of laws and deeds needed in the process: "He used to read all the time."[7]

The appreciation for notable persons of the past varied depending on who was telling the story. However, all accounts pointed to their ability to use writing and deal with legal matters for the community. Although they referred to the patronage of political figures or the aid of legal advisors, they underscored the personal merit of these local figures. Antonino Cuamatzi spoke of his father, Vicente Cuamatzi, who spent twenty years traveling regularly to Puebla or Mexico City with the municipal commission to undertake the affairs related to the "second trial" (1930s to 1950). The process entailed an endless sequence of paperwork to obtain a final resolution of Cuauhtenco's lands. It also meant confronting the previous generation of leaders. Vicente even managed to have the name of the village changed to San Felipe Cuauhtenco, apparently against the will of the *tiaxcas* of the elders who favored the Virgin of Guadalupe and wanted to keep the traditional name of the village, Cuauhtzincola.[8]

When the power of writing was held in individual hands and wielded for political ends, it could become a double-edged weapon. While some *tiaxcas* had used it to benefit the village, others pursued personal careers, held on to their posts for decades, or allied with external interests. During the twentieth

century, previous authorities were eventually displaced by a younger generation, those "who came behind them," which had also become versed in managing the town documents. José Muñoz, in his eighties when we interviewed
him, told us his version of the succession in the village. At the turn of the
century, Juan de la Rosa's group was heading the list, together with Agustín
Reyes. When they were ousted, Vicente Cuamatzi remained as the only *tiaxca*;
whatever he said would be done. By then "Juan de la Rosa was already ninety
years old; he used to wear white cotton pants and was quite curious," José
recalled. "Then it was our turn," he added as he named those who were associated with him.[9] He explained that they disagreed with the way Vicente
Cuamatzi was doing things, and objected that he would not take into account
their opinions. The group was tired of continuing with the fruitless process
of "trial after trial," actually long sequels of paperwork involved in obtaining
from the agrarian authorities of the federal government the adjudication of
the land after the legal settlement. The assembly decided to discharge Vicente
of his commission, and José Muñoz, along with others, took over the lead of
the village, undermining the power associated with the previous generation's
monopoly of legal processes. By then some of these younger men had learned
how to deal with the paperwork. In the late 1950s, the assembly agreed to
expropriate the land directly, distribute it to all *vecinos*, and allow everyone to
possess their individual plots and will them to their heirs.

Those villagers who entered the political realm were able to obtain a special know-how. Not only did they learn to speak and read Spanish but, more
significantly, they gained experience in navigating the various administrative
and judicial levels of the central government. These skills were distributed
unequally and not easily transmitted, even within families. Nahuatl continued to predominate in the daily life of the community, where there was little
need for writing. Local assemblies were conducted in both languages, yet the
minutes and other documents were written and read aloud in Spanish, and
spokesmen would take time to explain the terms to those who did not understand them. Many men still relied on the oral translations and explanations
yet acquired detailed knowledge of the content and import of the written
documents that were being presented, negotiated, and even signed. Dates
and boundary lines were confronted with knowledge passed down through
conversation with elders. Throughout these years, diverse sources were thus
woven into a fabric of local history that was shared by many, albeit—as in
academia—through different and at times conflicting versions. As I searched

the state archive's files for information on Cuauhtenco/Cuauhtzincola, documents dating from colonial times emerged that confirmed many of the local accounts. I realized that the interweaving of documentary and oral sources had been occurring for several centuries (Rockwell 2014).

THE VALUE OF LEARNING ON ONE'S OWN: *ME ACOMODÉ*

All these elders insisted with pride that they had learned to speak and write Spanish basically on their own. Learning to speak Spanish and to deal with writing through involvement in communal affairs largely explained the gap between minimal formal schooling and the mastery of oral or written Spanish they had achieved by the time I spoke with them, at the beginning of the twenty-first century. However, many seemed to highly value, retrospectively, even their brief time in school as the beginning of their current knowledge.

School experiences were variable. In the 1930s, as for decades before then, the village had an elementary school, although there were times when it was closed. According to the accounts, teachers were changed frequently, and some were remembered better than others. Some spoke Mexicano, but all were expected to enforce the use of Spanish in the classroom. The children nevertheless would tend to speak Mexicano among themselves, while attempting to repeat their lessons in the official language. School Spanish was probably highly scripted, ritualistic, and patterned after the written lessons. Initial instruction required children to trace letters put on the blackboard or presented on cards into the small copybooks that their parents could afford to buy. The government gave out readers, and the older students would copy lessons and learn to recite them. Better teachers are remembered as having explained, with some dramatic flair, the content of history lessons and the new constitutional rights. Some also taught songs and wrote skits for the children to perform for the community. Doing arithmetic was easier than writing, and was more readily useful. The children's participation was unequal, and perhaps few would complete their assignments. Some students survived the stressful ambience and continued, but many were promptly withdrawn and sent to help with household chores or care for animals.

It was unlikely that the knowledge of writing that the men we interviewed wielded as adults was due to those few years of formal instruction. Nevertheless, all emphasized "the rigor" of the exercises that their teachers had assigned them, as well as the severity of the punishments they meted out. Cipriano Galicia reported that he had attended classes for four years, without ever reaching the third grade, which was reserved—if we examine school attendance data—for the very few students who were ready to write on their own. Only after mastering calligraphy, including the difficult use of pens and inkwells, were any of them promoted to the fourth grade. None of their generation would go on to the higher grades available only in the municipal school. According to Antonino Cuamatzi, when he was a child there was no real obligation to enroll in school, even though it was legally compulsory; attendance was sporadic and irregular. He had been sent to first grade knowing no Spanish, but as his classmates teased him, he withdrew and his father sent him to tend the sheep. There was no need to be taught writing, so he claimed to have been *lírico* (lyrical); that is, he learned Spanish literacy on his own (Farr 1994). Antonino recalls that his father claimed that there would come a time when all children would be forced to attend school and not only go when they wanted to.[10] Victoria, Agustín Reyes's granddaughter, did not go to school and grew up without knowing how to read until later in life, although as she accompanied her grandfather, she began to understand Spanish. When she expressed her desire to attend school, her father reproached her and asked her whether what she wanted was to become a teacher. Her father trained her instead to do "manly" tasks, such as scraping the maguey plants to produce aguamiel.

Those who were most able to grasp school literacy, such as José Muñoz and Concepción Flores, did not necessarily come from families that had greater contact with Spanish, such as Antonino, but rather from more monolingual families. Their trajectories counter the purported determinism of cultural capital as an explanation of success in school. José, whose parents spoke no Spanish, explained: "I attended first grade and the second, but after second grade, they didn't send me due to economic difficulties."[11] However, he added, according to him and many other elders in the region, second grade at the time was equivalent to the sixth grade in the present-day schools his grandchildren attend.

Several elders valued another practice that had marked their school days: reading out loud. Given that students knew little Spanish, some teachers found it easier to have them copy words than to read texts in a language they could not speak. Teachers rarely had enough readers and so would circulate the few books among the class and collect them at the end of the day. They would ask students to review the lessons by themselves, and then they would pass individual students to their desk to read aloud; this moment was a stressful test in the pronunciation of sentences that students could read but did not necessarily understand. Others recalled that teachers instructed them to "respect every period and comma,"[12] as though written punctuation ruled the cadence of spoken language.[13] End of year public examinations entailed reading aloud in front of adults: "We had to read like lawyers [*licenciados*]" said José, "because if you made a mistake at any point in the text, you would not be promoted."[14] As most students were barely beginning to understand Spanish, reading aloud became a means for them to master the sounds of this foreign language. This task was probably the most difficult obstacle to continuing past third grade. In these classrooms, reading comprehension was less relevant, as it would be attained in the long process of dealing with Spanish after leaving school.[15] For many villagers, it would be later on, when life led them into domains where reading and writing Spanish were needed, that they would learn how to *juntar las letras* (join letters) in order to make sense of texts and compose their own documents. In the case of women, this moment sometimes arrived, as Paula Galicia told me, when they were pressed to help their own children with their homework.

Although this experience in schooling may have seemed precarious for many, for some it was enough to launch them on a lifelong path of learning and reading. Concepción's experience is revealing of such a trajectory.[16] He entered the elementary school in 1939 at the age of eleven, and the teacher, Benjamín Quiroz, let him sit with two older girls, fourth-graders, who were the granddaughters of Juan de la Rosa Cuamatzi and thus had more exposure to Spanish. They took it upon themselves to explain the lessons to Concepción, and so he was able to quickly go through the *Simiente* readers for the first three grades.[17] The teacher perceived his ability and took him to a regional reading competition, where he outdid the city students. However, according to his teacher, he was crossed out from the list for the state competition; Concepción imagines the dominant argument: "*[dirían] 'es un simple indito y nos viene a bajar nuestra sabiduría'... (se ríe) no... era... con mis calzoncitos de manta... así... de veras un pobrecito.*" ([They might say,] He is just a simple *indito* and he is coming to take [down] our wisdom [laughter] ... with my white cotton pants ... I was really a poor little boy.)[18] The teacher gave him a copy of the *Breve Historia de México*, the grade-school textbook published by the socialist author Teja Zabre in 1935. Concepción recalled verbatim parts of that text when I spoke with him. The following school year, Concepción returned, but a new teacher had arrived who did not treat them quite as well, and so at first he hid in a ravine to study on his own, until he was discovered and sent by his family to tend the sheep. Concepción retold all of this jokingly, fully aware that he had indeed mastered much of "their" knowledge and was then reading volumes of Tlaxcalan history, such as that of Muñoz Camargo.[19] With his sole year of schooling, Concepción was able to become a constant reader of historical books and documents and was recognized as the expert on the long-term struggles for communal land, called on to testify with government inspectors and engineers mapping the land.

In some cases, adults' efforts to learn on their own were quite impressive. Salvador Flores, for example, claimed that he had not gone to school even one day and did not know how to read; he didn't learn to speak Spanish until late in his twenties. Nevertheless, his knowledge of exact historical dates and regimes, his awareness of documents that might be found in the state archives, and his own management of community affairs and personal credentials was on par with the skills of many who had been to school. As studies have shown (e.g., Lave 2011), learning tasks through observation and practice has been documented in many situations; rural children especially have the ability to observe how work is carried out and then repeat the task individually. While growing up, Juan had learned to make charcoal: "What schooling?" he said. "I learned with my father, that's how I saw how it was done . . . it is not easy," he claimed as he described the details of the process. Salvador insisted that he wanted to learn to plow a field with oxen with his grandfather, but "It's on one's own" (*Ya es de uno*).[20] My colleague, Professor Ramos Rosales of Cuauhtenco, related this practice to learning one's first language, and saw how the same process was transferred to learning contents thought to be reserved to formal schooling. Throughout life, practice in a social domain served just as well for the appropriation of Spanish literacy and accounting.

Often referred to as *enseñarse uno mismo* (teaching oneself), this experience corroborated the argument that notable ancestors had probably acquired their knowledge with no schooling. Postrevolutionary discourse had largely erased from local memory the many previous communal attempts to hire teachers or request official schools, which are nevertheless recorded in archival sources.[21] Antonino recalled that his father, Vicente, used to boast of his own capacity for learning: "He used to have piles of papers, books, and newspapers around the house; he also used to write a lot. He carried some notebooks around . . . *era muy leísta* [in Spanish this sounds like "he was very readist," and it meant "he was an avid reader"] . . . I think he only went to school for a year and a half, maybe . . . but then he began to write [he signaled this with a gesture] . . . Everyone has a mind [*cabeza*], as I tell you, he really had a mind to learn . . . He would tell us, 'I had no father, but I can write, I can sing.' . . . He was very Catholic . . . Then they appointed him representative to follow the trials . . . and town agent . . . He began to go to Tlaxcala, and to speak with those guys in ties [*corbatudos*] . . . and so, that is how he began to get the gist of it [*agarrar la onda*]."[22]

When we asked José whether Juan de la Rosa Cuamatzi knew how to read and write, he reflected, "I don't know . . . but surely he did, for if he did not know . . . [he would have said,] 'Lyrically I cannot take on the responsibility to go to court, to stand before [a judge].' . . . He was great." (*No supiera . . . [diría] 'líricamente no me comprometo a hacer un juicio, a parar al frente.' . . . Fue grande.*)[23] Then José added some information on his own experience in contexts that required speaking or writing Spanish. He recalled that Vicente Cuamatzi had followed de la Rosa's group when he was young; that was when he first learned to deal with legal matters. Later, José himself had helped Vicente, which also allowed him to learn how to deal with documents.

Accounts such as these suggested that the ancestors who could speak, write, and read Spanish had learned on their own, just as these elders claimed to have done. Sometimes their personal history was summarized with a single sentence, as was the case of Juan Félix: "*Me supe acomodar.*" (I managed to accommodate myself.); or Concepción: "*Ellos usaban las letras, y yo la astucia.*" (They used letters, and I used cunning.)[24] The learning process invariably included the ability to *llevar las cuentas* (keep accounts) to keep track of the sales of charcoal or pulque or the local water fees. Even those who initially insisted that they did not know how to read and write described their activities in ways that implied knowledge of the documents involved in certain tasks. These ranged from keeping the books as religious *fiscales* to writing death certificates. When asked how they learned or who helped them, most would insist on their own *ingenio* (resourcefulness) and on their ability to accommodate themselves to the situation. Juan Félix repeated several times, "*Todos tenemos la crisma de dios,*" implicitly claiming that everyone is equally able to figure out how to learn and to reason, even without having much schooling.[25] Others used a more secular language. José Muñoz, after describing all the local commissions and positions he had held that required him to write diverse types of texts, returned the question: "How do you explain it? When I only went to school for two years . . . If I had finished third grade, who knows? I would have been a different person."[26] He compared his skills to those of younger persons who had gone on to secondary schools but who did *not* know how to handle village affairs. These skills were not easily acquired or transmitted and required some individual effort and persistence.

Other paths towards Spanish literacy were also possible. Antonino Cuamatzi, for example, married a woman from the village who had grown up in Cholula and knew Spanish; he first courted her with the help of a friend who could write love letters in Spanish. Later they taught each other their languages and insisted that their children learn both. Cipriano Galicia, as others, noted that he struggled with Spanish when he served in the army. At the time, they required all soldiers to copy the military regulations in a notebook. He recalls that some would ask their companions to copy the rules for them and then they would only sign them, but he was able to copy them by himself.[27]

According to Antonino, his father, Vicente—as well as other parents of his generation—had insisted that his children learn Mexicano; at the time they did not imagine that the language would ever disappear. However, Vicente, a devout and conservative Catholic, also insisted that the children learn to sing in Spanish (and Latin) during the mass, even though they may not have understood the words. Vicente, himself a singer, had collected sufficient money to purchase a piano and hire a music teacher to train children for the church choir. The tradition of forming choirs and bands for the patron saint fiestas was initially promoted by the colonial church and state but strongly backed in these villages. Certain villagers learned to read music and sing in liturgical songs; developing this skill had long been one of the paths to the acquisition of Spanish literacy, and it could eventually be remunerated.[28]

In other cases, learning Spanish accompanied the search for paid labor through networks that extended far beyond the limits of the community—toward other cities and states, and in a few cases to the United States. Jobs often required being able to get along in Spanish, without any formal training. In such cases, the expression *acomodarse* made sense. When Juan Félix had a job in public works with an engineer, he learned some accounting, and he was asked to become a collector, but his wife didn't want him to take on that responsibility (*no te comprometas*). Juan Muñoz's biography included a complex itinerary through a variety of jobs in which he eventually mastered first accounting and later writing. José faced several situations in which he had to move about in the world of bureaucratic writing before really learning how to compose a text. When he formed his own political group in the village, he bought a typewriter and learned how to use it; he moved his fingers over the table to mimic the movement of an expert typist, as he told us. He told of a time that he accompanied one of his more educated compadres to Mexico City to do some paperwork. The man already had his petition written up, but when he read it, José told him that the text was not composed in the best terms and suggested a new formulation. Accepting the task of rewriting the document, José asked permission to use one of the typewriters in the office. This was one of his first challenges. Later in life he served as the village *juez de paz*, and the day came when he had to write a death certificate; someone at the town court explained to him exactly how to write it the first time. "But then," he said, "how could I repeat the same thing over and over? I had to come up with new words in my own mind, depending on how I was going to write each certificate." José claimed that locals still ask him to help write up official documents, although he prefers not to be bothered and refuses to assume the power of the ancient *tiaxcas*.[29]

Archival data points to a fairly widespread ability to learn to both speak and write Spanish as adults with little, if any, formal schooling, at least from the nineteenth century on. Although the tally of signatures is not always sufficient evidence of the extent of basic literacy, it does signal a practice. In these Malintzi villages at the time of the revolution, more persons signed the petitions than those who just placed a cross beside their names written in by others. These autonomous processes of acquiring basic Spanish literacy in a world dominated by written documents undergird the numerous legal procedures (*trámites*) that *vecinos* in various parts of Mexico undertook to document and defend their land rights and their legal status as pueblos (Ruiz Medrano 2010). As in other regions, these were cases of "distributed literacy" (Curtis 2008); certain persons in each village would take on the task of learning the scribal skills needed for communal affairs, just as others were to become midwives or muleteers. Some translated the knowledge of writing into local prestige and assumed higher civil or religious cargos than persons with more formal schooling but less political experience. Others became well aware of all that was involved in dealing with writing and, when needed, resorted to younger scribes to do the actual writing, although they directed the logic of dealing with documents. In both cases, learning to negotiate with the official literate world was more important than the actual schooled skills of writing.

THE IMPORT AND AUTHENTICITY OF WRITTEN TEXTS

These testimonies might suggest that written language was an external phenomenon that the *vecinos* had to learn to face, particularly in the domains of religion, schooling, and governance. I argue, however, that there was an internal process of appropriation of writing in the communal context, and that literacy was transformed in the process. First, *vecinos* of the early twentieth century were fully aware of the struggles for land and political autonomy that had commanded and deployed documentary evidence, petitions, and settlement in litigations and administrative procedures since colonial times (Rockwell 2014). Indeed, in 1908, a request for the titles stored in the Archivo General de la Nación gave precise years, beginning with, "*Entre otras fechas recordamos para la búsqueda de los títulos los años de 1400 (época del rey Mexica)*."[30]

Counting on having some lettered *vecinos* who were able to follow the intricacies of the paperwork involved in these procedures was just as much a part of local culture as was having midwives and musicians. However, this was not simple; stories abound of loss and destruction of documents, as well as of treason. As for years there had been no town hall or registrar, documents were personally held and handed down, or hoarded, by the successive men commissioned to follow on with the "trials." Most elders I spoke to would speculate about the possible destiny of the papers collected by their lettered predecessors, such as Agustín Reyes and Vicente Cuamatzi, yet no one seemed to know where the papers ended up. Some expressed a justified reluctance to reveal the possible location or content of documents, or to show those they possessed, as though talking about them might bring about serious consequences, so responsibility was shifted to higher authorities. Others readily offered written evidence of their accounts: José offered a copy of the 1942 judicial resolution concerning the communal lands, and Antonino proudly showed us the receipt for the image of San Felipe that his father had bought in Puebla.

For a younger generation accustomed to municipal bureaucracies, photocopies, and digital databases, all of this seemed obsolete; however, the elders were still wondering what became of the original maps and deeds their ancestors had held. It was common among people of Cuauhtenco to know that there was a state historical archive nearby where all official documents were presumably stored. They would ask me what I had found there, and I did share relevant copies, particularly with Concepción, who had his own well-classified personal archive.

Particularly striking was the environment of mutual suspicion regarding property documents. The malicious use of documents by certain persons was a common theme. Several recounted the intrigues of Juan de la Rosa Cuamatzi's descendants, married to city-dwellers who tried to claim as their own the communal land of Cuauhtenco and were finally expelled from the town. This resonates with other studies of communities; since access to power was made possible through wielding the written code, some literate members would eventually break with their obligations to the community and use their skills in alliance with external interest groups (Gayol 2008; Rus 1994).

The conservation of personal written documents is an additional sign of the local appropriation of literacy. The practice spanned over lifetimes, as obtaining and preserving personal documents was essential to livelihood and was used to validate shared memories. Juan, who had told us that he had not learned to read, regretted that his parents had lost documents due to a household fire, yet this perhaps explains the extreme care that he took in saving his own in a carved wood chest equipped with lock and key. As he narrated experiences, he would take out documents: his military service identification, the U.S. temporary work permit (which had expired), the forestry permit necessary to collect firewood. As in most cases, the documents that were safely kept were not only those with a current use or value—such as land titles—but also those that signaled important moments in life or endorsed events to be recounted. He particularly valued his deeds, however, because, as he said, "Not even my children could take the plots away from me now."[31]

The legal procedures for producing local land titles dated from the early colonial period. Juan described in detail the formal aspects of the transaction when he bought a piece of land from his mother-in-law. Each party had witnesses, they verified on the site the dimensions and boundaries of the plot and drew a map, and finally the judge summoned them to sign the land title. The rhetorical formulae used when drawing up the document were similar to the ones that had been used for centuries (as found in archival files), and both parties knew them well; even those who did not know how to write paid close attention to the solemn reading of the titles. José also described in detail the procedure he used to follow as a village judge to issue land titles—and insisted that the documents he composed "had value, and it was no longer necessary to send them to the municipal office at Contla."[32]

Despite their recognition of the value of written documents, the members of this generation also expressed doubts about their validity. For instance, years after the trials, an engineer from the government of the state of Tlaxcala came to the community to demarcate the land belonging to each village. Juan and others had to show the engineer around the boundary markers. During a long conversation, Juan repeated to us in detail the long series of local names of particular gullies, roads, and lots (naming their owners) that marked the boundaries with neighboring villages. His capacity to recall the details was based on oral transmission, in Mexicano, of the topographical details that had been registered centuries before in colonial documents. Although there had been records used during the trials, Juan and other neighbors trusted memory over writing. For that reason, they recently took the younger generations on a tour to inspect, as in the colonial *vista de ojos*, the physical boundary marks of Cuauhtenco; they then produced an affidavit of the event.

Mistrust was particularly strong of documents produced in government offices. Juan told us that he had retrieved an updated birth certificate from the town hall records, but the name differed from the one he had used all his life. In order to get a corrected version, he sought out his baptismal certificate in the town church. He told the priest, "'This is the year, it has to be written in the books,' and that's how he found it."[33] Similar experiences had backed a collective action on the part of Cuauhtenco *vecinos*: a commission was able to negotiate directly with the governor the establishment of a public registrar in their own village in order to prevent such mistakes.

Concepción Flores expressed his mistrust as rage with what he perceived as fraudulent practices. In his view, the transactions of a group of newcomers who had established a barrio on village territory, and had then negotiated with the municipality to become autonomous, was fraught with false written claims. Among the irregularities that angered Concepción was the fact that they had come at night to mark the new boundaries rather than "in full daylight," in public. They had also produced false documents, such as deeds signed by a man who had died before the date on the contract, and state orders on the restructuring of their legal territory that had not been consented to by local authorities (Rockwell 2012). Such mistrust of official documentation produced through inept or fraudulent bureaucratic practices was extended to other works in print; Concepción thus expressed, regarding a book on the history of Tlaxcala, that of course it was not in the government's interest to include the successful feat of Juan de la Rosa Cuamatzi and his trial against the Porfirian governor Cahuantzi. His habit of doubting all written sources rang true with my own hard-earned training as a historian, and led me to reconsider the value of oral history.[34]

FINAL REMARKS

Although my contribution centers on a very small village in the smallest state of Mexico, the gist of these local histories resounds with many more collected around the world, connecting the various ways colonized peoples have engaged dominant literacies in multilingual contexts and appropriated writing in order to fend for themselves.

On one plane, these stories undermine some of the long-held certainties of the "literacy thesis." Collins and Blot (2003, chap. 2) summarize this thesis as the recurring perspective that elaborate alphabetic literacy rendered possible everything from permanence, extended memory, historical consciousness, and scientific doubt to linguistic reflection, abstract thought, and democracy. Stories such as those told in Cuauhtenco regard literacy practices and skills as consequences, rather than causes, of such processes. The capacity to retrieve and correct documents through memory practices that do not rely on writing is a remarkable situated knowledge, and counters the notion that only inscription lends permanence to facts. It leads us into a different field, in which, as Karin Barber (2007) argues, it is texts, whether oral or written, that make up the textures of memory and history.

On another plane, these stories suggest commonalities among conquered or colonized peoples—commonly called *indigenous* or *autochthonous* in many parts of the world. These peoples have been variously classified through racial, tribal, caste, religious, or linguistic categories, and political rights were often conditioned by the attributed labels. In Mexico, when the postrevolutionary government switched from racial to linguistic categories in the 1930 census, the immediate outcome was to both reduce and fragment the magnitude of the unsolved "indigenous problem" and to justify the educational program launched to "Castilianize" the remaining peoples in order to assimilate them into "Mexican" society.[35] Language itself was regarded as the principal barrier, yet many communities had a long history of dealing with the dominant polity and economy through that barrier, largely by tactically appropriating Spanish literacy.

Studies on literacy from many parts of the globe have brought to the fore similar patterns of how people have faced multiple and diverse scriptural economies.[36] Many suggest that groups engaging dominant scriptural economies that were established through imperial or state governing agencies, including schooling, face similar challenges and adversaries and use similar tactics to navigate the world and to counter dominant powers. States that consolidate power over heterogeneous populations by imposing standard languages and writing systems tend to degrade to an "oral" or "dialect" status the rich varieties of speech that exist in all societies. Terms such as "nonstandard dialects," "oral cultures," or "restricted literacies" produced in the academy have been used to account for poverty and school failure. Yet all humans possess a natural capacity—*la crisma de dios*—to make sense of language and to understand, beyond the simple facts of the written code, the forces and vulnerabilities of the written texts they must confront throughout life. This certainty is emerging as a common ground to contravene the effects of state and imperial classifications that restrict equal human rights.

ACKNOWLEDGMENTS

This chapter takes up and extends work previously published in Rockwell (2007; 2012; and 2014); those articles contain additional evidence for the arguments I set forth. I thank Natalia Mendoza for translations of the 2007 article, parts of which I have edited and used in this chapter. I also must acknowledge the invaluable collaboration of Professor Ramos Rosales Flores, bilingual teacher in Cuauhtenco, who accompanied me on the interviews.

NOTES

1. These include the groundbreaking work of Finnegan (1988), McKitterick (1989), and many others. See the summary of decades of discussion on the "literacy thesis" in Collins and Blot (2003, 9–29).
2. Attempts to revive the use of written Nahuatl have taken place in academic and literary spheres, but little has been reported on oral revitalization in the communities. In Tlaxcala, bilingual elementary and university teachers, including the Tlahtoltequitl group in Cuauhtenco, are undertaking revitalization work and publishing Nahuatl literature. Other initiatives include the Tosepan cooperative in Cuetzalan, the efforts of the Laboratorio de Lengua y Cultura Victor Franco, CIESAS, and the Instituto de Docencia e Investigación Etnológica de Zacatecas, among others.
3. Important studies include, among many, those published by Zavala (1996), Gonzalbo Aizpuru (1990), Lockhart (1992), Boone and Mignolo (1994), Ruiz Medrano (2010), Niño-Murcia and Salomon (2011), Rappaport (1994), and Rappaport and Cummins (2012).
4. Continuity and change in their customs and language in the region have been examined by Reyes García (1993), Nutini and Isaac (1974), Hill and Hill (1986), and Buve (1994), among others.
5. In this article I draw on conversations with Juan Felix Maldonado, Antonino Cuamatzi, José Muñoz, Concepción Flores, Cipriano Galicia, and Salvador Flores, held between 2005 and 2008. All interviews reported here were conducted

together with my colleague, Professor Ramos Rosales Flores, a bilingual teacher of Cuauhtenco, to whom I owe much of the interpretation.

6. According to the 1940 census, around half of the municipality of Contla's 6,500 residents lived in the head town, around 80 percent spoke Nahuatl, and over 25 percent of those over ten years old were literate, although few had gone past third grade. Well over half of the adult men worked for wages, at least part-time, primarily in textile factories or on haciendas, or were craftsmen. In the mountainous subject towns, men also cultivated domestic plots, tended magueys, and made charcoal.

7. Interview with Maldonado, June 9, 2005.

8. *Tiaxca* is the local title given to the elders (sometimes called *principales* in archival documents), who, having served in multiple posts/offices, were recognized as the informal authorities in the village.

9. Interview with Muñoz, June 25, 2005.

10. Of course, compulsory schooling laws had been passed in Mexico since the nineteenth century, and extended to six grades in 1934, but they were enforced only nominally.

11. Interview with Muñoz, June 25, 2005.

12. Ibid.

13. This had been a pedagogical doctrine from previous times (Viñao Frago 1999).

14. Interview with Muñoz, June 25, 2005.

15. Many studies have suggested that it was possible to learn to read aloud with minimal comprehension of the texts being read. On the practice of reading out loud in indigenous schools, see Rockwell (2004) and Acevedo-Rodrigo (2008).

16. Interview with Flores, March 19, 2007.

17. The series of *Simiente* readers were published by the Secretaría de Educación Pública in the 1930s and were models of the new socialist education methods.

18. Interview with Flores, March 19, 2007.

19. Diego Muñoz Camargo initially wrote what is now titled *Historia de Tlaxcala* in 1580; there have been several editions published since then.

20. Interviews with Maldonado, June 9, 2005, and with Flores, May 1, 2008.

21. As early as 1777, a document reports that all 110 Tlaxcalan towns claimed to have "*maestros de razón*" and children enrolled in "*escuelas de primeras letras.*" "Cuentas de los bienes de comunidad de los pueblos de este partido," Tlaxcala, AGN, Propios y arbitrios, 1777–1780, vol. 8, fols. L 70 and 170v. See also the cases of late nineteenth-century Oaxaca and Puebla, with abundant documentation on official schools, in Acevedo-Rodrigo's chapter in this book.

22. Interview with Cuamatzi, June 7, 2005.

23. Interview with Muñoz, June 25, 2005.

24. Interviews with Maldonado, June 9, 2005 and Flores, March 19, 2007.

25. Interview with Maldonado, June 9, 2005. "We all have the chrism of God"; literally, we are all anointed (baptized). However, in Spanish, *crisma* also refers in general to

cabeza, in the sense of brain; a frequent phrase is whether a person has or has not *cabeza* for schoolwork.

26. Interview with Muñoz, June 25, 2005.
27. Accounts in other villages add to the list of different occupations that led to learning on the job, including musicians, postmen, and railroad clerks.
28. Other testimonies confirm the association of literacy with musicians' guilds. However, some musicians learned to read scores well yet claimed they never learned to read texts in Spanish.
29. Interviews with Maldonado June 9, 2005, and Muñoz, June 25, 2005.
30. "Habitantes de San Bernardino Contla que se encuentran en el Distrito de Hidalgo piden testimonios correspondiente de los títulos primordiales de su pueblo," AGN, Buscas y Traslados de Tierras, 1908, vol. 38, file 10, fols. 36–39.
31. Interview with Maldonado, June 9, 2005.
32. Interview with Muñoz, June 25, 2005.
33. Interview with Maldonado, June 9, 2005.
34. Perspectives shared during various conversations held with Flores since 2008.
35. The population in Tlaxcala went from 55 percent "indigenous race" in the 1921 census down to a mere 18 percent of "speakers of Mexicano or Otomí" in the 1930 census.
36. Studies have been conducted on places as diverse as medieval Europe (Justice 1994; McKitterick 1989); early modern Europe (Davis 1975; Fabre 1993); colonial and postcolonial Africa (Finnegan 1988; Blommaert 2008; Barber 2007); Quebec and New Zealand (Curtis 2008; Kell 2011); the Andes (Niño-Murcia and Salomon 2011; Rappaport and Cummins 2012), and of course Mesoamerica (Lockhart 1992; Boone and Mignolo 1994; Kartunnen 1998; Morris 2007; Ruiz Medrano 2010).

REFERENCES

ARCHIVES

Archivo General de la Nación (AGN)

SECONDARY SOURCES

Acevedo-Rodrigo, Ariadna. 2008. "Ritual Literacy: The Simulation of Reading in Rural Indian Mexico, 1870–1930." *Paedagogica Historica* 45 (1): 49–65.

Barber, Karin. 2007. *The Anthropology of Texts, Persons and Publics: Oral and Written Cultures in Africa and Beyond.* Cambridge: Cambridge University Press.

Blommaert, Jan. 2008. *Grassroots Literacy: Writing, Identity and Voice in Central Africa.* London: Taylor and Francis.

Blommaert, Jan, James Collins, and Stef Slembrouck. 2005. "Spaces of Multilingualism." *Language and Communication* 25 (3): 197–216.

Boone, Elizabeth H., and Walter D. Mignolo, eds. 1994. *Writing Without Words: Alternative Literacies in Mesoamerica and the Andes.* Durham, NC: Duke University Press.

Buve, Raymond. 1994. *El movimiento revolucionario en Tlaxcala.* Tlaxcala: Universidad Autónoma de Tlaxcala and Universidad Iberoamericana.

Chartier, Roger. 1995. *Forms and Meanings: Texts, Performances and Audiences from Codex to Computer.* Philadelphia: University of Pennsylvania Press.

Collins, James, and Richard Blot. 2003. *Literacy and Literacies: Texts, Power, and Identity.* Cambridge: Cambridge University Press.

Curtis, Bruce. 2008. "On Distributed Literacy: Textually Mediated Politics in Colonial Canada." *Paedagogica Historica* 44 (1–2): 233–44.

Davis, Natalie Zemon. 1975. "Printing and the People." In *Society and Culture in Early Modern France*, 189–226. Stanford: Stanford University Press.

De Certeau, Michel. 1984. *The Practice of Everyday Life.* Translated by Steven Randall. Berkeley: University of California Press.

Fabre, Daniel. 1993. "Le livre et sa magie." In *Pratiques de la lecture*, edited by Roger Chartier, 231–63. Marseille: Payot et Rivages.

Farr, Marcia. 1994. *"En los dos idiomas*: Literacy Practices Among Chicago Mexicanos." In *Literacy Across Communities*, edited by Barbara Moss, 9–47. Cresskill, NJ: Hampton Press.

Finnegan, Ruth. 1988. *Literacy and Orality: Studies in the Technology of Communication.* Oxford: Blackwell.

Gayol, Víctor. 2008. "Los gestores de los indios. La relación entre las comunidades litigantes y los juzgados de la Real Audiencia a través de la correspondencia de Manuel Salvador Muñoz, indio cacique de Contla, 1788–1803." *Historias* (69): 37–55.

Gonzalbo Aizpuru, Pilar. 1990. *Historia de la educación en la época colonial. El mundo indígena.* Mexico: Colegio de México.

Hill, Jane H., and Kenneth C. Hill. 1986. *Speaking Mexicano: Dynamics of Syncretic Language in Central Mexico.* Tucson: University of Arizona Press.

Justice, Steven. 1994. *Writing and Rebellion: England in 1381.* Berkeley: University of California Press.

Kartunnen, Frances. 1998. "Indigenous Writing as a Vehicle of Postconquest Continuity and Change in Mesoamerica." In *Native Traditions in the Post-conquest World*, edited by Elizabeth H. Boone and Tom Cummins, 421–47. Washington, DC: Dumbarton Oaks Research Library.

Kell, Catherine. 2011. "Inequalities and Crossings: Literacy and the Spaces-In-Between." *International Journal of Educational Development* 31 (6): 606–13.

Kroskrity, Paul, ed. 2000. *Regimes of Language: Ideologies, Polities, and Identities.* Advanced Seminar Series. Santa Fe: School of American Research Press.

Lave, Jean. 2011. *Apprenticeship in Critical Ethnographic Practice.* Chicago: University of Chicago Press.

Lockhart, James. 1992. *The Nahuas After the Conquest: A Social and Cultural History of the Indians of Central Mexico, Sixteenth Through Eighteenth Centuries.* Stanford, CA: Stanford University Press.

McKitterick, Rosamond. 1989. *The Carolingians and the Written Word*. Cambridge: Cambridge University Press.

Morris, Mark. 2007. "Language in Service of the State: The Nahuatl Counterinsurgency Broadsides of 1810." *Hispanic American Historical Review* 87 (3): 433–70.

Niño-Murcia, Mercedes, and Frank Salomon. 2011. *The Lettered Mountain: A Peruvian Village's Way with Writing*. Durham, NC: Duke University Press.

Nutini, Hugo, and Barry Isaac. 1974. *Los pueblos de habla náhuatl de la región de Tlaxcala y Puebla*. Mexico: Instituto Nacional Indigenista.

Rappaport, Joanne. 1994. *Cumbe Reborn: An Ethnography of History*. Chicago: University of Chicago Press.

Rappaport, Joanne, and Tom Cummins. 2012. *Beyond the Lettered City: Indigenous Literacies in the Andes*. Durham, NC: Duke University Press.

Reyes García, Luis. 1993. *La escritura pictográfica en Tlaxcala*. Tlaxcala: Universidad Autónoma de Tlaxcala and Centro de Investigación y Estudios Superiores en Antropología Social (CIESAS).

Rockwell, Elsie. 2004. "Learning for Life or Learning from Books: Reading Practices in Mexican Rural Schools (1900 to 1935)." *Paedagogica Historica* 38 (1): 113–35.

———. 2007. "Relaciones con la cultura escrita en una comunidad nahua a principios del siglo XX: temas recurrentes en los relatos orales." In *Senderos de Ilusión. Lecturas populares en Europa y América Latina (del siglo XVI a nuestros días)*, edited by Antonio Gómez Castillo and V. Sierra Blas, 259–78. Gijón, Spain: Editorial Trea.

———. 2012. "Cultura escrita, historias locales y otra lógica ciudadana: relatos de los vecinos mayores de Cuauhtenco, Tlaxcala." In *Educación indígena, ciudadanía y Estado en México: Siglo XX*, edited by Marco A. Calderón and Elizabeth M. Buenabad, 93–118. Mexico: Benemérita Universidad Autónoma de Puebla and Colegio de Michoacán.

———. 2014. "Microhistorias de larga duración que enmarcan la 'Revolución Mexicana': La lucha de Juan de la Rosa y sus secuelas." In *México a la luz de sus revoluciones*. Vol 2, *Siglo XIX*, edited by Laura Rojas and Susan Deeds, 145–74. Mexico: Colegio de México.

Ruiz Medrano, Ethelia. 2010. *Mexico's Indigenous Communities: Their Lands and Histories, 1500–2010*. Boulder: University of Colorado Press.

Rus, Jan. 1994. "La comunidad revolucionaria institucional: La subversión del gobierno indígena en los Altos de Chiapas, 1936–1968." In *Chiapas: Los rumbos de otra historia*, edited by Juan Pedro Viqueira and Mario Humberto Ruz, 251–77. Mexico: Universidad Nacional Autónoma de México and CIESAS.

Viñao Frago, A. 1999. *Leer y escribir. Historia de dos prácticas culturales*. Naucalpan de Juárez, Mexico: Fundación Educación, Voces y Vuelos.

Zavala, Silvio Arturo. 1996. *Poder y lenguaje desde el siglo XVI*. Mexico: Colegio de México.

CHAPTER 6

COMMUNAL AND INDIGENOUS LANDHOLDING IN CONTEMPORARY YUCATÁN

Tracing the Changing Property Relations in the
Postrevolutionary Ejido

GABRIELA TORRES-MAZUERA

C OMMUNAL PROPERTY regimes are frequently associated with indigenous groups in contemporary Mexico and have been perceived as being
their dominant form of land tenure throughout the four centuries of
national history. Unsurprisingly, it is rarely highlighted how property relations
have altered over time within a changing legal framework that recognizes some
kind of communal landholding among indigenous people. In the same vein, it
is occasionally pointed out that the communal aspect has not always entailed
freedom of access, collective agrarian productive practices, or the inclusion of
all members of the community (or *pueblo*).

Current ideas of communal land tenure in Mexico comprise different layers
of meaning that I would like to consider: the common(s) as opposed to private property and as property ascribed to the majority. In the latter case, the
majority refers to the "common people," which, at some moment of Mexican
history, became equivalent to the Indian pueblo (*pueblo de indios*).[1] From the
perspective of property relations, the notion of communal landholding has dia-
metrically different connotations. During the nineteenth and early twentieth
centuries, this form of land tenure was seen as a "primitive" phase and one of
the major obstacles to progress, and was thus viewed in a negative light. Emilio
Rabasa, a distinguished intellectual and liberal politician, wrote in 1920 that "the
communal system . . . is the best for keeping the Indian in the vegetative life,

without waking in him the feeling of individuality . . . without personal rights or interests, under the pressure of the community, bound by caste and opposed to the civilized man" (cited in Mendieta y Nuñez 1975, 237). Nevertheless, this negative connotation turned into a more positive one with the expansion of the 1920s' postrevolutionary ejidos. Following the creation of collective ejidos under Lázaro Cárdenas's government in the 1930s, this form of communal property became a model of efficient and modern agricultural production that would subsequently be compared with the Soviet kolkhoz.[2] Finally, toward the end of the 1980s, a new theoretical model came to underpin the virtues of communal property, or the so-called commons, in Mexico, inextricably linking it to the ejido and the *comunidad*—both of which have been identified as efficient institutions in environmental conservation, particularly sustainable forest management.

The ejido and *comunidad* are two forms of landholding that, until 1992, have been distinguished from private property by their inalienability.[3] They represented the notion of communal continuity in two senses: as both a form of communal land tenure and a historical collective subject. Both exhibit a semantic duality similar to the notion of the commons (*el común*): not only as forms of landholding but also as a group of people in legal possession of collectively owned land or assets. This duality has resulted in many misunderstandings among the agrarian bureaucracy, scholars, and even peasants and ejido inhabitants, who defend their conflicting interpretations regarding who is the ultimate owner of ejidos, what type of property it is, and who can be considered to be part of the ejido or *comunidad*.

On the basis of fieldwork conducted between 2010 and 2013 in southern Yucatán, I propose to explore the property relations within four ejidos in order to question two basic ideas about communal landholding and the Mexican indigenous population that are prevalent in anthropological literature.[4] First, it has been argued that the postrevolutionary ejidos and *comunidades* are continuations of a certain type of colonial and/or pre-Hispanic communal landholding. This is a case more evident for the *comunidad*, which is frequently assumed to be "the form originally put forward as the means of recognizing the rights of indigenous groups to their lands . . . the characteristics attributed by the Agrarian Law to this form of tenure [the *comunidad*] *is that closest to the 'usages and customs' of indigenous groups*" (de Gortari 1997, 101; my emphasis).

Second, I will question the persistent association of indigenous usages and customs with world views (*cosmovisiones*) that are believed to determine property relations. Thus, in Yucatán, specialists subscribe to the idea that "ejido land belongs to everyone or, rather, to no one, given that appropriation of land falls outside the Maya worldview" (Quintal et al. 2003, 337).

This chapter is divided into three sections. I begin with a general description of the way in which the agricultural land in Yucatán was allocated during the twentieth-century agrarian reform, which explains the preponderance of ejidos throughout the region. Next, I show how postrevolutionary ejidos brought change and rupture in property relations among Maya-speaking peasants who were granted such lands. To this end, I describe the agrarian history of Tzucacab ejido to illustrate the changes wrought by legislation and the agricultural policy of the 1970s on the local Mayan norms ruling land access in southern Yucatán. The central aim of this section is to analyze the discrepancies between local norms and agrarian legislation as a consequence not so much of an incompatibility between an indigenous collectivist world view and a liberal individualist legislation but rather of the different dynamics of production that often come into conflict due to certain restrictions imposed by the ejido system. Finally, I describe the property practices developed in the southern Yucatán ejidos to explain what is common or collective about contemporary ejidos.

This work is part of a broader research project conducted in southern Yucatán, where 80 percent of the population speak the Maya Yucateco language but do not always identify themselves as Mayas, whereas government officials inexorably categorize them as Indians.[5] This apparent contradiction needs further explanation. Since the nineteenth century, most rural peasants in the Yucatán Peninsula who speak the Maya Yucateco language do not identify themselves as either Mayas, Indians, or indigenous people, but mainly as mestizos. A bloody regional war between 1847 and 1901, known locally as the Caste War, catalyzed the formation of mestizo as a new collective identity. To date, mestizos in Yucatán are Maya speakers who not only wear traditional dress and have Maya surnames but also have assimilated Hispanic and, more recently, Mexican cultural traits.[6] In the southern region of Yucatán, where the fieldwork was undertaken, people usually identify themselves as mestizos, but depending on whom they are interacting with, they may also use other identity categories. For instance, it was evident that when interacting with officials from the National Commission for the Development of Indigenous Peoples, many Maya-speaking peasants identified themselves as indigenous to gain access to government programs. Furthermore, people from the ejidos would also identify themselves by referring to their town of origin when interacting with people from different villages. Since the 1990s, some people have begun to identify themselves as Mayas in certain situations, particularly local intellectuals from the larger ejidos who wish to make clear reference to the wider movement (mainly in Latin America) vindicating indigenous culture. In this case, *Maya* is an identity mobilized by those who are well connected, informed, and politicized. In contrast, peasants from the ejidos who mainly speak the Maya language identify themselves as *mayeros*, denoting their lack of proficiency in Spanish and devaluing themselves in this context. Finally, it is important to point out that in rural areas, ejidatario is one of the main social identities as well as a social status.

LAND REFORM IN YUCATÁN: THE PREFERENCE FOR EJIDOS

Unlike Oaxaca, Guerrero, Chiapas, and other Mexican states with a high percentage of people identified as indigenous, only two (agrarian) *comunidades* in Yucatán were recognized as such throughout the twentieth century—an insignificant number compared to the 786 ejidos granted across the state. What factors determined the pattern of granting ejido land or the restitution and recognition of (agrarian) *comunidades* in Yucatán? Why are there not more *comunidades* in Yucatán, considering its villages date back to the colonial era, its population has been officially classified as indigenous, and its property relations are based on slash-and-burn cultivation? To answer these questions, I will refer to the case of Tzucacab, one of the four ejidos investigated between 2010 and 2013.

Anthropological and historical research has shown that land reform in Mexico (1915–1992) rarely involved the restitution of communal lands that had belonged to Indian pueblos during Spanish colonial rule. This finding contradicts the aforementioned belief that the *comunidad* would prevail as a form of land tenure in those regions where the indigenous population had historically settled. In contrast, our later discussion of the Tzucacab ejido reveals how the restitution of *comunidades* and granting of ejidos responded to different, independent factors in Yucatán.

In 1928, the village of Tzucacab officially received a land grant after some of its inhabitants applied for the restitution of the area locally known as Xulac, which they claimed to have "been working since time immemorial."[7] However, the legal owner, Miguel Araujo, contended that he had bought the land in 1901 at the end of the Caste War, during which it had been abandoned by its owners and subsequently cultivated by Tzucacab peasants.[8] Although the corresponding presidential decision rejected without any explanation the restitution of land, the 227 applicants from Tzucacab were granted 5,653.7 acres of unfarmed land to be taken from three neighboring properties.[9]

There are several possible reasons that may elucidate the agrarian bureaucracy rejection of the application for restitution of the Xulac land, which also may suggest why other pueblos around Yucatán were similarly impeded. First, there were the administrative or procedural obstacles: land restitution in Yucatán, and throughout Mexico, was complicated, as many pueblos either lacked the documentation proving legal title to what they considered were their communal lands or the documentation tended to be imprecise with regard to the land boundaries, which in many cases clashed with the claims of other pueblos. The difficulties increase when we consider that, until 1942, groups applying for restitution had to provide documentary proof not only of their immemorial land ownership but also that their loss had occurred after the so-called Lerdo Law was enacted on June 25, 1856 (Baitenmann 2011, 27).[10] While the inhabitants of Tzucacab failed to prove immemorial land ownership, they were granted an ejido.

In addition, we can hypothesize that Tzucacab inhabitants—and many other residents of Yucatán pueblos during the first three decades of land distribution—opted to apply for a land grant because the result was usually quicker and assured beforehand, since they only had to identify the land affected.[11] A further advantage of ejido grants was that the extent of the land was determined according to the needs of the applicants—in terms of the number of landless farmers and the quality of the land involved—and could even extend beyond the area for which proof of prior possession existed.

A complementary hypothesis to explain the general preference for ejido grants in Yucatán is that the process of restitution was complicated by the expansion of haciendas in the eighteenth century, followed by the social and territorial fragmentation of local populations during the Caste War of 1847. The war resulted in considerable population displacement, especially in certain parts of the peninsula, along with political divisions within communities, which later had a variety of effects on the land grant process during the early decades of the twentieth century (Rugeley 2009; Wells and Joseph 1996). Moreover, the Yucatán environment itself had precluded the development of communal land tenure during the colonial and independent periods; the better fertile lands were located in the monte (forestland) of the distant, untitled *terrenos baldíos* (wastelands) rather than on the surrounding lands legally owned by extended families and pueblos. Once the liberal government enacted the Lerdo Law, officials found that most peasants were occupying *terrenos baldíos* located far from the ejido villages, where they cultivated milpas (corn fields). Such circumstances made the task of locating the boundaries between communal and public lands almost impossible; furthermore, it was of no interest to peasant residents who, until then, had enjoyed secure access to the untitled forestland (Evans 2012; Ortiz Yam 2013).[12]

Finally, from the time of Governor Salvador Alvarado's administration (1915–1917), the discourse behind land reform in Yucatán was anticommunal and so unlikely to favor the restitution of former communal lands to pueblos. Similar to Venustiano Carranza and Álvaro Obregón, Alvarado regarded small private landholdings as key to rural economic development and ejidos as a necessary phase in the transition toward it, due to the cultural backwardness (in the view of these politicians) of the country's indigenous groups.[13] Similar to some owners of Yucatán haciendas at that time, Alvarado also associated lands held in common by pueblos as a primitive and unproductive form of land tenure. A case in point involves an application for restitution by the village of Hunucmá, described by Eiss (2010). The historic agrarian struggle of Hunucmá residents began in the nineteenth century, following the appropriation of communal forestlands by neighboring haciendas; this had developed into a demand for ejido grants by the 1920s, despite the protests of a large group of peasants who sought the restitution, and recognition, of what had once been Hunucmá's communal lands.[14] In this regard, it is interesting that the land struggle in Yucatán was never framed in terms of ethnic or indigenous claims, even during the administration of Governor Felipe Carrillo Puerto (1922–1924), who fostered a political discourse vindicating Mayan culture based on the legacy of the pre-Columbian Mayan civilization. From a broader perspective, land reform and ejido granting in Mexico can be considered part of an ambitious social and cultural revolution that implied indigenous population *mestizaje*. In this sense, before the 1992 legal reform, the agrarian legislation never explicitly mentioned the ethnicity of the grant recipients. It only made reference to the administrative organization of groups that could be considered as suitable to receive land (i.e., pueblos, rancherias, *congregaciones*, *tribus*) and to the social class of future ejidatarios: peasants.

It is therefore evident that, in many cases, the potential reasons for the preference for ejido grants were independent from the type of property relations involved, the way in which the land was exploited, or the ethnic background of the applicants. However, it did give rise to a distinction—a substantial one nowadays—between granted land and restituted, or recognized, land.[15] Such distinction, as I will show in the next section, went unnoticed by the inhabitants of southern Yucatán, as they were able to maintain property relations governed by customary norms for a long time, despite their incompatibility with those established by the agrarian legislation.

COMMUNAL LAND IN THE EJIDOS OF YUCATÁN: FROM THE INCLUSIVENESS OF THE MILPA TO THE EXCLUSIVENESS OF THE EJIDO

The communal dimension of postrevolutionary ejidos involved, in principle, not so much a method of collective land use but rather a form of ownership attributed to a collective member: the pueblo (Mendieta y Nuñez 1975, 237).[16] The presidential edicts in southern Yucatán regarding the creation of ejidos underlined their communal status in two ways: "for the purposes of protecting and defending the total extent of the land a communal title is granted," and, in addition, the ejido authorities "must organize communal exploitation of the granted land."[17] However, we will see that the significance of such edicts was negligible in terms of how Maya-speaking peasants who became ejidatarios organized subsequent access to ejido lands.

Initially, the postrevolutionary ejido was an organizational approach unknown to the Maya-speaking peasants and *milperos* (literally, corn growers) of southern Yucatán, for whom the land available for milpas at the beginning of the twentieth century was boundless.[18] It also implied a new concept of owner-ship that linked the social function of land to a hitherto-unheard-of approach to political community, which excluded any peasant or pueblo resident without legal recognition as an ejidatario. Before ejido grants, Maya-speaking *milperos* recognized open access to forestland—mainly federal property—for any peasant willing to grow milpa. According to the testimony of older ejidatarios from Maní, Tzucacab, and Huntochac, men would work individually, helped by their sons, the family grounds (*rumbos familiares*) situated either within the ejidos or on neighboring properties. Family grounds were areas appropriated by a single extended family (related through the paternal line) to grow milpa by means of land rotation and slash-and-burn clearance. A family's right to a given area was handed down from one generation to another but forfeited if it ceased to be cultivated (Duch 1995, 293; Flores 1997; Hernández Xolocotzi 1996; Quintal et al. 2003; Terán and Rasmussen 2009).

In Tzucacab, *milperos* chose milpas within the ejido boundaries and, until the end of the 1960s, there were no significant conflicts over access, since the ejido was large (5,653.7 acres) and then extended in 1956 by a further 9,884.2 acres. Until the 1970s, boundaries within the Tzucacab ejido between areas farmed under the slash-and-burn system were changeable and established by boundary paths and the presence of other milpas. The custom was that a *milpero* could farm anywhere that did not interfere with others, and that "once you've created your milpa, you had the right to continue acquiring surrounding land to make headway."[19] Thus, the extent of a milpa depended on the number of male family members in an ejidatario household.

During the initial years of the ejido, the status of the ejidatarios counted for little: although agrarian legislation had established a fixed number of ejidatarios with land rights, in practice, those who were not ejidatarios were also able to access the land. However, various factors led to conflicts and land disputes between groups of ejidatario and non-ejidatario peasants in Tzucacab.

A great transformation in agriculture production and property relations was initiated in southern Yucatán by the 1975 National Deforestation Plan, which aimed to clear the plains to enable the introduction of machinery for cultivating hybrid corn and irrigation channels for sustaining citrus trees and livestock. Between 1975 and 1985 in the so-called Southern Cone region, forty-two thousand acres were cleared (Rosales 1991). The clearance of the highland portions of ejidos brought about the first break with the milpa system, its "usages and customs" establishing that no *milpero* could clear an area larger than he, with his sons and relatives, could sow by hand (Villa Rojas 1978, 315).

These clearances also transformed the rules of the slash-and-burn system, introducing the potential for permanent possession of a "clean" area (a plot of land). Furthermore, agricultural production was modernized, and the ejidatarios became a powerful group within the village by forming rural production partnerships (RPPs). Such transformations were not the same in all ejidos, however; although following the same economic dynamic, each case demonstrates specific appropriation processes.

For instance, the 15,537.9-acre Tzucacab ejido comprised a variety of peasant groups farming their lands in an autonomous and uncoordinated way. The clearances and subsequent introduction of Banrural bank credits, however, triggered conflicts over boundaries between family grounds and fostered a new idea of land appropriation. Fidencio Canul, seventy-five-year-old ejidatario, recounts that during the 1970s, "There was a problem with the fellows in this village, because they were all there [referring to the place where he and his relatives farmed the milpa], and each one looking out for himself and knocking things down."[20] According to Fidencio's brother, David, "We started parceling . . . for each member, ejidatario, the forty-eight acres he was due [this area makes reference to Tzucacab land-granting presidential edict]" to resolve the boundary conflicts. He also recalled that, in 1975, a lawyer from the National Indigenous Institute (INI) helped with the process of "separating off the part that belonged to us."[21] Subsequently, a rural production partnership was formed and a Banrural credit applied for, which led to the marking out of a 720-acre area corresponding to the individual forty-eight acres granted to the fifteen ejidatarios of the RPP under the Tzucacab presidential edict. Several ejidatarios stated that registering their RPPs at the National Agrarian Registry in Mérida allowed them to define and legalize the land boundaries of their parcels.[22] In contrast, Arsenio Zapata reveals how his family and other ejidatarios did not join the partnerships, as their parents and grandparents believed to do so would be to "sell out to the government."They decided, therefore, to persevere with the traditional milpa system on lands left unoccupied by the RPPs. However, once there were no longer any "free lands," Arsenio's family decided to form the New Agrarian Reform group to legalize their possession of the offcuts (unused land) left by the existing RPPs.[23]

Thus RPPs became a means to confer legitimacy on the permanent appropriation of communal lands in the ejido by groups frequently comprising members of the same family, superseding other forms of productive organization and property relations such as the milpa and open access. It was at this point in Tzucacab that the ejidatarios gained status and exclusive access to the ejido land. In Tzucacab and the surrounding ejidos, enclosure of communal land thus gained social legitimacy, even among the *milperos* who once defended open access to the ejido.

Since the 1980s, conflicting principles regulating access to the forestlands have coexisted in southern Yucatán's ejidos. The milpa system traditionally entails open access and is used by both ejidatarios and non-ejidatarios to justify their actions and behaviors, but this norm coexists with that of maximizing individual profit, which justifies the individual appropriation of ejido lands.

This meant that inheriting ejido communal land became legitimate even though illegal, at least until the legal parceling of such land in 1998.

WHAT IS COMMUNAL OR COLLECTIVE IN THE EJIDO LANDS OF TWENTY-FIRST-CENTURY SOUTHERN YUCATÁN?

When I arrived in Yucatán in 2010 to undertake ethnographic research into the changes in ejido property relations caused by the 1992 reform of article 27 and the Program for the Certification of Ejido Land Rights and Titling of Urban House Plots (PROCEDE), I encountered some consensus among local anthropologists about the results. PROCEDE was designed to implement the "new" Agrarian Law of 1992, with the objectives, driven by a neoliberal agenda, of legalizing the alienation of ejido land, which, in order to be accomplished, required precise delimitation and partitioning into plots of ejido land. In Yucatán, its implementation between 1993 and 2006 was distinctive because the majority of ejidatarios decided not to divide their ejido lands. Their rejection of legal partitioning was interpreted by some scholars as indigenous resistance to the onslaught of neoliberal reforms; or, specifically, it was understood as the Mayas' defense of both communal ownership of the milpas and the community as a form of social organization.[24] Against this background, I selected a group of ejidos in southern Yucatán—one of the most "traditional" areas in the state according to both state officials and anthropologists—as the place to begin my fieldwork. One of the questions that guided my initial inquiries was, "What is communal or collective in twenty-first-century ejidos in Yucatán?"

On the four ejidos studied, *communal use* no longer meant open access to ejido lands for all inhabitants, because for most, communal ejido lands were parceled de facto. For example, since the introduction of orange trees to the Maní ejido in the 1970s, a number of areas designated as communal land by the agrarian law have been divided and assigned to those farmers, not necessarily ejidatarios, owning plots within an irrigated unit of land. These citrus orchards are for permanent individual use, thus signaling the enclosure of communal ejido land that has been capitalized through work. Another example of permanent land appropriation was found in the livestock-raising ejidos, such as Tzucacab and Huntochac, where the partitioning of communal lands, even to the point of fencing off plots, had been a frequent practice among ejidatarios for over three decades. Moreover, both legal restrictions and local norms imposed conditions on access and excluded anyone not belonging to what was considered to be the community, albeit this was inconsistent with the definition of who actually qualified as a member. For instance, on the Maní ejido, the *milperos* living in the village had right to access communal ejido lands: non-ejidatarios could cultivate a milpa in the ejido. Nevertheless, contrary to the law, local customs did exclude women, even those registered as ejidatarias.

Such a situation begs the question, Why was there opposition to the legal partitioning of communal lands during the PROCEDE program? According to agrarian visitors from the Agrarian Attorney (*Procuraduría agraria*), one factor that may explain this phenomenon is the control that certain local bosses in some ejido communities exerted over large areas of communal ejido lands.[25] One such case is on the 38,106.121-acre Chocholá ejido, where 565 ejidatarios—80.9 percent of whom are Maya speakers—opposed legal partitioning due in part to pressure from a group of livestock ejidatarios supported by the ejido commissioner at the time. These livestock ejidatarios, who owned four ranches covering an area of 5,436.3 acres, did not welcome legal partitioning that would have redistributed the ejido lands more equably among all the ejidatarios. However, opposition was also related to the defense of open access to ejido land by some groups of ejidatarios who argued to continue the sharing out of lands preserved, up to that point, for "the sons of the community"—referring to the sons of those ejidatarios who worked the communal ejido lands. This strategy had little effect on the way in which Chocholá—or most ejidos in fact—worked with PROCEDE to define who exactly belonged to the said community, as we shall see.

Many scholars have focused on the decisions about communal lands made through the PROCEDE program by ejido assemblies, arguing that the program threatens the "traditional life" of "indigenous peoples," assuming it would spell the end of communal land on ejidos—the locus of ejido community life. Few scholars have paid any attention to the decisions made by ejido assemblies that, in most cases, permitted the closure of the ejido community. In this respect, the events in Yucatán were no different from those across the rest of the country.

Until 1992, the only social category legally recognized by the state, as far as the possession of ejido land was concerned, was that of ejidatario; only they held the right to farm ejido land, participate in the ejido assembly, and make decisions on ejido affairs. The number of ejidatarios per ejido was fixed by presidential edict, based on the number of applicants and the amount of land necessary for the subsistence of a peasant family using certain production technologies.[26] Becoming an ejidatario thus necessitated not only technological change but also either the allocation of a larger portion of the ejido or acquisition of vacant plots, which arose regularly, for agricultural production. There were a number of different reasons for deregistering ejidatarios, including death, emigration, or ceasing to work the land themselves; ultimately, these actions came down to having abandoned the personal cultivation of the units granted for more than two consecutive years.[27] In addition to these legally recognized reasons, there were other nonlegal but locally accepted ones: the sale of plots or aggressive behavior might lead to expulsion from the ejido. Thus it was possible to withdraw membership from certain people to register others interested in becoming new ejidatarios. In general, those principally interested were individuals who had already spent some time working the ejido lands, such as *parceleros*, *posesionarios*, or *comuneros*, as authorized by the ejido assembly and commission.

The procedures relating to the revocation of rights and registration of new ejidatarios were periodically legalized by the government, which performed usufructuary investigations to update the register of ejidatarios and issue agrarian certificates to the newly registered ones (Nuijten 2003). The Agrarian Law of 1992 came to transform the practice of inclusion/exclusion: on the one hand, it brought an end to the usufructuary investigations, but on the other, it created a new legal entity of *posesionario* for those in possession of land who, up to that point, had no agrarian status. More importantly, the law granted the ejido assembly the authority to decide whether to accept new ejido members— ejidatarios, *posesionarios*, or *avecindados*—and so the ability to expand the ejido community.[28] It is interesting that despite these legal changes, some of the more important aspects were ignored at a local level.

Reviewing the number of ejidatarios in southern Yucatán before and after PROCEDE, we can see a reduction in the number per municipality (see table 6.1), most notably in Ticul, Teabo, Peto, and Tekax. Despite demographic growth in most ejidos, the total number of agricultural workers—ejidatarios, *posesionarios*, and *avecindados*—in these four municipalities also declined, which is also surprising in the light of the many vacancies compared with the number of ejidatarios established by every land grant. This also reveals the extent of transformation in the ejidos: the meaning of *the commons* changing from all inhabitants of the pueblo to only those who were ejidatarios.

TABLE 6.1. Number of Ejidatarios and Agricultural Workers Before and After PROCEDE by Municipality in Southern Yucatán

MUNICIPALITY	GRANTS & EXTENSIONS	PROCEDE			
	EJIDATARIOS	EJIDATARIOS	POSESIONARIOS	AVECINDADOS	TOTAL
Maní	652	592	266	0	858
Oxkutzcab	1,305	1,263	6	237	1,506
Tahdziu	421	420	0	0	420
Tzucacab	1,652	1,612	65	317	1,994
Akil	525	525	0	0	525
Chacsinkín	412	480	0	0	480
Dzan	646	646	0	0	646
Mama	276	283	0	0	283
Ticul	1,791	1,371	320	0	1,691
Tixmehuac	643	748	0	90	838
Teabo	758	394	0	17	411
Peto	3,107	2,756	293	15	3,064
Tekax	5,216	4,416	187	139	4,742[29]

On those ejidos that rejected PROCEDE's parceling of communal lands, all registered ejidatarios were issued with individual certificates that regulated their access to those lands and, for the first time, specified their percentage—calculated by dividing the total ejido area by the number of ejidatarios. Although not the intention, this led to the development of an individualist concept of communal ejido lands in southern Yucatán. In Tahdziu, where the ejido assembly voted to reject the PROCEDE parceling in 1998, the ejidatarios began to calculate the acreage to which they were entitled based on the percentage specified on their certificates, which many of those interviewed assumed to be equal to 33.3 acres. Consequently, the area that any ejidatario may work on the ejido has been limited to this size area and the precise location of a plot must be determined, especially in more recent years when some ejidatarios have received financial aid to sink a well.[30] This idea clearly confirms the increasingly prevalent practice of commodification and privatization of ejido land in the region. Individual property titles have resulted in a new concept of communal ejido land as divided or partitioned space allocated equally and exclusively to each ejidatario, and has made their status essential in gaining access to land. Therefore, thirteen years after the PROCEDE program, a group of Tahdziu ejidatarios is proposing the complete legal parceling of the ejido, arguing the need to define clearer and more circumscribed membership and access to ejido land.

In Yucatán, 231 ejidos decided to partition over 50 percent of their communal lands through PROCEDE. Most of these ejidos shared a common history of economic partitioning since the 1970s; however, this new partitioning included some elements unforeseen by agrarian officials and to some extent is contrary to the individualization embedded in the PROCEDE program. Referring back to Tzucacab, where the ejidatarios decided to abandon communal land and partition the entire ejido, a total of 394 plots, of which 368 were individual and 26 collective, were created. The area covered ranged from 2.17 to 91.4 acres per plot, although many averaged between 44 and 48 acres, while there were also plots between 2.4 and 12.3 acres never allocated to anyone. External observers do question the reasoning behind the irregular size and distribution of the plots in Tzucacab after PROCEDE.

As mentioned previously, the Tzucacab ejido was divided and allocated to ejidatarios even before the advent of PROCEDE in 1998. Moreover, there were a variety of property relations, determined by different criteria of use, control, and transfer of land, within the same ejido. On the one hand, there were the remains of the RPPs, formally dissolved in the 1990s, in terms of the ex-partners continuing to cultivate portions of the ejido's best land—such as cropland, pastures, or fenced-off land—and, in some cases, maintaining a degree of collective organization for production. On the other hand, some lands continued to be regarded as for communal use by the ejido—family grounds permanently allocated to certain ejidatarios and their families, and areas of variable quality (susceptible to flooding or forestland) freely accessible to ejido inhabitants. The latter was used by both ejidatarios and other members of the Tzucacab community for milpas, gathering wood, beekeeping, and hunting.

An initial solution to dividing such diverse lands among all members of the community was to divide each ejidatario's plot previously allocated to a partnership into productive zones, distinguishing between hilly scrub and cultivated pasture. Benito Chí, a Tzucacab ejidatario, explained that he therefore received three land certificates: one for 7.4 acres of arable land, another for an orchard of 37 acres, and a third for 32 acres of forestland.[31] However, this approach proved inadequate, since many ejidatarios feared that individual parcels placed them at a disadvantage due to variations in land and crop quality and proximity to a well or road. An ejidatario from the Miguel Alemán rural partnership pointed out that they decided to divide the arable areas according to the growth of the corn. First, lots were drawn for 7.4 acres each of areas with large corn plants; next, they divided those areas with medium plants into 37 acres each; and finally, they shared out the land with the smallest plants into less than an acre each. In some cases, though, an ejidatario ended up with six small plots, which proved a daunting task for those surveyors marking out the boundaries and issuing the corresponding land certificates. In addition, this was actually contrary to the objectives of the 1992 reform to article 27 and the PROCEDE program to prevent the creation of small holdings. The officials in charge of the program therefore proposed an alternative solution, issuing certificates for collective parcels and allowing ejidatarios as co-owners to maintain their complex land allocations. As such, the Lázaro Cárdenas Pozo 3 partnership retained the greater part of its land as a collective parcel for twenty-three ejidatarios, who agreed to an annual draw to allocate the different sections. Arrangements varied within each collective parcel according to the needs of its members, however; one case involved dividing one part on an individual basis and leaving the rest for communal use by all the co-owners; others were entirely divided among the individual co-owners, such as the 61-acre collective parcel in an irrigation unit shared out as 6.1-acre individual plots among the ten co-owners; while another approach created extremely small plots (less than 3.7 acres) shared among more than twenty co-owners. The aim of all these arrangements was to maintain access to a well for all the former partners of the dissolved partnerships. In Tzucacab, there also remained a number of small "vacant" plots—belonging to the ejido but unallocated to any one ejidatario—which were accessible to all inhabitants of the ejido for gathering wood, except that few people knew their precise locations, which were often hard to reach anyway.

Nevertheless, the collective parcel was an alternative to which the Yucatán ejidatarios resorted to escape complete individualized partitioning of the ejido.

Although more exclusive, being only accessible to co-owners, the collective parcel did allow flexible access to and use of existing land in southern Yucatán to continue in a way similar to that offered by communal ejido lands before partitioning.

FINAL CONSIDERATIONS

The possession of communal land in Mexico was associated with indigenous communities and became, at a certain time, an indicator of ethnic identity, while its legal framework was associated with a particular type of ownership. These associations have been so compelling that those specialists attempting to define the agrarian community—such as Warman (1985), de Gortari (1997), or Robles (2000)—have been obliged to begin by correcting this mistaken connection. Underlying this assumption is a belief that the ejido and community are a continuation of the colonial or even pre-Hispanic forms of communal tenure. With this perspective in mind, a large number of Mexican anthropologists and historians have equated ejidos with communities in an attempt to trace the historic continuity of the communal, thereby making the idea fundamental. By contrast, in this chapter I have attempted to explore the conformation and transformation of certain property relations in a region classified as indigenous, to which end I have sought to emphasize the rupture in property relations brought about by the ejido. As I have shown, based on the agrarian history of Tzucacab, the postrevolutionary ejido as a form of land tenure was a tool for social change that involved the substantial, long-term reconfiguration of local property relations. In addition, ethnographic observation in southern Yucatán also revealed distinct processes in ejido privatization involving a wide variety of social actors: *milperos*, livestock farmers, and fruit growers. These processes were both beyond the agrarian law and within its framework, but by the end of 1990 were formalized and fixed in individual or group privatizations of ejido plots by the PROCEDE program. Moreover, we should note the persistence of a certain viewpoint related to communal land tenure, whereby some ejidos have parceled all their lands; collective parcels are a creative response by Maya-speaking peasants that allows them to maintain flexibility and inclusiveness within a system (the ejido plot) aiming to regulate and individualize property relations.

NOTES

1. This dual meaning is more evident in Spanish, where the word *común* refers both to the people and to a form of property.

2. For a detailed description about the ideas of property and community behind postrevolutionary ejidos in Mexico, and the political motives that have shaped agrarian legislation, see Kourí (2015).

3. Agrarian law distinguishes between grants and restitution. Ejidos are lands never previously owned by pueblos that have been granted to them, while *comunidades* are some of the lands previously owned during the nineteenth century by *pueblos de indios* that are therefore restituted.

4. The fieldwork comprised both open-ended interviews about and ethnographic observations of ejido land access, transfer, and ownership, and involved local authorities, agrarian bureaucracy officers, ejidatarios, and inhabitants from Tzucacab, Huntochac, Maní, and Tahdziu. During my visits to the ejidos, I was also able to inquire about changes in agriculture and the implementation of the Program for the Certification of Ejido Land Rights and the Titling of Urban House Plots (PROCEDE) during the 1990s and 2000s. In addition to the fieldwork, I conducted interviews and participant observation at the National Agrarian Registry (RAN) and Agrarian Court—both located in Mérida, the state capital of Yucatán. Several lawyers and two magistrates kindly provided information and shared their perceptions about the conflicting situations related to ejido land transfers and the outcomes of the land reform in the Yucatán Peninsula.

5. The Maya Yucateco language is only one of the Mayan languages spoken in Mexico and Central America.

6. For a detailed account of the formation of the modern identity in the Yucatán Peninsula, see Gabbert (2001) and Quintal (2005).

7. Registro Agrario Nacional (RAN), Mérida, Tzucacab Carpeta Básica, file no. 23–25/10.

8. The Caste War (1847–1901) had broken out in the eastern part of the Yucatán Peninsula, where Maya-speaking peasants had enjoyed greater freedom from Spanish domination. It began as a political revolution involving both native village inhabitants and urban and rural dwellers of Spanish origin, but over time it was redefined as an ethnic conflict. For a detailed account of this event, see Rugeley (2009).

9. RAN, Mérida, Tzucacab Carpeta Básica, file no. 23–25/10.

10. The Law of Disentailment of Rural and Urban Properties of Civil and Religious Corporations of Mexico, sponsored by President Ignacio Comonfort and known as the Lerdo Law, decreed the end of corporate ownership and, in the case of communal land in Indian communities, its division and sale as private property.

11. The processes of restitution and land grants started at the same time, so that despite having insufficient proof for land restitution, landless applicants might still be granted ejidos.

12. I will return to this issue in the next section, where I discuss Maya peasants' appropriation of postrevolutionary ejidos.

13. It was only after the legal reform of agrarian law (Código Agrario) in 1934 that ejido land tenure became a permanent form of property (Azuela 2009, 91).

14. Nugent and Alonso (1994) discuss a similar case in the north of the country, where the inhabitants of Namiquipa, Chihuahua, refused to accept lands for which restitution had been applied as ejido grants.

15. This lies in the fact that the 1992 amendment to article 27 of the Mexican Constitution allows ejido land transfers while upholding the inalienable status of the (agrarian) community.

16. Until 1992, commons within the ejido were not defined as such in the agrarian law, although its features can be glimpsed by their absence: they are those undivided lands (pasture, woodland, and scrub) to which all members of the ejido in question have rights.

17. RAN, Mérida, Carpeta básica of the Maní, Tzucacab, and Tahdziu ejidos; emphasis added.

18. See the work of Duch (1995), Hernández Xolocotzi (1996), Rosales (1988), and Terán and Rasmussen (2009), whose ethnographic observations of Yucatan ejidos have shown the incompatibility between slash-and-burn farming and ejido tenure.

19. Interview with Samuel Caamal, a seventy-year-old ejidatario, December 13, 2010.

20. Interview with F. Canul, Tzucacab, December 14, 2012.

21. Interview with D. Canul, February 23, 2013.

22. It is notable that there is no record of these partnerships at the RAN in Mérida, because Banrural maintained its own register of partnerships, details of which it failed to share with the RAN.

23. Interview with A. Zapata, February 25, 2013.

24. See, for example, the works of Bracamonte (2007) and Quintal et al. (2003).

25. Santiago Aguilar and Wilberto Lozada, agrarian visitors from the Agrarian Attorney (Procuraduría Agraria) residence, Mérida, May 24 and November 23, 2010.

26. If farming became more intensive, or certain areas of the ejido were given over to crops, it was possible to increase the number of ejidatarios.

27. Article 85, ley Federal de la Reforma Agraria, 1971.

28. The *avecindado* was a legal entity whose rights had extended only to urban plots; the new agrarian law granted them rights to ejido lands via land transfer.

29. Padrón e historia de núcleos agrarios-Registro Agrario Nacional (PHINA): http://phina.ran.gob.mx/index.php#/.

30. This notion has no legal foundation and contradicts that of communal land set forth in the agrarian law: the total extent of the ejido lands includes areas that cannot be divided among individuals, such as paths and collective plots (school plots and plots shared by women from the ejido village); likewise, communal ejido land refers to management by a collective, not the allocation of land to individuals. In response to these misinterpretations, the RAN has recently omitted the percentage figure, substituting it with "Your use of common land is subject to the decision of the assembly."

31. Interview with Chí, Tzucacab, December 13, 2010.

REFERENCES

ARCHIVES

Registro Agrario Nacional (RAN), Mérida Yucatán

SECONDARY SOURCES

Azuela, Antonio. 2009. "El problema con las ideas." In *En busca de Molina Enríquez. Cien años de Los grandes problemas nacionales*, edited by Emilio Kourí, 79–125. Mexico: Colegio de Mexico.

Baitenmann, Helga. 2011. "Popular Participation in State Formation: Land Reform in Revolutionary Mexico." *Journal of Latin American Studies* 43 (1): 1–31.

Bracamonte, Pedro. 2007. *Una deuda histórica. Ensayo sobre las condiciones de pobreza secular entre los mayas de Yucatán.* Mexico: Centro de Investigación y Estudios Superiores en Antropología Social, Porrúa.

De Gortari, Ludka. 1997. "Comunidad como forma de tenencia de la tierra." *Estudios Agrarios. Revista de la Procuraduría Agraria* 8: 1–22.

Duch Gary, Jorge. 1995. "Los suelos, la agricultura y vegetación en Yucatán." In *La milpa en Yucatán: un sistema de producción agrícola tradicional*, vol. 1, edited by Hernández Xolocotzi, Baltazar Bello, and Tacher Levy, 97–107. Texcoco, Mexico: Colegio de Posgraduados.

Eiss, Paul K. 2010. *In the Name of El Pueblo: Place, Community, and the Politics of History in Yucatán.* Durham, NC: Duke University Press.

Evans, Sterling. 2012. "King Henequén: Order, Progress and Ecological Change in Yucatán, 1850–1915." In *A Land Between Waters*, edited by Christopher R. Boyer, 150–72. Tucson: University of Arizona Press.

Flores Torres, Jorge. 1997. *Los mayas yucatecos y el control cultural: etnotecnología, maya-economía y pensamiento político de los pueblos centro-orientales de Yucatán.* Mérida, Mexico: Universidad Autónoma Chapingo and Universidad Autónoma de Yucatán.

Gabbert, Wolfgang. 2001. "Social Categories, Ethnicity and the State in Yucatán, Mexico." *Journal of Latin American Studies* 33 (3): 459–84.

Hernández Xolocotzi, Efraím. 1996. "Racionalidad tecnológica del sistema de producción agrícola de roza-tumba-quema en Yucatán." In *La modernización de la milpa en Yucatán: utopía o realidad*, edited by Daniel Zizumbo, 187–93. Villareal, Mexico: Centro de Investigaciones Científicas de Yucatán.

Kourí, Emilio. 2015. "La invención del ejido." *Nexos*, March 24. http://www.nexos.com .mx/?p=23778.

Mendieta y Nuñez, Lucio de. 1975. *El problema agrario en México.* 13th ed. Mexico: Porrúa.

Nugent, Daniel, and Ana María Alonso. 1994. "Multiple Selective Traditions in Agrarian Reform and Agrarian Struggle: Popular Culture and State Formation in the Ejido of Namiquipa." In *Everyday Forms of State Formation: Revolution and Negotiation of Rule in Modern Mexico*, edited by Gilbert M. Joseph and Daniel Nugent, 209–46. Durham, NC: Duke University Press.

Nuijten, Monique. 2003. "Illegal Practices and the Re-enchantment of Governmental Techniques: Land and the Law in Mexico." *Journal of Legal Pluralism and Unofficial Law* 35 (48): 163–83.

Ortiz Yam, Inés. 2013. *De milperos a henequeneros en Yucatán, 1870–1937.* Mexico: Colegio de Mexico.

Quintal Avilés, Ella. 2005. "'Way yano'one' aquí estamos. La fuerza silenciosa de los mayas excluidos." In *Visiones de la diversidad: relaciones interétnicas e identidades indígenas en el México actual,* edited by Miguel Bartolomé, 291–371. Mexico: Instituto Nacional de Antropología e Historia (INAH).

Quintal, Ella F., Juan Ramón Bastarrachea, Fidencio Briceño, Martha Medina, Renée Petrich, Lourdes Rejón, Beatriz Repetto, and Margarita Rosales. 2003. "Solares, rumbos y pueblos: organización social de los mayas peninsulares." In *La comunidad sin límites. Estructura social y organización comunitaria en las regiones indígenas de México,* vol. 1, edited by Saúl Millán and Julieta Valle, 293–382. Mexico: INAH and Consejo Nacional para la Cultura y las Artes.

Robles, Héctor. 2000. "Propiedad de la tierra y población indígena." *Estudios Agrarios. Revista de la Procuraduría Agraria* 14: 1–25.

Rosales, Margarita. 1988. *Oxkutzcab, Yucatán 1900–1960. Campesinos, cambio agrícola y mercado.* Mexico: Centro Regional Yucatán and INAH.

———. 1991. "Mecanización y desarrollo en el sur de Yucatán." *Revista i'inaj del centro* 4: 12–21.

Rugeley, Terry. 2009. *Rebellion Now and Forever: Mayas, Hispanics and Caste War Violence in Yucatán, 1800–1880.* Stanford, CA: Stanford University Press.

Terán, Silvia, and Christian Rasmussen. 2009. *La milpa de los mayas.* 2nd ed. Mérida, Mexico: Universidad Nacional Autónoma de México; Yucatán, Mexico: Universidad de Oriente.

Villa Rojas, Alfonso. 1978. *Los elegidos de Dios. Etnografía de los mayas de Quintana Roo.* Mexico: Instituto Nacional Indigenista.

Warman, Arturo. 1985. "Notas para una redefinición de la comunidad agraria." *Revista Mexicana de Sociología* 47 (3): 5–20.

Wells, Allen, and Gilbert M. Joseph. 1996. *Summer of Discontent, Seasons of Upheaval: Elite Politics and Rural Insurgency in Yucatán, 1876–1915.* Stanford, CA: Stanford University Press.

PART II

SCIENCE

CHAPTER 7

FROM ANATOMICAL COLLECTION TO NATIONAL MUSEUM, CIRCA 1895

How Skulls and Female Pelvises Began to Speak the Language of Mexican National History

LAURA CHÁZARO

THE MUSEUM of Pathological Anatomy opened in 1853 as part of the National School of Medicine (Escuela Nacional de Medicina, hereafter ENM). At the museum, professors from the Department of Obstetrics who practiced at Mexico's charity hospitals collected female pelvic bones that had been diagnosed pathological. The pieces labeled "Mexican" or "jammed" pelvises originally belonged to patients who had suffered labor complications due to obstructions. In 1895, the National Museum (now Museo Nacional de Antropología e Historia) added these pieces to its anthropology collection along with skulls, skeletal remains, and other objects that represented Mexico's indigenous races.[1] According to anthropological and medical historians, these bones have garnered interest from a range of disciplines. But how did these human remains become a matter of medical and anthropological inquiries? Why were they classified as ancient and historical pieces politically worthy of being displayed in a national history museum?[2] What bridged the gap between a medicine museum and a history museum? Scientific practice may hold the answer to these questions. Anthropology, along with osteopathy and other medical practices, played a role in defining what we now refer to as "Indian" and "indigenous."

In this chapter, I will give an account of the anthropological and medical practices employed in the study of corporal variability. During the period of study, scientists understood variability as a consequence of pathologies, but after much debate, variability became naturalized as an expression of biological differences and racial hierarchies. Categories such as *indigenous, Mexican,* or *white* emerged when scientists attempted to understand variability, which is infinite, as a manifestation of race.[3] These categories were molded on corporeal differences—skin color, height to weight ratio, and bone morphology. Consequently, instruments and measurements were optimized to provide precise measurements of variations between skeletal remains.

With the intention of broadening the discussion on the historicity of categories such as *indigenous races* or *Mexican races*, I have searched a variety of locations, from hospitals to museums to archaeological sites, for skeletons that were prepared according to the practices of anatomy and anthropometric recognition. I will analyze those practices that reduced skeletons, heads, and pelvises to a series of numbers and indices. My interest in these pieces is in understanding the connection between measuring techniques and instruments used in medical situations, and the experience of race (indigenous or mestizo). The notion of being Indian or being mestizo acquired substance when bones became measurable aspects with length, width, and weight. If racial classification was once a mere idea or notion, it became a scientifically and politically legitimate fact when those bones came to represent the antiquity of the so-called Mexican race, became a part of history, and, thanks to naturalization, even played a role in predicting the future of national politics.

A study of the exchanges between the Museum of Pathological Anatomy and the National Museum reveals important details into how the medical school's pathological pelvis collection merged with the National Museum's bone collection. This unusual way of gathering those bones, pelvises, and skulls under the same roof was partially a result of political deals and discrepancies among physicians, anthropologists, and museum curators. Though they did not always agree on the matter, they all produced or adopted measurements that allowed them to supervise pathological variability and monitor atavistic inheritance, especially of indigenous female bodies, first in comparison to white remains, then to mestizo or Mexican remains. To this day, indiscernible traces of measuring charts with information on skulls and pelvic bones still exist, and at the same time, human variability remains a frequently used measurement. Biological averages and standards of normal or pathological functionality are still being produced. Indices and standards are often calculated in regard to presumed racial origins and sex. Even if measuring tools, measurements, the scientific workplace, and the way measurements are taken have changed, those first bones and measurements resonate in scientific practice and concepts. They are present in some of our most ingrained racism and prejudiced attitudes toward Indians.[4]

CORPORAL VARIABILITY AND PATHOLOGIES IN OBSTETRICS AND PATHOLOGICAL ANATOMY

In the early nineteenth century, medical practitioners in Mexico adopted an anatomic-clinical method that understood disease as a lesion located somewhere on the body. It soon became the dominant method at the ENM, founded in 1833. Known as the "clinical gaze," it used touch, smell, and sight to identify disease. Doctors were required to develop expert palpating and auscultating skills to assist in finding pathological symptoms—in this case, abnormal corporal variations. When speaking of pathologies, physicians used measured terminology to indicate differences in intensity, temperature, or irritation (Canguilhem 1995). The study of these corporal variations was crucial to clinics; it led to finding the subtlest differences between normal and diseased (Flores 1992, 475). While certain variations may have been regarded as peculiarities, those associated with sex and race were often considered the possible cause behind pathologies.

When it came to childbirth, nineteenth-century obstetricians associated pathologies with the uterus and the anatomy of female pelvises. A "happy" (dystocic) delivery, as they called it at the time, depended on the uterus performance, and it rarely failed. Medical intervention was only justified as a response to female "fragility." Women rarely accepted the presence of doctors during labor. Obstetricians competed with midwives, who practiced according to "indigenous" knowledge and were excluded from professional training reserved for men. Throughout the nineteenth century, midwives and obstetricians were constantly in conflict. While midwives sought access to university education, doctors struggled to access the rooms and bodies of women in labor (Carrillo 1999, 167–90).

Dr. Juan María Rodríguez, one of the most respected male midwives of the early 1860s, did most of his work at the ENM and the National Academy of Medicine (Academia Nacional de Medicina, ANM). He raised concern over the alarming frequency of "unhappy" deliveries occurring at the maternity hospital. His research led him to consider the possibility of defects in Mexican female pelvises. He wondered whether Mexican women endured labor dystocia as an effect of primitive racial inheritance in their bone structures. He analyzed the pelvises' anatomical dimensions and discovered what he called the "fatal secret" of Mexican female pelvises: a seemingly undetectable narrowing of the pelvis, which, during labor, revealed flawed anatomical configurations in women's bodies. He described these pelvises as "armored," or *acorazadas*. They featured a longer than normal pubis that reduced the distance between the coccyx and sacral region or sacrum. His students would later confirm these hypotheses at the maternity hospital, where they found pelvises measuring six to eight centimeters between the pubis and the sacrum; pelvises in European gynecology texts reflected an average of ten to eleven centimeters for the same measurement (Rodríguez 1872, 53–106). From this data, Rodríguez and his pupils concluded that the anatomical variation of Mexican female pelvises, compared to European women's pelvises, occurred because Mexican people had gone through continuous adaptation after white and indigenous races started to combine (Flores 1890, 294–344).

Doctors began to speak of the reduced width of Mexican pelvic structures after comparing them to imported anthropometric and somatometric measurements taken from women in operating rooms in Europe. Obstetricians typically used stethoscopes and specula to diagnose patients. If they suspected the possibility of a pathological constitution, they would turn to callipers or pelvimeters, also known as Baudelcoque's compass (1835), for additional measurements. These instruments measured the distance between the pubis and the coccyx and the width of the hips. Once they had those measurements, they were able to estimate the angles of the pelvic inlet, also known as *conjugata vera*.

As the armored pelvis hypothesis progressed, male midwives began to stress the importance of precise measuring. In addition to using the compasses mentioned above, they also used inner pelvimeters (graded rulers), which measured the lengths of the pelvic canal from the inside of the vagina. This arsenal of surgical and clinical equipment not only allowed them to explore potential pathologically configured pelvises, but it also meant this group of obstetricians was able to associate results with defects particular to Mexican women. However, how did they connect supposedly narrow pelvises to the notion of Mexican race? At the time, Rodríguez and his students were part of an elite of medical midwives that was both powerful and respected. Anyone who did not agree with their hypothesis went unheard (Olivares and González 1889, 266–72). The armored pelvises earned a top spot on the list of what Rodríguez (1872, 54) called "national pathologies." Those historically charged bone samples used in medical research ended up at ENM's anatomy museum.

Pablo Martínez del Río and Francisco Ortega, both professors from the Department of Clinical and Pathological Anatomy and doctors at ENM, created the Museum of Normal, Comparative, and Pathological Anatomy in 1853 (Flores 1992, 474).[5] They planned to collect original and plaster or wax models of anatomical specimens for an exhibition. They hoped their students would learn to distinguish between normal and pathological at first sight.

By 1872, the museum displayed a considerable amount of specimens, pieces from unusual or local cases prepared on site by professors and their students. They showed plaster and wax models as well as lithographs manufactured by French and English artists and artisans encountered at different world expos.[6]

Dr. Rodríguez managed the collection by dividing it into seven sections, from the anatomy of pathological organs to teratology, which was a collection of human and animal monstrosities or extreme deformities of beings for whom survival was "unviable."[7] Rodríguez located four "narrow" female pelvises in that section. Next to pelvises he placed lithographs, jars containing teratological organs, and malformed fetuses conserved in alcohol, most of which came from his personal collection.[8]

Medical knowledge from that period associated some pathologies and malformations with inheritance and with the evolution of race (López-Beltrán 2004; Ruiz 1990). Evolution was defined in regard to the "natural history" of race, especially in America. On this matter, Rodríguez rejected Charles Darwin's evolutionism and stood somewhere between Geoffroy Saint-Hilaire Jr. and J. B. Lamarck's theories. In short, Rodríguez—like many other physicians of his time—thought that modifications in individuals and species were the result of environmental influences. Monstrosities indeed happened during gestation, often because of random or unforeseen accidents (Gorbach 2008). Drawing on Saint-Hilaire, many believed that new races could stem from viable monstrous modifications. By contrast, Darwin rejected the possibility of abrupt changes in nature; his position was rather conservative. He saw evolution as a series of small leaps where only the ones that ensured survival remained (López-Beltrán 2006).

Darwin's work became known in Mexico in the late 1860s but took some time to become accepted. Physicians were sure that certain spontaneous and rapid disorders were accidents caused by the environment. A similar explanation emerged when it came to understanding supposed anatomical defects in female pelvises: external factors caused evolutionary throwbacks to an indigenous past and stopped that race and its descendants from developing any further, even when combined with other races (mestizos). By rejecting evolution through abrupt changes, as Darwin did, they denied any possibility of biological adaptation in indigenous individuals and their descendants (mestizos included) and barred them from finding their place in the nation's future (Ramírez [1878] 1989, 214–25).

Those physicians' evolutionism was inspired by the hypotheses of French hygienists who drew close associations between biology and morals. They claimed that certain moral practices spurred their patients' diseases. Disorders in children caused by parental alcoholism is a typical example (Lobato 1880, 362). According to medical practitioners, vice and poor general hygiene afflicted the indigenous population of that time and hence explained their children's "faulty constitution" (*defectos de conformación*). Race itself was the imprint of differences or variations on people's bodies, which in the long run caused pathologies.

Scientific interest in indigenous people's adaptation and normal reproduction abilities grew parallel to discussions on that topic among travelers, collectors, and museum curators. Outside of hospitals, museums became the place to debate biological and historical connections between the indigenous population of the past and the indigenous population of the present, including mestizos or descendants of mixed races. But which biological and moral attributes did mestizos inherit from their indigenous past?

In 1825, soon after Mexico became independent, government authorities grew interested in controlling illegal trade of so-called Mexican antiques, which included archaeological artefacts, codices, and jewelry. However, these antiques were not of defined monetary value. They were valuable as vestiges of the civilizations that populated America before colonial times (Achim 2013, 102–3). Only halfway through the nineteenth century did collectors and curators add Mexican bones and human remains to contraband, which were identified as evidence of ancient American civilizations, especially when remains came from sites near pyramids. As Achim (2017, 27) stated, even if science and collecting bones and antiques are now closely related, this connection did not exist in the past. It is worthwhile asking how antique dealers and collectors became associated with medical and anatomical practice.

While looking for Mayan stones and monoliths, explorer John Lloyd Stephens (1805–1852) and English artist Frederick Catherwood (1799–1854) purchased a skeleton whose skull, nicknamed Ticul, they sent to the American anatomist Samuel George Morton (1799–1851) for analysis (Achim 2017, 4–5). Morton, who was president of Philadelphia's Academy of Natural Sciences at the time, had published his best-selling *Crania Americana*, which appeared in 1839 (Díaz Perera 2008, 78–81). Like many pre-Darwinian anatomists, Morton's bone analysis was an attempt to end a current debate between those who claimed that human species resulted from various separate creations (a theory known as polygenesis) and those who argued that a single species produced all the others (monogenesis). Among anatomists and physicians, however, this debate became secondary to other more crucial questions: Where were the origins of American people? Were existing indigenous people, poor and degraded, descendants of the great builders who erected cities like Teotihuacán and Palenque? In this context of unanswered questions, skeletal remains were considered clues into the origin of America's ancient inhabitants. They were also likely answers to medical practitioners, collectors, and politicians' pressing questions regarding the (biological) connection between ancient Indians and what they called the Mexican race (López-Hernández 2009).

The Stephens-Catherwood case was typical: explorers and antique collectors exhumed bones and skulls to send to naturalists in museums outside of Mexico. To perform this task, they received instructions on how to take standardized measurements (although not always) of these objects. The instructions were almost always written in Europe (Zimmerman 1998, 70–73).[9] Thus, many skulls and skeletons that offered evidence or vestiges of the antiquity and origins of living indigenous people were relocated from Mexico to Paris, Berlin, or London, or to the United States, as would be the case with Morton and Stephens. Here we find proof that explorers and collectors looked at antiques from an anatomical point of view, as measurable and dissectible objects. The following segment depicts Morton and Stephens' observations on the skull from Ticul in 1841. The female skull, found in Yucatán, featured traits that Morton assigned to Americans: "The bones of the head, which are still partially separable at the sutures, are admirably characteristic of the *American Race*, as seen in the vertical occiput and the great interparietal diameter, which measures five inches and eight-tenths" (Morton 1842, 203–4).

Through anatomic analysis, Stephens and Morton confirmed that the history of the people who built pre-Hispanic cities was neither lost nor dead and that contemporary living Indians, by then degraded and impoverished, descended from that great race that once built magnificent temples (Achim 2017). Moreover, while the dilemma of polygenism and monogenism was still at the heart of the debate on the origins and antiquity of America's people, it also revealed the political roots behind this discussion.

Beyond Morton and other European colleagues, the interest in discussing the origins and evolution of American peoples in Mexico was not out of relevance to humankind in general but for its insight on race, the Mexican race in particular. In this context, both Alfredo Chavero (1841–1906), lawyer, archaeologist, and a member of the National Museum, and José Ramírez (1852–1904), naturalist, physician, and researcher of the National Medical Institute, deserve a mention. Regardless of whether or not they supported polygenist theories or Darwin's theories, Chavero and Ramírez sympathized with the notion that American races were autochthonous to America. They saw America's ancient indigenous people as the architects of great civilizations, as the ancestors of the contemporary indigenous population, and as historically and anatomically affiliated benefactors of modern mestizos. However, they did not entirely agree with European naturalists who claimed that American races "had originated with the migrations of some peoples from the Old World" (Ramírez [1895] 1989, 309). On this matter, Chavero (1886) was uncompromising: "If the black race inhabited and spread over the earth before others, on our continent it was but a migrating bird, and we must look for another race to call autochthonous. On our territory, we find, of course, the Otomi people . . . We then found two monosyllabic points of origin: the Otomis for the middle of our territory, and the Mayans to the south; and in the north we only find the line of Nahoa invaders" (114). Ramírez ([1895] 1989, 311) stated that natural history and medicine were proof that no analogies existed between American races and those of the Old Continent—not on phylogenetic, architectural, or sociological levels, and there were no anatomical or ethnological grounds for such analogies.

While there was never a consensus on this matter, Jesús Sánchez, also an ANM physician, conveyed Chavero and Ramírez's conclusions in the same terrain of medical and anthropological inquiries by asking, How is race related to pathological and degenerative phenomena? He made it clear that any attempt to approach the matter of atavisms and development implied touching on the subject of "extinction of inferior races, those less equipped to fight for their lives," which according to Chavero and Ramírez "is the case with our Indians" (Sánchez [1899] 1989, 321). At this point, dissecting, classifying, and measuring ancient and modern skeletons became shared practices between disciplines as variable as anatomy, archaeology, anthropology, and history. In practice, medical and anatomical dissecting tools such as the scalpel indeed coincided with anthropological tools used to compare, measure, and classify bones. For example, anthropologists and explorers measured skulls with the same tool used to measure pelvises in medicine. Over more than half a century, osteology instruments would provide information on the pathologies and normality of living and extinct races.

By the mid-nineteenth century, the study of race involved scalpels for dissection and goniometers and anthropometric rulers for measurement. Osteology, anthropometry, or anthropology of "Mexicans" was first practiced systematically during the French occupation, around 1862. After arriving with the army, French physicians inspired by the French Campaign in Egypt and Syria organized the Mexican Scientific Committee (Commission Scientifique du Mexique 1864). In association with Mexican doctors, the committee created a medical branch that offered studies in medical anthropology. As many in the field can attest, Jean Louis Armand de Quatrefages, then director of the Musée d'Histoire Naturelle in Paris, drafted the anthropology program—he was a true anti-Darwinian and monogenist and supported the idea of a single species and several races (Riviale 1999, 310).[10] From then on, medical practice included the study of human race: "L'exploration scientifique d'une contrée quelconque, au point de vue des sciences naturelles [for instance, medicine], comprend l'étude des races humaines qui s'y sont succédé et qui la peuplent encore" (Armand de Quatrefages et al. 1865, 19).

Armand de Quatrefage's instructions strived to regulate medical-anthropological practices for obtaining data on different races with the intention of sharing this information with museums, hospitals, and medical schools. Armand de Quatrefages saw dissecting and measuring as a way of comparing the sizes and proportions of body parts—the head (skull and face) and the skeleton (Armand de Quatrefages et al. 1865: 21; Armand de Quatrefages and Hamy 1882). He claimed, "au Mexique . . . Les populations mexicaines se partagent naturellement en trois grands groups: 1° les races indigènes; 2° les races étrangères; 3° les métis de ces diverses races" (Armand de Quatrefages et al. 1865, 22). Paul Maury, Pierre-Louis Gratiolet, and A. Berthold's descriptions of skulls (Gratiolet 1860; Berthold 1866) that supposedly belonged to ancient inhabitants are worthy of mention; so are Dr. Denis Jourdanet's thorax measurements (Jourdanet 1861). They were all members of the medical branch at the Commision Scientifique du Mexique.

Although officially the somatological anthropology program at the medical branch lasted only three years, Mexican physicians continued their studies in this field; they kept records of skeletons, ancient and modern skulls, and of their patients. Skeletons and data were added to the Musée d'Histoire Naturelle's collections, arranged by Armand de Quatrefages and his colleague, Théódore Hamy.

Armand de Quatrefages's instructions became part of greater somatological practice and its corresponding medical research methods. The word *race* acquired new dimensions; it became a source of data for clinical records and the object of somatological analysis. In 1872, physicians from the ANM who had once been members of the Commission Scientifique du Mexique enhanced their skills using measuring tools for long and short bones, as well as skulls. They strived to distinguish lineage and its transformations and wanted to identify the causes of degeneration among indigenous races and, through inheritance, among mestizos.

By the 1880s, study programs included Paul Broca's ([1864] 1879; 1875) *Instructions générales pour les recherches anthropologiques à faire sur le vivant* and *Instructions craniologiques et craniométriques* (Blanckaert 2009; Williams 1985, 331–48). Broca's work, like that of many others, was neither taken at face value nor did it build consensus among physicians and anthropologists. Alfonso Luis Herrera, Ricardo E. Cícero, and Nicolás León, the last three doctors in charge of the anthropology hall at the National Museum, claimed at different stages to have adopted Broca's method, adhering to its methods and using its unique anthropometrical instruments to measure skeletons and skulls (García Murcia, 2013). Broca's *Instructions* differed from Armand de Quatrefages's views not only in his support of polygenism but also in his physicalist approach, which focused on instruments. It would possibly explain the respect he garnered from those Mexicans who quoted him as a source of inspiration. As a way of accounting for different races (regarding conformation and variation), Broca's group adopted methods for measuring indexes and angles. Broca and Paul Topinard, Broca's most loyal supporter, refused to draw conclusions from single cases (the way physicians normally would) and insisted on collecting large amounts of measurements taken using repeatable procedures. They sought comparable averages and precise standards, regardless of who had obtained them.

Broca made a distinction between biological and morphological observations (for the living), where the first belonged to the study of functions and the second to an external description. When speaking of morphological observations, he emphasized that

Parmi les caractères morphologiques, il en est qui peuvent être déterminés par les mensurations, et qui constituent les *caractères anthropométriques*; ils ont le précieux avantage d'être exprimés en chiffres, de se prêter ainsi à des comparaison précises, et de se prêter surtout à l'application de la méthode des moyennes, que est la base la plus sûre de l'anthropologie. (Broca [1864] 1879, 28)

Broca's instruments, especially the goniometer, were widely accepted in Mexico. They were seen as a guarantee of accuracy and scientific rigor because they were said to enable measurements impossible to other instruments. The skull, a nonhomogenous variable entity, is impossible to measure lengthwise. As an example, Morton's way of measuring skulls for volume was completely different from Broca and R. Virchow's measurements (of ratios or angles) (Broca [1864] 1879, 41; Zimmerman 1998, 70).

ENM and the National Museum used facial and lateral goniometers to calculate Petrus Camper's, Georges Cuvier's, or even Broca's facial angles (Broca [1864] 1879, 39–40). Such was also the case for anthropometers, dynamometers, and breadth callipers. With the help of these tools, many bones, in and out of museums and hospitals, were typified as "Mexican."

NATIONAL MUSEUM BONE NARRATIVES, 1892–1895

A series of events in the 1890s would alter the fate of skeletal remains and skeletal measuring. In 1892, Alfredo Chavero and National Museum Director Francisco del Paso y Troncoso were invited to partake in the American Historical Exhibition, organized as part of the quadricentennial of the discovery of America celebrations held in Madrid. Having attended previous world fairs, they gained expertise in displaying indigenous races as a remarkable expression of the nation's past. On that occasion, they shipped skeletons and skulls used in science and anthropology to the exhibition in Madrid. The shipment included Tarahumara skeletal remains and bones found in Santiago Tlatelolco exhumed by Sociedad de Historia Natural (Natural History Society, hereafter SHN) contributors Dr. Manuel Villada, Dr. Manuel Ticó, and Dr. Aquiles Gerste (León 1919, 232). They had all published papers on the origins of man in *La Naturaleza* (*Nature*), SHN's journal, mainly in the anthropology section.

A few years later, in 1895, the Museum of Pathological Anatomy opened at San Andrés Hospital. That same year, pelvises believed pathological with atavistic inheritance were taken from the anatomy museum at ENM and sent to the anthropology hall at the National Museum (Lavista 1899, 351–55).[11] Also in 1895, the eleventh International Congress of Americanists, held in Mexico City, would become one of the most significant meetings of its time (Comas 1954). During preparations, del Paso y Troncoso led renovations in several National Museum halls, including the anthropology hall, founded in 1887 and since left practically abandoned. That year, Dr. Román Álvarez inaugurated the teratology hall (Herrera and Cícero 1895, iii).

Between 1892 and 1895, the National Museum received several anomalous pelvises, skeletons, and bones that had been labeled ancient by physicists. These bones had not been sent to museums in Europe, and as long as pre-Hispanic bone and antique trafficking persisted, the National Museum would accumulate them. Those bones remained in Mexico and affected the order of museum collections.

In 1895, the museum displayed its archaeology collection, which included the Sun Stone, on the ground level. The mezzanine and the upper levels housed the natural history collection, along with the anthropology, ethnology, teratology, and Mexican history collections (Gorbach 2008, 108–16). The story of the anthropology hall dates back to 1887. Over a period of a few months, Dr. Francisco Martínez Calleja served as professor of anthropology. Dr. Nicolás León (1859–1927) stated that Dr. Martínez Calleja and museum director Dr. Sánchez collected and exhibited "pre-Columbian Indian skulls along with a collection of plaster figures with representations of ethnic and pathological deformities, acquired in the United States" through a trader named Ward (León 1919, 231; García Murcia 2013, 69).

Needless to say, the structure and arrangement of the National Museum varied over time. National and foreign collectors, curators, explorers, and politicians experimented with different arrangements. Dominant versions came later in the twentieth century from a group of intellectuals born in the second half of the previous century who were also members of an educated and cosmopolitan elite faithful to the policies of President Porfirio Díaz (in power from 1876 to 1910). Members of the elite used the National Museum and many other places as a space for debating indigenous affairs; they worried over racial, historical, and political differences between the indigenous population and Mexicans, though they claimed at the same time to include indigenous people in their concept of "the nation" (Rutsch 2007, 60–71).

In 1895, Dr. Herrera and Dr. Cícero were asked to revitalize the museum's modest anthropology collection (Guevara 2002; Saldaña and Cuevas 1999, 309–32). By then, Herrera was a specialist in natural history and an active member of the SHN. He was interested in studying race, and he sympathized with Darwinian evolutionism, although he was critical of Darwin's natural selection theory. Cícero was a young physician who from 1895 onward had a brilliant career at the National Medical Institute's clinical laboratories and San Andrés Hospital.

Herrera and Cícero (1895) wrote *Catálogo de la colección de antropología del Museo Nacional*, a guide for visiting the collection, which also served as testimony of the anthropology hall's new arrangement. The text explains the three major subdisciplines of anthropology during that period that were used to organize the exhibition: 1) ethnology, 2) anatomical anthropology, and 3) physiological anthropology.

The ethnology section featured a photography collection, classified by Francisco del Paso, portraying images of indigenous peoples categorized in fourteen indigenous families (types) according to geography and language (Herrera and Cícero 1895, 5–83).[12] Texts and maps complemented the exhibit, displaying the regions they settled, their customs, and their traditional clothing (*trajes típicos*). The exhibition had references from a series of highly recognized texts from the time, such as Manuel Orozco y Berra's *Geografía de las lenguas*; Antonio García Cubas's *Atlas pintoresco*; Francisco Pimentel's *Las lenguas indígenas de México*; several articles from *Boletín de la Sociedad Mexicana de Geografía y Estadística*; and Domingo Orvañanos's *La Geografía Médica*. These texts, now considered expert literature in nineteenth-century historiography, described climates, customs, and languages.

Herrera and Cícero (1895) saw the museum's anatomical anthropology section as the most important of all. From their perspective, the objects and documents held there gave the *Catálogo* and the exhibition "strict scientific rigor," mainly because "this branch of science" was based on skeletal and cranial measurements (91). Inferring from the *Catálogo*, the exhibition displayed a considerable number of skulls and bones, many of which came from other existing collections. Among them, forty skulls, probably from Chichimec Indians, were part of a personal collection belonging to Protasio Tagle, a politician in Porfirio Díaz's regime.[13] Thirty-nine skulls from the Baumgarten collection, measured by the French physician Paul Maury, were also exhibited (137–52). Another twenty-six skulls came from Dr. Martínez Baca's collection, which he gathered from deceased inmates at the penitentiary in Puebla to prepare for criminological analysis. Pelvises from ENM's anatomy museum were displayed alongside those skulls (7–10; Martínez Baca and Vergara 1892). Skulls and bones exhumed by Dr. Ticó—as well as those collected by Colonel Joaquín Beltrán at Santiago Tlatelolco, Xico, Chalco, and Anacuco, all sites adjacent to Mexico City—were also displayed (Herrera and Cícero 1895, v-vi).[14] These bones, prepared by Herrera for exhibition, were exhumed while completing the Americanists' collection before attending the congress.[15]

According to Cícero and Herrera, biological anthropology created documents that provided bone measurements, mathematical descriptions, indices, and averages. Producing these numbers required anthropometric instruments. In the *Catálogo*'s introduction, the authors emphasized that they did not go into further detail on these measurements because "the tools needed for a study of this sort . . . unfortunately have not arrived yet [from Europe]" (Herrera and Cícero 1895, vii). However, the instruments would have been available at ENM or even at the National Museum. Museum inventories attest to the presence of at least some tools such as Adolphe Bertillon and Broca's breadth callipers and adjustable cephalometric square and Topinard's craniometer, cranial height callipers, and devices designed for measuring cubic capacity in Broca's area. According to information Herrera sent Dr. Villada (acting museum director), he did perform "craniometrical and chromascopic studies of the samples obtained at Santiago de Tlatelolco . . . by Dr. Broca's instructions."[16]

Under the title "Anatomical Anthropology," the *Catálogo* indeed describes a considerable number of model skulls made from plaster. Many of those, such as the "Neanderthal skull," the "Aymara skull," and the "Indian from Sacrifice Island," among others, were discussed individually. Every skull has descriptions of its race, some of which mention measurements, such as cranial capacity or dimensions, though the *Catálogo* does not specify whether it refers to plaster models or real bones (Herrera and Cícero 1895, 124–25).

The *Catálogo* then lists 118 skulls exhumed in 1895 in Santiago Tlatelolco, Chalco, Xico, and surrounding areas. Herrera prepared the skulls for the exhibition and, to preserve them, made several models in plaster.[17] Unlike previous occasions, they catalogued these skulls under inventory numbers instead of names. Although skulls were not recorded on a proper chart, they were numbered according to dimensions and entered on a table divided into columns. After the inventory number, the next column classifies them as brachycephalic or dolichocephalic under four possible degrees: sub, meso, supra, or ultra brachy-cephalic or dolichocephalic. The third column displays skull diameters (anterior-posterior and maximum transverse), and the final column shows cephalic index. These indices were calculated as the ratio between the two previous measure-ments, the way Broca did it (Broca 1875, 174; Blanckaert 2009, 126–27). Skulls were grouped into series according to their sex and where they were found. Two of those series came from Santiago Tlatelolco, with fifty-nine male and eleven female adult skulls. Then, regardless of sex, skulls were listed according to location; cranial deformations and mutilations were also recorded (Herrera and Cícero 1895, 124–36).

The *Catálogo* included only two craniometrical and skeletal measurement charts (Herrera and Cícero 1895, 131–36), taken from Théodore E. Hamy's book (Hamy 1885, 27, 37). The bones described in them were not part of the collection and belonged to the Musée d'Histoire Naturelle. Hamy took these measure-ments from skulls exhumed at ancient burial sites in Santiago Tlatelolco (chart 509) and from skulls that once belonged to persons of Otomi, Mazahua, and Mixtec origins (chart 523).[18] In these cases, indices and averages represented the real bones, which were missing. The authors published this data, which represented the missing bones, as a description of "Mexican" races. Under such a scope of numbers that spoke for bones (some of which were missing), readers (and maybe museum visitors, though we cannot know for sure) would have struggled to reach conclusions or establish comparisons between skulls, skeletal descriptions, and charts.

Evidently, bones matched to numbers could be standardized, compared, and averaged. In the process of standardizing and exchanging figures, the actual remains that "carried" Mexican history seem to have disappeared. Faced with these numbers, we are compelled to ask, What *are* Indians and races? Herrera and Cícero's generation was looking for a language that would allow them to read skulls and skeletons, to see the past of their mestizo present. Then, bio-logical anthropology produced a language of measurements and instruments, recognized as scientific and modern, like that of the most advanced nations. But this science had not been nationalized. Herrera and Cícero's "anthropology" pursued nationalist interests: collecting, measuring, and interpreting Mexico's indigenous skeletal remains, languages, and customs *in Mexico*. The problem then was how to bridge the gap between numerical language and what they called Mexican or mestizo race. On the one hand, they were dealing with num-bers, and on the other hand, race is unconcerned with measurements. Such is the case for Cícero's chart for classifying mestizos that appeared in the *Catálogo*. He claimed to use Broca's criteria to propose a classification where mestizos stemmed from "original" races—that is, the Spanish race, the indigenous race, and the black race—regardless of whether these races still existed. The resulting chart, a sort of blueprint describing kinship, did not reflect the same numerical complexity of cranial measurements (Herrera and Cícero 1895, 85, chart 804).

We can conclude that Herrera and Cícero did not lack anthropometric instruments; rather, they were looking to create instruments and measurement practices that were Mexican, not foreign. In an article written for their colleagues at *La Naturaleza*, though not for the general public, Herrera and Cícero severely criticized measurements of "Mexican skulls" published by foreign specialists. From their perspective, great anthropologists like Johann Friedrich Blumenbach, Morton, Hamy, and even Broca, among others, had based their studies on a few poorly informed cases:

> The number of Mexican skulls examined abroad is insignificant; none of them underwent rigorous comparisons in our country [. . .]. If Blumenbach, Retzius and other anthropologists had presented another 50 skulls, we would have a total number of 150 native skulls measured and studied abroad [. . .]. It is impossible to reach a general conclusion on the Mexican races based on the comparison of 150 samples scattered among several museums and measured by different anthropologists. (Herrera and Cícero 1896, 463)

If they considered current measurements unusable, they would have to look for new values to measure. Herrera and Cícero handed instructions to Mexican anthropologists as a guideline for the exploration and collection of more bones. They needed to complete the museum's collection, though they claimed, "We can assure without a doubt, it is the richest in the world, simply in remains of our aboriginal people, of course" (Herrera and Cícero 1896, 464).

They initially wanted new averages calculated, based on greater numbers. They recommended examining series of at least forty samples, twenty for each of the sexes. Given some samples were of undetermined sex, they suggested studying at least fifty skulls from each location. If they were to obtain statistically valid indexes and averages, they figured they would need to fade out minor individual deviations. Data collected from remains belonging to children and elders were unusable because they could not be compared to data from bones obtained at other localities. They called to nationalize those bones without disregarding anthropometric methods. In their words, they aimed to "know races, not individuals. [They refused to use] French craniometry, French anthropometry, French cranioscopy in Mexico, which is absurd" (Herrera and Cícero 1896, 465). According to Herrera and Cícero, the word *indigenous* or any other possible classification used at the time (based on origins, anatomy, or language) needed review under the scope of their instruments and measurement practices. By no other means could an explanation of the origins and atavistic features of indigenous people, as well as their possible tendency toward criminality, emerge. Above all else, they could then decide if modifications in Mexicans' osteological features were caused by inheritance or by the environment. They would be able to distinguish between mestizos' Spanish and indigenous inheritance. Indeed, no one from the exhibition questioned that the Indian race had a history of its own, different from that of Mexicans. And these certainties gave way to new forms of apprehension and doubt—how to measure distances and similarities between indigenous people and mestizos?

The exhibition's curators chose two studies as proof of biological anthropology's contribution to knowledge of indigenous races: Dr. Flores's study of female pelvises and Dr. Martínez Baca's prestigious work on the penitentiary of Puebla (Urías 2007). Both studies were based on bone, cranial, and skeletal measurements organized into charts with figures, and both used foreign and some local instruments.

During his work in the penitentiary, Dr. Martínez Baca used a vertical cephalometer or (Broca's) cephalometric square, which was very similar to the pelvimeter and the rulers that physicians used when measuring pelvises. Thanks to these techniques and instruments, the authors gave new material meaning to those criminals' skulls and women's pelvises. They became an indication of indigenous people's exposure to degeneration or stalled development and offered a way of evaluating the persistence of these conditions after races started to mix. Measurements that stood in representation of certain parts of dissected bodies proved that the "Mexican race's" indigenous side could produce degenerative variations. In his cranioscopy section, Dr. Martínez Baca claimed that

> because the validity of our study requires us to start by determining the race of skulls measured and displayed on Table III, we will say [the following about] the Mexican race, largest in number . . . the Totonac race . . . the Mixtec-Zapotec race, from the states of Guerrero and Oaxaca. . . . These races, quite degenerated after mixing, their social environment, and many other circumstances . . . have lost the signature of a pure race and have retained certain atavistic features, which allow

for us to classify and place them as members of primitive races soon to be extinct. (Martínez Baca and Vergara 1892, 41).

Criminal skulls and armored pelvises, exhibited physically and represented through charts, were distinguishable from European and Mexican skulls and pelvises thanks to their indigenous/sexual traits. They presented variations (biological or sexual) that made them different: "This would explain the conflict between those features that show how (Mexican) race is progressing, and others that belong to degenerating races . . . [with] such disproportion in cranial measurements, to the point of explaining the criminal nature of indigenous peoples" (Martínez Baca and Vergara 1892, 41).

The museum took on the important task of putting the notion of racial variability into practice through charts and numbers and shifting the legitimate boundaries that separated Indians from mestizos, expressed first as skulls and pelvises and then as numerical figures.

Variability was initially seen as pathological or as an affliction; it would soon be distinguished in relation to racial origins, where Europeans were considered the norm and the more evolved race. However, the point of reference for indigenous/female variability then shifted to Mexicans (mestizos of both Spanish and Indian descent) who became the norm/more evolved race. In bone measurements, variability and difference are always tentative and circumstantial values and are always subject to evaluation and verification.

From the *Catálogo*, we can gather that the museum displayed skulls, pelvises, skeletons, and measurements. These items somehow represented the substance of that Mexican race, which was capable, in comparison to Europeans and specifically indigenous people, of adapting perfectly to their environment. So who were those Mexicans? Or in anthropometrical terms, what were their measurements? How did they work? How did they breathe? The skeletons, physical expression of those Mexicans, were en route to being defined.

The "Physiological Anthropology" section (3), which would be the last part of the 1895 exhibition, contains charts obtained by Dr. Daniel Vergara López on the physiology of breathing at high altitude. By analyzing the correlation between inhaled oxygen and altitude, Vergara concluded that, far from lacking oxygen, Mexicans developed a perfect adaptation for breathing at altitude—2,250 meters above sea level. As a member of the National Medical Institute (Instituto Médico Nacional; 1889–1915), Vergara took anthropometric and physiological (chest and height) measurements such as oxygen intake and red blood cell counts from his patients, sick or healthy. In the lab at the institute or in the local Popocatepetl laboratory, his instruments showed that oxygen intake was the same at altitude or on European flatlands. The *Catálogo* told visitors that "Man can rely on a range of mechanisms for adjusting to Mexico's altitude, and no aspects of degeneration can be associated with contrary climacteric influences." He also added, "Modifications observed in Mexicans make them appear as possessing thoracic indices that show exceptional vigor" (Herrera and Cícero 1895, 92, 95).

Vergara's studies coincided with Herrera's stance on the transformation of human and animal races. In 1896, he published an article where he attempted to bring together the best of Lamarck and Darwin to prove that the environment had as much influence on the population as selection and inheritance. Despite their differences, both Herrera and Vergara thought that the indigenous race did not always transmit throwbacks or congenital malformations. The Mexican or mestizo population developed perfect biological adaptations to the environment and eliminated any hindrance to their progress. Inspired by contentions offered by French physician M. Duval, who in turn followed M. Wallace's transformism, Herrera claims that "with selection . . . there must be adaptation to the environment, and in turn, the anatomy, physiology, ethology, and so forth of adapted beings is also modified; a fact that has also been seen through direct observation" (Herrera 1896, 40).

If indigenous skulls and pelvises were under suspicion of involution, measurements showed the Mexican race's virile strength. However, Vergara's research did not include ancient skulls; his skeletal measurements focused mainly on thorax, height to weight ratio, visual acuity, and muscular strength (measured with a dynamometer). In this section of the exhibition, the skulls and pelvises on display seemed to challenge the notion of altitude-adapted man.

CODA: THE IDEAL ACHIEVED

The anthropology hall arrangement described in the *Catálogo* was short-lived. Just a year later, the collection diminished as the Tagle and Baumgarten collections went back to their owners. The remaining skulls were added to the anthropology department's collection; Cícero and Herrera left the museum and continued their careers as physicians. The anthropology laboratory, where they expected to conduct more measurements using instruments, was abandoned.

The anthropology hall's provisional vacancy ended in 1900 when Dr. León was appointed as naturalist assistant. León began his career at the Michoacán Museum, located in the city of Morelia. During the start of his time at the museum, as he describes it, he endeavored to start a collection and open a laboratory for biological anthropology, which he would later call physical anthropology. Through his excavations, he added to the anthropology collection. He classified skeletal remains and skulls according to race and "linguistic data . . . from our Republic's Indians, both pre-Columbian and contemporary."[19] He also added fetus skulls to the female pelvis collection, which he obtained and dissected through his obstetrician practice at the general hospital. In 1903, he created the Department of Physical Anthropology and he inaugurated the long-awaited Anthropometry Laboratory, where he cleaned, measured, and classified bones.[20] By 1907 he had collected thousands of bones but was dismissed from his position. In 1911, he returned to the museum as a professor of anthropology and reported the destruction of a large portion of his work in his absence. Nevertheless, he took back his place and by 1912 had measured one hundred skulls. From then until his death in 1929, León measured bones, classified indigenous peoples, and taught his students to use measuring instruments.

During those years, which coincided with the Mexican Revolution (1910–1920), León measured the bones in the collection with instruments designed by Broca and other anthropologists such as Alès Hrdlicka (1869–1943), whom he had met and invited to work at the National Museum, in 1902 and 1911, respectively.[21] Although León's work is not central to this chapter, it is important to highlight that the time he spent working at the museum allowed him to continue what had started with the 1895 exhibition: the material production of mestizos as agents of national history and as a contrast to indigenous peoples, who were seen as museum objects and atavistic agents that belonged to the past.

Race and sex do not exist per se. Women and Indians do not automatically materialize and become more or less valuable, with greater or smaller effect on the life of societies (Copjec 2006, 17; Dorlin 2006). Looking at the history of how those lost and forgotten skulls and pelvises were measured, we can conclude that the short time they spent at the National Museum provided a material testimony to what we now call "indigenous peoples," who have been the object of many political, agricultural, and cultural government plans. They will almost always be regarded as numbers that can be standardized, averaged, and compared. We as Mexicans, in every step and every action, bring out their true faces. And this finally accomplishes what one historian tried to achieve from craniometry: "to define our races, in the words of anthropology, to return them to their place, left so many years empty under Europe's scientific classification of peoples" (Romero 1895, 237).

ACKNOWLEDGMENTS

This chapter was translated from Spanish by Lucía Cirianni and Benjamín de Buen. I am grateful to Veronika Lipphardt, leader of the Twentieth-Century Medicine Research Group of the Max Planck Institute for the History of Science for her financial and intellectual support during a sabbatical leave in 2014.

NOTES

1. The National Museum was inaugurated in 1825. There are many valuable documents that tell the story of the National Museum; see Achim (2017) and Gorbach (2008).
2. See Zimmerman (1998), Star and Griesemer (1989, 387–420), Hopwood (1999, 462–96), Karp and Lavine (1991), Stocking (1983), Brown (1992, 57–80), Podgorny and Lópes (2008).
3. When I use the term *race*, I am referring to the vague way Mexican physicians and medical practitioners used this concept. The term once expressed a category of natural history, a functional and anatomical variation of the "human species," as described by French naturalists Jean Louis Armand de Quatrefages (1810–1892) and Théodore E. Hamy (1842–1908). It was a word for ancient indigenous peoples—Mayans, Aztecs—referred to also as nations.
4. Readers of this text will benefit from comparing my conclusions to Vivette García Deister's chapter also published in this book. For an illustrative example of the way in which racial differences were measured and brought to life in other parts of Latin America, see the case of Brazil in Peard (1999).
5. AHFM, FEMyA, file 488, box 5, Río de la Loza, "Reglamento del Museo Anatómico," 1871.
6. AHFM, FEMyA, box 192, "Informe Administrativo de 1874 para la compra de modelos anatómicos en cera e instrumental de cirugía," 1874.
7. AHFM, FEMyA, file 488, box 5, Río de la Loza, "Reglamento del Museo Anatómico de esta Escuela," 1871.
8. Reports mention phantoms, dissected and articulated pelvises, and uteruses "in normal state" used in obstetric and anatomy courses. AHFM, FEMyA, box 497, "La Junta directiva pide los inventarios de los instrumentos, aparatos y demás objetos," 1872, fols.17–22.

9. Several of these instructions, including Armand de Quatrefages's and Paul Broca's (1824-1880), were known in Mexico. By the end of the nineteenth century, Broca's were the most commonly adopted. R. Virchow's German instructions were also distinguished, as well as Adolphe Bertillon's work. According to Andrew Zimmerman, anthropologists in Germany decided on a single way of measuring skulls in the Frankfurt Agreement, signed in 1883. In Mexico, on the other hand, various instructions were used.

10. Armand de Quatrefages adopted a different vision from Broca, who was his rival and founder of the Société d'Anthropologie and the Faculté d'Anthropologie (1876). Armand de Quatrefages stated he was convinced by the catastrophists' work, considered compatible with the biblical version of creation. The text *Crania ethnica* (Armand de Quatrefages and Hamy 1882) became known in Mexico. Hamy entered the Musée in 1872.

11. AHFM, FEMyA, file 6, box. 266, Inventario del Museo Anatomo Patológico, 1905.

12. Descriptions of indigenous clothing can be credited to physician and museum director Francisco del Paso y Troncoso.

13. Protasio Tagle lent and later donated his collection to the museum. See AH-MNAH, June 14, 1895, vol. 9, file 84, fols. 212–15.

14. AH-MNAH, vol. 9, file. 83, De Alfonso Herrera a Manuel Urbina, Director del Museo Nacional, June 6, 1895, fol. 212.

15. It is impossible to know from the *Catálogo* exactly how many skulls were exhibited. There is an inventory of these bones in AH-MNAH, "Sección de Antropología. Informe, Junio de 1895," vol. 9, pp. 234–35; compare this to "Inventario del Museo," 1917, vol. 32, file 2, pp. 12–129.

16. AH-MNAH, Manuel Urbina y Díaz Millan, "Interpelación a Luis Herrera," vol. 9, November 20, 1895, file 85, fols. 216–17.

17. The museum's interim director, Dr. Manuel Urbina, opposed this effort. He feared skulls could deteriorate and ordered Herrera to stop making models. See AH-MNAH, "El Sr. Director interpela al C. Alfonso L. Herrera acerca de los trabajos que se están verificando," November 20, 1895, vol. 9, file 85, pp. 217–18r. Herrera followed Broca's technique by cutting skulls in half and casting a mold from gelatin, plaster, and water.

18. The *Catálogo* contained charts: 509 and 523 from T. Hamy (1885). Chart 513 was not published, perhaps due to a mistake. There is also chart 527, which displayed measurements taken by Desiré de Charney from living people. The final measurement chart is called *Huesos procedentes de las excavaciones hechas en Santiago Tlatelolco.*

19. AH-MNAH, Carta de Nicolás León al director del Museo Nacional, July 15, 1912, vol. 16, file 38, fol. 220.

20. Ibid.

21. AH-MNAH, "Informe de Nicolás León (1912) acerca de cómo se formó la colección de Antropología Física y su estado actual; así como su clasificación y actividades del Departamento," October 28, 1912, vol. 16, file 38, fols. 210–26.

REFERENCES

ARCHIVES

Archivo Histórico de la Facultad de Medicina de la Universidad Nacional Autónoma de México (AHFM)

Fondo Escuela de Medicina y Alumnos (FEMyA)

Archivo Histórico Museo Nacional de Antropología (AH-MNAH)

PRINTED PRIMARY SOURCES

Armand de Quatrefages, Jean Louis, and Ernest Th. Hamy. 1882. *Crania ethnica: les crânes des races humaines. Décrites et figurées, d'après les collections du Muséum d'Histoire Naturelle de Paris, Atlas*. Paris: Librairie Baillière.

Armand de Quatrefages, Jean Louis, Henri Milne-Edwards, Joseph Decaisne, Charles Sainte-Claire Deville, and Le Baron Félix Hippolyte Larrey. 1865. *Archives de la Commission Scientifique du Mexique*, vol. 1. Paris: Imprimerie Impériale.

Baudelocque, J. L. 1835. *De la compression de l'aorte: Un moyen propre à suspendre toutes espèces des pertes de sang chez les femmes*. Paris: Chez l'Auteur.

Berthold, Arnaud. 1866. "Descripción y estudio de un cráneo extraído de las tumbas de uno de los palacios de Mitla." *Anales del Museo Nacional de México* 3: 116–21.

Broca, Paul. (1864) 1879. *Instructions générales pour les recherches anthropologiques à faire sur le vivant*. Paris: G. Masson.

———. 1875. *Instructions craniologiques et craniométriques*. Paris: G. Masson.

Chavero, Alfredo. 1886. "La piedra del sol. Estudio arqueológico." *Anales del Museo Nacional de México* (3): 3–37, 110–24.

Flores, Francisco. 1890. "Ligeros apuntes de pelvimetría comparada." *Revista Mexicana de Medicina* (2): 294–344.

Gratiolet, Pierre-Louis. 1860. "Sur un crâne Totonaque." *Bulletin de la Société d'Anthropologie* 1: 562.

Hamy, Theodore Ernest. 1885. *Mission scientifique au Mexique et dans l'Amérique Centrale, première partie, 1885, 27 and 37*. Paris: Imprimerie nationale.

Herrera, Alfonso Luis. 1896. "El clima del valle de México y la biología de los vertebrados." *La Naturaleza*, 2nd ser., (2): 38–86.

Herrera, Alfonso Luis, and Ricardo E. Cícero. 1895. *Catálogo de la colección de antropología del Museo Nacional*. Mexico: Imprenta del Museo Nacional.

———. 1896. "Estudios de antropología Mexicana." *La Naturaleza*, 2nd ser. (2): 462–69.

Jourdanet, Denis. 1861. *Les altitudes de l'Amérique tropicale comparées au niveau des mers au point de vue de la constitution médicale*. France: Imprimerie Arbieu.

Lavista, Rafael. 1899. "Informe que rinde al C. Ministro de Instrucción Pública de las labores ejecutadas en el Museo de Anatomía Patológica, desde su fundación hasta la fecha." *Revista de Anatomía Patológica y Clínicas* 4 (9–10): 321–79.

León, Nicolás. 1919. "Historia de la antropología física en México." *American Journal of Physical Anthropology* 2 (3): 229–64.

Lobato, José Guadalupe. 1880. "Higiene. Sociología en sus relaciones con la demografía y demología mexicanas." *Gaceta Médica de México* (15): 357–72.

Martínez Baca, Francisco, and Manuel Vergara. 1892. *Estudio de antropología criminal. Memoria que por disposición del Superior Gobierno del Estado de Puebla.* Mexico: Imprenta, Litografía de Benjamín Lara.

Morton, S. G. 1839. *Crania Americana: Or, a Comparative View of the Skulls of Various Aboriginal Nations of North and South America. To Which is Prefixed an Essay on the Varieties of the Human Species.* Philadelphia: J. Dobson.

———. 1842. "Stated Meeting." *Proceedings of the Academy of Natural Sciences of Philadelphia* 1 (17–19): 203–4.

Olivares, Ambrosio R., and Manuel T. González. 1889. "Tocologia." *El estudio* 1 (17): 266–72.

Ramírez, José. (1878) 1989. "Origen teratológico de las variedades, razas y especies." In *La polémica del darwinismo en México. Siglo XIX*, edited by Roberto Moreno de los Arcos, 214–25. Mexico: UNAM.

———. (1895) 1989. "Las leyes biológicas permiten asegurar que las razas primitivas de América son autóctonas." In *La polémica del darwinismo en México. Siglo XIX*, edited by Roberto Moreno de los Arcos, 309–12. Mexico: UNAM.

Rodríguez, J. M. 1872. "Parto al término normal del embarazo." *Gaceta Médica de México* (7): 103–6.

Romero, José María. 1895. "Estudio craneométrico Zapoteca." Eleventh International Congress of Americanists, Mexico City, October 15–20.

Sánchez, Jesús. (1899) 1989. "Relaciones de la antropología y la medicina." In *La polémica del darwinismo en México. Siglo XIX*, edited by Roberto Moreno de los Arcos, 320–39. Mexico: UNAM.

SECONDARY SOURCES

Achim, Miruna. 2013. "Maleta de doble fondo y colección de antigüedades. Ciudad de México, 1830 ca." In *Museos al detalle. Colecciones, antigüedades e historia natural, 1780–1870*, edited by Miruna Achim and Irina Podgorny, 99–126. Rosario, Argentina: Prohistoria Ediciones.

———. 2017. *From Idols to Antiquity: Forging the National Museum of Mexico (1825–1867).* Lincoln: University of Nebraska Press.

Blanckaert, Claude. 2009. *De la race à l'évolution. Paul Broca et l'anthropologie française (1850–1900).* Paris: L'Harmattan.

Brown, Lee Rust. 1992. "The Emerson Museum." *Representations* (40): 57–80.

Canguilhem, Georges. 1995. *The Normal and the Pathological.* New York: Zone Books.

Carrillo, Ana María. 1999. "Nacimiento y muerte de una profesión. Parteras tituladas en México." *Dynamis. Acta Hispanica ad Medicinae Scientiarum Historiam Ilustrandam* (19): 167–90.

Comas, Juan. 1954. *Los congresos internacionales de americanistas. Síntesis histórica e índice bibliográfico general (1875–1952)*. Mexico: Instituto Indigenista Interamericano.

Copjec, Joan. 2006. *Imaginemos que la mujer no existe. Ética y sublimación*. Mexico: Fondo de Cultura Económica.

Díaz Perera, Miguel Ángel. 2008. "De viajeros y coleccionistas de antigüedades. Jean Frédéric Waldeck en México: Historia, origen y naturaleza del hombre americano en los albores de la modernidad." PhD diss., Colegio de Michoacán.

Dorlin, Elsa. 2006. *La matrice de la race. Génealogie sexuelle et coloniale de la nation française*. Paris: Éditions la Découverte.

Flores, Francisco de Asis. 1992. *Historia de la medicina en México. Desde la época de los indios hasta la presente*, vol. 3. Mexico: Instituto Mexicano del Seguro Social.

García Murcia, Miguel Antonio Abel. 2013. "La profesionalización de la antropología física en México: la investigación, las instituciones y la enseñanza (1887–1942)." PhD diss., Facultad de Filosofía y Letras, Universidad Nacional Autónoma de México (UNAM).

Gorbach, Frida. 2008. *El monstruo, objeto imposible. Un estudio sobre teratología mexicana, siglo XIX*. Mexico: Universidad Autónoma Metropolitana and Itaca.

Guevara, Fefer Rafael. 2002. *Los últimos años de la historia natural y los primeros días de la biología en México. La práctica científica de Alfonso Herrera, Manuel María Villada y Mariano Bárcena*. Cuadernos del Instituto de Biología, vol. 35. Mexico: UNAM.

Hopwood, Nick. 1999. "'Giving Body' to Embryos: Modeling, Mechanism, and the Microtome in Late Nineteenth-Century Anatomy." *Isis* 90 (3): 462–96.

Karp, Ivan, and Steven D. Lavine. 1991. *Exhibiting Cultures: The Poetics and Politics of Museum Display*. Washington D.C.: Smithsonian Institution Press.

López-Beltrán, Carlos. 2004. "In the Cradle of Heredity: French Physicians and 'l'hérédité naturelle' in the Early Nineteenth Century." *Journal of the History of Biology* 37 (1): 39–72.

———. 2006. *El sesgo hereditario, ámbitos históricos del concepto de herencia biológica*. Mexico: UNAM.

López Hernández, Haydée. 2009. "La construcción de la cultura madre en los estudios arqueológicos en México (1867–1942)." PhD diss., Facultad de Filosofía y Letras, UNAM.

Peard, Julian G. 1999. *Race, Place, and Medicine: The Idea of the Tropics in Nineteenth-Century Brazilian Medicine*. Durham, NC: Duke University Press.

Podgorny, Irina, and M. Margaret Lópes. 2008. *El desierto en una vitrina. Museos e historia natural en Argentina*. Mexico: Limusa.

Riviale, Pascal. 1999. "La science en marche au pas cadencé: les recherches archéologiques et anthropologiques durant l'intervention française au Mexique (1862–1867)." *Journal de la Société des Américanistes* (85): 307–41.

Ruíz, Rosaura. 1990. *Los orígenes del Darwinismo en México*. Mexico: Limusa.

Rutsch, Mechthild. 2007. *Entre el campo y el gabinete. Nacionales y extranjeros en la profesionalización de la antropología mexicana (1877–1920)*. Mexico: Instituto Nacional de Antropología e Historia.

Saldaña, Juan José, and Consuelo Cuevas. 1999. "La invención en México de la investigación científica profesional: El Museo Nacional." *Quipu. Revista latinoamericana de las ciencias y la tecnología* 12 (3): 309–32.

Star, Susan Leigh, and James R. Griesemer. 1989. "Institutional Ecology, 'Translations' and Boundary Objects: Amateurs and Professionals in *Berkeley's Museum of Vertebrate Zoology*, 1907–39." *Social Studies of Science* 19 (3): 387–420.

Stocking, Georges, Jr. 1983. "Essays on Museums and Material Culture." In *Objects and Others: Essays on Museums and Material Culture*, edited by Georges Stocking Jr., 3–14. History of Anthropology, vol. 3. Madison: University of Wisconsin Press.

Urías, Beatríz. 2007. *Historias secretas del racismo*. Mexico: Tusquets Editores.

Williams, Elizabeth. 1985. "Anthropological Institutions in Nineteenth-Century France." *Isis* 3 (76): 331–48.

Zimmerman, Andrew. 1998. "Anthropology and the Place of Knowledge in Imperial Berlin." PhD diss., University of California, San Diego.

CHAPTER 8

ANTHROPOLOGICAL DEBATES AROUND THE INDIGENOUS SUBJECT AND ALTERITY, 1940–1948

PAULA LÓPEZ CABALLERO

To define is, by its logical essence, to delineate the details that best fit within a concept not just for one given moment, but rather for all time. And the primary utility of a definition is grounded in its permanence.

—ALFONSO CASO 1948, 240

I N 1948 the Instituto Nacional Indigenista (INI, National Indigenist Institute) was launched in Mexico almost a decade after the creation, also in Mexico, of the Instituto Indigenista Interamericano (III, Inter-American Indigenist Institute), which resulted from the agreements made at the first Congreso Indigenista Interamericano (Inter-American Indigenist Congress) in Pátzcuaro in 1940 (hereafter, Congreso de Pátzcuaro). Beginning in that decade, policies directed toward the indigenous population of the country would be dominated by these two institutions. Particularly starting in the 1970s, their actions would face critiques, some of which would even come to conceive of them as promoting ethnocide in their policies. This critique of the *indigenista* project, however, originated within its own scholarly field and thus shares the bulk of its premises—above all, the supposition that *indigenista* policies and the INI were acting in relation to previously constituted and clearly identifiable social groups: indigenous people.

However, through previous work that sought to understand the conditions under which the INI initially began working in Chiapas State, it became clear—to my surprise—that a central problem directly engaging the institute's directives was that of determining who would be subject to their interventions: who was indigenous (López Caballero 2015). How could it be that almost half-way through the twentieth century the specialists dedicated to "acculturating" the indigenous population could not determine with any certainty on whom their work should focus? In effect, before developing an understanding of which policies were best in order to integrate indigenous people, the challenge for *indigenistas* was primarily to understand who was indigenous and what constituted their singularity, what made them different.

Furthermore, this problem was far from being unconscious or hidden, though it has gone practically unnoticed by historiography.[1] As we will see in this chapter, solely on a conceptual level, even before *indigenista* theory was confronted with the social realities of rural Mexico, the very category of *indigenous* constituted a spirited site of dispute. I will outline, then, an intense debate that took place during the decade of the 1940s between anthropologists and *indigenistas*, Mexicans and foreigners, primarily in articles published in the journal *América Indígena* (*Indigenous America, AI*), in relation to the problem of how to understand who is indigenous, what constitutes their alterity, and how that should determine what the state must do with those groups.[2] To examine these debates I borrow the concept of controversial space (Nudler 2004). This perspective allows me to demonstrate how each approach became more solidified in the heat of the debates themselves, even as each author exhibited certain tendencies.[3]

The controversy I reconstruct is of historical and current interest—in particular because it established the importance of self-identification as a central element of the identification of indigenous people, but above all, because on a global level a shift would be made from a concept of alterity based in features (phenotypic, cultural, etc.) to a definition of *indio* based on someone's belonging to the community. Thus, despite the fact that official *indigenismo* had been consensually condemned, its stamp on the category of *indigenous* remains present through, for example, the link that even today seems inherent between indigenous alterity and belonging to a collectivity.

INTER-AMERICAN *INDIGENISTAS* VERSUS CHICAGO ANTHROPOLOGISTS

In the following pages, I will give an accounting of a range of publications throughout the decade that culminates, in some measure, with the extremely well-known article by Alfonso Caso (1948)—founder and director of the INAH (Instituto Nacional de Antropología e Historia; National Institute of Anthropology and History) and future founder and director of the INI—titled "Definición del indio y de lo indio" ("Definition of the Indian and of Indianness"). The common ground that unites all the positions I will analyze here is the establishment of a field of political intervention; their task was to locate a series of problems (in this case marginalization, poverty, and the exclusion of important sectors of the national population) and their solutions. It was necessary to know who was indigenous, but it was equally necessary to know what to do with those persons.

After reviewing the nearly thirty issues of the journal *AI* that began in 1941 and extended through 1948, I established a typology of the articles.[4] The set of texts I will examine here belong to a subgroup I call theoretical-conceptual debates. The first article, written by the director of the III, Manuel Gamio, dates from April 1942.[5] In it, Gamio signaled that the first problem for *indigenista* institutions is to understand "the number of individuals in the continental population that might be correctly classified with the generic term *indios*" (1942a, 17). The most frequently used criteria up to that moment, Gamio notes, were linguistic and racial, but neither of those two options was sufficient—the first, because "it leaves out . . . many millions of individuals who only speak Spanish but who are indigenous based on their ethnic and cultural characteristics." As for the second, his objection was not conceptual (what race means, whether races exist or not, etc.) but rather "technical," since "in order to achieve such a purpose, one requires significant time and tremendous economic resources, and additionally, it is necessary for the technical difficulties (of measurement) one encounters to be overcome." The solution he proposed, therefore, was to classify "these social groups from the point of view of their respective cultures—that is, in accordance with the elements presented by their material and intellectual life" (1942a, 18).

Gamio expanded on this argument in at least two other articles, from July and October of that year (1942b and 1942c). In the first of these, he developed a concrete proposal for establishing who could be considered indigenous that consisted of "adopting a classification of cultural characteristics that might distinguish among characteristics that are properly indigenous . . . foreign characteristics . . . and mixed characteristics." Gamio associated "the indigenous" with two factors: pre-Hispanic legacy and "deficient biological development . . . the economic-cultural characteristics of which correspond to anachronistic and inferior evolutionary stages" (1942b, 15). Once it had been established, for instance, which sorts of objects were most predominant in each home, it could be "objectively" determined to which type of culture an individual belonged. His third article from that year (1942c) completed the argument. Once the cultural characteristics of each group had been established, Gamio wondered, "Who determines how many and which of these should be preserved, extirpated, corrected, or substituted, and how many or which should be introduced? Is it recommendable to leave such a daunting task to the exclusive criteria of indigenous people themselves?" (1942c, 17). His response was that it was not. In relation to certain issues, like health or education, the "conventional criteria" of indigenous people should be superseded by the anthropologist's "scientific criteria" (1942c, 22).

This set of articles has served to support certain norms or "common sense" that asserts that in Mexican anthropology race ceased to be an operative marker, having been supplanted by culture. In effect, Gamio defended the idea that an understanding of who is indigenous cannot be measured exclusively by racial, linguistic, or cultural criteria, but rather should be assessed using a combination of all of those elements, with principal importance placed on material culture. The overlaps among the terms he used, however, are remarkable: biological development, heritage, cultural characteristics, and poverty. Without a doubt, Gamio made a tremendous effort to systematize these notions, which nonetheless become confused—biologizing, in a manner of speaking, culture, and culturalizing poverty.

We might think that these articles were a response to a text published earlier by Robert Redfield[6] in English in March of 1940 (just one month before the Congreso de Pátzcuaro), titled "The Indian in Mexico"—an article that someone like Gamio, with ties to the North American academy, might easily have encountered.[7] In the intellectual context of the era, where the social reality of the Mexican rural world was conceived in terms of groups that were homogenous in and of themselves, with clearly discernible differences among them—even via use of biological criteria—Redfield's article stands out for its contrasting vision. The text begins with a categorical sentence: "In such a country as Mexico, where much racial intermixture has occurred . . . one cannot enumerate the Indians in a biological sense. Nor it is possible to count the Indians as a socially recognized group, as we do with Negroes in the United States, because in most parts of Mexico Indians are not so defined" (Redfield, 1940, 132).

In order to prove his argument, Redfield's article examined recent census reports, noting the difficulty they exhibited in tallying numbers of indigenous people; he offered testimonies from government officials and other authorities who demonstrated that the criteria for defining *indios* had more to do with class than with ethnic or racial groups, in the sense that these might be understood in the United States. Unlike Gamio, Redfield did not consider the problem of race to be one of measurement: for him, race was simply not an operative category of information and did not express any positive data in a society like Mexico. Additionally, Redfield (1940) indicated that the principal problem did not have to do with determining the origins of the elements of each group's social and cultural life, but rather with recognizing the predominant social fragmentation in the country. Thus, more than an issue of culture or of evolution, "The 'Indian problem' of Mexico is the problem of converting many little folk societies into a nation" (138).[8]

Both Gamio and Redfield agreed that the nation suffered a state of fragmentation due to the conditions of indigenous groups. The difference between them, though subtle, is that for Gamio (1942a, 18) the primary obstacle—also a primary virtue—preventing the integration of those groups was located in their own culture—that is, in the elements of their "material and intellectual culture," and hence his position has come to be known as "culturalist." Change must therefore operate through assessment and modification of elements social scientists consider necessary, but always from within indigenous cultures. Redfield, for his part, believed that the obstacles to integration were primarily located in the state's capacity to access isolated areas and integrate them efficiently. The transformation that must take place was that of the social and economic conditions in which certain sectors of the population lived, even if that might result in a change at the level of culture. Hence his position would be identified as "functionalist."

However, the field of *indigenista* thought was not limited to these two positions. At the end of that same year, Lucio Mendieta y Núñez (1942) would also put forth a reaction to Redfield's text.[9] The Mexican attorney contradicted Redfield, arguing that many groups "have remained at a level of isolation such that it has been possible to maintain an existence as distinct ethnic groups. Other indigenous races have intermingled, but the result . . . is always a type of *indio*" (65–66).[10] Mendieta y Núñez went even further in his conception of alterity as an inflexible biological issue:

In Mexico, since the colonial era and extending to the present day, there has not been intense racial mixing due to the following factors that would oppose such fusion: a) geographic isolation of *indios*. b) Cultural inferiority . . . c) Lack of physical attractiveness . . . d) Economic inferiority . . . e) Language . . . f) Endogamous customs. . . . In Mexico, to identify indigenous race and social class only leads to purposeful misrepresentations . . . because it artificially eliminates one of the principal terms of such identifications: that of race, which plays a central role. (66–67)[11]

Certainly, this position embodies one extreme of the debate, as it considers the alterity of people identified as indigenous to be innate (and contemptible). Even so, this biologizing concept of race did not elicit reactions or critiques that would be registered in publications. Though a person like Gamio would no longer defend the centrality of this idea of race as a principal "marker of alterity," neither would he deny its existence as positive data or as an explanatory factor. Mendieta y Núñez's position simply expressed a radical version of the perspective that Gamio had generalized and defended.

A fourth anthropologist would intervene with an article that was also published in *AI*, in the same month of October 1942. The text in question was titled "Ethnic Relations in Guatemala," by the anthropologist Sol Tax, who was at that time beginning his career.[12] It is not beyond imagination that this work should be the first, at least in the Latin Americanist sphere, to talk about ethnic relations. The type of publications that dominated at the time suggested that until that moment, the only elements that were "ethnic" (a term understood most of the time as referencing "race") were groups and their characteristics. The novelty in the title synthesized, in effect, an innovative perspective about the indigenous problem precisely as it was understood up to that point.

Tax reinforced the position of his mentor, Redfield, and began his argument asserting that "in the greater part of Guatemala, present-day distinctions *are not founded on biological race*" (Tax 1942, 44; emphasis added). Consequently, for Tax the indigenous problem is not a racial problem, as it might be understood in the United States, as the data allowing distinctions to be made between an *indio* and a non-*indio* were "independent of physical heritage" (45). Hence the problem at hand would, in Guatemala, principally be a question of inequality and lack of opportunities:

There is an Indian problem in Guatemala, but to understand it, and solve it, one must first cleanse his mind of the idea that it is a race problem. It is true that by and large the people who are called Indians in Guatemala are blood-descendants of American aborigines; it is also true that most of the non-Indians in Guatemala have more or less European blood. *It is not true that these facts are socially important.* (44; emphasis added)

This does not mean that Tax believed that race doesn't exist, nor that in Guatemala there was no inequality, discrimination, or disregard—often based in phenotype or skin color—toward those identified as *indios*. However, given that alterity was defined based on social rather than biological criteria, "Passage from one group to the other is possible; more than that, it tends to become automatic. An Indian who loses his Indian characteristics *is* a Ladino" (Tax 1942, 46).[13] In order to demonstrate his argument, Tax pointed out that though census counts did use the category of *race*, they distinguished solely between *indios* and Ladinos and included in the latter group Chinese, Lebanese, and, in fact, "white" people. In contemporary Guatemala, even in common language, only two categories of people exist: *indios* and Ladinos.

How does the distinction between one group and the other function? Language is one basic indicator, as is the type of clothing worn or participation in the religious-political life in the towns. For the author, the central point was that "all of the criteria mentioned are independent of physical heritage . . . the whole question of blood . . . is irrelevant in the distinction actually made." And his argument culminated with an example: "Once [this] is clearly understood . . . it need not seem strange that one of two brothers can be an Indian and the other, perhaps living in the same town, a Ladino" (Tax 1942, 45). Tax, like Redfield, concluded his work with a defense of the idea that the "indigenous problem" did not originate in elements intrinsic to groups thus designated (including "their" culture) but rather in the national context of unequal opportunities. Thus the most urgent task in terms of social transformation was to dismantle the associations among poverty, exclusion, and indigeneity.

Taking into account the generally accepted chronology, according to which race was never an operative criterion in discussions of indigenous people—and significantly, had been abandoned by the 1940s—the reactions against Redfield's and Tax's arguments are astonishing. At the end of Tax's article, the editors of *AI* decided to include a letter commentary penned by John Collier (1884–1968), a government official and self-taught anthropologist, of the same generation as Gamio, who was also the director of the Indian Affairs Bureau and a key political figure in inter-American *indigenismo*. Collier rejected Tax's hypotheses with a single stroke of the pen. For this government official, "The article seeks to abolish the factor of Indianhood from consideration, in treating of a country whose population is largely Indian. . . . Indeed, it used to be customary to abolish the Indian problem in just this way" (Tax 1942, 47). In other words, Collier seemed to indicate that it had been an advance to recognize the specificity of the problems indigenous people experienced, and that Tax's proposal was somewhat regressive.[14] He further established a more or less linear association between "race" and "Indianhood" to the extent that for him, to deny the existence of a racial problem, as Tax did, was equivalent to denying that there was an indigenous problem. In addition, the interpretation Collier offered would seem to invert Tax's entire argument:

> Nowhere is the Indian pragmatically speaking merely a pure-blood race. The Indian is defined . . . by blood, by language, by culture, and in some countries by a legal status . . . and to insist that the Indian does not exist or, as an Indian, should be ignored, unless his biological, linguistic, social, legal and economic identification are exactly coterminal, would be to confuse the subject hopelessly. (47)

Finally, he maintained that Tax's assertions contradict both the theses underpinning the III, the treaties among the countries that constitute it, and the presentations offered in Pátzcuaro, as well as "the total experience of countries like Mexico and the U.S." (Tax 1942, 48). Implicitly, then, Collier was confirming that Tax's critique hit the target dead on: his analysis of the ethnic situation in Guatemala destabilized and cast doubt on the entire project of a unified inter-American *indigenismo*, so dear to him (and to Gamio).

This critique was leveled so strongly that in the following issue of *AI*, in January of 1943, the editors published texts by various colleagues under the title "Comments on Dr. Tax's Article" (Redfield et al. 1943). The first to intervene was Redfield, writing in favor of the positions his colleague defended. His detailed missive offered three principal arguments in support of Tax's approach: (1) The situation of indigenous people in Guatemala was not the same as in the United States, particularly because it was more difficult to recognize an "indigenous problem" independent of social problems in general. (2) In contrast with the United States, where there were significantly fewer Indians, and those were extremely segregated—two reasons why a special program seemed to be more clearly justified—the indigenous population in Guatemala was the most intensely affected by inequality and would therefore be the greatest beneficiaries of a general social development program. (3) In Guatemala, unlike in the United States, Ladinos might be seen as equals with *indios*, for example, by the urban population. According to Redfield, this would be impossible in the United States, because "the important differences between groups in Guatemala are differences of culture. They are not differences of race. In our country the fact of Indian blood is of importance . . . No doubt the strength of race prejudice as between Negroes and Whites in our country has an influence on relations between Indians and Whites" (84).

Expressed in terms of my own analytical framework, what Redfield tried to demonstrate was that markers of alterity, those sociological data that identify someone as "other" (in this case, indigenous), along with their effects or consequences, are contextual, varying from country to country. It is fascinating, then, that Redfield was able to see that Collier was transplanting a "regime of alterity" specific to the United States to the Guatemalan context.[15] What was being argued, finally, was the question of the extent to which the regime of alterity that operated in the United States and that seemed to rule in the III might be applicable to Latin America: "In the U.S. there is a social barrier between racial groups that is based on awareness of differences in blood between members of the one race and members of another. This barrier is very strong in Negro-White relations; it is present in Indian-White relations. *It is practically absent in much of Guatemala*" (Redfield et al. 1943, 85; emphasis added).

What followed was a new and extremely brief response by Collier (two paragraphs). He insisted that inequality between *indios* and Ladinos went beyond the socioeconomic because the culture of *indios* was not valued. In order to enjoy opportunities, therefore, an indigenous person must abandon what in Guatemala was considered to be "Indianhood." But his central critique was that Tax "seems to presume that no inner or organic dynamic values exist within the Indian culture or life, which need to be studied, experimented with, and utilized as group values in the process of building both Indian life and the total life." (Redfield et al. 1943, 86). We can deduce that for Collier, this internal dynamic unique to indigenous cultures was a reality out of which *indigenista* interventions must be conceived and enacted.

The subsequent remarks came from a figure who is little known now but who held a relatively important position in *indigenista* circles in the 1940s: Emil Sady.[16] For him, there was a confusion around the definition of the "indigenous person," because though no one maintained that indigeneity was defined on a "purely racial basis," not even in the United States, it was still a mistake to organize development programs based on class, given that "the cultural characteristics of the population" must be taken into consideration as the central criterion (Redfield et. al. 1943, 88). His primary contribution was the identification of two positions that would be sketched out more and more clearly by two professional groups: anthropologists (Tax, Redfield) and government officials (Collier and Gamio). Significantly, the distinction he made between the two stemmed from their respective notions of change: for the first group, any innovation presupposed a break with the elements that tend to maintain the integrity and wholeness of a society; for the second, in "favor of cultural diversity," it was possible to introduce new elements without dismantling the structure of the culture (88). In my judgment, what distinguishes the two is the value placed on that culture: for the administrators if culture is lost, all is lost, and there cannot be justice for indigenous groups, as they will disappear. For the anthropologist, change is neither positive nor negative; it is simply inevitable if these groups' most basic needs are attended, instead of giving priority to the preservation of culture.

At the end of that year, in October of 1943, another article would appear, written by the also young anthropologist Julian Steward (1902–1972), who was of the same generation as Tax. His article attempted to mediate between these two positions. One primary confusion was that it had been assumed that when officials sought to protect "distinctive indigenous values" (Steward 1943, 324), they were referring to elements of pre-Hispanic culture, which would be an absurdity given that history had made of contemporary indigenous cultures an inseparable conglomerate of elements with multiple origins. Once this confusion was clarified, the conflict between the two groups was not so very great: "If, then, by Indianhood they mean not pre-Columbian customs and values but something that develops within native traditions and does not remain static or even stable, I see no great conflict with the anthropologists. For the latter does not maintain that acculturative forces will reduce the Indian to a dead level of national homogeneity" (324).

We shall summarize the controversy up to this moment, which has to do principally with the way indigenous alterity was understood (as a property, a level of biological development, a race, a cultural system, or a social position), with its transformation (inevitable, unidirectional, directable) and with its cultural expressions (as a system, a configuration, a set of practices, etc.). Mendieta y Núñez's most radical position, though no one attacked or discarded it, would not be taken up or defended by anyone else in the following years. One possible explanation is that there is no substantive difference between alterity as a concept of race and the biologized culture Gamio addresses, for example; the difference, rather, is one of degree. This is why Mendieta y Núñez's ideas could be heard and validated in this controversial space. Nonetheless, as we will see shortly, little by little they would be left behind. Gamio, for instance, whose position remained practically static over ten years, did not include a racial criterion in his final reflections.

Redfield and Tax perceived the alterity of indigenous people as a relative point of information when they signaled the importance of national contexts in their definition. This perspective, however, did not seem to have explicit impact on the debate. Of their proposals, only the most simplistic elements, almost the opposite of what the anthropologists signaled in their work, seemed to come to the fore—that is, the idea that in Mexico, unlike in the United States, the importance of biological mixing makes it difficult to formulate a clear distinction between indigenous and non-indigenous people (as if, in other situations, such an objective distinction would be possible).

BETWEEN RACE AND CULTURE: THE "INDIGENOUS COMMUNITY"

After a brief pause, for the remainder of 1943 until the beginning of 1945, the debate around the definition of *indigenous* reappeared very forcefully in *AI*, in April 1945, in the form of a detailed text published by Oscar Lewis, another young North American anthropologist also educated in Chicago, and Ernest Maes, a representative of North American *indigenismo* in Latin America (Lewis and Maes 1945). Their article entered the debate around these problems directly, no longer from a position of academic language and legitimacy but rather by fully inhabiting the vocabularies and necessities of *indigenistas* and administrators.

The first thing the III needed to do, the authors remarked, was to clarify how *indios* would be defined, and which categories of data were necessary for particular interventions. To that end, instead of discussing the scientific validity of the definitions that had been used up to that point in order to study the *indio* (physical-biological, social, etc.), the article's central objective was to "propose a definition that will be practical from the point of view of gathering statistical and cadastral data and usable in relation to the goals and purposes of the III" (Lewis and Maes 1945, 108).

Their critique around the definitions used both by anthropologists and by *indigenistas* is that these were based in the description of cultural features, the principal objective of which was to establish the alterity of indigenous people, particularly in contrast to non-indigenous people. The problem was that "neither the dances, nor the typical rites, nor the typical clothing—even when . . . these are cultural characteristics that clearly distinguish an indigenous community from a purely *mestizo* one—serve to help us understand the unique needs of these groups" (Lewis and Maes 1945, 111).

It was necessary, in contrast, to devise a practical definition that might be used by a government official or specialist, even if that functional definition did not allow for the establishment of limits that separated *indios* from non-*indios*. Such a definition should take into account not so much the unique attributes of indigenous people, or in the words of the authors, "the determining characteristics of what is indigenous," but more so the "most acute economic and social deficiencies" of the social groups (Lewis and Maes 1945, 113–17). What is interesting about this proposal—which might be understood as the simple transit from "culture" to "class"—is that it did not refuse, as Marxism or classical sociology would later on, the category of *indigenous*. In effect, what we have here, rather, is a mutation in the very interior of the category *indigenous*. To achieve this, the authors engaged in a kind of juggling act in order to attempt to articulate a notion of *indigenous* founded in alterity, which was central to the III as a practical notion in governmental terms: "According to our criterion, when a group has the maximum number of quantitative needs and deficiencies . . . alongside the maximum number of qualitative deficiencies, we are in the presence of a group that we might call indigenous" (115).

Nonetheless, Lewis and Maes ended up implicitly accepting the idea that socioeconomic position is not sufficient in order to characterize indigenous people, as this would further require a historical grounding: the four hundred years of colonial oppression. In conclusion, despite this return to the idea of a fixed constant that would characterize indigenous people—colonial oppression—the movement that Lewis and Maes proposed remains innovative and reinitiates the debate: No longer is the issue one of locating the limits that separate the indigenous from the non-indigenous, nor of identifying where the alterity of persons lies, but rather of which data might be useful in terms of the practical enactment of inter-American *indigenismo*. We might say, in short, that they moved from a definition that was attributive (in the sense that it appealed to or sought to define attributes of the indigenous, the fixed nucleus of its singularity) to a definition contemplated principally in function of who would use it, a realm more closely related to the ideas put forth by Redfield and Tax.

The next article to address this subject would appear in the first issue from 1947. The young self-taught anthropologist Julio de la Fuente (ca. 1905–1966) published an article that we can here understand as a first attempt at synthesizing the two approaches that up to that point had been antagonistic (de la Fuente, 1947a). In July of that same year, he would publish a second article relating to these topics; we will address both texts together (de la Fuente, 1947b). De la Fuente did not explicitly mention the debate that by that time had been going on for five years. Nonetheless, the elements and construction of the arguments he presented point to that debate with sufficient specificity such that we can include it here.

The author began by remarking that he did not agree that "it should be necessary . . . to define with precision, first and foremost, the groups that should be considered *indios*," precisely as Gamio proposed. However, he agreed with Lewis and Maes's proposal that the INI's target population should be defined on the basis of its socioeconomic needs. The reason he presented was tremendously innovative: "It is not always best to address the *indio* as such [due to the fact that many of them] have come to be non-*indios*" (de la Fuente 1947a, 63–64). A criterion was needed, then, that might take this shift into account. The rest of the article consists of arguments in support of this thesis.

De la Fuente (1947a) coincides with Redfield's critique of racial criteria, as he considers that these were of minimal significance and, further, that biological mixing had been a dominant process in the history of the population in Mexico. Nonetheless, in what we might read as a concession to Gamio, de la Fuente accepted that "racial attitudes" (or racist attitudes, we might say today) effectively existed with respect to certain phenotypical features or certain customs. The anthropologist goes on to critique the use of cultural criteria, due to the fact that it was often quite static, given that it was based in cultural features among populations that were experiencing intense cultural change. It was thus difficult to establish which cultural elements should be called indigenous alongside the enormous differences that existed within and among different indigenous groups (67–68). Furthermore, this criterion was an obstacle to an acknowledgement of what he called "El pase del indio" ("The *indio* pass"):

This pass is a daily occurrence and takes place when indigenous language and garments, principally, or a whole series of cultural attributes usually considered to be *indio* are disregarded. However, in many cases, it is not necessary to eliminate anything, insofar as *the 'indio' has not considered himself as such or has by now learned to consider himself a* campesino, *a worker, or a native of a specific region.* (68; emphasis added)[17]

In his second article from that same year, de la Fuente's (1947b) position seemed to become more nuanced. He explained that while his first text detailed the process through which an indigenous person in Mexico ceased to be identified as *indio*, this should not lead us to conclude that this was a generalized and homogenous phenomenon across the country, nor that it occurred with a speed such that it would become possible to speak plainly and simply about the "disappearance of the *indio.*" The anthropologist recognized that though certain areas of indigenous culture were being modified, there were attributes that "make [indigenous] subjects special, and different from the '*campesino*' population, and even more different from the urban population" (212). Hence changes in attire, language, and even self-identification did not automatically signal the disappearance of the *indio* as such.

Curiously, the alterity of indigenous people would appear once again as a fixed content, more in tune with Gamio's ideas about indigenous people and the policies the III should create for them. But, surprisingly, this assertion was employed by de la Fuente in order to support the arguments presented by Lewis and Maes, and even tacitly to contradict the director of the III. Given that cultural elements can change without the indigenous peoples disappearing, this author thus asserted, the criterion that should be the rule in relation to *indigenista* policies was that of the deficiencies and needs of the population.

To conclude, de la Fuente (1947b) signals "the relative inappropriateness of remedies and actions explicitly directed toward indigenous people in a process of change." And he proposes that "an *indigenista* policy in a country like Mexico should combine actions formally directed toward indigenous people, which give specific treatment to 'indigenous' characteristics, with actions directed to those [in the population] who are not explicitly 'indigenous'" (215).

We can see, then, that arguments and ideas that were already on the table for discussion are here formulated and utilized in an innovative way. Additionally, de la Fuente contributed new elements to this problematic: a critique of cultural criteria in societies that experience massive processes of change; a consideration, already articulated as a key factor, of the way individual persons perceive themselves; the idea that beyond a concept of *indio* there exists a plurality of forms of being indigenous; and finally, the movement that extends from alterity-as-culture to alterity-as-belonging.

De la Fuente reconsidered—practically, one by one—the critiques Redfield and Tax had leveled against authors like Gamio and Collier. Further, Tax's article had already outlined the way those individuals categorized as indigenous "felt," an element that for de la Fuente would constitute a central criterion of "Indianness" (we will see that Alfonso Caso would later enshrine this idea). Given the tremendous affinity between his ideas and those of the two North American anthropologists, why wouldn't de la Fuente's arguments receive similarly well-formulated critiques as did these earlier works?

One fundamental element is that despite all the critiques he revisited, and despite the fact that he was opposed to a specific policy directed toward indigenous people, he never denied the existence of specifically recognizable groups.[18] De la Fuente's two articles are significant precisely because in them the author successfully struck a balance between approaches that up to that point had seemed entirely incompatible: on the one hand, the acceptance of the existence of an indigenous subject with unique characteristics, and on the other, the idea that in order to be efficient, *indigenismo* must move beyond that cultural or substantial definition of the indigenous subject in favor of a practical definition that might encompass any person with certain needs.

If de la Fuente was the person who would "translate" the ideas—so provocative in their time—of the anthropologists from Chicago, moving just enough to be able to continue to assert those ideas and at the same time make them audible to the Mexican anthropological community, Gamio (1947), for his part, would publish one further text in the time period contemplated here. In this text, possibly in reaction to de la Fuente, he would reassert his ideas once again. Perhaps it was the Cold War looming ever closer just outside the threshold of this magazine that caused Gamio to denounce those who posited that class should be the principal criterion for public action, as "guided by the perspective of propaganda . . . inspired by fundamentally political aims." For those who thought this way, "The indigenous problem does not exist in reality," as they found indigenous people, like many rural people, to be in "equal or analogous conditions of economic misery and low levels of culture," and for that reason "they should be treated equally." Hence he asked:

Is it logical and possible that the mere fact that the two groups of individuals [Indigenous and non-Indigenous] . . . are said to be in equal or analogous conditions of misery, indicates that it is most effective to apply the same methods and treatment to both? . . . It is obvious that such a thing would be impossible, that it is necessary to develop different remedies for each group and that the Indigenous problem exists and has always existed. (283)

These considerations reiterate, almost word for word, ideas articulated at the beginning of the decade, and they reactivate an idea of alterity seen as intrinsic to indigenous people. The subtle but perceptible shift here is that, effectively, the idea of race fades more and more into the background, and the idea of needs is now foregrounded. Nonetheless, the updating or reformulation of these ideas would be a task not for Gamio but rather for one of his contemporaries, also a scientist and public official. What Caso would do with Gamio's ideas was equivalent to de la Fuente's work with the ideas of Tax and Redfield. His oft-cited article "Definición del indio y de lo indio," published for the first time in October of 1948, should thus be understood as an inheritance of this debate.[19] It would be this work that would serve as a guide for *indigenista* policies developed by the INI, at least until Gonzalo Aguirre Beltrán would develop his model around *"regiones de refugio."*

Caso (1948) began with an almost philosophical reflection about the difficulty of defining a process compared with a stable idea or a fixed object (cf. epigraph of this article). Once again taking up one of de la Fuente's central points (though without citing him), the challenge as Caso articulated it was how to define— and hence fix—something that is shifting. Like his predecessors, he formulated a critique of racial criteria or "biological meaning" as ways to define *indios*, in large measure due to the "mixing between *indios* and Europeans" (243)—once again, not due to the ineffectiveness of the concept. He even illustrated this idea with an example, apparently similar to one used by Tax: "In a single town, in a single family, one of the children might present indigenous somatic characteristics that are not discernible in another, and in contrast, this second child might have other indigenous characteristics that do not appear in the first" (243). The fundamental difference was that Tax was talking about sociological features (dress, language, etc.) while Caso referenced physical appearance.

Caso (1948) also points to the insufficiency of cultural criteria when he notes that the origin of a cultural object does not necessarily indicate without equivocation the identity of the person using it. Like Gamio, he recognized that linguistic criteria are the principal guide for knowing whether a person is indigenous or not. But this author added another element to this idea, one that was already present in de la Fuente's argument: "The consciousness of belonging or not to an indigenous group is . . . the most important feature . . . but . . . it is the most difficult to perceive" (245). This fourth criterion, which Caso called "psychological," would be the basis for his definition of indigenous people, and would provide the entry for this work and this author into the canon of *indigenismo* and of Mexican anthropology, despite the circularity of his assertion:

> An *indio* is someone who feels he belongs to an indigenous community. . . . We therefore arrive at the consideration that what is important to us is not to define an individual as *indio* or non-*indio*; . . . what is important to determine insofar as an *indigenista* policy for our population in intertropical America is, fundamentally, *the indigenous community* [which should be understood as] that community in which non-European somatic elements prevail . . . and which possesses the social feeling of an isolated community. (245–46; emphasis added)

Once a definition had been devised for the new subject on whom *indigenismo* would act, what remained was to establish what the necessities of that subject were: "The *indio*'s significant problems, at least in Mexico, are not just economic, but also fundamentally cultural." Hence his conclusion: "In short, what remains for us to offer the *indio* in order to resolve his problems is culture" (Caso 1948, 247).

To synthesize, the central concerns of Gamio's work (the need for a scientific and practical definition of indigenous people, the emphases he placed on culture as a solid nucleus of the distinction between indigenous and non-indigenous people, the benefits of specific interventions in the realm of culture in favor of groups defined as indigenous, etc.) would be updated in Caso's version, nourished by the critiques and contributions of de la Fuente, Tax, and Redfield: the difficulty of establishing with clarity who is indigenous and who is not, the idea that indigenous people are social subjects in constant change and are therefore difficult to fix within a single concept, and above all, the idea that self-perception is central to the establishment of borders between one group and another. Thus, we might almost suggest that this text by Caso is the translation of ideas posited by Redfield, Tax, and de la Fuente in the language and vocabulary of Gamio; the community, transformation, and self-identification those anthropologists proposed now served to defend the need, posited by the director of the III, for a definition of indigenous people and the centrality of culture—understood as elements that should be modified or preserved—in such a definition.

INSTITUTIONALIZING INDIGENOUS ALTERITY

Alongside the history of the institutionalization and professionalization of anthropology in Mexico and also parallel to the slow consolidation of an official *indigenista* policy, the controversies I have analyzed here demonstrate how the years that passed between the Congreso de Pátzcuaro and the creation of the INI are fundamental as well to the process of consolidation of a concept of *indigenous* that would last, in some measure, into the present time. At the intersection of a history of anthropological thought, an institutional history of *indigenismo*, and a conceptual history of the indigenous subject, the hypothesis I have tried to demonstrate is that the significance this term holds today acquired its most clearly defined delineations precisely during the period examined here, as part of the very process of institutionalizing the anthropological discipline and *indigenista* policies, and within the "controversial space" that has been analyzed here in detail.[20] During these debates, each position would undergo modifications, whether to become more radicalized or, as in the majority of cases, to discard or reformulate the extremes of each point of view that were most readily open to critique.

To attend to categories and their historicity allows for these to be constituted as analytical units per se, and for them to be interrogated around the distinct content that has been associated with a single word, rather than reproducing definitions, which are often atemporal. Thus the focal point is directed toward the uses actors make of categories, their tensions, and their transformations. Concretely, this perspective makes it possible to take into account at least three processes that occur within this debate. In the first place, the idea that biological (and cultural) mixing were distinctive features of the Mexican population would not successfully take root among *indigenistas*, nor would it impede the design of public policies directed exclusively toward the indigenous population. However, this idea—which, as we have seen, was consolidated, at least in part, in the interpretation Mexicans made of the ideas developed by the two anthropologists from Chicago—would occupy a central place within what would later be called the ideology of *mestizaje*. In the second place, we could observe that, though the term *race* was used less and less throughout the 1940s as a marker for the alterity of indigenous groups, the idea that inherited features existed did not completely disappear; now these were simply enumerated together within the term *culture*. Finally, an identification as "indigenous," as the term was eventually defined (and, in that measure, institutionalized) in Caso's article, would end up depending on a person's belonging to a collectivity, making it practically impossible to conceive of an indigenous person as an individual separated from their community. The othering of indigenous persons thus came to fix them not as part of a racial or ethnolinguistic group but as part of the community, a condition sine qua non for recognition of a person as such. These ideas prevail even to the current day, and are likely one of the longest-lasting legacies of *indigenista* policies.

In short, in this work I have attempted to make visible that concepts, too, are developed through processes; that is, I have attempted to make explicit the history of their contents, in particular at a moment when the term *indigenous* was incorporated into the vocabularies of public policy and science—a sociogenesis of the concept that moves beyond an objectivizing and ahistorical perception of this form of identification.

NOTES

This chapter was translated from Spanish by Jen Hofer. This chapter was originally published as "Dire l'altérité autochtone. Débats anthropologiques et indigénistes sur le sujet autochtone au Mexique (1940–1948)," *MOTS. Les langages du politique*, no. 115, November 2017, 145–64.

1. Globally, the history of anthropology and *indigenismo* jumps from the Congreso de Pátzcuaro (1940) to the creation of the INI (1948; cf. Téllez Ortega 1987; De la Peña 2014; Dawson 2004). But see Hewitt (1988), who focuses on the anthropological debates of the era, Faulhaber (2011) on the Smithsonian Institution in Mexico, and Giraudo (2014), who studies the Instituto Interamericano de Estadística (Inter-American Institute of Statistics), which at that same time was attempting to establish uniform criteria for census categories, particularly that of *indigenous*.

2. *América Indígena* was the foremost *indigenista* and anthropological journal of the time, published by the Instituto Indigenista Interamericano; the first issue dates from October 1941.

3. Oscar Nudler (2004) posits the concept of "controversial space" as an analytical unit privileged by the history of science. Its utility resides in a conception of the history of science as sequences of controversies, more than periods of stable and cumulative truths, as seems to be suggested by the idea of the paradigm proposed by Thomas Kuhn.

4. These articles can be classified in three ways: articles about the history of indigenous people (12 percent); articles that present ethnographic studies or case studies (30 percent); polemical articles (58 percent), which I then divide into two groups: programmatic texts and theoretical-conceptual debates. In this last subgroup we might also include another debate about the existence of races organized within a hierarchy, an issue that has already been studied by Giraudo and Martín-Sánchez (2013). It also

includes another debate between Lucio Mendieta y Núñez, Henrich Berlin, and Alfonso Villa Rojas, which has not been studied (between 1944 and 1945).

5. Manuel Gamio (1883–1960) undertook the first archeological and ethnographic project in Teotihuacán between 1917 and 1921. He published *Forjando Patria* (1916), which became one of the pillars of Mexican *indigenista* thought. His entry into the Instituto Indigenista Interamericano has yet to be studied, since his participation in the Congreso de Pátzcuaro and inter-American politics was minimal. See Legarreta (2016).

6. Robert Redfield (1897–1958) studied and worked at the University of Chicago. He began his fieldwork in Tepoztlán in 1926 for his doctoral thesis, which was published in 1930. That same year he began his research in the Maya region, where he met his future collaborator Alfonso Villa Rojas. Out of that research would emerge the foundational book *The Folk Culture of Yucatán*.

7. The article would be translated, published, and critiqued in 1942 in the *Revista Mexicana de Sociología*.

8. This argument is probably the foundation from which the idea developed that Redfield's functionalism saw the assimilation of indigenous people as the only inevitable future.

9. Lucio Mendieta y Núñez (1895–1988) studied at the Escuela Nacional de Jurisprudencia (National Law School) in 1915, and in 1917 began collaborating with Manuel Gamio at the recently founded Dirección de Antropología (Anthropology Administration). In 1939 he founded and began directing the Instituto de Investigaciones Sociales (Institute for Social Research) at UNAM and the *Revista Mexicana de Sociología*, in which the translated version of Redfield's article appeared.

10. From this quote we can assert that for Mendieta y Núñez, "ethnic group" and "race" were interchangeable terms.

11. The text concluded by denouncing Moisés Sáenz's projects, and in particular Morris Swadesh's first Proyecto Tarasco (Tarasco Project), which sought to build literacy in native languages.

12. Sol Tax (1907–1995) studied at the University of Chicago. In 1934 he got his PhD in anthropology specializing in Guatemala; he became a very close colleague with Robert Redfield. He taught at Escuela de Antropología (Mexico City) during 1942, and his work throughout the following two decades focused on the social organization and economic relationships among different Mayan groups.

13. This argument should not be confused or interpreted as a defense of a certain Latin American "racial democracy," a common interpretation in contrasting ideas about race in the United States and in Latin America. For a critique of this opposition, see Wade (1993). What Tax is proposing is that the logic of differentiation in Guatemala cannot be understood exclusively via the analytical tools used for United States society.

14. Perhaps Collier would read in Tax's argument a regurgitation of the old nineteenth-century liberal argument that rejected all recognition whatsoever of any type of sociocultural variation within the social body of citizens.

15. Regarding the term "regime of alterity": "We might advance the argument that each Nation-State creates and is simultaneously created by a *regime of alterity*, that is, by historicizing rhetorics that in the end confirm the 'truth' of the distinction that founds a national 'we' and a marginal and different 'other'" (López Caballero 2012, 130).

16. Sady was the representative of the United States National Indigenist Institute in Mexico. The institute was created in 1941, though it was always dependent on the Bureau of Indian Affairs, which Collier directed. Sady was his subordinate and ally in Mexico.

17. For the present author, an example of this would be the Zapotec people from the isthmus, whose preference is to refer to themselves using the name of the regions they are from—*juchitecos, tehuanos.*

18. Not to mention, of course, that in 1947 Julio de la Fuente did not have the same status or the same academic and symbolic weight as Sol Tax, and much less Robert Redfield; they were renowned academics, foreigners with the means to influence the development of Mexican anthropological research.

19. Published initially in *AI*, this article would appear in at least one anthology from 1951, in another from 1953 (Caso 1953), in another from 1954 (Caso 1954), yet another from 1971 (Secretaría de Educación Pública 1971), and finally one from 1996 (INI 1996). In addition to being referenced by *indigenistas* of the era themselves, Google Scholars registers more than three hundred citations from the text (https://scholar.google.com.mx/scholar?start=0&hl=en&as_sdt=2005&sciodt=0,5&as_vis=1&cites=17758834736026732244&scipsc). Among others, in chronological order, are Fabre ([1963] 1998), Stavenhagen (1969), Bonfil Batalla (1972), Knight (1990), De la Peña (1995), and Taylor (2009).

20. Even Knight's (1990) outstanding analysis seems to forget that "indigenous" was not the "object" of *indigenismo* but its product when he says that "the Revolution that began in 1910 could be fought and was fought on the basis of considerable Indian participation . . . but in the absence of any self-consciously Indian project" (76).

REFERENCES

PRINTED PRIMARY SOURCES

Caso, Alfonso. 1948. "Definición del indio y lo indio." *América Indígena* 8 (4): 239–47.

de la Fuente, Julio. 1947a. "Definición, pase y desaparición del indio en Mexico." *América Indígena* 7 (1): 63–69.

———. 1947b. "Discriminación y negación del indio." *América Indígena* 7 (3): 211–15.

Gamio, Manuel. 1916. *Forjando Patria. Pro-Nacionalismo.* México: Porrúa Hermanos.

———. 1942a. "Consideraciones sobre el problema indígena en América." *América Indígena* 2 (2): 17–23.

———. 1942b. "Las características culturales y los censos indígenas." *América Indígena* 2 (3): 15–19.

———. 1942c. "Calificación de características culturales de los grupos indígenas." *América Indígena* 2 (4): 17–22.

[———]. "Editorial." 1947. *América Indígena* 7 (4): 279–84.

Lewis, Óscar, and Ernest E. Maes. 1945. "Bases para una nueva definición práctica del indio." *América Indígena* 5 (2): 107–18.

Mendieta y Núñez, Lucio. 1942. "Notas sobre el artículo 'El indio en México' de Robert Redfield." *Revista Mexicana de Sociología* 4 (3): 63–68.

Redfield, Robert. 1940. "The Indian in Mexico." *Annals of the American Academy of Political and Social Sciences* 208: 132–43.

———. 1941. *The Folk Culture of Yucatán.* Chicago: University of Chicago Press.

———. 1942. "Del pensamiento sociológico actual: el indio en México." *Revista Mexicana de Sociología* 4 (3): 103–20.

Redfield, Robert, John Collier, Emil Sady, and C. Presnall. 1943. "Comments on Dr. Tax's Article." *América Indígena* 3 (1): 83–90.

Steward, Julian. 1943. "Acculturation and the Indian Problem." *América Indígena* 3 (4): 323–28.

Tax, Sol. 1942. "Ethnic Relations in Guatemala." *América Indígena* 2 (4): 42–48.

SECONDARY SOURCES

Bonfil Batalla, Guillermo. 1972. "El concepto de indio en América: Una categoría de la situación colonial." *Anales de Antropología* 9: 105–24.

Caso, Alfonso. 1953. "El Instituto Nacional Indigenista." *Accion Indigenista* no. 1.

———. 1954. *La política indigenista en México: métodos y resultados.* Mexico: Instituto Nacional Indigenista.

Dawson, Alex. 2004. *Indian and Nation in Revolutionary Mexico.* Tucson: University of Arizona Press.

De la Peña, Guillermo. 1995. *El cambio social en la región de Guadalajara: Notas bibliográficas.* Guadalajara, Jalisco: Universidad de Guadalajara.

———. 2014. "The End of Revolutionary Anthropology? Notes on *Indigenismo.*" In *Dictablanda: Politics, Work, and Culture in Mexico, 1938–1968,* edited by Paul Gillingham and Benjamin T. Smith, 279–88. Durham, NC: Duke University Press.

Fabre, Henri. (1963) 1998. *El Indigenismo.* Mexico: Fondo de Cultura Económica (Colección popular).

Faulhaber, Priscilla. 2011. "O Instituto de Antropologia Social (EUA, Brasil e México): Um artefato da Resposta Antropológica ao 'Esforço de Guerra.'" *Mana* 17 (1): 9–39.

Giraudo, Laura. 2014. "Entre 'atraso estadístico' e 'indigenismo científico': Uniformar los censos y definir a los indígenas en las Américas." In *La novedad estadística. Cuantificar, cualificar y transformar las poblaciones en Europa y América Latina, siglos XIX y XX,* edited by Jesús Bustamante, Laura Giraudo, and Leticia Mayer, 127–97. Madrid: Ediciones Polifemo.

Giraudo, Laura, and Juan Martín-Sánchez. 2013. "Dos debates medulares sobre el concepto de raza, 1943–1952." *Revista Mexicana de Sociología* 75 (4): 527–55.

Hewitt, Cynthia. 1988. *Imágenes del campo: interpretaciones antropológicas del México rural.* Mexico: Colegio de México.

Instituto Nacional Indigenista. 1996. *Homenaje a Alfonso Caso. Obras escogidas.* Mexico: Patronato para el Fomento de Actividades Culturales y de Asistencia Social a las Comunidades Indígenas.

Knight, Alan. 1990. "Racism, Revolution and *Indigenismo*: Mexico, 1910–1940." In *The Idea of Race in Latin America*, edited by Richard Graham, 71–113. Austin: University of Texas Press.

Legarreta, Patricia. 2016. "Ingeniería social en Mesoamérica. Revolución, intervención, desarrollo y cooperación internacional." PhD diss., Universidad Autónoma Metropolitana (UAM).

López Caballero, Paula. 2012. "Altérités intimes, altérités éloignées. La greffe du multiculturalisme au Mexique et en Amérique latine." *Critique internationale* 2 (51): 129–49.

———. 2015. "Las políticas indigenistas y la 'fábrica' de su sujeto de intervención en la creación del primer Centro Coordinador del Instituto Nacional Indigenista (1948–1952)." In *Nación y alteridad. Mestizos, indígenas y extranjeros en el proceso de formación nacional*, edited by Daniela Gleizer and Paula López Caballero, 69–108. Mexico: UAM and Ediciones Educación y Cultura.

Nudler, Óscar. 2004. "Hacia un modelo de cambio conceptual: espacios controversiales y relocalización." *Revista de Filosofía* 29 (2): 7–19.

Secretaría de Educación Pública. 1971. *Homenaje a Alfonso Caso.* Mexico: Secretaría de Educación Pública.

Stavenhagen, Rodolfo. 1969. *Las clases sociales en las sociedades agrarias.* Mexico: Siglo XXI Editores.

Taylor, Analisa. 2009. *Indigeneity in the Mexican Cultural Imagination: Thresholds of Belonging.* Tucson: University of Arizona Press.

Téllez Ortega, Javier. 1987. "La época de oro (1940–1964)." In *La antropología en México, panorama histórico.* Vol. 2, *Los hechos y los dichos (1880–1986)*, edited by Carlos García Mora, 291–338. Mexico, INAH.

Wade, Peter. 1993. "'Race,' Nature and Culture." *Man* 28 (1): 17–34.

CHAPTER 9

DISPLACEMENT, DEVELOPMENT, AND THE CREATION OF A MODERN INDÍGENA IN THE PAPALOAPAN, 1940S–1970S

DIANA LYNN SCHWARTZ

FROM 1953 to 1963, residents of the Papaloapan Basin moved household by household to new lands. Thousands were rescued by boat as their homes slowly flooded, dragging with them the transportable stuff of their daily lives—chickens, rustic furniture, elaborately embroidered *huipiles*—through the silted waters. Their relocation, precipitated by the building of a massive hydroelectric dam, presaged a new era in Mexico, with the undertaking of large-scale improvement projects in terms of both infrastructure and human capital. This was the beginning of Mexico's experiment in postwar development planning, an experiment in which social science would play a defining role.

As the Mexican government planned to convert this jungle backwater into an economically productive region, a cadre of anthropologists planned a relocation program to transform into modern citizens the population displaced by the dam. The roughly twenty thousand inhabitants of the region to be submerged by the reservoir waters were in their majority monolingual speakers of the Mazatec language and understood by government officials and anthropologists alike to be "indigenous," a designation I will explain in greater detail in the pages that follow. To most reformers, Mexico's indigenous populations collectively comprised a category apart from the rural population at large, as both the figurative heart of the Mexican nation and quintessentially pre- or even antimodern peoples. The central project of the anthropologists in the Papaloapan was to temper modernization: while seeking to preserve the essential indigenous qualities of the displaced population, they would incorporate tenets of modern life through improvement programs in the areas of public health, education, agriculture, and economic development more generally.

If economic development meant displacement for the local population, anthropologists in the Papaloapan believed a tailored modernization program could both offset the difficulties brought about by dislocation and remedy the apparent secular subjugation and oppression of indigenous peoples. Modernization among the *indígenas*, the anthropologists would have it, was to be most effective—and humane—if the displaced could retain their language and customs. But this project unsettled a longstanding trope of autarkic *indígenas* impervious to change and mobility, and begged the question: How could people undergo such a transformation and still retain that which made them indigenous? In other words, what would indigenous modernization look like? In this chapter I explore how the development programs of the Papaloapan Project called into question what it meant to be indigenous.

Scholars have enumerated in great detail the Mexican government's attempts during the first half of the twentieth century to incorporate the rural masses—and indigenous populations in particular—into the national mainstream. Starting in the 1920s, teachers tasked with making literate the denizens of the countryside also introduced public sanitation measures and new farming techniques among the rural poor.[1] Yet by the late 1940s, teachers were no longer the iconic lone warriors of nation building and state-led social reform. Historians have yet to explain the effects of comprehensive economic development projects in the countryside—which began in earnest in the late 1940s—and the ways in which such projects overlapped with and informed indigenous policy. An examination of the development programs in the Papaloapan (together comprising the Papaloapan Project) provides a window onto the confluence of midcentury developmentalism and changing conceptions of indigenous alterity.

After a catastrophic typhoon in September of 1944 left thousands dead and the entire regional capital of Tuxtepec, Oaxaca, under six feet of standing water, local residents, merchants, and politicians implored the federal government to find a permanent solution to the periodic flooding that had grown increasingly injurious to life and livelihood in the basin. President-elect Miguel Alemán, a native son with commercial and long-standing political ties in the region, made the improvement of the Papaloapan River Basin one of his first priorities not long after taking executive oath in 1946, with the creation of the Papaloapan Commission.

The commission was to carry out the "integrated" development of the river basin.[2] A committee of engineers determined that a dam would be the most effective means of flood control, but the commission designed a plan that would also fully integrate this tropical periphery into the nation in territorial, economic, and political terms. The river basin—plagued by waterborne illness, few and largely impassable roads, and with limited access to state services—had the potential to become a harbinger of the benefits of rural development (Rangel Cuoto 1946; William 1958). Turbines to harness the power of the Papaloapan River would electrify the region and Mexico City, and the yoked waters would irrigate the ranch lands of the lower Papaloapan Basin in the state of Veracruz.

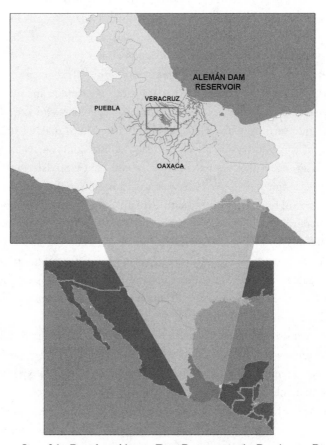

FIGURE 9.1. Site of the President Alemán Dam Reservoir in the Papaloapan River Basin

Highway and infrastructural communication expansion would fully link the sugar, beer, paper, and tropical commodity industries to domestic and international markets. And efforts to sanitize the region would promote colonization and population growth.

The people destined to lose their lands to the reservoir were a lesser concern to the commission planners, who deferred the resettlement planning and programming responsibilities to the anthropologists. Under the auspices of the recently created Instituto Nacional Indigenista (INI), these social scientists conducted fieldwork in the region, facilitated the relocation process, and carried out community development programs in the resettlement zones. As an institute whose purpose was to investigate problems and carry out improvement programs among the indigenous populations of Mexico, it seems of little coincidence that the INI was founded just one year after the creation of the Papaloapan Commission (1947), when the commission was in desperate need of personnel to prepare the evacuation of the population.[3]

As the first of its kind in Mexico—an experiment in integrated development and an application of anthropology for a culturally sensitive relocation and development program—the Papaloapan Project is an example of how "indigenous" citizens became objects of economic development. In the pages that follow, I trace the amorphous nature of indigenous alterity in the Papaloapan to suggest that *indigenous* was a political category, and its utility cemented through the realization of state-led regional development. The chapter is divided into three sections: in the first, I explain the relationship between the anthropological definition and practical use of indigenous alterity; in the second part, I explain the general contours of *indigenista* development in the Papaloapan; and in the third I turn to the case of a particular relocation community.

DEFINING THE *INDÍGENA*

As a discipline that professionalized and earned academic acclaim in the Americas through the study of the indigenous peoples of the hemisphere, anthropology was the human science with greatest repute in Mexico. Renowned archaeologist Alfonso Caso and labor leader Vicente Lombardo Toledano together successfully made the case to the Papaloapan Project directorate that, given their knowledge of indigenous culture and social change, anthropologists were ideally positioned to shepherd the displaced population into a modern existence

(Cometto 1984).[4] And so, beginning in 1949, a team of anthropologists under the direction of Alfonso Villa Rojas began their ethnographic reconnaissance of the Papaloapan.

Villa Rojas was at the forefront of a new generation in Mexican anthropology. Trained by Robert Redfield, Sol Tax, and Alfred Radcliffe-Brown at the University of Chicago, his approach departed from the ethnological recording of indigenous cultural markers typical of the previous generation, seeking instead to detail both cultural practices and social relations in the indigenous communities of the region.[5] This method, he and his colleagues suggested, would best inform a culturally appropriate and minimally harmful relocation process and resettlement program. As both a schoolteacher and Redfield's collaborator in Yucatán and Quintana Roo States, Villa Rojas had extensive field experience among the Maya, as did many members of his team. For Villa Rojas and his colleagues, generalized models of indigenous social relations were based on their observations of Mayan rural dwellers in southeastern Mexico and Guatemala. But it did not take long for the fact-finders to notice that Mayas were not analogous to Mazatecs.

In their revealing, if cursory, ethnographies and short reports of the late 1940s and early 1950s, students in the applied anthropology course at the National School of Anthropology and History (Escuela Nacional de Antropología e Historia), as well as more seasoned anthropologists on Villa Rojas's team, made note of the Mazatecs' individualism and "progressive" economic dispositions. The difference between non-indigenous male Ladinos or *gente de razón* and Mazatecs (*paisanos*) was not easily marked by dress or comportment. And while some ethnographic reports indicated that the minority Ladinos categorically subordinated their Mazatec neighbors, others observed that Mazatecs were also merchants and indiscriminately exploited both fellow Mazatecs and even Ladinos for personal economic gain.[6] Such conclusions accompanied a wave of Mesoamerican scholarship that sought to identify elements compatible with modern life among indigenous peoples, and located "capitalist" and "progressive" dispositions among indigenous villagers (Tax 1953; Redfield 1950).[7] But the idea of indigenous folk as equally forward-looking and open to change as their non-indigenous neighbors in the country or compatriots in the city did not easily fit into a targeted program to modernize indigenous inhabitants of the Papaloapan Basin.[8]

At the heart of the cognitive dissonance between documented evidence of indigenous peoples as socially and economically heterogeneous, on the one

hand, and the idea of homogeneity, on the other, was the problem of definition: What did it mean to be indigenous? Was it not the case that Mexico's
indigenes were rural dwellers living in misery, subject to the machinations and
abuses of more powerful mestizos/Ladinos? The quest to identify what set the
indigenous population apart from rural Mexicans more generally had begun
long before this anthropological intervention in the Papaloapan, but the new
INI had to justify its intervention among specifically *indigenous* citizens and
therefore define its target population. In 1948 Alfonso Caso pronounced what
became the INI's official definition of the *indígena*, explaining the relevance
of language use and cultural heritage but above all affirming that an indigenous person was one who felt him or herself part of an indigenous *community*
(Caso 1948, 239).[9]

Most curious about Caso's definition was its supposed reliance on the ascription of an individual *indígena*, despite the fact that the Papaloapan indigenous
peoples themselves did not actively articulate an explicitly indigenous community identity before the INI designed and implemented programs in their home
municipalities or hamlets. Identification with a particular locality was most
common (the ejido and/or hamlet), and not infrequently an ethnolinguistic
identification as well (Mazatec), but *indigenous* appears to have had little purchase for locals prior to the Papaloapan Project.[10]

The idyllic peasant community, subject of tomes and essays during the first
half of the twentieth century, served as an antidote to the ravages of capitalism and excesses of modernity. In popular culture, politics, and academic writing, peasant (campesino) and indigenous communities were often conflated,
though it was frequently assumed that the tradition that governed social norms
of Mexico's rural communities originated in Mesoamerican indigenous practices (Kourí 2002; Kourí this volume; Guardino this volume). Members of a
single indigenous community in particular were presumed to share a common
past, a past that was historically rooted in the land. Thus, anthropologists in
the Papaloapan were concerned with the disruption displacement would cause,
and in particular the possibility of what they called community disintegration.

A number of the communities to be displaced by the dam lacked such a
shared past. Of the lands to be flooded by the reservoir, close to half were
ejidos—communally held lands granted by the federal government—or agrarian communities awaiting their ejidal grant. A portion of the ejidos had been
granted in the 1920s or 1930s, but many had been formed in the 1940s, and
several received their grant title on the eve of evacuation (Schwartz 2016, chap.

2). The ejido's requisite twenty male agrarian committee members who worked otherwise idle land at least seven kilometers from the population center was not easily achieved on the first attempt; as a result, would-be male ejidatarios, often with female partners and children in tow, frequently migrated in search of a committee or existing ejido that best suited their needs. The experience of Panuncio Cadeza, a Mazatec speaker displaced by the dam who served as an INI promoter and later INI-designated resident head of a resettlement community, best illustrates the tenuous and ephemeral nature of ejidal communities. As told to the journalist Fernando Benítez, for reasons both personal and political, Cadeza helped form, abandoned, and joined multiple agrarian committees or ejidos in the hopes of securing land to farm for his family's sustenance (Benítez 1970). If a long-term common sense of territorially based community was shaky among ejidatarios, it was likely just as difficult to come by for sharecroppers, *jornaleros* (wage laborers), and even small private-property holders.

Perhaps the promise of land redistribution and a handful of agrarian-based unions or peasant leagues gave rural dwellers who tilled the land a shared sense of campesino solidarity with their neighbors, but to what extent did they belong to an *indigenous* community, at least as anthropologists understood it?[11] Though state agrarian officials often recorded information about ejido petitioners' *raza* or took note when a majority of petitioners did not speak Spanish, the archive leaves few indications that membership in a specifically indigenous community was prevalent in the *vaso*—the area to be subsumed by the dam's reservoir.[12] To be sure, a conclusive reading of in-group identity of the *vaso*'s residents during the 1950s is outside the scope of this study. Rather, I suggest that anthropologists—and perhaps other agronomist and engineering experts working in the Papaloapan as well—simply presumed a static indigenous community identity to be not only present but also intrinsic to social relations among the people to be displaced.

INDIGENISTA DEVELOPMENT

The activities of the INI Coordinating Center in the Papaloapan reached all the hamlets (*poblados*) of the basin affected by the dam.[13] Its staff toured the *vaso* in an attempt to convince residents that relocation was, more than a mere necessity, a choice that would provide a better future for their families. Coordinating center personnel planned the relocation and shuttled residents throughout the basin over the course of the evacuation, but its deepest interventions were carried out in the newly created resettlement zones.

The ethnographic fact-finding missions carried out under Villa Rojas's direction were meant to inform resettlement and development plans that would modernize Indians while maintaining their indigenous alterity. At the heart of this task was a problem of definition: even if anthropologists could successfully discern indigenous from non-indigenous qualities, certainly some aspects of so-called indigenous life were incompatible with the modernization program. The exploiter/exploited binary was not easily drawn along ethnic lines. A case in point was the problem of the oft-despised cacique of anthropological and historical lore, often depicted as a social leech draining an equitable existence from indigenous nuclei. Such political bosses, however—many of them indigenous go-betweens themselves—were also key intermediaries for the anthropologists and gatekeepers for the assimilation of new "modern" aspects of life into indigenous society.[14]

The evacuation necessitated the assistance of local intermediaries, and the social and economic programs the coordinating center was to carry out in the relocation communities would require more than informal indigenous language-speaking allies. Anthropologist residents of the center enlisted *promotores*, or "promoters," to assist in the areas of health, education, agriculture, and local economic development. In the Papaloapan, as in other areas within the ambit of INI Coordinating Centers, promoters worked in conjunction with anthropologist residents in relocation communities. Their role had the potential to provide them a privileged political and economic position both within the community and vis-à-vis state institutions.[15] But not all promoters were indigenous language speakers, not all indigenous language-speaking promoters were Mazatec, and—most importantly—not all Mazatec promoters possessed the cultural credentials to be successful brokers.

What is more, promoters' training materials throughout the 1950s proffered contradictory explanations about the differences between *indígenas* and "us" (mestizos). Despite the nuanced explanations of differences in socioeconomic status in the ethnographic reports, Mazatecs were all dubbed farm workers ("todos trabajan en el campo"), while their hygiene habits were just like those of other campesinos.[16] Perhaps any kind of improvement program will likely invoke one-dimensional and incomplete characteristics or labels to identify the target population, but in this case it seems the conflict between research findings and policy prescriptions is best explained by the specific context of *indigenista* development. That is to say, the coordinating center's task was ostensibly to modernize the *indígena* while preserving indigenous alterity, but because, as I indicated above and the editors of the present volume outlined in the introduction, indigenous alterity was amorphous, ephemeral, and polyvalent, the effect of the center's actions was to ossify the category as a foil for modernization.

The coordinating center's plans for the resettlement zones were vague, often more perfunctory than premeditated, and aimed principally at triaging the deleterious political and economic effects of dislocation. The *indigenista* component of their work—that is, the work that would ostensibly foment culturally sensitive economic development and social integration—was as elusive as the definition of *lo indígena*. As early as 1953, while conducting ethnographic studies in the *vaso*, the young anthropology student Rodolfo Stavenhagen (1953) predicted that this "reintegration" process would transform the indigenous population into "campesinos," "*obreros*" (workers) or "*proletarios*"—social categories that would require both the adoption of the "psychology and perspective" of these respective groups or social classes and the position such groups occupied in the economic, political, and social structures of the country (35). "If social anthropology persists in being applied to the groups in the process of change exclusively for their quality as 'indígenas' and does not prepare them as capable and efficient members of the classes of which they will form a part," he warned, "it can cause grave harm to the development of the affected groups, as well as to the country in general" (Stavenhagen 1953, 35). Yet Stavenhagen's observations about the inherent paradox of *indigenista* work omitted another possibility: that many *indígenas* did not think of themselves as such, and likely already identified as campesinos.

The center and Papaloapan Commission created five resettlement areas for the displaced residents, where promoters would increasingly become essential—and permanent—fixtures of daily life. The first of the improvement programs carried out were health campaigns, which brought mixed results during the first years of life in the relocation zones. Resistance to some foreign healing practices—inoculation and the use of oral medication such as Paludrine or antibiotics—was frequent, even with the assistance of bilingual Mazatec health promoters. While some evacuees welcomed the use of pharmaceuticals and vaccinations to damper tropical viral outbreaks and prevent the spread of Old World diseases, averseness to blood drawing and inoculation remained high, and local healers held their ground as the ultimate authorities on human health concerns.

Both before the evacuation and in the first decade following relocation, health officials were most successful in their efforts when they convinced and enlisted *brujos*—so-called "witch doctors"—to incorporate modern medicine into their practice. For example, reticent residents, even those who were outright hostile toward the practices of the center's health brigades, had a change of heart when their local healer administered malaria treatments.[17] The center's staff complemented most existing health practices among indigenous residents, as opposed to replacing them entirely with "modern" medicine.[18] One *curandero*, according to anthropologists, a Mixtec Indian from a region outside the river basin, was much sought after in the relocation community of La Joya. His longstanding use of an edited volume on medicinal plants from Mexico's flagship national university, the UNAM (Universidad Nacional Autónoma de México), earned him high regard among the center's anthropologists.[19]

The coordinating center's educational interventions also required the complicity of local intermediaries but went a step further in valorizing a long-recognized defining feature of indigenous identity: language. The reach of rural schools had expanded in the Mexican countryside since the 1920s—though they had existed in some regions since the nineteenth century—as a nation-building enterprise that promised literacy, life, and hygiene skills, and nationalist, civic socialization; but the coordinating center schools' mission, on the other hand, was to promote bilingual education with the immediate goal of teaching indigenous literacy.[20] Anthropologists were not alone in believing that command of the Spanish language, both written and spoken, was the key to fully integrating indigenous citizens into the Mexican nation. Their approach to literacy, however, followed contemporary psychological and linguistic scholarship that explained language as intrinsically related to culture and personality. A lack of state support throughout the 1940s undermined approaches to indigenous literacy in Mexico pioneered by linguist Morris Swadesh and colleagues in the Tarascan Project of the 1930s.[21] Now the INI had the institutional power to impose such methods, and the expansion of primary education in the Papaloapan would include bilingual education efforts.

In 1955 the coordinating center serviced 1,450 monolingual students, and the initial efforts would follow the mandate of the rural education plan drawn between the coordinating center and the Mexican Ministry of Education (Secretaría de Educación Pública, SEP).[22] In Nuevo Paso Nacional, location of the coordinating center and home to a cosmopolitan blend of professionals, merchants, and upwardly mobile Mazatecs from the region, bilingual educators

used the Freinet technique—a child-centered, storytelling, print-making pedagogy—to promote indigenous literacy. North American expatriate public health
nurse Lini De Vries was awestruck by what she witnessed during her first visit
to a local schoolhouse in 1955: "With pride, children were learning their own
legends and history as told by the old story-tellers. These accounts were now
being read on mimeographed sheets in both languages—Mazateca [sic] and
Spanish, as well as contemporary knowledge—all taken home to their families"
(De Vries 1969, 127).[23]

Parents, however, did not always agree with the INI staff's educational policy
or pedagogy. In community schools where students spoke the same linguistic
variant, Mazatecs often balked at time wasted in teaching their children to read
and write in their mother tongue instead of Spanish (Luna Ruíz 2003, 161–62).[24]
And regardless of whether or not teachers spoke Mazatec in the classroom,
in some instances parents derided the educators' use of the Freinet method,
which to them seemed a series of games inappropriate in a serious learning
environment.[25] To the local population, the benefits of an educational modernization program tethered to one of the primordial markers of indigenous alterity
were not self-evident. If not all parents were enthusiastic about their children
learning to read and write in Mazatec, perhaps indigenous language literacy
was not an essential quality for retaining the sense of integrated community
the anthropologists considered so crucial for an effective resettlement program
(Acevedo-Rodrigo, present volume).

The impact of parental activism indelibly shaped the civic culture of the
resettlement zones. Together with parent committees (*Comités de padres de
familia*), various coordinating center schools implemented free breakfast programs and employed *faenas*, or community collaborative labor projects, to build
outdoor courts suitable for volleyball and basketball. This latter endeavor served
to encourage intercommunity sports competition throughout the new settlements. The *faena*, an old practice frequently used to carry out public works projects when government moneys were scarce, was here invoked to promote locally
based sport—a modern form of sociability.[26] Parents encouraged vocational
training sponsored by the coordinating center as well, which by the end of the
1950s included courses in haircutting and hygiene, as well as dressmaking with
sewing machines and woodworking at the center's carpentry shop.

Of the varied improvement programs carried out by the coordinating center
in the relocation communities, education was the most specific and targeted
area in which there was an attempt to preserve and promote indigenous culture

(specifically, language) and community. To be sure, if the value of indigenous literacy was not necessarily a shared belief among relocated Mazatecs, community members themselves were infrequently initiating the community-building activities, which were largely organized and encouraged by the resident anthropologists. The newfangled community, then, may have been as indigenous as it was not, as modern as it was traditional.

At midcentury, modernization and development may have included human capital improvement programs, but their heaviest connotation was economic. The INI's economic development programs at the community level were based almost exclusively on agricultural improvement. While a small but significant portion of those affected by the construction of the President Alemán Dam were artisans or merchants, the vast majority dedicated their lives to working the land. INI staff in particular envisioned indigenous smallholders producing for subsistence as well as for local, regional, domestic, or even international markets. With the right amount of outside mediation and *indigenista* know-how, planned agricultural development could give rise to financially solvent indigenous yeoman farmers. Agricultural improvement programs, more so than health or education efforts, further linked locals to an expansive *indigenista* institutional apparatus, yet in and of themselves such programs did not salvage purportedly indigenous practices in the fields of animal husbandry or planting technique.

The coordinating center introduced commercial tropical crops, followed by improved rice and maize seed and new breeds of chicken, hogs, and cattle in the relocation zones. While the crops did not always bear fruit and animal husbandry created greater dependency on the center's veterinary scientists and agronomists, staff reported overall acceptance of and interest in such remunerative activity among the local population.[27] In the late 1950s, the coordinating center added local agricultural promoters as part of the expanding INI bureaucracy. Trained in the agricultural sciences, these interlocutors became the principal agents of agrarian modernization in the relocation zones, providing instruction to residents, inoculating (pigs and chickens) against cholera and other curable illness, and replacing the ambulatory Papaloapan Commission or coordinating center engineer as a local and permanent technician.

Such changes in local INI administration echoed broader institutional changes that had lasting effects in INI Coordinating Centers throughout Mexico. A closer examination of the practices of locals, *promotores*, and anthropologists alike best illustrates how communities took shape upon resettlement, and the ways in which economic development practices reconfigured indigenous alterity. It is to this detail that we now turn.

THE NEW COMMUNITY

Settlers arrived for the first time to the *predio* of Yogopi in the late winter of 1955. Improvised roads led them to a plot in the overgrown jungle, where no one had confirmed the land was either bountiful or sufficiently flat for farming. Nonetheless, the newcomers razed the landscape *a machetazos* to prepare and sow modest plots that would later provide their first harvest.

The construction of a new community was an exercise in rudimentary urban planning. Lacking definitive plans—and resources—to establish an ideal rural indigenous community, INI Coordinating Center resident anthropologist Rodolfo Stavenhagen organized on the Yogopi lands the pueblo of Nuevo Ixcatlán. From its inception, he raised a schoolhouse and general supply store, and—controversially—a church. That a state agency, in this case the INI, would erect a church for any polity seems anathema to Mexico's strict separation of religious practice and official political action, but religious spaces and objects were essential for a successful relocation. Like the Ixcatecos, residents of the affected municipality of San José Independencia also demanded a designated space in the relocation hamlet of "Nuevo" San José for the veneration of their saints. There, resident anthropologist Maurilio Muñoz naively assumed relocation campaigns would be most effective if the saints moved first (Muñoz 2009, 123–24).

As more families arrived to Nuevo Ixcatlán, the community was segmented into colonias, doubling as both colonies and neighborhoods. Residences were segregated based on the appraisal of the household lands and appurtenances in old Ixcatlán: those with less than ten hectares could be accepted as ejidatarios in Nuevo Ixcatlán, but those with more than ten hectares in their old community would move to a specific area destined for smallholders.[28] Both the center and the commission promoted ejidal membership among the relocated of the lowest means. Perhaps membership in an ejido constituted a more consistent relationship of patronage with the growing Mexican state. Yet in the face of "community disintegration," it seems likely that planners saw in ejidal membership a solution that would both provide access to existing state agricultural support and encourage collective allegiance that could over time gently transform indigenous community alliances into an ostensibly more egalitarian, modern form of agricultural organization.

In November of 1955, Stavenhagen and the coordinating center spearheaded a new wave of agricultural programs to increase the locals' purchasing power and better integrate them into regional, domestic, and international markets. This joint effort between the coordinating center, the Papaloapan Commission, and the secretary of agriculture fostered a rubber nursery, which now had enough small trees to plant 150 hectares. This, with another sixty sacks of raw peanuts, would provide residents with a rotation of crops "as remunerative as tobacco."[29] These smallholders and ejidatarios, perhaps, would finally be able to participate in tropical commodity production and sale that could make them financially self-sustaining and provide them with disposable income. As we shall see, the problems relocated residents faced made for precarious economic sustainability and illusory community integrity.

Though in Oaxaca the Ixcatecos belonged to the *municipio libre* (free municipality) of San Pedro Ixcatlán, in Veracruz they had been demoted to an *agencia municipal*, a department with little local autonomy in fiscal and political matters. The municipal presidency saw in Nuevo Ixcatlán a "juicy source of economic exploitation," and implemented a tax schedule for so-called "public services" that Stavenhagen read as malintentioned. It was indispensable, the anthropologist opined, to protect the relocated population from "abusive interventions contrary to their interests," at least until the pueblo could defend themselves.[30]

While Nuevoixcatecos implored Stavenhagen to protect them from the reach of Playa Vicente, Veracruz—their newfound *jarocho* municipality with what locals and anthropologists identified as a largely non-indigenous constituency—Stavenhagen's and the coordinating center's reports during the first decade upon relocation leave no trace of a long-term plan to promote political autonomy among the Nuevoixcatecos or other relocated populations. The ad hoc nature of the anthropologists' work in the relocation zones suggests that they contained potentially volatile political and economic situations, as opposed to proffering a specific plan for community politics that would promise sustained economic development and a coherent sense of Mazatec community belonging or identity.

As employees of the INI, resident anthropologists wore a number of hats—and as Stavenhagen himself later reflected, were themselves caciques of a sort—but their collective role in rooting indigenous culture and economic development in new territory was largely ineffective in ameliorating the political and economic inequalities they found so abhorrent in the old lands.[31] Stavenhagen had attempted to induce more communally oriented, egalitarian political participation and economic practices in Nuevo Ixcatlán, but to his surprise locals were not interested in and even opposed his designs for local participatory democracy.[32]

Toward the end of the 1950s, political conflicts and economic problems continued unresolved in Nuevo Ixcatlán. In the summer of 1961, the center's legal department consistently intervened in instances of theft, beating, and kidnapping. As it trained promoters to provide legal aid to Nuevoixcatecos, the department's involvement in community affairs only increased. The legal department head even went so far as to suggest to the Coordinating Center director that in the next elections in Nuevo Ixcatlán, he should secure in office an *agente municipal* of Nuevo Ixcatlán sympathetic to the center's plans.[33]

The power of intermediaries grew in the early years of the 1960s, as they assumed many of the agricultural-related duties of the resident anthropologists. Between 1962 and 1963, one local promoter doubled as his relocation community's resident anthropologist while also serving within the community's local political leadership. Local leaders and other INI staff slowly displaced anthropologists as the resident representatives of the coordinating center. Yet this is not to imply that the coordinating center, or the INI more broadly, was undergoing a democratic transformation. The INI created its own Agrarian Department (Departamento Agronómico), which at the behest of the coordinating center effectively displaced the Papaloapan Commission and Federal Agrarian Department officials (of the Departamento Agrario) as the bulwark of agronomic expertise.[34]

By the early 1960s, in the area of agricultural science, the INI had become a formidable agent of development and management of the "indigenous" countryside. Yet the question remains: What really was *indigenista* about the scope of the INI's work in the Papaloapan? Regardless of their landholding status, locals were increasingly referred to as campesinos, signaling not only the significance of their occupation in agricultural work but also the moot relevance of their qualities as *indígenas* in the agricultural development programs.

CONCLUSION

Within a few years after relocation, the power monopoly of local or regional merchants had disappeared only to be replaced by coordinating center staff—resident anthropologists (consisting of both indigenous locals and anthropologist outsiders), indigenous agricultural promoters, or agents of the INI's Economic Promotion Department. That is to say, economic strongmen lost their prominence, not necessarily to a mass of would-be yeoman indigenous farmers, but to *indigenista* economic managers, a number of whom were themselves Mazatec-speaking locals.

The work of the INI in the Papaloapan was premised on particular ideas about what it meant to be indigenous and how indigenous citizens could be effectively included in Mexico's modernizing efforts. To allege that midcentury social scientists and planners presumed indigenous people were inherently antimodern and in need of state-led improvement projects to lift them from backwardness is nothing new. What is noteworthy, however, is that the very parameters of who was indigenous or what constituted an indigenous community were blurry to historical actors themselves, and were redefined through the Papaloapan Project. The notion that indigenous peoples were static in terms of time and space contradicted the reality anthropologists found on the ground in the Papaloapan, and yet projects that targeted "indigenous" communities proliferated and the INI bureaucracy grew. Indigenous modernization in practice had the effect of reifying the very category of *indigenous* while maintaining its elusive definition. This chapter has attempted to show that the INI's development efforts in the Papaloapan were ineffective in realizing the mission of indigenous modernization in part because the indigenous—as both individual and community—was illusory.

In the wake of the INI's economic improvement programs, the term *indígena* as a decisively ethnic referent faded from view. The cumulative effect of modernization programs under the auspices of the INI was a static, political notion of *indigenous* as both a foil for and a justification of the institution's particular economic development schemes.

NOTES

1.   See, for example, Vaughan (1997), Lewis (2006), Acevedo-Rodrigo (2012), Civera (2011), and Loyo (2006).

2.   Inspired by the New Deal era Tennessee Valley Authority, the "integrated" river basin development model saturates the literature published by Mexico's National Irrigation Commission (first called the Comisión Nacional de Irrigación and later christened the Secretaría de Recursos Hidráulicos). Some choice examples are Orive Alba (1945), Comisión del Papaloapan (1949), and Rangel (1946). In fact, by the late 1950s, the concept of integrated river basin development was a global

phenomenon, exemplified most clearly by the UN's 1958 report on the subject. See United Nations (1970).

3. Estrada Tena (2003, 108) in fact argues that the Papaloapan Project itself was the impetus for the INI's creation.

4. Interview with Alfonso Villa Rojas, September 22, 1983, quoted in Cometto (1984, A5).

5. Villa Rojas to Robert Redfield, April 3, 1950, Robert Redfield Papers, box 38, fol. 8. These ideas are also explored in López Caballero, this volume.

6. See Cámara (1955); Sergio Morales, "Informe que presenta Sergio Morales al Instituto Nacional Indigenista acerca de un viaje de estudio que hizo a la Cuenca del Papaloapan bajo su patrocinio," 1951, in Alfonso Villa Rojas Papers, box 11, file 62; Agustin Romano, "Informe para el Instituto Nacional Indigenista relativo al viaje de estudio realizado por los alumnos de los cursos de antropología aplicada en la zona de la Cuenca del Papaloapan," November 1951, in Alfonso Villa Rojas Papers, box 11, file 63; Stavenhagen (1953). The clearest physical marker of being indigenous among women was use of the *huipil* with embroidery specific to a community (either the municipal head town or hamlet), though for a number of reasons this was also an elusive indicator of indigenous identity, particularly after relocation when other styles of dress became readily available and more affordable than huipiles.

7. Kummels (2013) discusses the tension in the mid-twentieth century in which Tarahumaras both exhibited qualities desirable for modernity and were "threatened" by modernity itself.

8. Though anthropologists in the Papaloapan do not make much of it in their notes and reports, Ladinos themselves might often be, as the conservative definition of the word implies, Mazatec in some circumstances and non-Mazatec in others—so-called *revestidos* whose group identity could shift accordingly. See Torres Cantú (2010)

9. My emphasis.

10. I have come to this conclusion after a thorough perusal of the INI anthropologists' reports and field notes, as well as complaints and petitions from residents from the affected municipalities in the Archivo Histórico de Temazcal (hereafter, AHT); the papers of Presidents Manuel Avila Camacho, Miguel Alemán Valdés, and Adolfo Ruíz Cortines at the Archivo General de la Nación, Mexico; and the land petition and grant archives for populations affected by the dam at the Archivo General Agrario, Mexico (hereafter, AGA), among others.

11. Peasant leagues such as Ligas de Comunidades Agrarias in the district of Tuxtepec and the state of Oaxaca were active in the Papaloapan region long before the construction of the dam and were one of the ejidatarios' primary means of advocacy.

12. On noting the *raza* of the petitioners (Mazateca), see Censo General Agrario Primera Pochota, La Primera Pochota, Ixcatlán, Oaxaca (n.d.), file 23/122239, Dotación de Ejidos, AGA.

13. Beginning in 1951, the INI installed coordinating centers in areas understood as indigenous zones to carry out various sorts of improvement programs in their

area of influence. Lewis (2011) has written about the first center, formed in San Cristóbal, Chiapas. López Caballero (2015) also treats the creation of the first coordinating center.

14. As documented by Rus (1994), this was also the case in the INI Coordinating Center in San Cristóbal de las Casas, Chiapas, and most likely in other areas of INI interventions in the countryside as well.

15. On the role of intermediaries in the colonial period, see Yannakakis (2008). Literature on nineteenth-century popular liberalism also mentions intermediaries' place in the implementation of liberal reforms. See Caplan (2009), Thomson (1999), Mallon (1995), and McNamara (2007). For the early nineteenth-century genesis of liberalism in the Spanish-American world, see Quijada Mauriño (2006). On the twentieth century, see Dawson (2004).

16. Charlas con los promotores culturales del Papaloapan, Visitas a los hogares (n.d.; likely 1959), 1–2, AHT, box 25, file 255.

17. Meeting minutes, January 27, 1956, AHT, box 16, file 1969.

18. Such public health practices were not uncommon in other reaches of the Americas. See Palmer (2003).

19. Diario de campo, 1958, AHT, box 3, file 23.

20. The coordinating center's bilingual literacy policy was an institutional mandate within the INI more broadly.

21. This reference to second language education is ubiquitous throughout Centro Coordinador Indigenista del Papaloapan (CCIP) internal memos and reports. See also INI/CCIP "Empleo de las lenguas vernáculas en la enseñanza," taken from the UNESCO document of the same name, originally published in 1953, AHT, box 69, file 696. The notion of "culture and personality" as interrelated aspects of human life came to prominence in anthropological circles with Benedict's 1934 publication. Throughout the 1940s and 1950s, culture and personality studies applied aspects of psychological theory and method to anthropological research, bearing a heavy mark on studies of culture change, particularly among "backward" or "primitive" societies. On the Tarascan Project, see Swadesh (1939).

22. Ricardo Pozas to Jefe del Depto. de Estadística Escolar, SEP, September 2, 1955, AHT, box 18, file 200.

23. Brought to Mexico by Spanish Republican refugees Patricio Redondo and José de Tapia Bujalance, who had landed in Veracruz, the Freinet approach to pedagogy was established in a series of schools in the basin.

24. Indigenous literacy efforts were unsuccessful in a number of relocation communities where children hailing from different municipalities spoke mutually unintelligible linguistic variants of the Mazatec language. In 1955, the CCIP's director of education, Isabel Horcasitas de Pozas, decided to focus literacy efforts on Spanish language literacy, which resulted in her dismissal. Regarding relations between indigenous language speakers and Spanish language instruction, see chapters by Ariadna Acevedo-Rodrigo and Elsie Rockwell in this volume.

25. "Junta del Consejo Correspondiente a Noviembre," November 25 (n.d.; likely 1956), AHT, box 16, file 169.
26. I thank Ariadna Acevedo-Rodrigo for bringing this to my attention.
27. Informes de Rodolfo Stavenhagen, Maurilio Muñoz, Panuncio Cadeza, 1955-56, AHT, box 101, file 1016; Ing. Saturnino Fuerte to Miguel Mejía Fernández, August 5, 1963, and Ing. Saturnino Fuerte to Promotor Panuncio Cadeza Montor, April 6, 1963, AHT, box 7, file 67.
28. Ricardo Pozas to Pedro Betanzos, Policía Rural, April 18, 1955, AHT, box 24, file 253.
29. Junta del Consejo, November 25, 1955, AHT, box 16, file 169.
30. Stavenhagen Informe No. 4, October 16, 1955–January 31, 1956, AHT, box 101, file 1016.
31. Stavenhagen, interviewed by Cristiana Cometto, October 19, 1983, in Cometto (1984); interview with Rodolfo Stavenhagen, August 17, 2013. Field notes of other resident anthropologists indicate the same: see the reports of Carlos Incháustegui, 1956-58, AHT Caja 16 Expediente 177, and Muñoz (2009).
32. Interview with Stavenhagen, August 17, 2013.
33. Sandoval Prats to Rodríguez Ramos, January 6, 1961, AHT, box 83, file 815; Ignacio Patlán Romero, Jefe del Depto Legal to Mejía Fernández, October 16, 1961, AHT, box 100, file 990.
34. Fuerte to Cadeza, August 8, 1963, AHT, box 7, file 77; Director Alfonso Caso, "Reglamento de la Comisión Técnica Consultativa," June 1, 1963, Departamento de Agronomía (INI), July 17, 1963 "Instructivo para el manejo de las semillas enviadas en paquete especial del laboratorio INI," and "Método de control y combate del barrenador del nudo vital del arroz," AHT, box 7, file 80.

REFERENCES

ARCHIVES

Alfonso Villa Rojas Papers, Fondo Alfonso Villa Rojas, Biblioteca Juan Comas, Instituto de Investigaciones Antropológicas, Universidad Nacional Autónoma de México, Mexico City

Archivo General Agrario (AGA), Mexico City

Archivo General de la Nación, Mexico

Archivo Histórico de Temazcal (AHT), Comisión Nacional para el Desarrollo de los Pueblos Indígenas, Oaxaca City

Robert Redfield Papers, University of Chicago Special Collections, University of Chicago, Illinois

SECONDARY SOURCES

Acevedo-Rodrigo, Ariadna. 2012. "Ciudadanos indígenas: la construcción de derechos y obligaciones en la relación de los pueblos indígenas escuelas, 1875–1940." In *Edu-*

cación, ciudadanía y estado en México: Siglo XX, edited by Marco Calderón and Elizabeth Buenabad, 25–51. Mexico: Colegio de Michoacán and Benemérita Universidad Autónoma de Puebla.

Benedict, Ruth. 1934. *Patterns of Culture*. New York: Houghton Mifflin Harcourt.

Benítez, Fernando. 1970. *Los indios de México*, vol. 3. Mexico: Ediciones Era.

Cámara, Fernando. 1955. "Deplácement e réinstallation de groupes indigène au Mexique: Le Plan du Papaloapan." *Civilisations* 5 (2): 203–29.

Caplan, Karen. 2009. *Indigenous Citizens: Local Liberalism in Early National Oaxaca and Yucatán*. Stanford, CA: Stanford University Press.

Caso, Alfonso. 1948. "Definición del Indio y lo Indio." *América Indígena* 8 (4): 239–47.

Civera, Alicia. 2011. "La reforma integral del campo mexicano a través de la escuela rural posrevolucionaria: la relevancia de la enseñanza agrícola y el cooperativismo, 1921– 1945." In *Campesinos y escolares: la construcción de la escuela en el campo latinoamericano, siglos XIX y XX*, edited by Alicia Civera Cerecedo, Juan Alfonseca Giner de los Ríos, and Carlos Escalante Fernández, 303–48. Zinacantepec, Mexico: Colegio Mexiquense.

Cometto, Cristiana. 1984. "Il progetto della Valle del Papaloapan, Messico: It ruolo dell'antropologia in un programma di suiluppo." Master's thesis, Universia' Degli Studi di Roma, Facoltà di Lettere, Istituto di Etnología.

Comisión del Papaloapan. 1949. *El Papaloapan, obra del Presidente Alemán; Reseña sumaria del magno proyecto de planificación integral que ahora se realiza en la Cuenca del Papaloapan*. Mexico: Secretaría de Recursos Hidráulicos, Comisión del Papaloapan.

Dawson, Alexander S. 2004. *Indian and Nation in Revolutionary Mexico*. Tucson: University of Arizona Press.

De Vries, Lini. 1969. *The People of the Mountains: Health Education Among Indian Communities in Oaxaca*. Mexico: Centro Intercultural de Documentación.

Estrada Tena, Valeria Elizabeth. 2003. "Gestión de cuencas fluviales en México. Un acercamiento a la historia de la Comisión del Papaloapan, 1947–1985." Bachelor's thesis, Universidad Nacional Autónoma de México, Facultad de Filosofía y Letras.

Kourí, Emilio. 2002. "Interpreting the Expropriation of Indian Pueblo Lands in Porfirian Mexico: The Unexamined Legacies of André Molina Enríquez." *Hispanic American Historical Review* 82 (1): 69–117.

Kummels, Ingrid. 2013. "Indigenismos populares y trasnacionales en torno a los tarahumaras de principios del siglo XX: la concepción de la modernidad a partir del deporte, la fotografía y el cine." *Historia Mexicana* 62 (4): 1551–607.

Lewis, Stephen. 2006. "The Nation, Education, and the 'Indian Problem' in Mexico, 1920–1940." In *The Eagle and the Virgin: Nation and Cultural Revolution in Mexico, 1920–1940*, edited by Mary Kay Vaughan and Stephen E. Lewis, 176–95. Durham, NC: Duke University Press.

———. 2011. "Modernizing Message, Mystical Messenger: The *Teatro Petul* in the Chiapas Highlands, 1954–1974." *The Americas* 67 (3): 375–97.

López Caballero, Paula. 2015. "Las políticas indigenistas y la 'fábrica' de su sujeto de intervención en la creación del primer Centro Coordinador del Instituto Nacional

Indigenista, 1948–1952." In *Nación y alteridad: mestizos, indígenas y extranjeros en el proceso de formación nacional*, edited by Daniela Gleizer Salzman and Paula López Caballero, 69–108. Mexico City: Universidad Autónoma Metropolitana and Ediciones Educación y Cultura.

Loyo, Engracia. 2006. "El conocimiento del indio. Nuevo camino para su asimilación (1930–1940)." In *Historias, saberes indígenas y nuevas etnicidades en la escuela*, edited by María Bertely, 69–94. Mexico: Centro de Investigaciones y Estudios Superiores en Antropología Social.

Luna Ruíz, Xicohténcatl Gerardo. 2003. "De la Cuenca a la selva. Política pública y reubicación en una comunidad indígena: San Felipe Zihualtepec, Oaxaca." Bachelor's thesis, Escuela Nacional de Antropología e Historia.

Mallon, Florencia. 1995. *Peasant and Nation: The Making of Postcolonial Mexico and Peru*. Berkeley: University of California Press.

McNamara, Patrick. 2007. *Sons of the Sierra: Juárez, Díaz, and the People of Ixtlán, Oaxaca, 1855–1920*. Chapel Hill: University of North Carolina Press.

Muñoz Basilio, Maurilio. 2009. *Fuentes para la historia del indigenismo en México. Diarios de campo de Maurilio Muñoz en la Cuenca del Papaloapan (1957–1959)*. Mexico: Comisión Nacional para el Desarrollo de los Pueblos Indígenas.

Orive Alba, Adolfo. 1945. *La política de irrigación*. Mexico: Turanzas del Valle.

Palmer, Steven Paul. 2003. *From Popular Medicine to Medical Populism: Doctors, Healers, and Public Power in Costa Rica, 1800–1940*. Durham, NC: Duke University Press.

Quijada Mauriño, Mónica. 2006. "La caja de Pandora. El sujeto político indígena en la construcción del orden liberal." *Historia Contemporánea* (33): 605–37.

Rangel Cuoto, Hugo. 1946. *El desarrollo regional integral en la síntesis del programa del gobierno del Sr. Lic. Miguel Alemán: El sistema Valle de Tennessee*. Mexico: Talleres Gráficos de la Nación.

Redfield, Robert. 1950. *A Village That Chose Progress: Chan Kom Revisited*. Chicago: University of Chicago Press.

Rus, Jan. 1994. "The '*Comunidad Revolucionaria Institucional*': The Subversion of Native Government in Highland Chiapas." In *Everyday Forms of State Formation: Revolution and the Negotiation of Rule in Modern Mexico*, edited by Gilbert Joseph and Daniel Nugent, 265–300. Durham, NC: Duke University Press.

Schwartz, Diana Lynn. 2016. "Transforming the Tropics: Development, Displacement, and Anthropology in the Papaloapan, Mexico, 1940s–1970s." PhD diss., University of Chicago.

Stavenhagen, Rodolfo. 1953. "En la Cuenca del Papaloapan: aspectos de la antropología social aplicada." *Tlatoani*, 2nd ser., (7): 30–35.

Swadesh, Morris. 1939. "Proyecto de plan de educación indígena en lengua nativa tarasca." *Boletín Bibliográfico de Antropología Americana* 3 (3): 222–27.

Tax, Sol. 1953. *Penny Capitalism: A Guatemalan Indian Community*. Washington, DC: Government Printing Office.

Thomson, Guy P. C. 1999. *Patriotism, Politics, and Popular Liberalism in Nineteenth-Century Mexico: Juan Francisco Lucas and the Puebla Sierra*, with David G. La France. Wilmington, DE: Scholarly Resources.

Torres Cantú, Briceidee. 2010. "Comerciantes, caciques y chikones. La cultura regional de tres localidades afectadas por la presa Miguel Alemán." Master's thesis, Colegio de Michoacán.

United Nations. 1970. *Integrated River Basin Development: Report of a Panel of Experts.* New York: United Nations Department of Economic and Social Affairs.

Vaughan, Mary Kay. 1997. *Cultural Politics in Revolution: Teachers, Peasants, and Schools in Mexico.* Tucson: University of Arizona Press.

William, Winnie, Jr. 1958. "The Papaloapan Project: An Experiment in Tropical Development." *Economic Geography* 34: 227–48.

Yannakakis, Yanna. 2008. *The Art of Being In-Between: Native Intermediaries, Indian Identity, and Local Rule in Colonial Oaxaca.* Durham, NC: Duke University Press.

CHAPTER 10

ENCAPSULATED HISTORY

Evon Vogt and the Anthropological Making of the Maya

JOSÉ LUIS ESCALONA VICTORIA

NTHROPOLOGY HAS played a fundamental role in the production of *indigenous alterity*—that is, of the indigenous as a popular social category that has strongly influenced the contemporary history of several groups, territories, and goods. In Mexico, this alterity-making process was influenced partly by interactions between Mexican and foreign anthropologists, thereby involving metropolitan institutions in Europe and the United States. My purpose in this chapter is to examine a particular moment in this history: the production of *the Maya* as developed by anthropologist Evon Z. Vogt.

In historical accounts, the initial point in the "discovery" of the Maya was the publication, in 1841, of *Incidents of Travel in Central America, Chiapas, and Yucatan*, by John Stephens and Frederick Catherwood ([1841] 1969). At that time, only a few, little-known documents broached the idea of an advanced American civilization in the region (particularly Dupaix 1834). Stephens and Catherwood's book was the first on the topic to be published and widely distributed (Lerner 2011). However, *Maya* in this text referred only to the language spoken by people in Yucatán.[1] The next generations of explorers and academics (e.g., Sylvanus Morley or Eric Thompson), following Stephens's intuitions, made selective connections between this language and other contemporary spoken ones (e.g., Manuel Orozco y Berra or Carl Hermann Berendt), as well as between this language and glyphs that had been printed on paper and carved in stone (e.g., Tatiana Proskouriakoff or Yuri Knorosov). They also connected ancient and contemporary populations, thereby giving birth to the idea of a millenarian civilization called the Maya, who were still alive. That is why the ethno-eponym *Maya* is problematic, rejected, and disputed, even in Yucatán, where it is supposed to have originated (as much ethnography and history confirms: Redfield 1941; Castañeda 2004; Evans 2004; Eiss 2008; Lerner 2011).

In most historical accounts, the predominant archeological and epigraphic narrative depicted disciplinary progress in terms of the "discovery" or "deciphering" of peoples and writings.[2] There is no doubt that we can use these terms, particularly in reference to the breaking of the Maya code—equated by Coe (1992) to scientific DNA decoding and the conquest of outer space. What I suggest here is that one of the main results of the aforementioned process of discovery and deciphering was *the production of indigenous alterity*. Firstly, these results marked the history of anthropology as a sort of conceptual production: the category *Maya* was established, as was Americanistic museography and anthropology as a university discipline, which embraced particular styles of ethno-narratives, as we will see below. Secondly, the varied objects (stones, ceramics, instruments, documents, and glyphs, as well as live languages and peoples) that came out of this anthropological production were charmed with a second life, as articulated in narratives that broadly influenced the contemporary production of popular ideas about heritage and culture in a way that was unknown in the mid-nineteenth century. Two well-known institutions in North American anthropology, established in the mid-nineteenth century in Cambridge, Massachusetts—The Peabody Museum of Archaeology and Ethnology and the Department of Anthropology at Harvard University—played a lively part in the history of the category *Maya* and the ethno-narratives about Maya people. It is possible to see a part of this long and colorful history in the work of Evon Z. Vogt (1918–2004).

A professor of anthropology at Harvard (1954–1989), and director of the Harvard Chiapas Project (1959–1984), Vogt's usage of the category of *Maya* in the 1960s (to refer to a living American civilization, known to specialists but with obscure zones yet to be discovered) had been in circulation for barely one century. Vogt was convinced that he studied the Mayan culture, and that his own work was a contribution to increasing our understanding of this civilization. At the same time, anthropologists like Vogt developed a particular kind of ethnography with a focus on alterity and uninterrupted links between ancient and present peoples (a focus that I call "encapsulating" history, borrowing a term used by Vogt to explain "Maya" practices; more on this below). This type of ethnographic practice ultimately produced ethno-narratives of contemporary populations that didn't exist before the nineteenth century.

The relevance of such ethno-narratives, printed in books and journals for consumption by anthropologists and, eventually, lay public, is that they have been widely spread by different modern mass media technologies, from school textbooks to museums, pictures, and films.[3] Moreover, the production and consumption of indigenous alterity have been a key part of broad processes of mediation (Escalona 2001), ideological interpellation, and governmentality (Castañeda 2004). Thus, particular trends in the field of anthropology participated in the production of a new political epistemology of the present times and their relationship to the past, in the era of mass media and the production of popular cultures.

VOGT, HARVARD, AND THE MAYA IN THE 1960S

In the 1960s, an ambitious anthropological project was underway in the highlands of Chiapas, Mexico: the Harvard Chiapas Project. Since 1957 Vogt had visited the area twice and selected Zinacantan, a rural municipality, for developing ethnographic research. Afterward, Vogt fostered several undergraduate and graduate students of different disciplines and universities in the United States, funded by Harvard and, mainly, other sources.[4]

In 1955, Vogt arrived in Chiapas for the first time, thanks to Mexican anthropologists and *indigenistas* Alfonso Caso (then the general director of the National Indigenist Institute [Instituto Nacional Indigenista, or INI]), Gonzalo Aguirre Beltrán, and Alfonso Villa Rojas (who headed the Centro Coordinador Tzeltal Tzotzil of the INI in Chiapas).[5] However, Vogt developed a different agenda from that of the INI, which was a governmental agency for the integration of the indigenous population into national society. The Mexican anthropologists from INI found that Indians' situation of poverty and marginalization emerged from the relations with local political and economic elites—a view that caused offense among these elites. By contrast, Vogt, Rus (2004) suggests, tried to stay neutral on these issues by focusing on "Indian communities" instead of analyzing regional and historical dynamics that could reveal political subordination and exploitation (de la Fuente 2009).

Vogt conducted fieldwork with a very particular interest: the Mayan culture. Three influences seem to explain his concentration on this issue. The first was Vogt's recognition that the Harvard Chiapas Project had its origins in the comparative project developed by members of the Laboratory of Social Relations at Harvard.[6] The second influence was his experience doing ethnography in New Mexico and Arizona (Vogt 1994, 59). However, other anthropologists' long-established fascination with the Maya contributed remarkably to Vogt's perspective as well. He had been in contact with this captivation first at the University of Chicago, where anthropologists like Robert Redfield and Sol Tax[7] had been teaching, and later on in the Peabody Museum at Harvard University, which had been founded a century earlier (1866).[8] This fascination with the Maya is seen in Vogt's writings from the sixties and early seventies (Vogt [1966] 1992; 1971; and mainly 1969a and 1969b).

ZINACANTEC CULTURE

In his monograph *Zinacantan* (1969a), Vogt noted the Mayan area from the south of Guatemala to the peninsula of Yucatán, inhabited by more than two million contemporary Maya. He pictured Zinacantan as a Maya municipality because the people spoke a Mayan language (Tzotzil) and dwelt in a Mayan settlement (with about two hundred inhabitants), which consisted of a ceremonial center with a cabildo, Catholic churches, a school, and stores, as well as a set of dispersed hamlets (with a total of about 7,600 inhabitants) and several sacred water springs, caves, and mountains in between. In Vogt's view there were four strongly intertwined ethnographic subjects: patterns of settlement, social structure, ritual organization and performance, and cosmology. These elements comprised a single consistent social system with regular principles, similar to a computer program, which Vogt identified as Zinacantec culture (Vogt 1969a, 571, 577). The first principle he put forward was the replica. Zinacantec settlement pattern, he argued, would be an aggregate of ascendant and compressing settings, from the households (three rooms around a patio with a cross in the middle, per family), to clusters of houses (according to patrilineage), to hamlets around specific water springs and lands, and finally including the whole municipality. Social relationships followed the same aggregate shape: families and lineages shared lands and waters in much the same way as the patrilineages in a given hamlet or *paraje* shared a specific set of family names.

Similar patterns were also found in the larger patriclans, or *fratrias*, that shared life in the *municipio*. The seat of the municipality was described as a ceremonial center, occupied by those holding temporary or enduring religious and civil posts (though most of the post holders returned to their hamlets at the end of their terms). Ritual activities of different scales, such as ceremonial meals and pilgrimages, replicated one another. During ritual feasting, for instance, a table was placed in an east-west orientation, with a pink-and-white tablecloth, a bottle of local aguardiente, and a bowl of salt. Post holders joined together around the table to greet, honor, and toast each other in strict hierarchical order. From the household to the greatest municipal pilgrimages, all followed the same ranked order, with lower positions heading the ceremony, and always moving in a counterclockwise direction. The ceremonies varied in size and complexity but followed the same pattern in ways that replicated one another.

A second principle is what he called encapsulation. It refers to the way in which the local culture incorporated new elements from governmental agencies and anthropologists, such as innovations introduced by the INI. This happened, for example, as the INI built the first school in Paste' in 1955. A fight that occurred near the locality caused the inhabitants to build an altar with crosses (*kalvario*), and thus the school area became a stopover point during pilgrimages. The same happened when the Pan-American road passed by the hamlet Na Chih, where the inhabitants, after several car accidents, erected shrines as a way to prevent new accidents from occurring. When a house for the Harvard Project was built in Paste' in 1960, an altar or shrine was also placed there. From Vogt's perspective, these altars and *kalvarios*, as well as the incorporation of places/things and innovations, were forms of encapsulation. He projected this process back in time, proposing that it would have occurred several times in the past, when external elements had been introduced. Encapsulation, according to Vogt, allowed the integration of innovations within Zinacantec cultural logic. One example of the process as described by Vogt is the Catholic cross, as now used in Zinacantan: it is painted green and festooned with pine foliage. Other examples include the notion of *kalvario* (a term clearly borrowed from Spanish Catholic doctrine), the worship of saints in churches (saints of European origin, but reputed to have appeared nearby), and the family names used in the patrilineal system.

The regular cultural principles that he had observed, said Vogt (1969a, 588–89; 1969b; 1971), inform us about social life among the ancient Maya. First, and following other scholars, he argued that similarities in linguistic and cultural patterns showed the contemporary Maya to be descendants of a single, ancient proto-Maya community.[9] Next, Vogt asserted that there were parallels between pre-Columbian and contemporary settlement patterns: both had hamlets scattered about ceremonial centers containing pyramids (in the past), and churches and sacred mountains (in present times).[10] In addition, it was probable that the organization based on patrilineages and patriclans, and invested with functions of authority to regulate access to land and water, was prevalent throughout the Mayan area. Finally, the old pyramids and stelae (as well as the sacred mountains, their supposed modern-day replicas) could be associated with tribal ancestors and lineages, and thus become objects of worship and pilgrimages (Vogt 1969a, 591–92).[11]

A privileged ethnographic object thus arose: the so-called cargo system. Vogt described that system as consisting (in the case of Zinacantan) of a set of temporary posts, hierarchically ranked in four levels: *mayordomos*, *alféreces*, *regidores*, and *alcaldes*. It was complemented by a minor series of permanent posts. Temporary posts were assigned to the peasantry from different patrilineages and hamlets; thus cargo holders were required to move to the seat of the municipality for the duration of their ceremonial responsibilities. This system ensured that all of the patrilineages, hamlets, and families eventually took part in the ceremonial life, and alternated between the main village and the smaller localities of the same municipality. Thus Vogt proposed that the cargo system showed integrating functions.[12] He added that none of these cargos involved power; they were only ritual positions.

ENCAPSULATED HISTORY

From Vogt's perspective, there may have been permanent settlers, ritual specialists, and artisans in the old Mayan centers; however, there could also have been an abundant floating population that occupied short-term posts in ritual activities that were invested with service but not with power. The rotation of such responsibilities among the patrilineages integrated the latter by tying them to a common center. Vogt based his ideas on descriptions (by Diego de Landa, and analyzed by Coe: Vogt 1969a; de Landa [1941] 1966) of ceremonies in Yucatán at the time of the Spanish conquest. At the root of Vogt's view of Zinacantan's contemporary ceremonial life and cargo system was a picture of the ancient Maya as bearers of rituals and counters of cosmologic time (Thompson [1954]

1966). This interpretation, shared by other specialists as well, was threatened in the 1960s by improvements in archaeological research and in the reading of glyphs carved in stone and printed on paper. These improvements enabled scholars to understand historical accounts of ruling families, thereby revealing the importance of politics, war, commerce, and government in ancient societies (Fash 1994; Graham [1994] 1999; Proskouriakoff [1994] 1999; Willey [1994] 1999; Drew 1999). At the same time, alternative perspectives arose (in some cases, among the Harvard Project's own students) from research that used nascent ethnographic approaches to study contemporary peasantry in the area. For example, new studies on the origins, current functioning, and contradictions of the so-called cargo system emphasized the historical factors that had produced and shaped it, as well as its corporative and conflictive character (see, for instance, Cancian 1965; Rus and Wasserstrom 1980).

For Vogt, preexisting Maya culture prevailed, and more recent historical developments were encapsulated by it. This is not to say that Vogt was ignorant of the importance of some historical facts in local social transformations; the conquests (both by Spaniards, and before them, from Central Mexico), independence, and nation-state formation are present in Vogt's accounts, but in a particular form that, borrowing from Vogt's own analysis of the Maya, I describe as analytically encapsulated. In his monograph, Vogt (1969a) spent several pages reviewing the available sources for the history of Mexico and Chiapas and made notes on what he called the ethnohistory of Zinacantan and the origins of the contemporary cargo system in colonial times. Vogt even underlined changes that affected religious life in Zinacantan. In later years, a few of the Harvard Project's former students would consider all these historical changes seriously.[13] However, Vogt considered these changes to be of little relevance to his analysis of Zinacantan culture. In his view, history consisted of a series of interferences that would be encapsulated by local cultural logics through erecting altars and by inserting places and objects into the ritual geography and paraphernalia. Why did Vogt have this attitude toward history?

One explanation could be that most of the fundamental studies of the history of Chiapas were still to come.[14] The lack of reliable, available sources may well have contributed to Vogt's underestimating the effects of Chiapas's history upon Maya communities. However, the minor importance of history in Vogt's anthropological style might also be understood in the light of another factor: the fascination with "the Maya."

VOGT AND THE MAYANISTS

In the 1960s, the category of *Maya* was firmly established in anthropology, linguistics, and archaeology, as well as in *indigenista* politics, literature, photography, museography, and tourism.[15] But at the same time, the Maya were still an "enigma," as said by Thompson ([1954] 1966, 11):

> Why? How? What? When? Like the soporific rhythm of a Pullman car passing over points and rail joints, the questions repeated themselves as I dozed in my hammock. How did this civilization arise? Why, unlike any other civilization in the world, did it come into being in tropical forest? When did it flourish? What hidden forces made it succeed? Why is it so like, but also so unlike, the ancient civilizations of the Old World? The questions danced across the vaulted room.

At that time, several books provided broad overviews of the latest findings concerning the Maya civilization, based on decades-long research by Harvard and Chicago Universities and the Carnegie Institute. Examples of such books are *The Maya and their Neighbors* (Hay [1940] 1962), written by students of Harvard professor Alfred Tozzer; *The Ancient Maya* (Morley 1946); and *The Rise and Fall of Maya Civilization* (Thompson [1954] 1966). On the other hand, Robert Adams (1961; professor at the University of Chicago and visiting professor at Harvard during the summer of 1966) had been focusing on settlement patterns; that was also the main perspective for Gordon R. Willey (archaeologist at the Peabody Museum and promoter of settlement-pattern analysis at Harvard). They probably had a remarkable, direct influence upon Vogt's interest in settlement patterns in Chiapas. While the Harvard Chiapas Project was in progress, the University of Chicago developed its own Chiapas project (Man in Nature), led by Professor Norman McQuown (McQuown and Pitt-Rivers [1970] 1989).

Some of these archaeologists, like Morley and Thompson, had also explored Mayan epigraphy. Between 1960 and 1967, a few articles on Mayan epigraphy were published by Tatiana Proskouriakoff, an architect and artist who became an epigraphist while doing reproductions of Mayan writings for several research projects, particularly for Morley. During the time of her publications, she was a collaborator at the Peabody Museum. Her work is highly valued for its contribution to breaking the Maya code; she proposed that writings in stone revealed histories of ruling linages and elites, instead of being merely cosmogonic and ceremonial signs (Proskouriakoff [1994] 1999; Graham [1994] 1999; Willey [1994] 1999; Coe 1992).

Vogt paid little attention to Proskouriakoff's thesis.[16] However, Vogt continued to seek dialogue with the chief explorers, discoverers, and decipherers of the Maya.

In 1961, Vogt asked several of those experts who worked in the United States to attend the symposium New Perspectives in the Study of Maya Culture, which was to be part of the American Anthropological Association Conference (Philadelphia, November 16–19). Vogt selected McQuown, Julian Pitt-Rivers, and Adams, from the University of Chicago, in addition to Kimball Romney from the University of California in Berkeley (linked to the Chicago Chiapas Project); Duane Metzger (a Chicago student); and himself. McQuown and Adams answered Vogt's invitation and recommended that he include two outstanding students at Chicago: Edward Calnek and Terence Kaufman. Calnek was doing archival research on preconquest Indian history; Kaufman worked on glottochronology and on McQuown's idea of "proto-Maya," which McQuown had proposed as a tool for classifying Mayan languages better and more completely.[17] Adams, who was conducting archaeological fieldwork in Iran by that time, replied to Vogt with a letter expressing a concern that he shared with McQuown and Pitt-Rivers: that there would be a "bothersome hiatus" in the symposium between preconquest history and the present days.[18] Adams also suggested that that hiatus would in some way be compensated by the participation of Calnek, who could talk about the impact of the Spanish conquest in Chiapas.[19] Vogt did not respond to this warning and kept working on his own idea: to summarize the research methodologies applied in the study of Mayan culture (without historians). It was the same perspective that Vogt used in planning a subsequent conference for the succeeding year.

With funding from the Wenner-Gren Foundation for Anthropological Research, Vogt organized the symposium The Cultural Development of the Maya in September 1962, in Burg Wartenstein, the foundation's castle in Austria. The idea was to bring together specialists from all over the world to analyze the Mayan culture from the viewpoint of a genetic model (i.e., comparing the developments of the same Mayan cultural base produced by different influences and contacts).[20] The invited speakers for this occasion were Willey and Proskouriakoff, from the Peabody Museum; McQuown and Tax, from the University of Chicago; and Thompson, from Harvard. In addition, Vogt invited Henning Siverts, from the University of Bergen in Oslo, Norway (who had been doing fieldwork in the Chiapas municipality of Oxchuc), and Knorosov, from the Institute of Ethnography of the University of Leningrad, in the Soviet Union, who was well recognized among epigraphists at that time for a recent article in which he proposed a method for reading the Mayan glyphs. Other participants were Alberto Ruz Lhuillier, archeologist of the Instituto Nacional de Antropología e Historia (or INAH, National Institute of Anthropology and History) in Mexico, who was the chief of the Zona Maya at INAH between 1949 and 1958, and also director of the Seminario de Cultura Maya (Mayan Culture Seminar) at the Universidad Nacional Autónoma de México (National Autonomous University of Mexico) in 1960. The list of speakers also included Alfonso Villa Rojas (from INI, Mexico); Wolfgang Haberland, from Hamburg Museum of Ethnology and Prehistory; Franz Termer, from the Museum of Hamburg; and Gunter Zimmerman, from the University of Hamburg.[21] The list of specialists whom Vogt invited to the symposium showed his own interest in being among the most renowned scholars in the field of Mayan culture, first in the United States and Mexico, and later on in the whole world.

LONG COUNT CALENDAR

In 1966, the Peabody Museum celebrated its one hundredth anniversary, and Vogt participated in organizing the festivities.[22] The spacious hall of Central America was well prepared, and various Mayan objects and replicas were exhibited. Unlike the first exhibitions (Watson 2001), this one provided visitors with a script following the logic of so-called cultural areas. Vogt was a member of the museum, where he discussed different subjects with archaeologists and epigraphists he knew personally. At his retirement in 1989, he established an office behind a space where there are today copies of the wall paintings in Bonampak, Chiapas. Perhaps Vogt considered himself part of that history of explorers and travelers who turned into anthropologists and archaeologists and contributed to creating a more complete notion of the Maya, supported by monographs, documents, and archaeological artefacts, both originals and replicas. What is interesting about this notion of the Maya is that it did not exist when Stephens and Catherwood traveled through the region twelve decades earlier.

As said above, these explorers had crossed Central America, finding buried cities in the jungle and in the mountains; in 1841 they published their account of the trip, called *Incidents of Travel in Central America, Chiapas and Yucatan*. It was a very popular text, written by Stephens, and illustrated by Catherwood ([1841] 1969). The book was read by many later archaeologists working in the area. A couple of paragraphs in that book stand out because of their connection to the processes set up then for the production of the "Maya":

All day I have being brooding over the title-deeds of Don Jose Maria, and, drawing my blanket around me, suggested to Mr. Catherwood "an operation." (Hide your heads, ye speculators in up-town lots!) To buy Copán! remove the monuments of a by-gone people from the desolate region in which they were buried, set them up in the "great commercial emporium," and found an institution to be the nucleus of a great national museum of American antiquities! But query, could the "idols" be removed? They were on the banks of a river that emptied into the same ocean by which the docks of New-York are washed, but there were rapids below; and, in answer to my inquiry, Don Miguel said these were impassable. Nevertheless, I should have been unworthy of having passed through the times "that tried men's souls" if I had not had an alternative; and this was to exhibit by sample: to cut one up and remove it in pieces, and make casts of the others. The casts of the Parthenon are regarded as precious memorials in the British Museum; and casts of Copan would be the same in New-York. Other ruins might be discovered even more interesting and more accessible. Very soon their existence would become known and their value appreciated, and the friends of science and the arts in Europe would get possession of them. They belonged of right to us, and, though we did not know how soon we might be kicked out ourselves, I resolved that ours they should be; with visions of glory and indistinct fancies of receiving the thanks of the corporation flitting before my eyes, I drew my blanket around me, and fell asleep. (115–16)

Only hours later, Stephens bought Copan for fifty U.S. dollars. In histories of the region's archaeology and epigraphy, Stephens and Catherwood are considered to be the initiators of modern archaeology on the Maya (Morley 1946; Thompson [1954] 1966; Coe [1966] 1999; 1992; Drew 1999). They were indeed, with one caveat: they did not mention the Maya. Stephens discussed the different theses that were being debated at that time about the possible origin of these jungle cities and suggested that the people who built them had to be from America (i.e., not from Phoenicia, Egypt, Israel, Greece, India, or China) and that they had to be the ancestors of the people presently living in the region (despite the contrast between the grandeur of the ancient cities and the simplicity of the contemporary localities). Furthermore, Stephens and Catherwood ([1841] 1969) suggested that the similarities between glyphs found from Honduras to Yucatán, as well as information from old documents, showed that the ruined cities buried in the jungles of Central America were the remains of one and the same civilization.[23] Stephens and Catherwood ([1843] 1996) used the term *Maya* to refer to three specific things: the kingdom of Mayapan at the time of the conquest; the language written with the Latin alphabet in documents found in Mani, Yucatán; and a language spoken by natives of the Yucatán Peninsula.[24] That was the extent to which the term *Maya* was used in describing what was then known, two decades before the foundation of the Peabody Museum in Cambridge, and the modern explorations of the ruins and settlements in Central America and Yucatán.

In conclusion, the narrative of the Maya culture as an ancient American culture/civilization that had survived until the present day appeared gradually, on the basis of explorers' work oriented and financed by businessmen and members of scientific associations who simultaneously created American anthropology, epigraphy, and archaeology. In the 1960s, scholars continued this quest, organizing congresses at universities, museums, and castles. They also made pilgrimages, not only to the ceremonial centers but even to Leningrad to meet Professor Yuri Knorosov, who made very few appearances outside of his city. Vogt and his wife traveled there in the sixties, as did Coe in 1989 (Coe 1992). Vogt found a place for himself in this field when anthropology already existed as a university degree: he had been a ranger in the southwest of the United States and came into contact with the anthropology of Chicago and Harvard through ties to anthropologists who visited the area where he was born. By then, it was possible to talk about the Maya with a familiarity that earlier generations had lacked, and Vogt managed to get funding for studies, congresses, and publications. Anthropologists who participated in this enterprise located themselves at some point on a scale of what they called "civilization" or "modernity." They had themselves sometimes observed it during trips in the Maya area, such as when Thompson ([1954] 1966) talks about a tourist guide who, upon returning to Guatemala City, considers himself civilized compared to the jungles through which the guide had traveled to reach Tikal; or when Redfield thinks about Mérida as a point of entrance of the European cultures. Vogt (1994) thought the same about the town of San Cristóbal de Las Casas, in Chiapas, wherein he had very good relations with members of the local elite.

The consequences of this production of the Maya are embedded in the creation of anthropology as a university discipline but also in different ethnographic styles. Vogt developed his anthropological project in close dialogue with archaeology and epigraphy because it was considered to be part of a much vaster enterprise: the discovery-deciphering of the great American civilizations. There were particular ethnographic objects of study, as in the case of religion, or what was considered to be its equivalents—ritual practices and cosmogonic ideas—as well as in case of the paraphernalia associated with the organization of ritual work (called the cargo system). The type of encapsulating-history view was also an expression of the long-lasting fascination with the Maya.

But in addition, the decades-long process of producing "the Maya" was an important impulse for making popular narratives on American civilizations by applying technologies of mass reproduction. First were printed images and books (like *Incidents of Travel* by Stephens and Catherwood), but then appeared exhibits and collections of objects and replicas (as those preserved in the Peabody Museum of Harvard), as well as archives, drawings, photographs, and films (Evans 2004; Lerner 2011). Seen from the wider perspective, the production of indigenous alterity has been part of a broader process of ordering the social world, in this case through the use of an ethno-eponym inserted in distinctions between the primitive and the civilized or tradition and modernity; that order is presented to us as objectivized reality through finished narratives in the form of books, archaeological sites, and museums. Doing anthropology of alterity enables us to understand the process by which these ethno-eponyms and their contemporary objectifications were produced.

ACKNOWLEDGMENTS

This chapter was translated from Spanish by the author and revised by James Smith. I want to thank the David Rockefeller Center for Latin American Studies, Peabody Museum of Archaeology and Ethnology, and Harvard University Archives for the facilities to access documents. I thank specially William and Barbara Fash for their support and advice during my research.

NOTES

1.   The notion of *Maya* appeared very early in the history of Yucatán, and was used by Diego de Landa ([1941] 1966) in his *Relación de las cosas de Yucatán* to name the area of the peninsula corresponding to the ancient Mayapan realm and a language spoken in a particular area of the north of Yucatán. But it was not employed by de Landa as social category or ethno-eponym. He normally used the terms "*naturales*," "*indios*," or "gentiles" to refer to the natives. At the dawn of the nineteenth century, Dupaix traveled through Tabasco and Yucatán, visiting lost cities in the jungle, and suggested that a single language could be found, with regional stylistic differences,

in a large area from Honduras to Yucatán. However, his observations remained in unpublished bureaucratic reports until thirty years later, in 1834.

2.   See, for instance, Coe ([1966] 1999 and 1992), Morley (1946), Thompson ([1954] 1966), and more recently Drew (1999) and Fash (1994), among others.

3.   Lerner (2011), for instance, writes of old objects and sites transformed into archeological parks, museum exhibits, and tourist locations, including locales that one day appeared as representing "twentieth-century Maya," as in a National Geographic article published in 1961 (2). Images of the Maya were created by modern visual media and its consumers in the era of modern primitivism. The starting point of the history of mass reproduction was nineteenth-century antiquarians' use and consumption of lithography or daguerreotypes, ambrotypes, the camera lucida, and other early photographic technologies (8, 17).

4.   These were the National Science Foundation, National Institute for Mental Health, Wenner-Gren Foundation, and Carnegie Institute. During some of the years between 1961 and 1967, the Harvard Chiapas Project was part of the Columbia-Cornell-Harvard Summer Field Research Program for undergraduate students' research training. The program managed three fieldwork stations: San Cristóbal de Las Casas, Chiapas, Mexico (Harvard); Riobamba, Ecuador (Columbia); and Vicos, Peru (Cornell). In 1962, the University of Illinois took over the Riobamba station, and Columbia moved its own to Bahia, Brazil. "Columbia-Cornell-Harvard Summer Field Studies Program. Report and proposal" and "Columbia-Cornell-Harvard-Illinois Summer Field Studies Program Report and Evaluation of the First Three Years," box 2, file: Columbia-Cornell-Harvard-Illinois Summer Field Studies Program—1962; "Columbia-Cornell-Harvard-Illinois. Summer field Studies Program, 1964–1965. Sponsored by the National Science Foundation," box 1: Summer Field Training Program '64, Harvard University Archives (HUA), HUGFP 140.75, "Evon Z. Vogt, Papers relating to the Harvard Chiapas Project. 1959–1975."

5.   For the history of *indigenista* policy in Mexico, see Rus (1976).

6.   The Department of Social Relations for Interdisciplinary Social Sciences Studies, also known as the laboratory, was created in 1946 to promote collaboration among the departments of anthropology, psychology, and sociology. The laboratory's best-known member was sociologist Talcott Parsons. It was also headed by anthropologists like Clyde and Florence Kluckhohn, as well as Vogt (Keller and Keller 2001). Unsurprisingly, the first version of the Chiapas Project was entitled "Mexican Cultural Change: Comparative Analysis of the Processes of Cultural Change in Tzotzil and Tzeltal Indian Communities in Chiapas, Mexico," reflecting the topic and perspective of the laboratory's project (Vogt 1994, 82).

7.   Robert Redfield had worked in Yucatan; Sol Tax worked in Guatemala and made his first visit to Zinacantan when he was teaching at the Escuela Nacional de Antropología e Historia (ENAH, National School of Anthropology and History in Mexico) from 1942 to 1943. He went to Zinacantan with a group of students

from Chicago University and the ENAH (García Méndez 2002; Vogt 1994, 83). See also López Caballero in this volume.

8. George Peabody (1795–1869), a powerful businessman and banker in the United States and England, financed the foundation of the Peabody Museum of American Archaeology and Ethnology in 1866. He also established an endowment for the first professorship in anthropology at Harvard to prepare curators and explorers who would be dedicated to organizing, increasing, and analyzing the collections. With this and additional investments, the Peabody Museum began the enterprise of discovering the unknown ancient American civilizations (Browman and Williams 2013, 39–45).

9. Various spoken languages were classified as belonging to the Maya-Kiché linguistic family since the mid-nineteenth century (Orozco y Berra 1864; Brinton 1881; Johnson [1940] 1962), but glottochronology and the idea of a proto-Maya original language for analyzing historical differentiation was used up to the middle of the twentieth century (McQuown and Pitt-Rivers [1970] 1989).

10. Vogt (1969a, 589–91; 1969b, 138) argued that compact patterns of settlement—like those around the Atitlan Lake in Guatemala, Amatenango, and Aguacatenango in Chiapas, or on the peninsula of Yucatán—were the result of atypical circumstances, colonial as well as geographic and historical. In contrast, Zinacantan's settlement pattern would reveal the precolonial pattern. However, analyses published both before and after Vogt (Redfield 1941; Fash 1994) made this argument undermine his idea about the "typical" Mayan settlement by showing that there is more variability and complexity in settlement patterns among the so-called Mayan towns than Vogt had recognized.

11. "Since in various types of ceremonies observed today (such as curing ceremonies, and rituals for renewal of the year), the contemporary (Zinacanteco) Maya make ritual pilgrimages to these sacred mountains, it seems highly likely that the Ancient Maya also came from their hamlets into the ceremonial centers either to pay homage to the pyramid associated with their particular lineage or to make the rounds, paying homage to all of the pyramids that represent their tribal gods" (Vogt 1969a, 595). Vogt argued, following Thompson ([1954] 1966), that in the lowlands, this role was played by the natural wells (*cenotes*) rather than mountains and caves.

12. The integrative-functions thesis for the cargo system was taken from Manning Nash (1958) and reworked later by Frank Cancian (1965). However, for Vogt this thesis was a key to solving the question of how ancient scattered Maya peasantry remained integrated to ceremonial centers.

13. Cancian (1965), for instance, pointed out the contrast between the cargo system's financial organization and strict religious character and what happened at the dawn of the twentieth century, when available resources grew because of the governmental land repartition. The long list of people waiting for a cargo, which involves spending money on fiestas, could be understood as a sign of insufficiency (not everyone is going to be able to participate anymore), and not of cultural vitality, as Vogt maintained. Some years later, Rus and Wasserstrom (1980) analyzed

how the cargo system may have acquired its current form as a result of economic and social changes in the nineteenth and twentieth centuries, thus confronting Vogt's view of the cargo system as based on pristine cultural principles.

14. As Robert Wasserstrom claimed in 1983 (vii), a close examination of local history had not been published until 1973, by Murdo MacLeod in his *Spanish Central America: A Socioeconomic History, 1520–1720.*

15. Thompson ([1954] 1966, 3–4) compares the Tikal that he found during his first visits there to how it looked years later: "Now the University of Pennsylvania Museum is making large-scale and exciting excavations there, converting the site into a magnificent showplace, and adding each season to our stock of Maya knowledge. A hotel has been opened and tourists flock there in large numbers. Guides escort them around the ruins, imparting much unrelated information. This heady knowledge can be imbibed freely by the pilgrim realizing that two hours later, in the modern bars of Guatemala City, he can return to what he calls civilization."

16. "Proskouriakoff (1960) has suggested that the figures on Maya stelae are portraits of reigning lords, but couldn't they equally plausibly be interpreted as ancestral gods?" (Vogt 1971, 38).

17. As mentioned above, by that time there was already a classification of most of the living languages from Yucatan to Guatemala (Orozco y Berra 1864; Brinton 1881; Johnson [1940] 1962). In-depth analysis of languages had led to a more precise classification by families, while glottochronology helped to reconstruct historical relations among them.

18. Adams, who did archaeology in Highland Chiapas, would later become secretary of the Smithsonian Institute in Washington, DC (1984–1994).

19. "If we concern ourselves with the impact of the whole program, your outline leaves a bothersome hiatus between the preconquest period and the present. An integrated approach, one that would really permit communication between the panelists, might better stress some historical problem to fill the hiatus. I have in mind Ed Calnek, who, with many months of work on the documents under his belt, is uniquely qualified in this field." Letter, from R. M. Adams to Evon Z. Vogt, February 2, 1961, HUA, HUGFP 140.75, "Evon Z. Vogt. Papers relating to the Harvard Chiapas Project. 1959–1975," box 1, file: "AAA Session on Chiapas November 1961." Calnek (1962) defended his dissertation shortly afterward.

20. For more details, see Vogt (1971).

21. HUA, HUGFP 140.10, Evon Z. Vogt, Miscellaneous Correspondence and Other Papers 1954–1976, box 4 of 6, file: "Maya Conference at Castle, September 1962." Only eleven invitees arrived. Contributions were gathered and published in a bilingual edition as *Desarrollo cultural de los Mayas* (Vogt and Ruz 1971).

22. Archaeologists and epigraphists use the name *long count calendar* to identify the system to count linear time, which does not repeat days. It was found in different areas of Middle America, mainly in old "Maya" cities.

23. Stephens even had the intuition, later shown to be incorrect, that some similarities between signs in stones in Copan and the Mexican Central Plateau suggested that

there were similar writing systems and spoken languages in those separate areas (Stephens and Catherwood [1841] 1969).

24.   Stephens and Catherwood were also interested in a different kind of objects: bones (See Cházaro in this volume).

REFERENCES

ARCHIVES

The Harvard University Archives, Cambridge, Massachusetts (HUA)

Evon Z. Vogt's Archives, Peabody Museum of Archaeology and Ethnology at Harvard University, Cambridge, Massachusetts

BIBLIOGRAPHY

Adams, Robert McKormick. 1961. "Changing Patterns of Territorial Organizations in the Central Highlands of Chiapas, Mexico." *American Antiquity* 26 (3): 341–60.

Brinton, Daniel G. 1881. "The Names of the Gods in the Kiche Myths, Central America." *Proceedings of the American Philosophical Society* 19 (109): 613–47.

Browman, David L., and Stephen Williams. 2013. *Anthropology at Harvard: A Biographical History, 1790–1940*. Cambridge, MA: Peabody Museum Press.

Calnek, Edward. 1962. "Highland Chiapas Before the Spanish Conquest." PhD diss., University of Chicago.

Cancian, Frank. 1965. *Economics and Prestige in a Maya Community: The Religious Cargo System of Zinacantan*. Stanford, CA: Stanford University Press.

Castañeda, Quetzil E. 2004. "'We Are Not Indigenous!' An Introduction to the Maya Identity of Yucatan." *Journal of Latin American Anthropology* 9 (1): 36–63.

Coe, Michael D. (1966) 1999. *The Maya*. Reprint, London: Thames and Hudson.

———. 1992. *Breaking the Maya Code*. New York: Thames and Hudson.

de la Fuente, Julio. 2009. *Monopolio de aguardiente y alcoholismo en los Altos de Chiapas: un estudio "incómodo" de Julio de la Fuente (1954–1955)*. Mexico: Comisión Nacional de Desarrollo de los Pueblos Indígenas.

de Landa, Diego. (1941) 1966. *Landa's Relación de las Cosas de Yucatán: A Translation*. Papers of the Peabody Museum of American Archaeology and Ethnology, Harvard University, vol. 18. Reprint of the first edition, edited with notes by Alfred M. Tozzer. New York: Kraus.

Drew, David. 1999. *The Lost Chronicles of the Maya Kings*. Berkeley: University of California Press.

Dupaix, Guillaume. 1834. *Antiquités mexicaines, relation des trois expéditions du capitaine Dupaix, ordonnées en 1805, 1806 et 1807, pour la recherche des antiquités du pays, notamment celles de Mitla et de Palenqué. . . .* Facsimile. Gallica: Bibliothèque Nationale de France. http://gallica.bnf.fr/ark:/12148/bpt6k5725493t.

Eiss, Paul K. 2008. "Constructing the Maya." *Ethnohistory* 55 (4): 503–8.

Escalona, José L. 2001. "Pluralismo y mediaciones: imaginario sociopolítico en Chiapas." In *Dilemas del estado nacional*, edited by Salvador Maldonado, 55–76. Mexico: Colegio de Michoacán.

Evans, Tripp. 2004. *Romancing the Maya: Mexican Antiquity in the American Imagination, 1820–1915*. Austin: University of Texas Press.

Fash, William L. 1994. "Changing Perspectives on Maya Civilization." *Annual Review of Anthropology* 23: 181–208.

García Méndez, José A. 2002. "La antropología estadounidense en Chiapas: los proyectos Harvard y Chicago." *Revista Cuicuilco* 9 (24): 297–312.

Graham, Ian. (1994) 1999. "Tatiana Proskouriakoff, 1909–1985." In Proskouriakoff (1994) 1999.

Hay, L. Clarence, ed. (1940) 1962. *The Maya and Their Neighbors*. Reprint, Salt Lake City: University of Utah Press.

Johnson, Frederick. (1940) 1962. "The Linguistic Map of Mexico and Central America." In Hay (1940) 1962, 88–114.

Keller, Morton, and Phyllis Keller. 2001. *Making Harvard Modern: The Rise of America's University*. New York: Oxford University Press.

Lerner, Jesse. 2011. *Maya of Modernism: Art, Architecture and Film*. Albuquerque: University of New Mexico Press.

MacLeod, Murdo J. 1973. *Spanish Central America: A Socioeconomic History, 1520–1720*. Berkeley: University of California Press.

McQuown, Norman, and Julian Pitt-Rivers. (1970) 1989. *Ensayos de antropología en la zona central de Chiapas*. Reprint, Mexico: Instituto Nacional de Antropología e Historia.

Morley, Sylvanus G. 1946. *The Ancient Maya*. Stanford, CA: Stanford University Press.

Nash, Manning. 1958. "Political Relations in Guatemala." *Social and Economic Studies* 7 (1): 65–75.

Orozco y Berra, Manuel. 1864. *Geografía de las lenguas y carta etnográfica de México*. Mexico: Imprenta de Andrade y Escalante.

Proskouriakoff, Tatiana. (1994) 1999. *Historia Maya*. Reprint, Mexico: Siglo XXI.

Redfield, Robert. 1941. *The Folk Culture of Yucatan*. Chicago: University of Chicago Press.

Rus, Jan. 1976. *Managing Mexico's Indians: The Historical Contexts and Consequences of Indigenismo*. A revised special paper presented to the Department of Anthropology, Harvard University; San Cristóbal de las Casas, Chiapas, Mexico, May.

———. 2004. "Rereading Tzotzil Ethnography: Recent Scholarship from Chiapas, Mexico." In *Pluralizing Ethnography: Comparison and Representation in Maya Cultures, Histories and Identities*, edited by John M. Watanabe and Edward F. Fischer, 199–230. Santa Fe, NM: School of American Research.

Rus, Jan, and Robert Wasserstrom. 1980. "Civil-Religious Hierarchies in Central Chiapas: A Critical Perspective." *American Ethnologist* 7 (3): 466–78.

Stephens, John Lloyd, and Frederick Catherwood. (1841) 1969. *Incidents of Travel in Central America, Chiapas, and Yucatan*, vol. 1. Reprint, New York: Dover Publications.

———. (1843) 1996. *Incidents of Travel in Yucatan*. New ed. Washington, DC: Smithsonian Institution Press.

Thompson, J. Eric S. (1954) 1966. *The Rise and Fall of Maya Civilization*. 2nd ed. Norman: University of Oklahoma Press.

Vogt, Evon Z., ed. (1966) 1992. *Los Zinacantecos. Un pueblo Tzotzil de los altos de Chiapas*. Reprint, Mexico: Instituto Nacional Indigenista.

———. 1969a. *Zinacantan: A Maya Community in the Highlands of Chiapas*. Cambridge, MA: Belknap Press of Harvard University Press.

———. 1969b. "Introduction." In *Handbook of Middle American Indians*, edited by Robert Wauchope and Jay I. Kislak. Vol. 7, *Ethnology*, edited by Evon Z. Vogt, 3–17. Austin: University of Texas Press.

———. 1971. "The Genetic Model and Maya Cultural Development." In Vogt and Ruz 1971, 9–48.

———. 1994. *Fieldwork Among the Maya: Reflections on the Harvard Chiapas Project*. Albuquerque: University of New Mexico Press.

Vogt, Evon Z., and Alberto Ruz L., eds. 1971. *Desarrollo cultural de los Mayas*. Mexico: Universidad Nacional Autónoma de México.

Wasserstrom, Robert. 1983. *Class and Society in Central Chiapas*. Berkeley: University of California Press.

Watson, Rubie. 2001. *Opening the Museum: The Peabody Museum of Archeology and Ethnology*. Occasional Papers, vol. 1. Cambridge, MA: Peabody Museum of Archeology and Ethnology, Harvard University. Reprinted from *Symbols*, Fall 2001 Issue, a publication of the Peabody Museum and the Department of Anthropology, Harvard University.

Willey, Gordon R. (1994) 1999. "Prefacio." In Proskouriakoff (1994) 1999, 9–10.

CHAPTER 11

IN SICKNESS AND IN MYTH

Genetic Avatars of Indigenous Alterity
and the Mexican Nation

VIVETTE GARCÍA DEISTER

GENOMICS PROJECTS AS STORYTELLING PRACTICES

I
N MANY current investigations about genomics, DNA is conceptualized
as a text authored by natural selection, one through which we read about
our history and tell stories about our past, present, and future. In order to
facilitate research that may shed light on the demographic history of humans
and their evolutionary patterns of diversification, researchers collect biological
samples (DNA) from diverse populations around the world. Indigenous populations have been of particular importance to genetics researchers since the
mid-twentieth century. The notion that DNA of indigenous peoples offers a
privileged historical window into the past because of their "primitiveness" motivated projects that set out to map human genetic diversity in the global south
by sampling "isolated indigenous populations" deemed valuable for their relative
"purity" or closeness to nature.[1] Building on the metaphor of DNA as text in
connection with indigenous "purity," in the 1950s and 1960s, Brazilian geneticists
sampled "the isolate, and the primitive, viewed as away from the influences of
the socioeconomic and demographic influences of the nation state" (De Souza
and Santos 2014, 98). Colombia's Human Expedition, which ran from the end of
the 1980s through the first half of the 1990s, sampled mainly black and indigenous groups in "the hidden Americas," seeking some sort of correlation between
perceived cultural and biological characteristics and genetic structure (Restrepo,

Schwartz-Marín, and Cárdenas 2014). In Mexico, medical geneticists working in the 1960s considered indigenous DNA samples as historical-epidemiological records capable of shedding light on matters of national public health (Suárez-Díaz 2014). This historical logic of DNA is still current, and has been further exacerbated by the idea that the propensity to diseases such as type 2 diabetes, which affects a large portion of the Mexican population, can be traced back to indigenous DNA.

I am particularly concerned in this text with the kinds of stories that genomic scientists in Mexico tell based on their analyses of indigenous DNA. I build on other scholars' examination of genomics projects as "storytelling practices" and their conclusion that despite using cutting-edge technologies, such projects many times end up enacting older stories that privilege Eurocentric views and bodies over indigenous ones. This relationship is epitomized in the title of Reardon and TallBear's (2012) article: "Your DNA Is *Our* History." They argue that Native American DNA is claimed (by white people) as a resource for understanding white people's history. It is not unusual that DNA stories about Latin American populations also end up recreating received narratives of local colonial history. For example, of the 384 Mexican American women's mitochondrial genomes recently sequenced by a group of researchers in Texas, 320 were identified as having Native American ancestry. This was interpreted as "indicative of directional mating involving preferentially immigrant [European] men and Native American women" (Kumar et al. 2011, 3). Research protocols that involve estimation of ancestral contribution via maternal or paternal DNA lineages lend themselves to what López-Beltrán (2011) has called obvious and blunt gendered narratives of molecular phylogeny that resemble "self-fulfilled prophecies" of sexual-genetic asymmetry or bias. Similarly, by comparing genomic narratives of *mestizaje* in Mexico, Colombia, and Brazil, Wade (2013, 206) identifies the repeated finding that "in present-day populations of people labeled by geneticists as 'mestizos' . . . maternal lineages are characterized by high levels of . . . Indigenous ancestry, while paternal lineages show high frequencies of European ancestral genetic markers." Sommer (2010) has conceptualized the retrospective tracing of genealogies and geographical origins from the historical record offered by DNA as "cultures of remembrance" that tend to interpret genetic DNA in the light of established historical narratives. These observations notwithstanding, the study of the human genome as an archive of human history is claiming a place in historical investigations, to the extent that "'genetic history' is evolving into a separate subdiscipline" (De Chadarevian 2010, 304).

Estimation of genomic ancestry is central to DNA storytelling. There are specific parts of the human genome considered to be highly informative about an individual's molecular past. Specific gene variants (small sequences of DNA) that have been previously recognized to be associated with distinct geographic ancestries are called ancestry informative markers, or AIMs (Fullwiley 2008). Based on these, scientists seek explanations of human evolutionary diversification and propensity to disease. The concept of ancestry used by genomic scientists may seem ambiguous, for ancestry can be assessed at different levels: it may refer to our closest ancestors, such as parents or grandparents, or it may refer to our most distant ancestors, such as the earliest hominids or the first Homo sapiens. The description of ancestry estimation provided by the American Society of Human Genetics is useful for the purpose of disambiguation:

> Ancestry estimation has enormous value in human genetics research, illuminating patterns of past human migration and providing a background pattern of human genetic variation that is essential for inferences about the past action of natural selection and genetic disease association. Genetic ancestry assessment often addresses the *intermediate levels of ancestry* that are usually imprecisely defined and identified [in genomic research and direct to consumer/recreational ancestry testing]. *It is exactly this intermediate level of ancestry*, however, that may be *especially informative for identification of the genetic basis for complex disease*, as it provides a combination of advantages of pedigree analysis and association testing. (American Society of Human Genetics 2008; emphasis mine)

Ancestry estimation is performed, then, to infer biogeographical origins or population admixture for different research purposes, be they anthropological or biomedical. In every case, identification of particular ancestry (for example, African or Amerindian) is always uncertain and statistical (one person may have 14 percent African or 56 percent Amerindian ancestry with a certain level of confidence and statistical error). Ancestry estimation is of particular relevance for studying admixed populations whose origins tend to be broken down geographically (for example, as a mix of European and African components). Because Mexico's demographic majority has been considered to be admixed or mestiza (a combination of European, Amerindian and, to a lesser extent, African components) since postrevolutionary times, estimation of the indigenous contribution to contemporary mestizo genomes is seen as offering a window into a preadmixture past. The Mexican mestizo, as it was conceived by postrevolutionary ideologues and is now taken up by biomedical researchers, seems ripe for this kind of analysis, and has become increasingly relevant as an object of study for different genomics projects, both nationally and internationally.

One research project that gained prominence in Latin America on account of its high visibility was the one carried out by Mexico's National Institute for Genomic Medicine (INMEGEN) between 2004 and 2009. This national institute of health was conceived from the start as a kind of science-government coalition formed to preempt possible threats to Mexico's "genomic sovereignty" (Benjamin 2009; Schwartz-Marín and Silva-Zolezzi 2010; López-Beltrán and Vergara-Silva 2011). INMEGEN has elicited from scholars in the science studies community diverse examinations and analyses—for instance, its role in establishing links between race and nation while simultaneously seeking to guarantee that the nation "exercise custodianship over genetic resources of its people" in accordance with "postcolonial sensibilities" (Wade, García Deister, et al. 2014, 500). The institute's flagship project, the Mexican Genome Diversity Project (MGDP), sought to develop a "map of the Mexican genome" that would contribute not so much to accomplishing nuanced DNA stories about who we Mexicans are as to providing a base for understanding the genetic basis of disease. Nevertheless, as we will see, both aims are mutually dependent, for the question about national identity is implicated in the question about the biomedical effects of *mestizaje* (García Deister 2012; García Deister and López-Beltrán, 2015).

In a previous publication I have argued that looking at biomedicine and genomics is important for understanding the work that the notion of *mestizaje* is doing in the twenty-first century (García Deister 2014). Here I take this approximation further by examining how mestizo genomics takes up and reconfigures ideas of what being *indígena* means. Based on an ethnography of a genomics laboratory, on an ethnography of national and international conferences in medical genomics, and on interviews with scientists, this text argues that current genomics practices in Mexico tell two kinds of interrelated stories: stories about the recent evolutionary past, and stories about disease. Two specific articulations of indigenous alterity (one mythical, the other pathological) are central to deciphering these molecular archives and their relevance for narratives about identity and nation. In the following section I concentrate on a particular reading of genomics that organizes scientific approximations to indigenous groups. Then I provide empirical data that support the thesis that genomics practices are contributing to contemporary understandings of indigenous alterity in Mexico.

MESTIZO GENOMICS: "ANOTHER VIEW OF *LA CONQUISTA*"

In Mexico, the term "Mestizo genomics" (Wade, López-Beltrán, et al. 2014) is used to describe the way local population genomes are being mapped with the objective of tracing ancestries and identifying genetic variants linked to disease. The processes involved in these practices—which include identification, categorization, sampling, and collection—offer elements that can help us understand the way certain categories used to describe human diversity (categories that long preexist the advent of contemporary genetics) have been both assimilated and changed in contemporary science. One of these categories is the notion of *indígena*, which has been the focus of anthropological and genetic considerations for at least a century, serving as a referent that gave the discourse of national identity in the revolutionary regime (1920–1950) a seemingly scientific dimension (Saade Granados 2009). During the twentieth century, the scientific discourse on human population genetics in Mexico was often evoked to legitimate the project of assimilating indigenous others into the mestizo body of the nation, and provided a substantial "natural" basis for official notions of national identity, indigenous alterity, and *mestizaje*. For example, the Indian-mestizo dichotomy used to organize ethnic and political interactions was reinforced through biomedical markers that produced differentiated descriptions of these two categories (López-Beltrán and García Deister 2013). As argued by Suárez-Díaz (2014), the work of some geneticists was explicitly linked to the goal of socioeconomic improvement of marginal (*indígena*) populations, which, it was officially hoped, would eventually lead to the erasure of ethnic boundaries and the homogenizing of the nation by the creation of a united Mexican people. In the developmental policies that were implemented by post–World War II Mexican governments, indigenous alterity was ideologically subordinated to an imagined mestizo homogeneity. The reality of otherness was accounted for, then, by its "medicalization"—a view of it as inherently deviant from a healthy norm—which tacitly lent cover to the perpetuation of racialized representations of the "developing" world (Escobar 1995).

Drawing from ethnographic research on biomedicine, this chapter aims to add to the collective debate about how we understand and conceptualize indigenous alterity within a scientific discourse in which the nation continues to play a pivotal role in a global context (Wade, García Deister, et al. 2014; Kent, Santos, and Wade 2014). Genetic science, as we have seen, is not averse to narratives that frame *mestizaje* as a genetic blending of European whites and indigenous peoples caught up in the cultural and social exchanges that resulted from a history of conquest. This focus on genetic admixture is clearly imbued with nationalist overtones that may be traced back to mestizophilia (Stern 2000), or to an ideology of homogeneity characteristic of centralized nationalist discourse (Hobsbawm 1995). But despite the mestizo's current centrality as an object of study—or perhaps one can even say because of it, because of the defining opposition that it necessarily generates—genetic science continues to underwrite the characteristics of the country's indigenous others. In other words, institutional science continues to provide a place for indigenous alterity in contemporary mestizo genomics.

Central to INMEGEN'S MGDP is, once again, the idea that DNA sequences are special kinds of historical documents—ones that we can read with an increasingly higher degree of resolution with the advancement of sequencing technologies. In a conference on genomic medicine sponsored by INMEGEN, a molecular psychiatrist explicitly considered the study of genetic admixture of Mexican mestizo populations to "provide another view of *La conquista.*"[2] A nationwide research project designed to access the molecular footprint of this two-world encounter was set in motion in 2004.

Because of the difficulty of sampling true ancestral populations (such as those migrating from Asia to America across Beringia during the Upper Paleolithic), scientists rely on samples from what they consider to be closely related populations, which they use as proxies (for example, contemporary West African Yoruba stands in for the African reference population in most genomic studies). In the process of collecting Amerindian samples for the MGDP, researchers designated thirty unrelated Zapotec individuals from a community in Oaxaca's Sierra Norte as direct descendants of the pre-Columbian inhabitants of the country who are supposed to have maintained a biological and cultural continuity with their ancestors. A contemporary indigenous group (representing one among over sixty different ethnolinguistic groups) was used as proxy for the ancestral Amerindian population (Silva-Zolezzi et al. 2009).[3] The four major criteria for inclusion of indigenous donors were: being born in the state of recruitment; having two parents and four grandparents also born in the state; and speaking the Zapotec language, a linguistic marker to which the donor, the donor's parents, and the donor's four grandparents must conform. The selection of indigenous donors was based on both line of descent and on sociocultural criteria that are also used in population censuses to designate ethnic membership. The strategy of using language to define the ancestral constituent of the Mexican population is consistent with a form of mestizo nationalism that "promotes an understanding of Indianness as lodged in the metaphorical gut, heart, tongue, soul, and blood of the nation and national selves" (Tarica 2008, 2; see also García Deister 2014). Ascribing a different time and a restricted space to the Zapotecs is in agreement with twentieth-century mestizo nationalism which, supported by state *indigenismo*, successfully plotted the assimilation of indigenous cultures by regarding them as primitive or at least unsynchronized with respect to the rest of the population (Tarica 2008).[4] It also erases a historical past of admixture among indigenous populations and ignores the creative redefinitions of contemporary indigenous identities (Navarrete-Linares 2009).

The results reported in 2009 showed that the contributions to the ancestry of Mexican mestizos were, on average, 55.2 percent Amerindian, 41.8 percent European, and 3.5 percent African. This information, it was claimed, would be useful for understanding the genetic basis of diseases that affect the Mexican population and for optimizing the design and analysis of future studies seeking to identify disease-related genes (Silva-Zolezzi et al. 2009). A journalist considered these results to be a "confirmation of the obvious": "The study . . . reminded us that we are in fact a coffee with milk nation. White? Only if we are referring to chlorine-washed diapers, for we are all the way we are: mestizos, mixture of ethnic groups, cauldron of heterogeneous pasts, between forced and random combination of genes here and there, with a dash of salt and two of sugar" (Salazar 2009).

After having been repeatedly exposed to it for over a century, the image of *mestizaje* has become internalized in the collective imaginary of Mexicans to such an extent that genomic data that statistically documents it becomes, on this journalist's account, little more than state-of-the-art technology in the service of producing truisms. So why has Mexico boarded the global bandwagon of human genomics and begun actively rereading the story of *mestizaje* in molecular idiom?

While the focus of the MGDP is on mestizo DNA, results of the genomic analysis indicate that genetic differences among Mexican mestizos are mainly due to differences in their Amerindian contributions. INMEGEN researchers see the "Amerindian portion" of the genome (presumably inherited from a founder Native American population) as conferring on mestizo genomes different qualities of *mestizaje*. One general conclusion that researchers drew from this study was that by contributing Amerindian ancestry to Mexican mestizos, *indígenas* make the former genetically unique. The uniqueness of the Mexican population is thus predicated on the singularity of the biological processes that have taken place in Mexico, resulting in the phenomenon of a distinctive national type.[5] But this inference incorporates a pathological dimension as well, for the Amerindian portion of the genome also carries the genetic variants that make mestizos susceptible to a variety of diseases that are highly prevalent in the Mexican population today, such as diabetes. The implication is that the legacy of the *indígena* to the mestizo type, in combination with a nutritional environment vastly different from that of the original indigenous diet, has created a public health crisis. In the following section I explore the discourse and practices around this "Amerindian portion"—what is said about it and the ways in which it is defined and approached. It is in this space of inquiry that the two genetic avatars of the *indígena* become visible.

GENETIC AVATARS OF INDIGENOUS ALTERITY

The Oxford English Dictionary defines *avatar* as an incarnation, embodiment, or manifestation of a person or idea. When I speak of genetic avatars, I refer to genetically mediated manifestations of the notion of the Indian. Two theoretical approaches inform my use of *avatar*. One is articulation theory (Clifford 2001); the other is hybridity (García-Canclini 1995). Articulation allows us to understand acts of borrowing, interpretation, and reconfiguration (cf. TallBear 2007; 2013) of concepts, precision instruments, and practices that render the Mexican population "as ancestrally rooted in time and space" but always with respect to "the same three parental populations" (Wade 2014, 219), which is where hybridity becomes relevant. Percentage allocation to different ancestral components is invariably done according to a "trihybrid model" of Mexican (European, Indian, and, to a lesser extent, African) *mestizaje* that seems to imply poles of purity while at the same time acknowledging processes of trans-bio-culturation that bring forth the mestizo/a hybrid "all the way down" (Rosaldo in García-Canclini 1995, xv). Articulation theory, which tries to move beyond static, essentialist, and dichotomous views of indigenous alterity, paradoxically allows us to identify the ways in which Indian qualities are genomically fixed and objectified "with apparent exactitude" (Wade 2014, 219). Attention to hybridity, on the other hand, allows us to identify actors' fascination with admixture and the interpretive flexibility with which they apply notions of purity and *mestizaje*.

I now turn to the mythical avatar of indigenous alterity. One of the lead researchers of the MGDP at INMEGEN said in an interview in 2010 that Xavier Soberón, the recently appointed director general, had asked her to select three indigenous samples for whole genome sequencing. But how would indigenous samples be selected? "Perhaps [we should include] Mayas, Tepehuanos, and either Zapotecas or Mixtecos," she said.[6] A bioinformatics researcher later commented, "Being *indígena* per se does not warrant sequencing. Having 93 percent Amerindian ancestry and possessing a rare variant—now that would justify selection of the sample. Whom and why matter; it must be an informed decision . . . Guaranteeing the existence of mitochondrial and Y-chromosome Amerindian haplotypes would be necessary."[7] The discussion about how many samples, and which ones to include, lasted many months. As a result of the first and second phases of the MGDP, INMEGEN was in possession of several hundred indigenous samples from different ethnic groups. When the director of INMEGEN first approached the researchers, three individuals selected from this pool of samples were thought to be an adequate choice. But the diversity of *indígena* samples became manifest as further genetic analyses were carried out. Some samples clustered together and far away from those belonging to other subpopulations, thus indicating homogeneity. But certain individuals overlapped with those of another group; some samples labeled as *indígena* even overlapped with the mestizo sample population. "They are all ethnic groups with varying degrees of *mestizaje*. Should we select a sample that is halfway between mestizos and *indígenas*, or one that is the farthest away from mestizos? I think we should aim for an intermediate one."[8] There was also talk of increasing the number of *indígena* samples to be sequenced: two Zapotecs (from MGDP), one Maya (different source), and one Totonaca (different source). The issue of discussion then became the provenance of the samples: where, how, why, and in what terms were they collected? The change of director general at INMEGEN had brought about the hiring of a molecular anthropologist and a medical geneticist, both of whom had developed their own sampling strategies of indigenous populations and were asked to participate in the project. Would these different samples, all obtained under different circumstances, criteria, and research protocols, be comparable?

Further along in the deliberation, a researcher from a neighbor laboratory at INMEGEN arrived with a sample he had collected himself from a domestic worker, arguing that she was a true representative of Mixtecos from Oaxaca.[9] The number of samples to be sequenced increased (rather authoritatively) to five, and new concerns regarding the sample's provenance emerged. "[This researcher] brought us a supposedly Mixteca sample. He wanted to have it sequenced. So we analyzed the sample. ADMIXTURE indicates that it is 93 percent Native American, but we do not know, genetically, how Mixteca it is because we do not have a Mixteco reference population to compare it with.[10] We have doubts about whether it is a good candidate for sequenciation."[11] Other researchers also expressed reservations about the design of the project. A molecular anthropologist was worried about the urgency with which libraries of readily available indigenous samples were being sought, with hardly any attention to collection protocols (beyond the existence of an informed consent) and without ethnographic input. Concerns not only about the reasons for selecting certain samples but also the ethnic groups from which blood was originally collected further burdened the venture. Finally, when the allegedly Mixteca sample was run against other *indígena* populations, it did not behave as expected: "We have reasons to believe that the sample is Totonaca, not Mixteca, because it appears to be very close to the Totonaca cluster. Also, it appears to be halfway between Tepehuanos, Mayas, and Zapotecas. But we do not know if it represents a member of an intermediate population or if it is an outlier[12] of one of these populations."[13]

The race to sequence the (at the time) first contemporary Amerindian genome differed from the previous project of mapping the mestizo genome in several ways. "At first we did not use particular labels for the samples (such as Mayas or Zapotecos). We were concerned in the first phase of the MGDP with being able to tell apart *indígenas* from non-*indígenas*."[14] Being *indígena* at that time translated into not showing indication of *mestizaje* at the genetic level (that is, presenting Amerindian ancestry in both mitochondrial DNA and Y-chromosome DNA). With the realization that all *indígena* populations present some degree of *mestizaje* (one that can be identified by increasing the number of genetic markers sought in the nuclear DNA), the notion of indigenous alterity seemed to require further qualification and nuance. This turned out to be an obstacle for the selection of *indígena* samples to be sequenced, for the ideal indigenous type—the one defined, also genetically, in opposition to the mestizo—was nowhere to be found. "In the race towards publishing the first indigenous genome, perhaps the most important part is not being the first one to publish, but rather having an interesting question. Many times, next-generation sequencing technologies are used without an interesting question to answer."[15] The problem was that this undertaking had originated not in a research question but rather in a preassembled concern with the Indian as a relational variable. The motivation for sequencing *indígenas* was to "rescue" the indigenous component of the mestizo population, to provide a document that would allow researchers to characterize the Amerindian peculiarities of the mestizo genome with greater detail. It was "the natural next step after doing GWAS [Genome Wide Association Studies[16] on mestizo genomes]."[17] In other words, the project was secondary to and, to a certain extent, a subsidiary of the practices of mestizo genomics.

Even as the *indígena* sequencing project was indefinitely postponed (partly due to the unresolved selection of samples collectively deemed appropriate for sequencing, and partly due to technological setbacks having to do with proper calibration and operation of sequencing technology), this episode of my ethnography illustrates how hegemonic and rather static narratives about *mestizaje* are successfully drawn into genetic research. As we have seen, the genetic articulation of indigenous alterity partly requires that contemporary *indígenas* are fixed within a different sociogeographic space and time and thus made available to be regarded as proxies of a pre-admixture past. The mythical avatar contributes to the narrative that while mestizos have become modernized, the *indígena* has remained in an ancestral state, which reproduces marginalizing assumptions about education, potential, and ability (the selection of a domestic worker's sample for sequencing saliently exemplifies this).[18] There is also an expectation that cultural alterity of people identified as indigenous is somehow identifiable in the genome. This practice is built upon a preexisting, nongenetic category of the Indian, inscribing it in genomic science itself, where it is barely visible but conceptually powerful, sustaining the founding myth of the Mexican nation: that all Mexicans descend from a European (more specifically, Spanish) father and an indigenous mother.

Let us now examine the pathological avatar of indigenous alterity. In the publicity about the MGDP, emphasis was invariably placed on the localization of the gene variants (presumably of Amerindian ancestry) responsible for the high prevalence of obesity and diabetes among Mexicans. The map of the Mexican genome was meant to help derive future treatments that will target populations that have been made vulnerable by admixture with indigenous genes, as well as the marginal "pure" indigenous population. INMEGEN currently collaborates with a researcher from UNAM's School of Chemistry who has named the library of gene variants she has assembled over three decades of sampling different indigenous groups the *Genoteca indígena* (so far, thirty-one out of sixty-two ethnolinguistic groups are represented in the *genoteca*). The aim of her research is to understand "why we Mexicans are so vulnerable to suffering from diseases like diabetes, and why it affects us in such a different way than [the ways in which it affects] Caucasians, Africans, and the Chinese" ("Genoteca indígena" 2013). The genetic particularities of *mestizaje* in Mexico (that is, derived from the average mix of 70 percent Amerindian, 25 percent European, and 5 percent African ancestry—although the percentages mentioned by this researcher change from one interview to the other) provide content to the idea of the Mexican not only as mestizo but also as obese and diabetic.

A word this scientist coined for naming these genetic peculiarities is "*etnosoma*" (or ethnosome). Although never formally defined, and (to my knowledge) never used in peer-reviewed publications, she often uses the word in conferences addressed both at specialized and wider audiences (I heard it for the first time in the international conference Genomics, Obesity, and Diabetes, sponsored by INMEGEN on August 17, 2011). The ethnosome is, according to this scientist, "derived from the notion of ethnic group," onto which an odd variation of the suffix -omics (used to designate the objects of study in the field informally referred to as "-omics," i.e., genomics, metabolomics, etc.) is applied. Attempting an etymological analysis of the neologism, we can break it up into the Greek *ethnikos* and *somatikos*, which leaves us with the idea of an ethnic body, an indigenous type that is very much in accord with the way in which, judging from her academic talks, the investigator conceptualizes indigenous alterity. For her, "our beautiful indigenous people" are in fact isolated populations, carriers of detrimental genetic variants, and bearers of disease that is frequently embodied, hence the title of one of her latest talks: "Maya Diabetes: Past, Present and Future in One Dimension" (April 23, 2015). But the word *ethnosome* is also revelatory of the way in which indigenous groups are approached by biomedical investigators vested in diabetes research: once again appealing to an expected correlation between genetic and cultural traits, the aim is "to get to know the [indigenous] genomes in order to get to know the [indigenous] groups."[19] If we know what "disease genes" look like, and these can be found in Amerindian genomes, then DNA stories of Indianness as molecular disease can be narrated. In this case, rather than displacing the contemporary *indígena* to a distant past (as with the mythical avatar), the study of present-day indigenous groups and Amerindian portions of mestizo genomes synchronizes pre-admixture indigenous alterity with contemporary ideas of Mexico as a sick nation. In this diseased nation in which 4.5 million children and 48 million adults are obese, and over 9 percent of the population is diabetic, indigenous genes are scrutinized as a "key to diabetes and obesity," one that will help us to "understand the genetic background that may be responsible for susceptibility to diabetes" ("Genoma indígena" 2011).

The pathological avatar has also made its way into the research assumptions of neurogeneticists. The genetic study of neuropsychiatric disorders in the Mexican mestizo population is also linked to the metaphor of DNA as a text of the past. By relating bipolar disorder and schizophrenia to admixed ancestry, neuropathology is temporally traced back to the very "trauma" of *La conquista*, when Spanish males forced themselves on indigenous females and a new breed of intermediate beings was born. This pathological avatar is a reverberation of twentieth-century appreciations of Mexicans as psychologically deviant (Ramírez 1977) or, at least, prone to identity crises (Ramos 1934; Paz 1950).[20]

The story of the first events of interbreeding between Spanish males and indigenous females can also be told via nuclear-mitochondrial DNA interactions. This is the way in which a Mexican scientist specializing in ancient DNA makes sense of linkage-disequilibrium analyses in admixed populations. This scientist's own projects of (1) characterizing Native American genome variability to assess the effects of population admixture with special focus on nuclear-mitochondrial interactions, and (2) assessing the role of nuclear-mitochondrial interactions in complex diseases, are strongly interrelated. They are both based on a hypothesis regarding differential adjustment between mitochondrial DNA (from maternal inheritance) and nuclear DNA (the result of recombination of maternal and paternal DNA during sexual reproduction) over recent evolutionary time (five hundred years ago). When speaking about this moment in evolutionary history, this scientist sketched for me a map of the world on a white piece of paper (figure 11.1). He drew arrows to indicate human migrations from Africa, Asia, and, more recently, from the Iberian Peninsula to North America. The protagonist of his illustrated story of migration was DNA, which also "recombined and populated" North America. He spoke of admixture in terms of European (Spanish) DNA and Native American DNA.

On this interpretation, when a population has had a long history of isolation and has not received external nuclear or mitochondrial DNA elements, the population's mitochondria and nuclei appear to be synchronized, which leads to favorable physiological conditions. But when a different genetic lineage carrying new genetic variants arrives on the scene, as occurred when the Spaniards reached America, a mixture is created in the cell nucleus (as a result of sexual

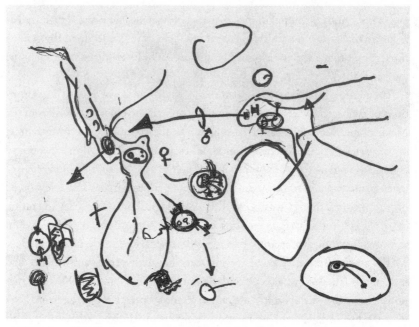

FIGURE 11.1. Sketch done by a genomicist to explain the admixture resulting from the arrival of Spaniards to America five hundred years ago in terms of interactions between European (Spanish) DNA and Native American DNA (interview June 10, 2010).

reproduction) that does not take place in the mitochondria (because mitochondrial DNA does not recombine and is transmitted maternally from one generation to the next). The result is dissonance or desynchronization between a population's mitochondrial (Native American) and nuclear (Spanish) DNA, which can bring forth physiological disruption and, hence, an increased susceptibility to disease. Indigenous alterity in this case surfaces as a maternally inherited molecular disruptor capable of reigniting the age-old trope of the diseased political body of the Mexican nation.

CONCLUSION

The assertion that the *indígena* contributes Amerindian ancestry to Mexican mestizos, thus making them genetically unique, has the effect of displacing the contemporary *indígena* to a distant five-hundred-year-old past: the mythical avatar. A complementary thesis states that the *indígena* carries the genetic variants that make mestizos susceptible to obesity and diabetes: the pathological avatar. Today's Mexican mestizo is tomorrow's diabetic due to vulnerabilities stemming from the admixtures of the past. But also, the past is resurfacing today as a prognostication of the events to come: indigenous groups in contemporary Mexico are being studied by genomics as carriers of the pathologies of yesteryear that will reemerge in the future.

This thematic has a long history in Mexican intellectual culture, where the *indígena* is variously seen as a weakness in the Mexican fabric, which accounts for Mexican backwardness, or as an iconic figure for ceremonial use that makes *indígenas* exceptional even as the living correspondents of the figure are marginalized (Earle 2007). These two seemingly contradictory strands in Mexican self-reflection actually reinforce one another and have a place in genomics research.

The examples shown exist within a historical horizon that extends the present both into the past—where at some level "pure" units of Europeans and Amerindians met—and into the future, where the results of that meeting have produced population-wide vulnerabilities to obesity and diabetes. Through these temporal displacements, the search for Amerindian markers fuels practices of corroboration of deeply embedded historical narratives. Pre-Hispanic indigenous alterity is genetically recovered and glorified as a source of genetic exceptionalism, whereas its current presence in Mexican genomes is considered to require biomedical intervention.

ACKNOWLEDGMENTS

I am grateful to Ariadna Acevedo-Rodrigo, Paula López Caballero, and Santiago Molina for their very useful comments on earlier drafts of this chapter. The ideas expressed here are also indebted to the conversations and exchanges with team members from the projects acknowledged below, especially Carlos López-Beltrán and Peter Wade. Francisco Vergara-Silva has also been a valuable interlocutor on these topics. The empirical material discussed in this article arises out of two projects: "Race, Genomics and *Mestizaje* (Mixture) in Latin America: A Comparative Approach," funded by the Economic and Social Research Council (U.K.; grant RES-062-23-1914), and "Public Engagement with Genomic Research and Race in Latin America," funded by the Leverhulme Trust (grant RPG-044). The projects were based at the University of Manchester and ran from January 2010 to March 2013. They were directed by Peter Wade and involved collaborative work with teams in Brazil (led by Ricardo Ventura Santos), Colombia (led by Eduardo Restrepo), and Mexico (led by Carlos López-Beltrán).

NOTES

1. See Reardon (2001) and M'charek (2005) for critical examinations of the international Human Genome Diversity Project, which capitalized on this idea of isolation and purity.
2. "International Meeting on Genomic Medicine: Challenges in Research and Social Impact," October 21, 2010.
3. There are important methodological reasons for extracting DNA from contemporary groups in order to build a reference population rather than seeking extraction of DNA from ancient Zapotec tombs, for example. First, the quality and quantity of DNA that can be extracted from ancient bones or teeth is highly contingent. Differences in the conditions of the environment in which remains are found, as well as in the kinds and number of manipulations they have been subject to over hundreds of years, may greatly affect the outcome of DNA extraction and analysis. The sources of possible contamination are many and unspecified, which renders the endeavor both technically challenging and epistemologically suspect. Second, even if the conditions in which alleged Zapotec remains are found were ideal for uncontaminated conservation and they were processed with state-of-the-art ancient DNA extraction technology, researchers need to know the number of individuals that make up their reference population in order to guarantee statistical robustness. Precise delimitation of the number of different Zapotec individuals comprising an ancient reference population is extremely difficult to achieve, and subject to archaeological and historical interpretation (both in terms of individuality and in terms of ethnic adscription, since migration is well documented among pre-Hispanic groups). Also, obtaining the necessary number of samples of different Zapotec individuals (in the same archeological site) to conduct statistical analysis may prove impossible. Third, an additional criterion for inclusion of samples in a reference population is that they derive from biologically unrelated individuals (the reason for this has to do with avoiding genetic bias due to endogamy); given the known demographics of ancient Zapotec groups, and the unknown relationships among individuals' remains, this condition is practically impossible to ensure.
4. See Schwartz's and López Caballero's chapters in this book.
5. See Kent et al. (2015) for a comparison between two genomic national types: Mexico's "Genoma Mexicano" and Brazil's "Homo Brasilis."
6. Interview, June 28, 2010.
7. Interview, February 17, 2011.

8. Interview, June 28, 2010.

9. The apparent ease with which this researcher established a correspondence between indigenous alterity and domestic work is widespread among the urban elites in Mexico City. This connection has its roots in a pigmentocratic system that draws indigenous rural women to work for "white" households in urban areas, under conditions in which their cultural and economic exclusion is not only maintained but also actively reinforced.

10. ADMIXTURE is one of the most commonly used software tools for statistical estimation of individual ancestries.

11. Interview, November 26, 2010.

12. An outlier is considered to be a statistical anomaly. It may be due to variability in the measurement or it may indicate experimental error, and it is sometimes excluded from the data set. Deletion of outlier data is a controversial practice in human genomics.

13. Interview, February 17, 2011.

14. Interview, September 24, 2010.

15. Interview, February 17, 2011.

16. Genome-wide association studies (GWAS) is a method that scans an entire genome in the search for small variations, called single nucleotide polymorphisms, or SNPs (pronounced "snips"), that occur more frequently in people with a particular disease than in people without the disease. Each study can look at hundreds or thousands of SNPs at the same time. Researchers use data from this type of study to pinpoint genes that may contribute to a person's risk of developing a certain disease. Scientists consider such studies to be particularly useful in finding genetic variations that contribute to common, complex diseases, such as asthma, cancer, diabetes, heart disease, and mental illnesses, although there is much debate on whether or not these methods are actually valuable for risk prediction.

17. Interview, February 17, 2011.

18. Such articulation of indigenous alterity further allows for the notion of "genetic patrimony"—coined by INMEGEN's medical-political elite as a legal and discursive resource—to emerge under the form and structure of a myth. Genetic patrimony plays a role in the creation of an imagined genetic community (decanted in the category *Mexican mestizo*, as defined by geneticists) by advancing the idea that there exists a catalog of goods that belong to all Mexicans, and that those who symbolically and normatively possess such goods are included in the national community (Azuela 2009). Under this logic, a "unique genome" derived from admixture between European and Native American populations five hundred years ago, is interpreted as one of these patrimonial goods. What Antonio Azuela calls the "juridification" of national patrimony is linked with the legislation of national goods that was set forth by the Mexican state toward the end of the nineteenth century and became stronger with postrevolutionary nationalism during the twentieth century (see also Cottom 2008). Article 27 of the Mexican Constitution is,

judicially, the main passage point for all matters related to national goods, including natural resources (e.g., oil) and rural property (e.g., ejido). But juridification of the so-called "Mexican genome" in the role of patrimonial goods passes not through the laws that legislate over property but rather through a law that regulates another fundamental right: the right to health (article 4 of the Mexican Constitution). Mestizo genomics is considered, under this legal scheme, as a national health good (Petryna 2009), and protection of genetic patrimony is allegedly achieved through the exercise of so-called genomic sovereignty.

19.   Interview with biomedical geneticist, August 17, 2011.

20.   A recent (largely derivative) take on these kinds of arguments is developed in Basave's (2010) *Mexicanidad y esquizofrenia*. See Yépez's (2010) *La increíble hazaña de ser mexicano* for a more sardonic result of the same strategy. Both books were published in 2010, the year celebrating the centennial of the Mexican Revolution and the bicentennial of Mexican independence.

REFERENCES

American Society of Human Genetics. 2008. "Ancestry Testing Statement." http://www .thegeneticgenealogist.com/wp-content/uploads/ASHG.pdf. Accessed May 18, 2015.

Azuela, Antonio. 2009. "Durkheim y la tentación contractualista. Notas sobre la dimension mítica del patrimonio nacional de México." In *¿Por qué leer a Durkheim hoy?*, edited by Juan Carlos Geneyro, Antonio Azuela, and Juan Carlos Marín, 59–96. Mexico: Instituto Tecnológico Autónomo de México and Editorial Fontamara.

Basave, Agustín. 2010. *Mexicanidad y esquizofrenia. Los dos rostros del mexiJano*. Mexico: Océano.

Benjamin, Ruha. 2009. "A Lab of Their Own: Genomic Sovereignty as Postcolonial Science Policy." *Policy and Society* 28 (4): 341–55.

Clifford, James. 2001. "Indigenous Articulations." *Contemporary Pacific* 13 (2): 468–90.

Cottom, Bolfy. 2008. *Nación, patrimonio cultural y legislación: los debates parlamentarios y la construcción del marco jurídico federal sobre monumentos en México, siglo XX*. Mexico: H. Cámara de Diputados, LX Legislatura, and Miguel Ángel Porrúa.

De Chadarevian, Soraya. 2010. "Genetic Evidence and Interpretation in History." *BioSocieties* 5 (3): 301–5.

De Souza, Vanderlei Sebastiao, and Ricardo Ventura Santos. 2014. "The Emergence of Human Population Genetics and Narratives About the Formation of the Brazilian Nation (1950–1960)." *Studies in the History of Biological and Biomedical Sciences* 47: 97–107.

Earle, Rebecca. 2007. *The Return of the Native: Indians and Myth-Making in Spanish America, 1810–1930*. Durham, NC: Duke University Press.

Escobar, Arturo. 1995. *Encountering Development: The Making and Unmaking of the Third World*. Princeton, NJ: Princeton University Press.

Fullwiley, Duana. 2008. "The Biologistical Construction of Race: 'Admixture' Technology and the New Genetic Medicine." *Social Studies of Science* 38 (5): 695–735.

García-Canclini, Néstor. 1995. *Hybrid Cultures: Strategies for Entering and Leaving Modernity*. Minneapolis: University of Minnesota Press.

García Deister, Vivette. 2012. "Palabra clave: mestizaje." *Revista Cronopio*, September 26. http://www.revistacronopio.com/?p=8903. Accessed May 18, 2015.

———. 2014. "Laboratory Life of the Mexican Mestizo." In Wade, López-Beltrán, et al. 2014, 161–82.

García Deister, Vivette, and Carlos López-Beltrán. 2015. "*País de gordos/país de muertos*: Obesity, Death and Nation in Biomedical and Forensic Genetics in Mexico." *Social Studies of Science* 45 (6): 797–815.

"Genoteca indígena recopila ADN de mexicanos." 2013. *El Universal*, December 31. http://www.eluniversal.com.mx/ciencia/2013/genoteca-indigena-adn-mexicanos-82420.html. Accessed May 18, 2015.

"Genoma indígena es clave de diabetes y obesidad." 2011. *El Universal*, August 30. http://www.eluniversal.com.mx/articulos/65769.html. Accessed May 18, 2015.

Hobsbawm, Eric J. 1995. *Nations and Nationalism Since 1780: Programme, Myth, Reality*. Cambridge: Cambridge University Press.

Kent, Michael, Vivette García Deister, Ernesto Schwartz-Marín, Ricardo Ventura, Carlos López-Beltrán, and Peter Wade. 2015. "Building the Genomic Nation: *Homo Brasilis* and the *Genoma Mexicano* in Comparative Cultural Perspective." *Social Studies of Science* 45 (6): 839–61.

Kent, Michael, Ricardo Ventura Santos, and Peter Wade. 2014. "Negotiating Imagined Genetic Communities: Unity and Diversity in Brazilian Science and Society." *American Anthropologist* 116 (4): 736–48.

Kumar, Satish, Claire Bellis, Mark Zlojutro, Phillip E. Melton, John Blangero, and Joanne E. Curran. 2011. "Large Scale Mitochondrial Sequencing in Mexican Americans Suggests a Reappraisal of Native American Origins." *BMC Evolutionary Biology* 11 (1): 293.

López-Beltrán, Carlos, ed. 2011. *Genes (y) mestizos: Genómica y raza en la biomedicina mexicana*. Mexico: Ficticia Editorial.

López-Beltrán, Carlos, and Vivette García Deister. 2013. "Scientific Approximations to the Mexican Mestizo." *História, Ciências, Saúde—Manguinhos* 20 (2): 391–410.

López-Beltrán, Carlos, and Francisco Vergara Silva. 2011. "Genómica nacional: El inmegen y el genoma del mestizo." In López-Beltrán 2011, 99–142.

M'charek, Amade. 2005. *Human Genome Diversity Project: An Ethnography of Scientific Practice*. Cambridge, MA: Cambridge University Press.

Navarrete-Linares, Federico. 2009. "Crisis and Reinvention: The Redefinition of Indigenous Identities in Contemporary Mexico." In *Indigenous Identity and Activism*, edited by Priti Singh, 53–79. Delhi: Shipra Publications.

Paz, Octavio. 1950. *El laberinto de la soledad*. Mexico: Fondo de Cultura Económica.

Petryna, Adriana. 2009. *When Experiments Travel: Clinical Trials and the Global Search for Human Subjects*. Princeton, NJ: Princeton University Press.

Ramírez, Santiago. 1977. *El mexicano, psicología de sus motivaciones*. Mexico: Grijalbo.

Ramos, Samuel. 1934. *El perfil del hombre y la cultura en México*. Mexico: Colección Austral.

Reardon, Jenny. 2001. "The Human Genome Diversity Project: A Case Study in Coproduction." *Social Studies of Science* 31 (3): 357–88.

Reardon, Jenny, and Kim TallBear. 2012. "Your DNA Is Our History: Genomics, Anthropology, and the Construction of Whiteness as Property." *Current Anthropology* 53 (S5): S233–45.

Restrepo, Eduardo, Ernesto Schwartz-Marín, and Roosbelinda Cárdenas. 2014. "Nation and Difference in the Genetic Imagination of Colombia." In Wade, López-Beltrán, et al. 2014, 55–84.

Saade Granados, Martha. 2009. *El mestizo no es 'de color.' Ciencia y política pública mestizófilas (México, 1920–1940)*. Mexico: Escuela Nacional de Antropología e Historia and Instituto Nacional de Antropología e Historia.

Salazar, Horacio. 2009. "El genoma del mexicano." *Notas de la ciencia.* http://www.milenio.com/node/214857. Accessed May 14, 2009.

Schwartz-Marín, Ernesto, and Irma Silva-Zolezzi. 2010. "'The Map of the Mexican's Genome': Overlapping National Identity, and Population Genomics." *Identity in the Information Society* 3 (3): 489–514.

Silva-Zolezzi, Irma, Alfredo Hidalgo-Miranda, Jesus Estrada-Gil, Juan Carlos Fernandez-Lopez, Laura Uribe-Figueroa, Alejandra Contreras, Eros Balam-Ortiz, et al. 2009. "Analysis of Genomic Diversity in Mexican Mestizo Populations to Develop Genomic Medicine in Mexico." *Proceedings of the National Academy of Sciences* 106 (21): 8611–616.

Sommer, Marianne. 2010. "DNA and Cultures of Remembrance: Anthropological Genetics, Biohistories and Biosocialities." *BioSocieties* 5 (3): 366–90.

Stern, Alexandra. 2000. *Mestizophilia, Biotypology, and Eugenics in Post-revolutionary Mexico: Towards a History of Science and the State, 1920–1960*. Chicago: University of Chicago.

Suárez-Díaz, Edna. 2014. "Indigenous Populations in Mexico: Medical Anthropology in the Work of Ruben Lisker in the 1960s." *Studies in History and Philosophy of Biological and Biomedical Sciences* 47: 108–17.

TallBear, Kim. 2007. "Narratives of Race and Indigeneity in the Genographic Project." *Journal of Law, Medicine & Ethics* 35 (3): 412–24.

———. 2013. "Genomic Articulations of Indigeneity." *Social Studies of Science* 43 (4): 509–34.

Tarica, Estelle. 2008. *The Inner Life of Mestizo Nationalism*. Minneapolis: University of Minnesota Press.

Wade, Peter. 2013. "Blackness, Indigeneity, Multiculturalism and Genomics in Brazil, Colombia and Mexico." *Journal of Latin American Studies* 45 (2): 205–33.

———. 2014. "Race, Multiculturalism, and Genomics in Latin America." In Wade, López-Beltrán, et al. 2014, 211–40.

Wade, Peter, Vivette García Deister, Michael Kent, María Fernanda Olarte Sierra, and Adriana Díaz del Castillo Hernández. 2014. "Nation and the Absent Presence of Race in Latin American Genomics." *Current Anthropology* 55 (5): 497–522.

Wade, Peter, Carlos López-Beltrán, Eduardo Restrepo, and Ricardo Ventura, eds. 2014. *Mestizo Genomics: Race Mixture, Nation and Science in Latin America.* Durham, NC: Duke University Press.

Yépez, Heriberto. 2010. *La increíble hazaña de ser mexicano.* Mexico: Editorial Planeta.

EPILOGUE

BEYOND ALTERITY, BEYOND OCCIDENTALISM

"Indigenous Other" and "Western Self" in Mexico

PAUL K. EISS

THERE MAY be no better way to begin a reflection on the place of the "indigenous other" in Mexico than with a reading of Guillermo Bonfil Batalla's ([1987] 1996) classic study, *México profundo*.[1] *México profundo* unfolds as an epic tale of a five-hundred-year confrontation between two civilizations: a popular culture rooted in "Mesoamerican ways of life" (xv), which he terms "México profundo," and another imposed from above by advocates of a Western, modernizing project. Bonfil Batalla calls the latter "the imaginary Mexico"; "It is imaginary not because it does not exist," he writes, "but because, based on it, there has been an effort to build a Mexico different from Mexican reality" (161). The text is by turns anthropology, history, and political manifesto. The first part provides a broad survey of contemporary Mexico, which the author calls a "schematic x-ray view" (xviii) of the basic characteristics of "México profundo" and "imaginary Mexico" (xvi) and their "permanent confrontation" (xv) in Mexican society. The second part is a history of Mexico from the conquest to the present. It traces the transformation of Mesoamerican peoples into "Indians" subject to colonial domination, and the various reformulations of "imaginary Mexico" as a project, from colonial exploitation and missionization, to the creole and liberal modernizing movements in the wake of independence, to revolutionary and postrevolutionary regimes, with their attempts to develop and to redeem indigenous populations. *México profundo* concludes with Bonfil Batalla's political appeal—in the mid-1980s, a time he characterized as one of deepening crisis in "imaginary Mexico"—for a new "civilizational project" (158) that might overthrow the culture of the dominant classes. Thus "México profundo" might be reclaimed as a step toward the "recovery of a true, deeply rooted nationalism" (xii) that could provide for an "authentic future" (xix) of Mexico as a pluralistic society and a real democracy, rather than an imaginary, Western one imposed from without.

The "profundo" in "México profundo" is significant. The metaphor of depth suggests that what is at issue is not merely a kind of identity but the geography that undergirds it: that of "Mesoamerica." Mesoamerican civilization, for Bonfil Batalla ([1987] 1996, 12), arose from a "millennial interrelationship of man with nature." Agricultural practices, material life, and even cultural forms were shaped by Mexico's geography and environment, and in turn shaped them. With the emergence of the region's "mother culture" (5)—the Olmecs—key aspects of Mesoamerican culture were consolidated, establishing the "internal coherence of the cultures of Mesoamerican origin, a coherence explained by the world-view they conserve" (xviii). Mexico's contemporary indigenous populations have retained that "coherence," which Bonfil Batalla identifies with a series of social characteristics and transcendent cultural values: the concentration of indigenous populations in certain geographical regions; age-old agricultural systems like milpa, and diet and tools that continued preconquest Mesoamerican practices; ritual practices that governed work and relationships with the natural world, and a cohesive sense of cosmic order and a harmonious relationship with nature; confinement of women to reproductive and household work; communal property, and mechanisms governing the distribution of land and other resources to family heads; an emphasis on community service and obligations; and the devaluation or stigmatization of individualistic accumulation of property and wealth. Even present-day mestizo populations that did not identify themselves as indigenous or speak an indigenous language retained aspects of indigenous culture as a "multitude of isolated traits" (1). Hence Bonfil Batalla denominates such rural populations, and even those who had migrated to barrios in urban centers like Mexico City, as "de-Indianized Indians" (17). Despite losing their identity, they retained the "cultural repertoire, the way of life" of "México profundo" (17). For Bonfil Batalla, Mexico's Mesoamerican civilization, its indigenous heart and geographical body, were thus omnipresent, leaving its imprint even outside populations denominated as "indigenous." "We constantly have in front of us," he writes, "a material vestige, a way of feeling and of doing certain things, a name, a food, a face" (10).

If "deep" Mexico references a human geographical entity—an indigenous civilization shaped by and rooted in the Mesoamerican landscape—it might seem that the other Mexico, labeled as "imaginary," would lack such a taproot. But to the extent he discusses "imaginary Mexico," Bonfil Batalla ([1987] 1996) also makes reference to it in geographic terms: as "the West." He relates the history of Mexico as a constant confrontation between "Indian Mesoamerica and the Christian West" (57), with the latter vaguely demarcated as the place of genesis of an ideology starkly at odds with Mesoamerican civilization. It is a place where the natural world is "seen as an enemy," where "greater human self-realization is achieved through greater separation from nature" (27), and where the "individualistic acquisitive perspective of modern capitalist society" (36) reigns supreme. Most explicitly, Bonfil Batalla locates the origins of "imaginary Mexico" in reconquest-era Spain, where the characteristics of "dominant Western ideology" (75) were accentuated in ways that stressed the natural superiority of the West and denied the humanity of those outside the West. Hence the reason Bonfil Batalla labels "imaginary Mexico" as such is not that it has no geographical locus, but rather that in Mexico—located outside "the West"—it is simply misplaced. Whether in the fevered desires of creole elites for wealth and modernity or in the glorification of *mestizaje* and development measures instituted by revolutionary and postrevolutionary leaders, the "ways of the West" were imposed (105); "imaginary Mexico" came to Mesoamerica as an "imported product" (103). Hence Bonfil Batalla calls, in the conclusion of his work, to overcome the "antagonistic duality" (58) of "Mexico profundo" and "imaginary Mexico" by replacing it with a "new civilizational project" (158) and an "authentic decolonization" (167). Thus, "imaginary Mexico" might be expelled for good, and with it the "arrogant assumption that one's own, Western way of understanding is the only certain and true one" (160).

In its projection of two Mexicos, inalterably opposed to each other—and underlying those Mexicos, two distinct civilizations and geographies, Mesoamerican and Western—*México profundo* is a work characterized at the deepest level by what anthropologist Fernando Coronil (1996) called "Occidentalism." In "Beyond Occidentalism," a trenchant critique of scholarly considerations of alterity and practices of othering, including Edward Said's *Orientalism* (1978), Coronil attempts to redirect attention from constructions of "the Orient" as the other to the "conceptions of the West animating these representations," and enabling the "representational practices that portray non-Western peoples as the Other of a Western Self" (52, 56). Coronil emphasizes that such categories are "geohistorical" in nature (55), portraying the West and its others in terms of fixed geographic referents that belie their internal complexity and obscure the dynamic historical relationships that crosscut such static, bounded spatial reifications. Most importantly, such geohistorical constructs had a hidden "politics." Whether directly or indirectly, Occidentalist representational practices supported "Western hegemony" by tending to "1) separate the world's components into bounded units; 2) disaggregate their relational histories; 3) turn difference into hierarchy; 4) naturalize these representations; and thus 5) intervene, however unwittingly, in the reproduction of existing asymmetrical power relations" (57). Coronil discusses three different modalities of Occidentalist representations of self and other—the "dissolution of the Other by the Self," the "incorporation of the Other into the Self," and "the destabilization of the Self by the Other" (58). The last of these modalities might well be taken to describe Bonfil Batalla's attempt to reclaim "México profundo" and exorcise "imaginary Mexico." Like the texts Coronil placed under that rubric, *México profundo* might be characterized as a work that "polarize[s] contrasts between cultures that are historically interrelated . . . exalting their difference, erasing their historical links, and homogenizing their internal features, unwittingly reinscribing an imperial Self-Other duality even as it seeks to unsettle colonial representations" (68).

It might seem a bit of a detour to have begun a commentary on this important collection of essays with an extended discussion of *México profundo* and Coronil's critique of Occidentalism. Yet I would argue that both of those texts help to foreground Paula López Caballero's and Ariadna Acevedo-Rodrigo's call to challenge the common sense of scholarship on Mexico's indigenous populations by moving beyond alterity, or more specifically, by questioning and historicizing the automatic ascription of alterity to indigenous populations, thus approaching indigenous alterity not as an "explanation but as an object to be explained." Bonfil Batalla's text is a demonstration of how the specific elements or dimensions of alterity attributed to indigenous populations (in terms of social organization, land tenure, culture, world view, orality, etc.), and addressed separately by the contributors to this volume, are tightly and systematically integrated in the conceptualization of "the indigenous" as a referent and an assumed object of study. Moreover, *México profundo* makes clear how *indigenous* is not just a category of identity but rather a geohistorical category. It is an argument or assumption about how the world is or should be organized as much as it is a category of ascribed or avowed identity. As Coronil argues—and I hope my reading of *México profundo* suggests—the ascription of alterity also involves the reinscription of a reified version of a Western self, as what Coronil (1996, 56) called the "dark side" of representations of the Orient as "other," or here the indigenous as other. Can we ever go "beyond alterity" without at the same time going "beyond Occidentalism"? Do the studies presented in this collection, with their laudable commitment to moving beyond alterity, also challenge the dark side of the indigenous other—namely, the Western self?

I would argue that taken as a whole, the essays in this collection do level such a challenge. They move not only beyond alterity but also beyond Occidentalism, in at least two ways. First, all of these historical and anthropological studies of indigenous populations have moved from assuming alterity—of a kind that distinguishes that which characterizes the indigenous other from that which is *external* to it—to exploring the differentiation *within* indigenous populations. As the opening chapter of the section on "Land and Government," Emilio Kourí's comprehensive survey of practices of landholding in indigenous villages of the colonial period strikes against ingrained assumptions of communalism, cohesion, and egalitarianism as characteristic features of indigenous populations, and hence, implicitly, of privatization, competitive individualism, social differentiation and hierarchy in the outside non-indigenous social world where "Western" values presumably prevailed. Kourí demonstrates that land use even in pueblos characterized by corporate landholding was "hierarchical and profoundly inequitable" (31), with a system of both "differential" and "private" rights governing the usage of land and other resources. While Kourí is perhaps too quick to dismiss native communalist rhetoric as "fantasy" and as an "imagined communalist ethos" (52), his essay does suggest that distinctions between communal and private use of land, between equitable or inequitable distribution of resources, and between hierarchical or egalitarian relations of power were not drawn at the boundary between indigenous pueblos and the world that surrounded them but rather were drawn within the pueblos themselves, as factors of differentiation, contradiction, and sometimes conflict between inhabitants of the pueblos, as much as between pueblo residents and outsiders.

Similarly, in an ethnographic study of ejidos and land use among Maya-speaking populations in southern Yucatán, Gabriela Torres-Mazuera disputes assumptions common in scholarly studies of the ejidos and privatization measures, which tend to distinguish sharply between (indigenous) communal possession of land and (Western) forms of individual property. Such studies tend to oppose positive law or state order and indigenous *usos y costumbres*, and to assume continuity between contemporary ejidos and pre-Hispanic forms of communal land tenure (i.e., swidden milpa agriculture). Instead, Torres-Mazuera depicts the agricultural landscape as a complicated patchwork that defies easy distinctions between "indigenous" communal practices and those of capitalist, state-sponsored, or "Western" origin. Ejidal organization, for instance, provides a framework for excluding some *milperos* from access to lands they had formerly cultivated; groups that reject the option of individually titling ejidal lands through PROCEDE—a phenomenon widely represented by scholars as rooted in the indigenous communalist rejection of private property—nonetheless adopt the logic of commodification, quantification, and privatization in regulating the use of ejidal lands. Here, as in Kourí's contribution, oppositions that might have seemed to demarcate the boundary between indigenous and non-indigenous worlds are instead revealed to be lines of differentiation *within* indigenous populations. Thus Kourí and Torres-Mazuera both call into question any attempt to demarcate categorically delineated indigenous and non-indigenous or "Western" worlds, practices, or geohistorical entities.

Other chapters in this section build on such arguments by challenging the tendency to ascribe stereotypical features to indigenous political conduct as insular and localistic, with a focus on traditional and customary practices—and expressed via oral forms of communication and cultural transmission—to the exclusion of political engagements beyond the village level, in the mestizo, urban, and lettered contexts of national life. Hence Peter Guardino, in an exploration of "indigenous peasant political culture" (76), questions the localism, or campanilismo, typically ascribed to indigenous rural populations. The social structure and concrete interests of residents of those communities, and the conflicts that often unfolded around the cargo system, justice of the peace appointments, and liberal reform measures, made it "inevitable that some peasants would look outside their villages for solutions to their problems" (74). There was no contradiction between intense involvement in local concerns and engagement with the wider polity. Similarly, in a study focused on the Gulf Coast during the War of Independence, Michael Ducey demonstrates that the political involvements of indigenous communities defied easy categorization. Sometimes engaging in guerrilla insurgency, and sometimes supporting counterinsurgent campaigns, they made political choices and deployed political rhetoric that expressed a heterodox notion of citizenship—one that could embrace emergent concepts of national identity and political rights even as it remained deeply rooted in the social and political realities of the colonial *pueblos de indios*.

Ariadna Acevedo-Rodrigo makes the flip side of this argument in a discussion of liberal republican schools in indigenous communities in Oaxaca and Puebla. National-level educational reforms and discourse—though seemingly distant from and largely unapplied to indigenous communities by federal authorities—were brought to those communities, or at least some of their members, through the action of state and municipal officials. Though limited in extent and constituency, those schools, like the kinds of political conduct described by Guardino and Ducey, manifested not the exclusion of indigenous populations from national publics and political discourse but rather what Acevedo-Rodrigo calls their "subordinate inclusion" within them. Finally, there is Elsie Rockwell's discussion of how Tlaxcalan elders engage with Spanish literacy—both in the past, from colonial times forward, and in the present. Rockwell dispenses with the assumption of indigenous orality, showing an engagement with Spanish language and literacy that manifests strategic involvement in multiple "scriptural economies" (145). Rockwell ethnographically depicts a world where the dividing line between Spanish and Mexicano languages, and between orality and literacy, is a constantly crossed, internal line of differentiation within Tlaxcalan society rather than a boundary dividing an indigenous other, inside, from an Occidental lettered city outside its bounds.

Taken as a group, in short, the essays presented in the "Land and Government" section make a significant move *away* from a social and political paradigm of alterity—that is, one that attributes consistent internal characteristics to indigenous populations and communities and simultaneously circumscribes a literal (geographic) and figurative boundary between them and non-indigenous external actors, entities, institutions, or contexts that are characterized by opposite characteristics. What they shift *toward*, instead, is a social and political paradigm of difference—one that situates those lines of differentiation *within* indigenous communities, and that at the same time admits an indigenous presence or effect in presumably external entities, like the state and the wider polity. To put this differently, the separation of other and self, indigenous and non-indigenous into reified geohistorical entities—to recall Bonfil Batalla, "México profundo" versus "imaginary Mexico," or "Mesoamerica" versus "the West"—cedes place to a project of historicization that dissolves those boundaries in a way that recalls Coronil's (1996, 73) suggestion "that their difference be historicized rather than essentialized, and that their boundaries and homogeneity be determined, not assumed."

There is, moreover, a second way that the essays in this collection—and particularly those presented in the section on "Science"—move not only beyond alterity, but beyond Occidentalism. As López Caballero and Acevedo-Rodrigo indicate in their introduction, several of these contributions demonstrate how, in particular social and historical contexts, the contents of the marked category of indigenous are "fixed," thus exposing the historicity and constructedness of indigenous alterity. This is certainly true. But equally fixed, however, is an unmarked Western or Occidental self, which is implicitly constructed, stabilized, or confirmed in such processes of indigenization. This is clear, for instance, in López Caballero's exploration of Mexican and U.S. anthropological debates over "what constitutes [the] alterity" (200) of indigenous populations around the time of the founding of the INI. Anthropologists and public officials debated various factors or measures of indigenous alterity—biological, cultural, social, historical, psychological—and their implications for various indigenist policies targeting such populations. But at the same time, they confronted the problems of differentiating indigenous from Ladino or mestizo populations or persons, even within the same family or community. For anthropologists, the problem of the "disappearance of the indio" (i.e., of his/her passing out of that marked category of alterity into one of unmarked Mexican national selfhood) was inextricable from the problem of defining "indigenous" culture or identity.

A similar point is made by Diana Schwartz in her study of resettlement programs targeting Mazatec communities displaced by hydroelectric development. Schwartz demonstrates the disconnection between the *indigenista* rhetoric and policies of anthropologists and project directors (which posited Mazatec populations in generic, static, and stereotypical terms as indigenous populations "historically rooted" in communal lands) and the displaced population itself. That population was not only composed of both Mazatec speakers and mestizos but was also quite socially and economically diverse in occupation, in ways that crosscut generic expectations of them as indigenous others. This heterogeneity was complicated further by the somewhat contradictory attempts of anthropologists and officials to preserve the indigenous qualities of displaced populations, even as they sought to inculcate the "tenets of modern life" (223). Over time, via the application of agrarian and developmental policies and institutions, those populations increasingly identified, and were categorized, as campesinos, with the term *indígena* tending to "fade from view" as an ethnic referent. As Schwartz argues, the "static, political notion of *Indigeneous*" deployed by officials was a "foil . . . and a justification" (237) for development schemes that tended to recategorize resettled aid recipients as ethnically unmarked (and hence Westernized or modernized) Mexican campesinos.

As the essays by both López Caballero and Schwartz demonstrate, the fixing of distinct categorizations of the indigenous other and the Western (mestizo, Ladino, campesino) self unfolds not only as a process of identity construction but also as a geohistorical operation. It is a kind of fixing that relegates the indigenous other to the past, even as it firmly situates the Western self in a temporal movement from present to the future—a counterpoint, perhaps, to Bonfil Batalla's identification of "México profundo" with an ancestral Mesoamerican past and "imaginary Mexico" with Western modernity. That temporal operation, which consigns the indigenous other to the past and the Western self to the future, recalls *Time and the Other*, Johannes Fabian's (2002) critique of anthropology's colonialist epistemology. Fabian calls the systematic refusal of anthropologists to recognize and engage with their interlocutors as contemporaries the "denial of coevalness" (25). The remaining essays in this collection, which deal with scientific discourses relating to the indigenous other, demonstrate that exactly such a denial, and the consequent relegation of the indigenous other to a distant ancestral past, is a systematic dimension of the fixing of distinct indigenous and Occidental identities in time and space. In her exploration of the formation and study of skeletal collections in the late nineteenth century, for instance, Laura Cházaro demonstrates that when medical pathologists and physical anthropologists worked at measuring and determining the characteristic of indigenous "races," they did so in conjunction with the study of their presence of those groups within, or distinction from, a "Mexican" national race. "indigenous" skulls and pelvises became "museum objects" belonging to the past, while "mestizo" remains emerged from procedures of measurement and classification marked as "more evolved" and as "agents of national history" (192), rather than as remnants of an archaic past.

A similar process of temporal differentiation unfolds in very different cases explored by José Luis Escalona and Vivette García Deister. Escalona considers the consolidation of the category *Maya* in cultural anthropology and museography, and particularly in the work of anthropologist Evon Vogt in the 1950s and 1960s. Vogt's work helped to substantiate an axiomatic conception of Maya culture—both in the distant past and in the present—as a coherent system of ritual and cosmological principles. Critical to such an ethnographic construction of Maya alterity, and of the presumably uninterrupted links between ancient and present day peoples, was what Escalona calls "encapsulated history": the way in which modern-day practices, or practices introduced from a surrounding non-Maya world, presumably were encapsulated and, in effect, indigenized, by "local cultural logics" (250). In short, the substantiation of a systematic representation of the Maya as indigenous other, and hence as existing outside and before Western time and history, was predicated both on its projection back into an ancient past and on the encapsulation of any sign of their present-day interconnection, and coevality, with a non-indigenous exterior. Likewise, in her study of ancestry estimation and "cultures of remembrance" (264) in the work of contemporary Mexican genomic scientists, García Deister demonstrates how estimations of the indigenous contribution to contemporary mestizo genomes are perceived as "offering a window into a pre-admixture past" (265). In their studies of genetic material from contemporary indigenous populations, and their possible linkage to pathological outcomes in those groups or mixed populations, genomic scientists fix indigenous genetic lines in a "different socio-geographic space and time . . . as proxies of a pre-admixture past" (273). The narratives such studies support, García Deister argues, present contemporary indigenous populations as mired in an ancestral state that contributes to their ongoing biological pathologies and social marginalization. Conversely, the genetic material of contemporary mestizos is taken as emblematic of Mexico's present and future.

In at least these two ways, by reframing external boundaries of alterity into internal lines of difference and by historicizing the production of geohistorical alterity, the contributors to this collection not only move explicitly "beyond alterity" but also, at least potentially, beyond Occidentalism. I will conclude with a question that follows from these observations: Why does this matter? In a world where *indigenous* and *Western* are still terms used in ways that imply alterity and sameness—in a world whose map, both geographical and conceptual, remains drawn by and around those geohistorical reifications and where the legacies of imperialism and colonialism continue to affect and constrain the life chances of many of those categorized as indigenous—what difference does a collection like this make? Is this a purely academic exercise, or does it contribute to a politics of knowledge that might seek not only to describe the world but also to change it?

It is clear that *México profundo* was meant, above all, to chart exactly such a politics. In his attempt to valorize and reclaim "Mesoamerican civilization" and its legacies, Bonfil Batalla ([1987] 1996) levels a political challenge at the way "México profundo" has long been made into an exploited and denied other. He seeks to embrace it as the self and to turn the tables on an "imaginary Mexico," an assumed Western self that now becomes the other. He presents a way forward—the validation and prospective advent of a truly pluralistic nation in Mexico—in strikingly geohistorical terms. Thus he separates out the entwined histories of Mexico past and present as distinct geographically situated civilizations and fixed geographic referents: "Mesoamerica" and "the West." In the future he evokes, "Mesoamerican civilization" finally might have the "place it deserves, a place that allows it to view the West from Mexico" (175). In essence, Bonfil Batalla seeks to overthrow the domination of Western modernity—that is, the domination of "imaginary Mexico" over "México profundo"—by reversing the polarities of self and other. Here, in some ways, Bonfil Batalla might be seen as converging with identitarian political movements that have found such a polarity, and the essentialisms it implies, to be strategically useful in the struggle for social justice and for indigenous recognition and rights.[2]

Yet in retaining the polar opposition between self and other, even with reversed terms, Bonfil Batalla may well remain trapped within Occidentalist representational strategies that Coronil (1996) describes as "constitutive of [Western] modernity itself" (78). Could recreating the opposition between self and other, even in the service of a movement on behalf of indigenous populations, indirectly serve what Coronil calls the "foundational premises" of a global imperial order (73), dispelling "imaginary Mexico" only to conjure forth a new world of opposed "civilizations" with essentialized traits, severed connections, obscured histories? In "Beyond Occidentalism" Coronil calls for more than merely destabilizing—but then restabilizing—the relations between Western self and its others; more, even, than exposing the historical connections and relationships that Orientalism and Occidentalism tend to efface, or historicizing the production of self/other categorizations. Above all, Coronil seeks to foster the emergence of a "decentered poetics that may help us imagine geohistorical categories for a nonimperial world" (52), one that affords not only a critique of past or present but also alternatives for the future, and a challenge to the global and asymmetrical power relations that continue to haunt a neocolonial world long after colonialism's demise. He seeks a way to free the living, both colonizer and colonized, from the "nightmare of the past" (81), but he also seeks a way to imagine a new relationship between history and geography, a new way to "articulate the future historically" (80) once the present is freed of the prison of Occidentalist categories and representational schema.

What then, are the politics of this volume, with its attempt to move beyond alterity? What resources or suggestions might it offer in a time in which, as the editors of this volume note in their discussion of the 2010 Mexican national census, ever greater numbers of Mexican citizens are asserting indigenous identity, but in ways that break with long-held, stereotypical assumptions equating indigeneity with alterity? What lessons, insights, or inspiration might the Tlaxcalan elders, or younger generations in the Malintzi region or elsewhere, draw from *Beyond Alterity* as they consider their own politics and their own poetics? These questions are imperative to ask, but perhaps answering them is beside the point. The point may well be this: such questions are not to be resolved by those of us who have defined, deployed, or studied "the indigenous" in past or present. They may well be decided by those of us who have borne the weight of that category in the past and will live our way through it in the future, whether within, across, or beyond, its confines and horizons.

NOTES

1. My citations are from the English translation, Bonfil Batalla ([1987] 1996). As in the translation I employ the terms "México profundo" and "imaginary Mexico" here.
2. The translator of *México profundo* makes such a claim. He presents the work as a manifestation of its author's unwavering belief that "Indian peoples have the right to control their own destiny," and considers the book's initial publication just a few years before the outbreak of the Zapatista movement to make it "prophetic in retrospect" (Dennis 1996, ix, vii). For a historical examination of Bonfil Batalla's involvement in and communications with indigenous movements for self-determination in the 1970s and 1980s, see Muñoz (2016).

REFERENCES

Bonfil Batalla, Guillermo. (1987) 1996. *México Profundo: Reclaiming a Civilization*. Translated by Philip A. Dennis. Austin: University of Texas Press. Originally published as *El México Profundo, una civilización negada*. Mexico: Editorial Grijalbo.

Coronil, Fernando. 1996. "Beyond Occidentalism: Toward Nonimperial Geohistorical Categories." *Cultural Anthropology* 11 (1): 51–87.

Dennis, Philip A. 1996. "Translator's Foreword." In Bonfil Batalla (1987) 1996, vii–x.

Fabian, Johannes. 2002. *Time and the Other: How Anthropology Makes Its Object*. New York: Columbia University Press.

Muñoz, María L. O. 2016. *Stand Up and Fight: Participatory Indigenismo, Populism, and Mobilization in Mexico, 1970–1984*. Tucson: University of Arizona Press.

Said, Edward. 1978. *Orientalism*. New York: Pantheon Books.

CONTRIBUTORS

Paula López Caballero is a historian and anthropologist working at the Center for Interdisciplinary Research of the Universidad Nacional Autónoma de México (UNAM). She is the author of *Indígenas de la Nación*, first published in France (2012) and now translated for the Fondo de Cultura Económica (2017). Her work has been awarded with the Premio Universidad Nacional en investigación en Humanidades (2017). It deals with the long-term processes and contemporary practices of social differentiation, which define who and what is "indigenous" as a part of the nation and state formation.

Ariadna Acevedo-Rodrigo is professor of history at the Centro de Investigación y de Estudios Avanzados (Cinvestav) in Mexico City and specializes in the intersections between education and politics. She coedited *Ciudadanos inesperados. Espacios de formación de la ciudadanía ayer y hoy (Unexpected Citizens: The Making of Citizenship Past and Present)*, published by Colegio de Mexico in 2012, and is currently writing a monograph entitled *Lingering Liberalism: "Indians," Education and Government in Puebla, Mexico, 1875–1940*.

Emilio Kourí is professor of history and director of the Katz Center for Mexican Studies at the University of Chicago. He is the author of *A Pueblo Divided: Business, Property, and Community in Papantla, Mexico* (Stanford University Press, 2004) and editor of *En busca de Molina Enríquez: Cien años de Los grandes problemas nacionales* (Colegio de México and Katz Center for Mexican Studies, 2009).

Peter Guardino is professor of history at Indiana University. His first book, *Peasants, Politics, and the Formation of Mexico's National State: Guerrero 1800–1857,* was published by Stanford University Press in 1996, and a Spanish translation appeared in Mexico in 2001. His second book, *The Time of Liberty: Popular Political Culture in Oaxaca, 1750–1850,* was published by Duke University Press in 2005, followed by a Spanish edition in 2010. His most recent book is *The Dead March: A History of the Mexican-American War,* published by Harvard University Press in 2017.

Michael T. Ducey is the author of *A Nation of Villages: Riot and Rebellion in the Mexican Huasteca, 1750–1850* (Arizona University Press, 2004), a study of the role of indigenous villagers in Mexican state formation during the period of the emergence of the nation-state. He is currently writing a history of the independence movement in the Gulf region of Mexico while also coordinating a project on political transformations in rural towns in central Veracruz. Formerly an associate professor of history at the University of Colorado, Denver, where he also founded and directed the International Studies Program, he is now a researcher at the Instituto de Investigaciones Histórico-Sociales of the Universidad Veracruzana.

Elsie Rockwell is professor at Cinvestav in Mexico City. She has done extensive research in both the history and anthropology of education, and published in English, Spanish, French, and Portuguese. She received the Francisco Javier Clavijero Award of the Instituto Nacional de Antropología e Historia (Mexico) in 2008, and the Spindler Award from the American Anthropological Association in 2013.

Gabriela Torres-Mazuera is associate professor at the Centro de Investigaciones y Estudios Superiores en Antropología Social (CIESAS) in Mérida, Yucatán. Since 1996 she has participated in different research projects drawing on the conformation of rural and urban spaces in Mexico. Her book, *La ruralidad urbanizada en el centro de México,* published by UNAM in 2012, won the Arturo Warman prize that year. Her current research project deals with the changing roles of land tenure and local institutions in the Mexican countryside.

Laura Cházaro is professor at Cinvestav in Mexico City. She is the author of several books and articles on the history of science in Mexico and is currently preparing a book and a catalogue on the instruments used in Mexican physiology to be published by the Facultad de Medicina at UNAM.

Diana Lynn Schwartz is an Andrew W. Mellon Postdoctoral Fellow at the Center for the Americas at Wesleyan University. She has a PhD in Latin American History from the University of Chicago. Her doctoral dissertation examines the displacement and resettlement of indigenous inhabitants of the Papaloapan River Basin in southern Mexico, led by the newly created Instituto Nacional Indigenista, in the wake of a hydroelectric development project. At the intersection of *indigenismo* and developmentalism, the Papaloapan case serves as a vantage point to analyze the interplay between anthropology, government, and indigeneity in 1940s–1970s Mexico.

José Luis Escalona Victoria is professor at CIESAS in San Cristóbal de las Casas, Chiapas. A revised version of his PhD thesis was awarded the Arturo Warman prize (2006) and published in 2009. His numerous publications in English, French, and Spanish discuss power relations in the Altos de Chiapas region of Mexico, with particular emphasis on a critical analysis of what the author terms the "ethno-argument": the causality that the Mexican anthropological tradition attributes to social identity, particularly that of indigenous peoples.

Vivette García Deister is associate professor in science and technology studies at the Facultad de Ciencias, UNAM. She is a biologist with postgraduate studies in the philosophy of sciences (2009, UNAM), and author of the book chapter "Laboratory Life of the Mexican Mestizo" in Peter Wade et al., *Mestizo Genomics* (Duke University Press, 2014). Her main areas of research are biomedical and forensic genetics in Mexico. She critically analyzes mestizo and indigenous bodies as objects of investigation in contemporary genomics and the impact of these investigations on notions of identity and nation.

Paul K. Eiss is an associate professor of anthropology and history at Carnegie Mellon University. His book, *In the Name of* El Pueblo: *Place, Community, and the Politics of History in Yucatán*, was published by Duke University Press in 2010. Currently he is working on two projects: an analysis of the rhetoric of self-defense in contemporary Mexico, and a historical study of *mestizaje*, performance, and the politics of translation in Yucatán.

INDEX